'MIDDLE SAXON' SETTLEMENT AND SOCIETY

Duncan W. Wright

ARCHAEOPRESS ARCHAEOLOGY

Archaeopress Publishing Ltd

Gordon House
276 Banbury Road
Oxford OX2 7ED

www.archaeopress.com

ISBN 978 1 78491 125 6
ISBN 978 1 78491 126 3 (e-Pdf)

© Archaeopress and D Wright 2015

Printed in England by Holywell Press, Oxford

This book is available direct from Archaeopress or from our website www.archaeopress.com

Table of Contents

List of Figures

I

List of Tables

Acknowledgements

I wish to express my most sincere thanks to all of those who have supported and encouraged me during the production of this book. In particular I would like to express my deep gratitude to Professor Julia Crick and Professor Stephen Rippon, for their invaluable input and advice. I would also like to thank the staff and students of the Archaeology Department at the University of Exeter, especially Professor Oliver Creighton, who has provided much guidance and encouragement. My appreciation is expressed to Professor John Blair who read and discussed my work, and provided many useful comments. I am also thankful to Professor Helena Hamerow, who examined this work as a doctoral thesis, and gave extremely helpful insight and feedback. My thanks are also expressed to the members of staff at the various Historic Environment Records that were utilised, whose help was utterly essential for the completion of this work. I am grateful to those friends, in Exeter, Bristol, and elsewhere, who have offered encouragement throughout. Last but certainly not least, I would like to thank the entirety of my family for their constant love and support — this book is dedicated to them.

Chapter I:
Introducing Middle Saxon Settlement

The early medieval period has long been central to the way in which the settlement history of England is understood. Less than a century ago, the prevailing scholarly view held that the village landscape of England was a product of the first Germanic migrants, who felled dense woodland and established a settlement form that endured into the present day (e.g. Seebohm 1883). Similarly, the majority of researchers believed that 'Anglo-Saxon' incomers also brought with them a new approach to agriculture, introducing the ploughing of intermingled strips within expansive open fields, which replaced the pre-existing 'Celtic' arrangements of small cultivated 'infields' (e.g. Gray 1915). By introducing such novel farming regimes, it was asserted, these peoples created the open fields which characterised much of the English countryside until the transformations of the enclosure movement that began in the sixteenth century. Such views of the landscape were but one facet of a more overarching attitude, which considered that the beginnings of English history was rooted in the arrival of the 'Anglo-Saxons', and not in the establishment of Roman Britain (Higham 2010, 2). Alongside the overhaul of settlements and field systems, the introduction of Old English language and place-names, and the adoption of Christianity were in effect viewed as part of the same process: the making of England (e.g. Green 1892).

Such perceptions of the rural landscape have since been dismissed by subsequent generations but, as the 'nucleated' villages that characterise much of midland England are now widely regarded as a product of the tenth century, the idea of the early medieval period as transformative has persisted. Modern researchers have access to a growing body of data that allows the settlement landscape of pre-Conquest England to be viewed with ever-increasing clarity, as local and regional studies contribute to a gradually more comprehensive understanding of the national picture. The development of a more nuanced chronological framework has proved particularly beneficial, allowing archaeologists to associate changes to the countryside with their social context more closely. Perhaps the most significant 'hangover' of the earliest research into the 'Anglo-Saxon' heritage of the English landscape, however, is the enduring influence of historic methods and texts. It is by no quirk of circumstance that many archaeological studies of 'Anglo-Saxon' England have focussed on the last two centuries before the Conquest, featuring as it does some of the most extensive archaeological evidence, but also access to written records unparalleled elsewhere in the early medieval period. The historical figures of the 'Late Saxon' period also continue to loom large, and although earlier leaders such as Offa and Rædwald are well-recognised, the influence of Alfred and the later kings of Wessex remain especially prevalent within published research and the popular consciousness. The archaeology of 'Early Saxon' England, taken to denote the two centuries following the withdrawal of Roman administration, has also proved a fertile area of scholarly interest, and it was research into the cemeteries and grave goods of this period that particularly laid the foundations of 'Anglo-Saxon' archaeology as a self-contained discipline (see below).

Current early medieval landscape archaeology is no exception to these more general trends, with the importance of 'Late Saxon' England as a period which imparted lasting change upon the character of the countryside especially emphasised. The majority of active scholars view the villages of England as a product of the ninth century at the very earliest, with new settlement forms introduced in what has been termed the 'village moment'—a contradictory term which in fact denotes a protracted process which is argued to have lasted several centuries (e.g. Taylor 1983; Lewis *et al.* 1997; Roberts and Wrathmell 2000; Page and Jones 2007). At the other extremity of the period, the landscape during the earliest centuries of early medieval England has also proved a fruitful area of academic interest. Researchers have attempted to delineate the character of this transitional period between the breakdown of administration in Roman Britain and the development of alternative social and economic systems that manifested themselves in new forms of material culture. In terms of settlement and landscape archaeology, the extent to which occupation centres and agricultural regimes underwent transformation in this 'Early Saxon' period continues to draw focus (e.g. Cool 2000; Christie 2004; Dark 2004), with the impact of migration receiving particularly detailed analysis (e.g. Faull 1977; Hodges 1989; Härke 1990; Higham 1992). Such discourse is usually accompanied by more fundamental debate regarding the appropriate interpretation of material culture, and the ways in which archaeology can provide an insight into the rapidly changing composition of society in the early post-Roman centuries (e.g. Hills 2011).

Sandwiched between these two more commonly-researched periods, the archaeology of 'Middle Saxon' England has traditionally been treated as something of a poor relation by comparison. Chronologically too distant to be integrated into debates on migration and early post-Roman upheaval, whilst also lacking the more lasting material culture and documented sources of the 'Late Saxon' period, the settlement archaeology of the mid-seventh to mid-ninth centuries has in the past been an area of scholarly neglect. Assisted by access to written sources brought about by the development of the Church from the late sixth century, historians have typically engaged more readily than archaeologists with 'Middle Saxon'-period England (e.g. Stenton 1970; Brooks 1984; Hanson and Wickham 2000). Recently, however, and partly as a consequence of such historical enquiry, archaeologists have begun to appreciate the research potential of pre-Viking societies. Over the past two decades, a gradually increasing quantity of academic investigation has focussed specifically on 'Middle Saxon' settlement archaeology, so that there now exists a substantial body of research on the subject (e.g. Hamerow 19991; Brown and Foard 1998; Reynolds 2003; Rippon 2010).

Developments outside of academia have contributed significantly to this improved research environment, specifically the increased extent and detail of commercially-led archaeology projects. The introduction of statutory heritage protection in the early 1990s has resulted in a marked increase in excavation of 'Middle Saxon' settlements: material which had previously rarely drawn interest on the basis of its perceived research value alone (e.g. Mortimer 2000; Hardy *et al.* 2007). Despite the progress both in scholarly interest and the archaeological data now available for study, significant uncertainties continue to surround research into 'Middle Saxon' settlement and landscape. In many parts of the country a lack of chronological precision, chiefly the result of un-diagnostic ceramics, results in a limited understanding of the early medieval settlement sequence. These conditions frequently lead to the amalgamation of 'Middle Saxon' and 'Early Saxon' material, as the mid-ninth century onward is again underscored as the period in which occurred more meaningful changes to the countryside. Many researchers also persist in undermining the potential insight that 'Middle Saxon' archaeology provides to its immediate historical context. Seventh to ninth-century settlement material is instead more commonly deployed in order to explain later landscape character, as scholars regularly seek to discern the origins of medieval villages and fields (e.g. Jones and Page 2006, 222).

This book seeks to redress precisely these imbalances by focussing primarily on the archaeology of 'Middle Saxon' settlement, with the primary aim of demonstrating the ways in which such material can provide a picture of contemporary social, economic and political conditions. Within this overarching aim, this research encompasses a number of more specific objectives, first among which is a re-examination of the character and chronology of early medieval settlement change. In particular this volume will question what has become the prevailing view that it was the later ninth to eleventh centuries that saw the first fundamental transformation of rural settlements, and that before *c.*850, few significant developments occurred in the countryside. A further objective of this book is to assess whether there is regional variation in archaeological evidence relating to 'Middle Saxon' settlement, and analyse whether these inconsistencies represent actual differences in the character of the rural landscape between the seventh and ninth centuries, or are more of a product of alternative research traditions.

The significance of data derived from development-led projects, many of which remain unpublished in Historic Environment Records (HERs), will be particularly prevalent, as excavations within currently occupied villages have revealed material especially informative for early medieval settlement studies. Research in this volume is concentrated on understanding the 'Middle Saxon' countryside of five counties in central and eastern England: Northamptonshire, Oxfordshire, Wiltshire, Cambridgeshire and Norfolk. These counties together represent a study area of extreme diversity and topographical complexity, providing ideal conditions to explore the way in which physical conditions may have influenced 'Middle Saxon' communities. Whilst it will be clear that the topographical backdrop shaped the relationship between people and their landscape, the most prominent theme of this book is one of comprehensive transformation to settlement that occurred across all types of countryside. The most important factor influencing such widespread change, it will be shown, was fundamental and deep-rooted stratification that was taking places across society.

Before investigation can begin in earnest, however, it is essential to place these objectives in their wider research context. The remainder of this chapter is therefore dedicated to a critical assessment of existing research, allowing the significance of the contributions made in this book to be appreciated more fully. Such an analysis of previous works facilitates the establishment of more specific aims, outlined in Chapter II, together with a description of the methodologies adopted. Following presentation of the county-based material in Chapters III to VII, this piece will then present a detailed discussion of its findings and their wider significance in Chapter VIII. The book will subsequently close with a brief concluding chapter, which will reemphasise the key points of the work.

DEFINING THE 'MIDDLE SAXON' PERIOD

It is exceptionally difficult to attribute a name to the period between the end of Roman administration in Britain and the Norman invasion that is not affiliated with a specific perspective (see Hills 2011). The traditional term 'The Dark Ages', describing the hiatus of 'classical culture' has been wholly rejected by academics, yet remains in popular use elsewhere. 'Medieval' and 'Middle Ages' are equally unhelpful idioms, both of which also allude to an interim period separating phases of greater social complexity (Gerrard 2003, xi; Hills 1999, 176-8). In England, the time between the withdrawal of Roman authority and 1066 is most commonly known as the 'Anglo-Saxon' period, based largely on the apparent influence of 'Germanic' peoples from the fifth century. Yet, whilst scholars are in near unanimous agreement that there was some influx of groups from the continent at this time, the extent and character of migration remains a source of significant contention (e.g. Scull 1992; Higham 1992). Compounding such uncertainty, the term 'Anglo-Saxon' carries significant racial and ideological weight, whilst promoting the study of England in isolation, rather than in its wider geographical context (Reynolds 1985, 400-2).

For the most part, scholars have failed to consider the way in which 'Anglo-Saxon' has been used in the past and its changing significance through time, with the terminology often employed without apparent consideration of its possible connotations. As early as the eighth century, the inhabitants of what we now call England were using the simple word 'English' (OE *Angli* or *Anglici*) to refer to themselves (Reynolds 1985, 398). Particularly during the nineteenth century, 'Anglo-Saxon' was used to refer both to early medieval people and the nation, thus providing a common biological and cultural descent for the contemporary English. Indeed, the overall historiography of 'Anglo-Saxon' England is characterised by misuse in order to fulfil often hegemonic political and ideological agendas. Susan Reynolds (1985, 414) has suggested that such an inheritance results in a viable case for terminological change in the current literature, whilst conceding that this course of action is probably over-presumptuous and unrealistic. 'Early medieval' is, nevertheless, a preferable term, and one which possesses fewer political implications, and a less dubious background of usage.

'Early medieval' is now generally used for the fifth to eleventh centuries, but 'Anglo-Saxon' remains too imbedded in the existing literature, and indeed the popular mindset, to be completely overhauled. Whilst 'early medieval' is therefore preferred, this book will also occasionally utilise 'Anglo-Saxon' to refer to archaeological material that has been interpreted as 'Germanic' in character, but continue to place it within apostrophes to emphasise its subjective nature. Similarly, as this research is dedicated to the archaeology of the fifth to seventh centuries and not the entirety of the early medieval period, the term 'Middle Saxon' will also be employed, but as a period term only. 'Early Saxon' (*c.*400-650), 'Middle Saxon' (*c.*650-850) and 'Late Saxon' (*c.*850-1066) continue to be used in archaeological research, especially in eastern England (Reynolds 1999, 23; Rippon 2008, 8). These approximately equal periods at first appear convenient, but are essentially derived from historical contexts. The end of 'Middle Saxon' England for instance, is generally taken as the period in which the Scandinavian presence became more permanent, with the first overwintering of an army recorded at Thanet in 853 (ASC A for 850).

This tripartite system is therefore not ideally suited to archaeology, which traces social and cultural change gradually rather than by discrete historical events. Without due caution, archaeological researchers can be misled into neglecting the broader chronological significance of their results due to a tendency of adopting a 'period-specific' approach. Although this book retains the established tripartite approach common in the current literature, it does so with an awareness of its provisional character, whilst also actively seeking to deconstruct misleading

chronological boundaries both as lived experience and as subject for study. For this very purpose, 'Early Saxon', 'Middle Saxon' and 'Late Saxon' will again remain in apostrophes throughout the volume. With these chronological divisions, and their inherent difficulties and constraints in mind, this chapter now turns to a critical assessment of past approaches to 'Anglo-Saxon' studies, and more specifically previous research into early medieval settlement and landscape archaeology.

VIEWS OF 'MIDDLE SAXON' SETTLEMENT

Background

The perception of 'Anglo-Saxon' England, as with all studies of the past, has often been conditioned by contemporary social, religious and political ideology, as much as by available forms of evidence. Indeed, the historiography of 'Anglo-Saxon' studies represents a conspicuous example of the way in which the writing of history is marked by the contemporary society in which it was produced (Hills 2003, 21-2). Such influences cannot be completely avoided in modern research, yet critical assessment of previous traditions is essential in order to gauge the way in which they influence current thinking. Whilst the relatively recent development of 'Middle Saxon' settlement archaeology as a distinct area of study would form a rather brief analysis, the modern discipline actually owes much of its practice to the more established and broader studies of 'Anglo-Saxon' history and archaeology. Beginning with a review of the earliest investigators of early medieval societies, this chapter will subsequently assess the development of both disciplines, albeit with a greater emphasis on archaeological studies, culminating with an appraisal of the central perceptions and debates that currently characterise 'Middle Saxon' settlement and landscape archaeology.

'Anglo-Saxon' Archaeology: Development of a Discipline

Perhaps the most significant continuing influence that the earliest investigation of 'Anglo-Saxon' archaeology has had upon current research is the almost singular emphasis placed on evidence from burials and cemeteries. Indeed, the lasting bias toward funerary material has even led some scholars to suggest that current knowledge remains restricted merely to furnished graves of the fifth to seventh centuries (Reynolds 2003, 98-9). The first recovery of early medieval graves occurred as early as the thirteenth century, but it was not until the eighteenth century that the first 'Anglo-Saxon' burials and churches were positively identified. In addition to their conspicuous character in the landscape, early investigators benefited from an ability to associate furnished burials with the details outlined in early charters (Dickinson 1983, 33). The latter half of the eighteenth century denoted a phase of intense investigation which lasted well into the Victorian period, as antiquarians became increasingly aware of the potential insight that investigation of the landscape could produce. In Kent, for instance, the Reverend Bryan Faussett apparently excavated over seven-hundred graves between 1757 and 1777, including twenty-eight in one day. Unfortunately, the attention to detailed documentation paid by Faussett was seldom replicated elsewhere, and the speed and cavalier attitude of most investigations led to the destruction of numerous sites without record (Arnold 1997, 3-4; Gerrard 2003, 5-15).

It was not until the second half of the nineteenth century that the discipline of 'Anglo-Saxon' archaeology, being the systematic investigation of early medieval remains, became more firmly established. At this time, historical research throughout Europe was largely dedicated towards defining the history of 'nations', and the creation of origin narratives for rapidly expanding states. Situated at the centre of a global empire, England required historical vindication for colonial attitudes and racial preconceptions. The value of English liberty was therefore seen as derived from 'Anglo-Saxon' democracy as an imperial myth of a superior Germanic race, ideally suited to rule other peoples, was developed. The idea of a Teutonic inheritance was one of two national myths central to English history, the other being origin stories surrounding the inhabitants of Troy and their supposed connections to Arthur and 'Celtic' Britain. It could even be argued that the perception of a singular 'Anglo-Saxon' nation and people was cultivated as early as the sixteenth century, in response to the rise of English imperial status (MacDougall 1982, 1-2). Racial applications to history during the nineteenth century were not therefore novel, but rather represented an intensification of a tradition that had persisted for several centuries. Irrespective of their exact origins, the approaches to 'Anglo-Saxon' studies that became so prominent in the Victorian period had a profound impact on subsequent generations, shaping attitudes that remained embedded in the collective subconscious of the English people (Gerrard 2003, 12-5; Hills 2003, 35; Stafford 2009b, 10-16).

Despite the significant interest in furnished burials during the nineteenth century, investigation of settlement sites in the same period was almost non-existent. Amongst the rare works on early medieval settlements, Stephen Stone recognised four 'Anglo-Saxon' 'dwelling places' in Oxfordshire during the 1850s (Stone 1859a; 1859b). Significantly, Stone initially noted the location of sites on the basis of crop-marks that he had detected on horseback, but also realised that density of artefacts in the ploughsoil were further indicators of previous settlement sites. The general principle of these prospection methods are now prominent in modern archaeology as aerial and fieldwalking survey, and using such approaches Stone was able to identify a series of 'pits', probably representing the remains of *Grubenhäuser* (Stone 1859a, 94; Tipper 2004, 15). Such research into settlement remained exceptionally slight in comparison to work on funerary sites, however, and by the end of the Victorian period typologies and chronological models were being developed from recovered grave goods. Typical of the colossal undertakings of data presentation that were produced around this time

are publications such as Gerard Baldwin-Brown's *The Arts in Early England* (Baldwin-Brown 1915).

Published at around the same time as Baldwin-Brown's work, was E.T. Leeds' *The Archaeology of Anglo-Saxon Settlements*, which represents the first notable attempt at amalgamating the archaeological evidence for 'Anglo-Saxon' society (Leeds 1913). In addition to data synthesis, Leeds' work was also amongst the first to specifically define the theories and methods of contemporary archaeology as the author perceived them (Arnold 1997, 8). Leeds, and other practitioners like him, were desperate to raise the profile and integrity of archaeology, and did so by attempting to corroborate the historical record with material culture. The result often undermined the original contribution of material studies, and more broadly the overarching value of archaeological approaches (Dickinson 1983, 34). One should not be over-critical of such pioneering works of the discipline, however, and it should be considered that approaches such as Leeds' merely reflect the document-driven agendas that characterised archaeological research throughout much of the twentieth century. Indeed, the syntheses of material and mapping of burial types and finds undertaken at this time formed the cornerstone of 'Anglo-Saxon' archaeology for much of the coming century, as demonstrated by David Wilson's *Anglo-Saxon England* which despite being published in the 1970s, retained a chronology that was still largely indebted to the research of individuals such as Leeds and Baldwin-Brown (Wilson 1976).

Acting as a guide for the budding discipline of archaeology, without doubt the early medieval text most utilised by any form of 'Anglo-Saxon' research has been Bede's *Historia Ecclesiastica Gentis Anglorum* (*HE*) ('Ecclesiastical History of the English People'). Completed in the first quarter of the eighth century, Bede's polemic remains the most influential source of any kind used by early medieval scholars (Jones and Page 2006, 6-7). In addition to details of the 'Anglo-Saxon' conversion and growth of the early Church, the *HE* also provides a descriptive account of the 'Early Saxon' migration, or the *Adventus Saxonum*. In an account based largely on the British cleric Gildas' *De Excidio Britonum* (*DEB*) ('The Ruin of Britain'), Bede depicted invading Germanic peoples driving west the 'wretched survivors' of the native Britons (*DEB*; Rippon 2000, 47; Yorke 1999, 26). In early archaeological studies, these accounts were ostensibly verified by material remains, such as the recovery of 'Germanic' artefacts from grave goods, but were also seemingly evidenced by the high proportion of Old English place-names and linguistic heritage (e.g. Myres 1969). It would be unfair to suggest that all early scholars agreed with this model, as researchers such as John Kemble attempted to 'retell' the accounts of early post-Roman Britain (Kemble 1849). Using archaeological material from the continent, Kemble was determined to demonstrate that written accounts of the *Adventus* were 'devoid of historical truth in every detail' (Kemble 1849, 16). Although extremely significant, such attempts to buck the prevailing paradigm were few and generally poorly received, and the largely uncritical use of written documents to interpret material evidence persisted well into the twentieth century (Sims-Williams 1983, 1-5).

More significant to the development of landscape archaeology as an independent discipline, researchers from the late nineteenth century also began to amalgamate historical evidence with topography. John Green's *The Making of England* for example, contained headings such as 'Conquest of Our Berkshire', as researchers attempted to map early migration against features in the countryside, particularly villages and fields. Whilst studies such as Paul Vinogradoff's (1892) *Villeinage in England* took as read that open fields and nucleated villages were the product of the earliest 'Anglo-Saxon' migrants, the publication of Howard Gray's *English Field Systems* firmly correlated landscape types with particular ethnic groups (Gray 1915). Gray's seminal publication ensured that the racial and ethnic makeup of 'Early Saxon' communities was seen as the causal factor behind England's regional settlement and landscape variation for the next fifty years. It was not until the 1920s that the first systematic excavation of an 'Anglo-Saxon' settlement was undertaken on the outskirts of the village of Sutton Courtenay (Leeds 1923; Williamson 2003, 10).

Early medieval settlement remains were first identified at Sutton Courtenay—then in Berkshire but now in Oxfordshire—by Dr. C.W. Cunnington who informed E.T. Leeds, then Keeper of Antiquities at the Ashmolean Museum. Excavations were begun by Leeds who undertook work in sporadic fashion between 1921 and 1937 in advance of phases of gravel quarrying (Leeds 1923; 1927; 1947; Chapter IV). The 'rescue' character of the work recovered only limited evidence, yet the positive recognition of features represented the only evidence for non-ecclesiastical Anglo-Saxon structures at the time (Hamerow 1991, 1; 2002, 7; Tipper 2004). In a significant departure from the previously positive views of 'Anglo-Saxon' culture, interpretation of the settlement at Sutton Courtenay, and similar sites excavated around the same time, such as Waterbeach, Cambridgeshire, (Lethbridge 1927) and Bourton-on-the-Water, Gloucestershire (Dunning 1932), were partly influenced by contemporary attitudes. The collapse of Anglo-German relations brought about by the First World War probably led to the interpretation of the ephemeral and apparently rudimentary archaeological deposits in a particularly negative manner. Leeds therefore interpreted *Grubenhäuser* as of a 'rude nature' and, disregarding the possibility that the structures might have been used as material dumps, concluded that the occupants lived 'amid a filthy litter of broken bones, of food and shattered pottery' (Leeds 1936, 25-6). Similarly, the settlement at St Neots, Cambridge was described by the excavators as 'miserable huts in almost as primitive a condition as can be expected' (Lethbridge and Tebbutt 1933, 149). The perception of rudimentary 'Anglo-Saxon' daily life persisted for several decades, as part of a wider belief that cultural affinities could be linked to architectural style and excavated ground plans (Reynolds 2003, 98).

In spite of these early efforts, and partly as the result of Second World War, investigation of early medieval settlements continued to progress at an exceedingly slow rate during the 1940s. Further global conflict promoted further reconsideration of England's 'Anglo-Saxon' heritage, as scholars reacted against fascist concepts of nation and race. The *Adventus* again served as the focus for the definition of new attitudes, and from the 1970s migration began to be rejected as an explanatory model for material change (Hodges 1989; Chapman and Hamerow 1997, 3). This reaction against 'invasion neurosis' was initially and unintentionally sparked by David Clarke's (1966) paper on prehistoric migration, and although initially slow to react, early medievalists also began to voice doubt over how material culture change was understood (Hills 2003, 37; Stafford 2009b, 16). Several studies began to emerge arguing for hybridisation of 'Anglo-Saxon' and 'British' peoples, and for the existence of only small 'Anglo-Saxon' warrior elites, based particularly on evidence from burial grounds of the fifth and sixth-centuries. Contributions from settlement researchers arrived somewhat later, such as Phillip Dixon's (1982) study illustrating an apparent lack of continental precursors for the byre-less 'Anglo-Saxon' house (Hamerow 1997, 34-38).

Increasing Awareness: New Research of the Early Medieval Landscape

Although hostilities with Germany had again resulted in a more critical approach to understanding the English past, paradoxically, it was the period immediately after the Second World War that 'Anglo-Saxon' settlement archaeology began to develop as a more coherent discipline (Loyn 2007, 9). The excavation of the extraordinary ship burial in Mound 1 at Sutton Hoo, Suffolk, on the eve of war in 1939 brought 'Anglo-Saxon' archaeology into the popular imagination, acting as a stimulus for further research (Bruce-Mitford 1974; Lapidge 2002, 19). In spite of the continuing focus on burial material, the 1950s ushered in something of a qualitative transformation for 'Anglo-Saxon' settlement archaeology. Excavation of the palatial complex at Yeavering, Northumberland, by Brian Hope-Taylor from 1953 had a particularly positive impact for early medieval settlement studies, demonstrating that conspicuous displays of wealth and status were not solely restricted to the burial tableau (Hope-Taylor 1977). Yeavering's initial identification on aerial photographs was also significant, illustrating the new means available to archaeologists attempting to study early medieval settlements on a landscape-scale. Such methods were further supplemented by improved excavation techniques, many of which were developed on the continent, such as open area investigation and *pro forma* recording, all of which resulted in marked improvements in available archaeological data (Tipper 2004, 15).

Only two years after Hope-Taylor began excavating at Yeavering, W.G. Hoskins published *The Making of the English Landscape*, regarded by many as the founding text for historic landscape studies (Hoskins 1955). There can be little doubt over the influence of this work, although modern landscape archaeologists have debated the merits of Hoskins' approach (e.g. Fleming 2007 vs. Johnson 2007). Perhaps Hoskins' most significant contribution to archaeological studies was the emphasis that he placed upon the landscape as 'the richest historical record that we possess', regarding the countryside itself as an artefact worthy of study in its own right (Hoskins 1955, 14; Rippon 2000b). In spite of such recognition, the view of the early medieval landscape amongst scholars at this time remained largely the same as researchers from the preceding generation. The document-led approach to archaeological material used by doyens such as Leeds was embraced by individuals such as J.N.L. Myres. Using the distribution of pottery largely derived from cremation burials, Myres' *Anglo-Saxon Pottery and the Settlement of England* attempted to illustrate the 'invasion routes' of the 'Early Saxon' period (Myres 1969). Whilst utilising the significantly increased corpus of archaeological data at their disposal, academics therefore continued to assert the traditional view of England's historic landscape as the product of the earliest Germanic migrants.

Challenging Traditions: New Ideas of Early Medieval Settlement

If the post-War period represented a quantitative transformation for medieval settlement archaeology, then the 1970s was marked by a revolution (Williamson 2003, 13), as a series of sites were excavated predominantly on a 'rescue' basis. As infrastructural developments placed the archaeological record under increasing threat, the organisation 'Rescue' was formed in 1972 with the aim of recording sites at risk. Large-scale excavations, particularly of urban sites such as London, Ipswich and York transformed understanding of early medieval trade and urbanism (Gerard and Rippon 2007, 535), but in rural areas too, there was a growing awareness of the potential for destruction to significant material posed by development and industry. Fewer more important sites were investigated at this time than Mucking in Essex, the scale of excavation at which remains unparalleled by any early medieval settlement in England (Jones and Jones 1974; Jones 1980; Hamerow 1991).

At Mucking, the extent of excavations revealed an unambiguous picture of a transient settlement type, identifying for the first time what is known on the continent as *Wandersiedlung* or 'wandering settlement' (Hamerow 1991, 13). The dating of occupation layers at Mucking, in addition to the apparent lack of high status buildings created initial speculation that it was a 'pioneer' site: a first landing place for storm-tossed peoples arriving from the continent (Hamerow 1991, 8). Preliminary interpretation almost exclusively concentrated on the earliest settlement phases, despite evidence for occupation until at least the beginning of the eighth century. The recovery of Ipswich Ware, then dated to c.650-850, and two 'Middle Saxon' sceatta finds suggested that although Mucking may have been occupied as early as the fifth century, habitation in

the area perhaps continued as late as the ninth century (Rippon 2007, 172). Probably the most important initial outcome of the excavations at Mucking and comparable sites such as West Stow in Suffolk, was that they clearly demonstrated that 'Early-Middle Saxon' settlements were of a different character to historic villages (West 1985).

The material from such excavations also began to be supplemented by new forms of archaeological evidence from the 1970s onwards— most significantly from fieldwalking surveys. The development of landscape archaeology around this time led to the recovery of artefactual material from ploughsoil through the systematic 'walking' of fields, particularly in east midland counties such as Northamptonshire. In the countryside around existing villages, this novel survey method began to detect concentrations of early medieval ceramics, consisting almost exclusively of organic-tempered ware, datable only to a very broad c.450-850 phase or 'Early-Middle Saxon' period (e.g. Foard 1978; Hall and Martin 1979; Chapter III). The existence of settlement centres underlying such pottery concentrations was often demonstrated by subsequent excavation which regularly identified occupation structures. Similar to the more extensively excavated settlement at Mucking, habitation at such sites appeared to be relatively short-lived. Indeed, the quantity of discrete pottery scatters located by fieldwalking also indicated that, akin to Mucking, these settlements possessed a dispersed pattern with a tendency to shift across the landscape over time (Ford 1995).

The evidence from fieldwalking and targeted excavation therefore demonstrated without doubt that the earliest medieval settlements were of vastly different character to later medieval villages. The traditional model of village origins was thus clearly no longer tenable, leading to the development of a new interpretive framework. In arriving at this conclusion, of equal importance to the fieldwalked finds of 'Early-Middle Saxon' organic-tempered ware, was an almost complete lack of later material from the same artefact scatters (e.g. Foard 1978; Hall 1981). This evidence implied the replacement of transient, scattered farmsteads at some point in which 'Early-Middle Saxon' ceramics were in use, but before the introduction of 'Late Saxon' wares, a point recognised by some early fieldwalking pioneers such as David Hall (Hall 1981, 37). It is somewhat baffling, however, the prevailing view that emerged from the late 1970s was that village formation dated to sometime *after* the mid-ninth century, with most arguing for a protracted 'village moment' process perhaps continuing as late as the thirteenth century (e.g. Lewis *et al.* 1997, 198). Until relatively recently, the earliest material derived from investigations into both currently occupied villages and deserted sites was also invariably 'Late Saxon' in origin, ostensibly supporting a late date for early medieval settlement change (e.g. Chapman 2010).

As Stephen Rippon (2010, 54) has observed, central to divergent interpretations are the different datasets that scholars utilise; with fieldwalking evidence pointing to a *terminus ante quem* of *c*.850 for the creation of historic villages, but a body of material derived from villages apparently providing a *terminus post quem* of *c*.850 for the same process. Whilst this book is not primarily concerned with explaining the origins of later medieval landscape and settlement character, central to the village origin debate is the way in which the 'Middle Saxon' countryside, and indeed 'Middle Saxon' society itself, is perceived. The revisionist model of the late 1970s, which remains the prevailing one amongst scholarship today, suggests albeit implicitly that the landscape of England remained largely unchanged until at least the ninth century (e.g. Lewis *et al.* 1997, 79-81; Dyer 2003, 21). Over the last two decades, however, the archaeological dataset relating to 'Middle Saxon' settlement has increased dramatically and, whilst such material continues to be most commonly filtered into village origin debates, the breadth and quality of material also lends itself to alternative research aims.

OUT OF OBSCURITY: RECENT 'MIDDLE SAXON' SETTLEMENT RESEARCH

The last two decades undeniably represent the most significant period for the emergence of 'Middle Saxon' settlement studies with regard to sheer increase of available data. Earlier work had provided some important foundations, however, as a number of investigations throughout the 1970s and 1980s hinted at a more complex 'Middle Saxon' settlement hierarchy than that typically envisaged. At Cowdery's Down, Hampshire, for instance, excavation revealed a sixth and seventh-century complex consisting of a series of large halls and rectilinear enclosures, demonstrating a significant degree of permanence and spatial demarcation (Millett and James 1983). Sites apparently illustrating a similar degree of planning were also identified at Foxley, Wiltshire, and Catholme, Staffordshire (Hinchcliffe 1986; Losco-Bradley and Kinsley 2002). More recently, detailed excavation at West Heslerton, North Yorkshire, also showed exceptionally long-lived occupation apparently zoned into discrete areas (Powlesland 1990). The importance of the seventh and eighth centuries as a transformative period was also highlighted by what has become known as the 'Middle Saxon shuffle' model (Arnold and Wardle 1981). Based on excavated 'Early Saxon' settlements such as Mucking in Essex, West Stow in Suffolk and Chalton in Hampshire, archaeologists Christopher Arnold and Ken Wardle argued for a dislocation in occupation sites around the late seventh century, as 'Early Saxon' settlements located on lighter soils and higher ground were abandoned in favour of richer soils in river valleys (Arnold and Wardle 1981; see also Moreland 2000, 86-7).

The 'Middle Saxon shuffle' has since been subject to major critique, based largely on the data used to develop the model. Helena Hamerow (1991; 2002, 121-4) has demonstrated that many shifting settlements have probably only been partly investigated, and that other phases of occupation may lie beyond excavated the area in many cases. The apparent dislocation visible in some sites, she

argues, is therefore a product of research conditions rather than an actual marked change in the settlement sequence. In the case of Mucking, Rippon (2008, 171) has proposed that settlement may have shifted from the gravel terrace to the lower-lying site occupied by the parish church through a process of continued and gradual migration. Such re-assessments reflect heightened awareness amongst scholars of the range of archaeological evidence available to them, which has led to an increased concern for 'Middle Saxon' settlement studies more generally. Whilst the material upon which the 'Middle Saxon shuffle' is based thus renders it largely untenable as a concept, the idea of settlement transformation before the mid-ninth century has not been wholly disregarded.

Based on a multi-disciplinary project in the Nene Valley of Northamptonshire, Tony Brown and Glenn Foard argued again for a crucial modification of the settlement sequence in the 'Middle Saxon' period, but associated such change more convincingly with the development of historic villages (Brown and Foard 1998). The pair claimed that, based on evidence from the Raunds area in particular, some historic villages developed as part of a two-stage process, with the initial 'nucleation' phase occurring probably in the seventh or eighth centuries, followed by a later process of restructuring which created the historic village form (Brown and Foard 1998, 80; Parry 2006; Audouy 2009; Chapman 2010). The evidence on which Brown and Foard based their idea is explored more thoroughly in Chapter III, but of central importance to their hypothesis was the archaeological data derived from investigation in and immediately surrounding Raunds village itself. The research potential of such investigation within village environs has been recognised by archaeologists for some time, but was first demonstrated clearly by the investigators of the Shapwick Project, Somerset (Aston and Gerard 1999; Gerard 1999; 2007). The excavation of small test-pits in empty plots and gardens of still-occupied villages has since been adopted by a number of research projects, such as the Whittlewood Project, Northamptonshire (Jones and Page 2006), and the Higher Education Field Academy (HEFA) project, run by the University of Cambridge (Lewis 2007; 2010).

Based on test-pits in a number of villages, the researchers of the Whittlewood Project cautiously suggested that some historic centres possessed 'pre-village nuclei', with origins datable to the pre-ninth century (Jones and Page 2006, 222). Outside of Northamptonshire, the research of the HEFA project has been far more critical of the potential significance of 'Middle Saxon' settlement material from current villages. Based on test-pit excavations of fifty-one villages across nine counties in central and eastern England, Carenza Lewis concluded that, with the exception of Essex and South Suffolk, there seems to be little evidence for any co-location between sites of the 'Early-Middle Saxon' period, and later-occupied villages (Lewis 2010, 103). As Chapter II of this volume shall shortly demonstrate, however, there are a number of fundamental problems surrounding the methodology employed by the

HEFA project, and thus the conclusions reached by the investigators remain open to question. Central to such methodological issues are the way in which HEFA defines 'Currently Occupied Rural Settlements' or 'CORS', and the adequacy of limited test-pitting for the identification of often ephemeral 'Middle Saxon' settlement deposits (see Chapter II).

It is not only research-orientated projects that have investigated village environs though, as the last two decades have witnessed a major increase in commercial investigation of currently-occupied rural settlements. From 1991, the introduction of statutory heritage protection for the historic environment, first represented by Planning Policy Guidance (PPG) 16, and more recently by Planning Policy Statement (PPS) 5, has transformed archaeological practice across the United Kingdom. The legal obligation of contractors to mitigate for damage or loss to the historic environment, has led to an unprecedented increase of archaeological projects in advance of development. Many such projects which have recovered evidence for early medieval settlement have been subject to full publication, such as Yarnton, Oxfordshire and Higham Ferrers, Northamptonshire (Hey 2004; Hardy *et al.* 2007). The majority of development-led commercial archaeology projects remain unpublished, however, with reports instead archived in the National Monuments Record (NMR), and regional HERs, as well as in some online sources such as OASIS managed by the University of York. Academics have been slow to realise the significance of this body of so-called 'grey-literature', and although attitudes are slowly improving (e.g. Hamerow 2010), the quantity of data produced by commercial units continues to far outstrip related scholarly research.

'Middle Saxon' settlement research therefore currently stands at something of a cross-roads. Whilst research-orientated projects have laid a firm foundation, rehearsing the evidence from the same corpus of sites and landscapes will undoubtedly lead to stagnation in our growing understanding of the early medieval countryside. The current economic environment has resulted in decreased funding for academic field-projects, making the marked expansion in the dataset from development-led investigation all the more crucial to furthering research. It is therefore through a combination of the academic endeavour outlined above, and the unpublished 'grey-literature' that new insights of the early medieval landscape are most likely to be developed. The more detailed methods by which this research will approach the data are discussed in the following chapter.

CONCLUSION

The above analysis of previous and current 'Middle Saxon' settlement research illustrates a number of central themes that will be explored by this book. The most fundamental debates regarding early medieval landscape studies remain centred on village origins, particularly the emergence of 'nucleated' settlements that came to characterise much of central England. This research is not primarily concerned with explaining such divergence of settlement form, but of key relevance to such debates is the implicit way 'Middle Saxon' settlement and society is viewed in such models, and indeed by scholars generally. Following the development of fieldwalking in the late 1970s, the prevailing interpretation amongst scholars continues to assert that villages emerged during a protracted 'village moment' process which began around the mid-ninth century at the very earliest. The preoccupation with village origins in such interpretive frameworks has led to a neglect of earlier developments, however, as the pre-ninth century landscape is amalgamated into a broad 'Early-Middle Saxon' period.

By the 1980s, the traditional view of the early medieval landscape had been firmly rejected, and the 'Late Saxon' period heralded as the time at which significant changes to the English countryside first occurred. From as early as the 1970s, however, a number of excavation programmes already began to reveal 'Middle Saxon' settlements of appreciable variety and complexity, suggesting that the significance of the pre-ninth century period could not be wholly disregarded. The persisting emphasis placed by modern scholarship on the ninth century and later period, however, is part of a more deep-rooted interest in 'Late Saxon' England, inherited from the document-driven agendas that characterised early archaeological research. The vast increase of available written sources, coupled with the more durable material remains of 'Late Saxon' society certainly provide improved research conditions, but this has been to the detriment of the period immediately preceding it. Whilst the continuity and migration debates of the 'Early Saxon' period have also attracted academic investment, until relatively recently the 'Middle Saxon' period had somewhat fallen through the cracks.

The last two decades have led to a transformation of 'Middle Saxon' archaeology, however, both in terms of the available data, and the scholarly focus now afforded the discipline. The onset of statutory heritage protection has been fundamentally important in providing a rapidly growing body of material for study, the most prominent of which has been utilised by academic research. The 'grey-literature' relevant to early medieval settlement remains largely untapped by researchers though and as the corpus of commercially-led work continues to exceed research-led fieldwork, academic understanding of the archaeological material will become increasingly polarised without more active engagement. Concentrating on five counties within central and eastern England, this book will therefore counter the existing research trend by placing far greater emphasis on the 'grey literature' in order to provide a greater understanding of settlement and landscape in the 'Middle Saxon' period. In particular it will focus on contributing to the central debate of early medieval landscape studies, regarding the degree of transformation and complexity that can be viewed in the 'Middle Saxon' countryside. It will be demonstrated that the enduring scholarly focus on village origins undermines the significant changes that 'Middle Saxon' communities underwent—changes that are indicative of deep-rooted developments in society.

Particularly prominent in this volume, is the contribution both of the 'grey literature' and of published sources of 'Middle Saxon' settlement evidence from still-occupied villages. Such data is naturally of essential relevance to debates regarding village origins, and indeed does hint at a relationship between 'Middle Saxon' and later settlements. This theme will be investigated further in the coming chapters, but the focus of discussion will remain upon the central aim of providing an insight of 'Middle Saxon' society through study of seventh to ninth-century settlement remains. This agenda will be addressed through a series of case studies that address these objectives, which will provide a greater understanding of the countryside throughout the period which in turn will fulfil the key aim of providing greater comprehension of the social, economic and political environment of 'Middle Saxon' England. The following chapter details the methods by which the archaeological data for this book was acquired and assessed. Of vital importance is the way in which 'currently occupied' settlements are defined and understood, in order to research the potential relationship between 'Middle Saxon' settlement and existing villages critically. Chapter II also presents a discussion of the way in which alternative forms of data to archaeology have been used by this research, with particular detail given to the deployment of written sources.

Chapter II
Approaches and Methods

Based on a thorough critique of previous and existing approaches to early medieval settlement studies, the previous chapter delineated the main focus of this book and its broader research context. The primary aim and a number of related objectives have been established, as this work seeks to provide an insight into 'Middle Saxon' society, through detailed study of seventh to ninth-century settlement remains from five counties across central and eastern England. The transformation of the 'Middle Saxon' countryside remains a central debate within pre-Conquest settlement studies, with the prevailing opinion amongst scholars asserting that key changes only occurred from the mid-ninth century onward, at the very earliest. Contrary to this outlook, this book will demonstrate an increasingly complex and rapidly developing settlement hierarchy before the mid-ninth century, providing a unique insight into contemporary economic, social and political conditions in 'Middle Saxon' England. Now that the fundamental aims and objectives of this research have been outlined, this chapter will delineate more specifically the approaches and methods used to accomplish them. Beginning with a definition of the study area, this chapter will then describe the methods by which the archaeological data relating to the five counties was gathered. Given that currently-occupied settlement research represents such a significant contribution to this book, the chapter will subsequently undertake a critical analysis of the way in which data from such contexts is defined and quantified. The piece will close with a brief discussion of the way in which alternative sources to archaeology are used by this research.

INTRODUCING THE STUDY AREA

The study area of this book comprises five counties in central and eastern England, listed here in order of presentation: Northamptonshire, Oxfordshire, Wiltshire, Cambridgeshire and Norfolk (Figure 2.1). This study area therefore forms a broad transect running from the North Sea in Norfolk, to Wiltshire, the south-eastern point of which is located less than 10km from the English Channel. The counties were chosen on the basis of a number of factors. Topographical conditions were amongst the foremost considerations, as it was deemed that only through study of a diverse geographical area could 'comprehensive transformation...across all types of countryside' be demonstrated (Chapter I, X). The five counties chosen therefore possess marked landscape variation, and include countrysides such as the chalk downlands of Wiltshire, the Fenlands of eastern England, and the broad, fertile floodplain of the Thames in Oxfordshire.

Previous investigation was also another significant factor, as this book sought to study an area which possessed a mixture of research traditions. Counties such as Norfolk and Northamptonshire, for instance, which have been subject to a substantial number of fieldwalking projects, has not been replicated everywhere, such as in Wiltshire which has experienced far less archaeological investigation overall. The landscape of Oxfordshire has similarly been subject to relatively few systematic fieldwalking surveys, but in the Thames floodplain in particular, a number of large-scale excavations have yielded significant early medieval settlement evidence. Incorporating areas with varied histories of archaeological study allows models regarding the early medieval landscape, typically developed in well-research midland counties such as Northamptonshire, to be compared and contrasted with the material evidence from regions with a less-impressive record of previous investigation. On the basis of such mixed research profiles, this book will assess the way in which existing traditions influence the way in which early medieval settlement has been perceived in different parts of central and eastern England.

The third and final consideration for choosing a study area was purely based on practical implications, and particularly the quality and accessibility of HER data. Although all unitary authorities possess an HER, the functioning and management of individual archives varies hugely. Many HERs have made a significant quantity of their material available online, such as Norfolk which allows full record searches to be conducted. Other HERs operate a largely paper-based search system, the use of which is far more difficult and time-consuming, such as Northamptonshire. That Northamptonshire was researched regardless was due to its central role in the development of early medieval settlement studies, and the extent and detail of available data. This reflects the balanced approach that was required when defining counties for research, with a combination of the above factors contributing to the final selection of the study area.

The following chapters will explain the character of each region in detail, but it is important to note here the arbitrary nature of counties as units for 'Middle Saxon' settlement study. Certainly in the Wessex region it is possible to trace the concept of shires (OE *scir*) as far back as the eighth century, where they likely formed early taxable units for the provision of renders to centres, which themselves formed a focus both for royal accumulation and 'shire' identity (Yorke 1995, 87). It is only following the West Saxon re-conquest of the eastern Danelaw in the early

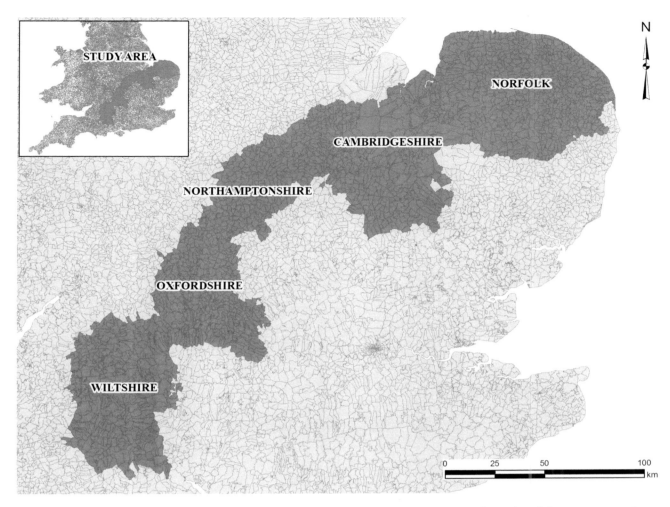

FIGURE 2.1: THE FIVE COUNTIES THAT COMPRISE THE STUDY AREA AND THEIR LOCATION WITHIN THE SOUTHERN BRITAIN (INSET). SOURCE FOR MAPPING: HISTORIC PARISHES OF ENGLAND AND WALES ONLINE

tenth century, however, that county-based administration became ubiquitous across central and southern England, allowing their form and function to be viewed with greater clarity (Oosthuizen 2001, 52). The relationship between shires and 'Middle Saxon' landscape arrangements is therefore uncertain, and the counties were utilised largely on the basis that they remain the essential framework utilised by HERs. The choice between adopting historic or modern county boundaries as study areas was based upon the coverage of the relevant HER, made explicit in each chapter.

DATA COLLECTION

Once the five counties that comprise the study area had been defined, each of the HERs was subject to a comprehensive search for data relating to 'Middle Saxon' settlement. Having established the extent of 'Middle Saxon' settlement records, the quality and relevance of each 'grey-literature' report was individually assessed. In addition to the unpublished material derived from HERs, a comprehensive search of the published literature was also carried out. It is this combined evidence, from both the unpublished 'grey-literature', and the more widely-recognised material in-print, that forms the basis of

evidence used by this book. Founded on the data searches in the five HERs in particular, however, it became quickly apparent that a significant quantity of the 'Middle Saxon' settlement material relevant to this research was derived from archaeological investigations within currently-occupied rural centres. It was considered that this initial observation required further analysis, and crucially quantification, so that the regularity with which 'Middle Saxon' material found in villages could be determined with greater clarity. The following section details the way in which this aim was achieved using the Archaeological Investigations Project (AIP) archive, in addition to explaining how 'currently-occupied' has been used in previous studies, and the way in which it is defined by this research.

'CURRENTLY-OCCUPIED' SETTLEMENT RESEARCH

As discussed in the previous chapter, scholars have become increasingly aware of the research potential of 'currently-occupied' settlement investigation (Chapter I, p28-31). Perhaps the longest- running research of still-occupied rural settlements is that of the Higher Education Field Academy (HEFA) scheme, organised by the University of Cambridge. First piloted in 2005 and having just completed

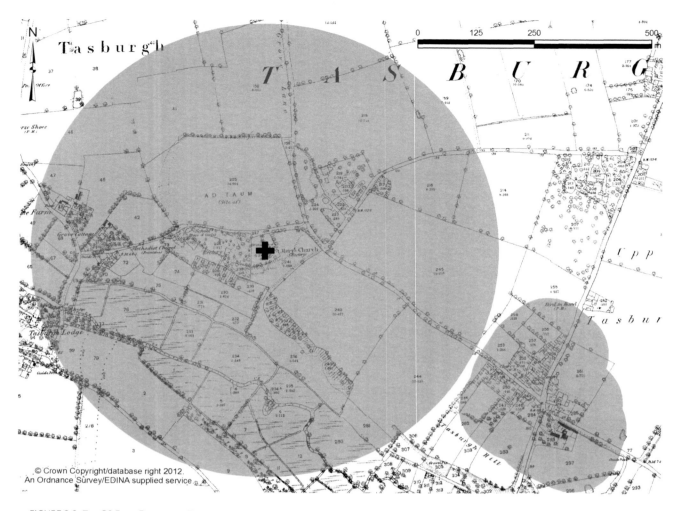

FIGURE 2.2: THE OS FIRST EDITION OF TASBURGH, NORFOLK. THE TWO ZONES SURROUNDING THE PARISH CHURCH (CROSS) AND HISTORIC VILLAGE CENTRE ENSURES THAT SETTLEMENT DEVELOPMENT AT BOTH LOCATIONS IS CLASSED AS 'CURRENTLY-OCCUPIED'

the tenth consecutive season of study, the key observation made by the HEFA project for this research, is that there appears to be little relationship between 'Early-Middle Saxon' activity and 'currently-occupied' settlements (Lewis 2010, 103). Closer inspection of the methods used, and the way in which 'currently-occupied' is defined by the HEFA scheme, however, questions the validity of such an analysis. Critique of previous approaches also forms a platform from which this book can develop a more coherent research methodology.

Involving local community groups and young people, the fieldwork conducted by HEFA comprises excavation of 1x1m archaeological test-pits, dug to depths not exceeding 1.2m. Such restricted areas of investigation are not suited to the identification of 'Middle Saxon' settlement deposits, which are typically characterised by ephemeral remains often difficult to identify, even through open-area excavation. With depth of excavation set by health and safety regulations, it is also questionable whether the test-pits in many cases reach stratigraphic horizons in which 'Middle Saxon' deposits are likely to be encountered. Indeed, it is a notable outcome of this research that the

most compelling 'Middle Saxon' settlement evidence from currently-occupied villages is derived from development-led investigations, excavating far more extensive areas and to greater depths than the HEFA test-pits.

Another significant observation of the HEFA research is the way in which 'currently-occupied' is defined by the investigators. Basing their areas of excavation on largely practical considerations, the members of the HEFA project excavate test-pits in unoccupied plots or areas of private and public land where permission has been granted. Whilst this results in a useful random sampling strategy, considerable quantities of the test-pits examined are located in areas outside of what might be realistically classed as 'historic' village centres, such as recently-developed suburban areas. Projecting the location of test-pits excavated in the village of Great Sheldon, Cambridgeshire onto the Ordnance Survey First Edition (dated to 1885) for instance, it is clear that the majority of locations are in areas that were not 'currently-occupied', even in the middle of the nineteenth century (Figure 2.2). The use of the term 'CORS' (Currently-occupied Rural Settlements) is therefore misleading, as although excavation may be undertaken within areas of modern-day settlement, the locations of many test-pits investigated by HEFA could not be classified as part of a historic village core.

A final, rather obvious, point to be made regarding the lack of observed 'Early-Middle Saxon' material by the HEFA scheme is that an absence of evidence does not determine a lack of previous activity. Excavating test-pits of such limited scale, it is possible that even through investigation of significant numbers of trenches, that extant 'Middle Saxon' deposits remained undetected. These circumstances are made apparent by reviewing the 2010 HEFA Report published in Medieval Settlement Research, which notes that test-pits excavated in the village of Cottenham, Cambridgeshire detected no 'Middle Saxon' remains whatsoever (Lewis 2011, 50-2). As this work will demonstrate, though, more extensive development-excavation in other parts of the village has identified substantial pre-ninth century settlement remains, underscoring the caution with which the conclusions made by the HEFA project must be treated (Chapter VI, p206-12). Similarly, the lack of post-medieval activity in a trench does not determine that to this part of the village had become deserted at this time, and so similar caution is urged for earlier periods. This critique of the current practice of the HEFA scheme, perhaps the most well-known 'currently-occupied' rural settlement investigation in England, provides a number of important conclusions for this research. Most importantly it demonstrates that test-pits are not appropriate for the identification of early medieval settlement remains, and that when studying village environs usage of the term 'currently-occupied' must be made explicit. As it was necessary for this research to quantify the regularity with which 'Middle Saxon' settlement deposits are located within existing villages, the following section describes the way in which 'currently-occupied' was defined, based on lessons derived from the above critique.

'CURRENTLY-OCCUPIED': QUANTIFYING AND QUALIFYING

The Archaeological Investigations Project (AIP) was established as a joint project between English Heritage and Bournemouth University, with the intention of providing a national database of all conducted archaeological fieldwork. The AIP now holds records for all investigations undertaken between 1990 and 2009 for each of the five counties studied by this book. The coverage of the AIP provides an ideal database with which to quantify the frequency of 'Middle Saxon' settlement finds within 'currently-occupied' rural centres. It cannot be claimed that the AIP is a completely comprehensive database, as many notable investigations conducted over the past three years are not included, but its analysis nevertheless provides a valuable guide with which to define the co-location of 'Middle Saxon' settlements with existing villages.

This book created a database of 'currently-occupied' village excavations for each of the five counties, consisting

of archaeological interventions classified by the AIP as 'evaluations' or 'excavations', but excluding projects listed as 'test-pits' or 'watching briefs'. It was deemed that the latter two categories were likely too restrictive to determine the presence or absence of 'Middle Saxon' occupation deposits with a suitable degree of confidence, and thus only the records from more extensive 'currently-occupied' excavations were assessed. As this exercise was aimed primarily at providing a measure of 'currently-occupied' settlement research, analysis was undertaken only of interventions dated between 1990 and those most recently archived by the AIP. This approach therefore emphasises in particular the contribution of development-led archaeological projects, and the significance of the material that such interventions have produced. The term 'rural' also required definition, and for this purpose any centre that had been subject to an English Heritage Extensive Urban Survey was not regarded as a 'rural' settlement. Although not included as part of the AIP 'CORS' assessment, 'Middle Saxon' settlement evidence from places which later developed as towns form an extensive and important corpus, and thus are referred to in the discussion.

The above review of past research also demonstrated that 'currently-occupied' has been used by some investigators as a rather loose term, lacking critical definition. It is clear that the results of excavation within unambiguously areas of modern development, in particular, add little to our understanding of the relationship between 'Middle Saxon' settlements and the later historic landscape. This research therefore adopted a stricter definition of 'currently-occupied' in order to understand with greater clarity, the relationship between early medieval and later settlement. The Ordnance Survey First Edition maps of the mid nineteenth century represent the first comprehensive topographic survey of England, with a consistency of recording which far surpasses the marginally earlier tithe maps and apportionments. OS First edition surveys therefore represent our oldest source of nationwide and reliable mapping, providing an accurate record of the historic landscape as it looked in the nineteenth century. Rather than determining 'currently-occupied' on the basis of the modern landscape, this research mapped the AIP data against OS First Editions. This methodology therefore situated archaeological investigations within the earliest compressive and accurate geographical record of the historic landscape, removing the influence of the unprecedented expansion of rural settlement growth dated to the last one-hundred and fifty years.

Contrary to the methodology adopted by the HEFA project, the approach used by this book therefore delineates historic 'cores' far more precisely, allowing a more comprehensive analysis of the relationship between 'Middle Saxon' and later settlement forms to be reached. Utilising OS First Edition Revisions in the rare instances when First Editions were not accessible, an arbitrary curtilage of 100m was created around village centres and tenements, with a further 500m zone surrounding any existing parish church, together creating a 'core area' of historic settlement. The inclusion of the additional zone surrounding the parish church is due to the clear significance of such centres in the development of early medieval settlement sequences. In many regions studied in this book, but particularly in Norfolk, the parish church stands in isolation, positioned in a discrete location to the historic settlement centre (Figure 2.3). It was deemed essential to this research that archaeological investigations undertaken at both foci were assessed in such instances, and thus a curtilage around both settlement and church was created. Investigations recorded by the AIP that were undertaken within either of the zones were classed as 'currently-occupied', and the results analysed for the detection or absence of 'Middle Saxon' activity. Where present, 'Middle Saxon' activity was divided between purely artefactual material, and evidence for structural features. The following five county-based chapters each possess an analysis and interpretation of investigations into currently-occupied rural settlements, based on the above methodology. In addition to the AIP analysis and assessment of the material culture from the five counties, this research also engaged with non-archaeological evidence in order to provide as comprehensive a study as possible. The following section details the way in which these alternative sources were utilised, before this chapter closes with some concluding remarks.

BEYOND ARCHAEOLOGY: THE USE OF OTHER SOURCES

As Chapter I demonstrated, throughout its development early medieval archaeology has been closely related to other disciplines, especially document-based research. Although initially slow to engage with the 'post-processual' school of thought developed primarily by prehistorians, from the early 1990s medieval archaeologists began to assess more critically the use of written sources. Studies such as David Austin's (1990), demonstrated the problems and restrictions of using documentary data to lead medieval archaeological research, instead asserting that the material record could be utilised as the 'primary text' (Austin 1990, 10). Whereas some have, somewhat over-zealously called for the near-total disregard of documentary material (e.g. Alternberg 2003), a more productive line of enquiry consists of archaeological-orientated investigation, supplemented by alternative sources where available.

Such an approach maintains the material record as the 'primary text', whilst engaging with other sources to compare, contrast and contextualise the findings of archaeology-led research. Apart from Bede's *HE*, our main source of information relating to the 'Middle Saxon' landscape is the corpus of diplomas, writs and wills, known collectively as charters (Yorke 1995, 54). From the late seventh century onwards, scribes began to formulate official records detailing the transfer of privileges, relating to particular estates, in order to create a lasting legal record. The Church was at the forefront of this movement, adopting the established principles of Roman land law, recording the creation of administrative units derived from

royal patronage that were free from the burdens of tax (Hooke 1998, 85).

The written texts of charters typically comprise two parts. The legal record detailing the grantor and the grantee, which usually also mentions the size of the estate and the appurtenances to which the recipient will obtain rights. In addition to the legal script, significant quantities of charters are accompanied by boundary clauses also known as perambulations, allowing the extents of an estate to be identified on the ground (Jenkyns 1999, 97). These clauses are the element of charters most frequently used by archaeologists, as they provide a written record of physical features that may potentially leave an archaeological signature. Deployment of charter evidence is not as straightforward as is often made out however, and archaeologists remain guilty of treating the material in an often uninformed and uncritical manner. Amongst the central problems of charter data is that few early medieval texts survive in their original form, and we possess even fewer that originate from before the mid-ninth century. Scholars are instead mostly dependent upon versions copied into monastic cartularies, causing numerous problems for modern research (e.g. Stenton 1953; Brooks 1974; Wormald 1984).

In addition to the miscopying and misinterpretation of text by later scribes, often only sections of the earlier document were reproduced, and boundary clauses, usually written in the vernacular, were often edited out by post-Conquest scribes unfamiliar with Old English. 'Improvement' of charters by later scribes is also common, changing earlier church-dedications for current ones, for example, or interpolating other material to help ensure rights and privileges. Outright forgeries are usually relatively easy to dismiss as such, but more difficult to interpret are substantially genuine charters which have received various interpolations (Yorke 1995, 55). The coverage of charter evidence is also uneven across England, with research in the east of the country particularly impinged on by an extremely lacunose record. Indeed, of the thirty-five boundary descriptions in manuscripts widely accepted as genuinely dating before *c*.900, twenty-six relate to land in Kent, and only one to Wessex (Jenkyns 1999, 97).

The body of 'Middle Saxon' documents therefore represent a tiny percentage of the charter data relating to the early medieval landscape of England, and it must be remembered that such early records are of distinctly different character to 'Late Saxon' texts. Pre-tenth century boundary clauses typically include only brief Latin statements of location, and the evolution from such documents into the detailed vernacular descriptions characteristic of the tenth century is difficult to trace (Hooke 1998, 85-6). The limited and fragmentary corpus of likely genuine 'Middle Saxon' boundary clauses has led to the widespread back-projection of details contained in later clauses, particularly from the well-documented counties of central-southern England. Whilst present understanding of the early medieval landscape derived from charter evidence is

FIGURE 2.3: THE OS FIRST EDITION OF GREAT SHELFORD, CAMBRIDGESHIRE, WITH THE LOCATIONS OF TEST PITS DUG AS PART OF THE HEFA PROJECT MARKED AS DOTS. ALTHOUGH IN THE MODERN LANDSCAPE ALL OF THE TEST-PITS ARE LOCATED IN 'CURRENTLY-OCCUPIED' AREAS, WHEN PLOTTED AGAINST EARLIER MAPPING IT IS CLEAR THAT MOST ARE NOT LOCATED IN OR EVEN ADJACENT-TO OCCUPIED AREAS.

therefore essentially of 'Late Saxon' and 'Wessex-centric' character, the ideas developed from documented locales are often projected into regions lacking written evidence (e.g. Hooke 1988; 1994; Eagles 1994).

Such attitudes undermine the potential for alternative social and landscape conditions in parts of England outside of the heartland of Wessex, and assume a national consistency of estate structure that may simply not have existed. In addition to the problems of transferring models spatially, the tendency of researchers to uncritically back-project later charters to reconstruct earlier landscapes is also fraught with problems. Such methods presume stability of landscape administration sometimes over several centuries, viewing the early medieval communities and their agricultural regimes in largely static terms. This book will challenge this outlook, adding to the growing body of archaeological and other research, suggesting that the early medieval landscape of England was subject to radical transformation in its physical and administrative constitution between the seventh and ninth centuries. The evidence from clearly 'Middle Saxon' charters will not be disregarded, however, but akin to other sources such as place-name material and linguistic data, will be used to supplement the picture derived primarily from archaeological evidence.

CONCLUSION

This chapter has outlined the methods and approaches of this book, detailing the extent of the chosen study area and providing a rationale of how it was assessed. The five counties chosen by this book present an opportunity to investigate an area of great topographical and social variety, whose separate components have been subjects to different modes of study. The data from HERs forms a central part of this work, but of equal importance is the way in which 'currently-occupied' rural settlements are defined. It has been demonstrated that previous approaches to currently-occupied villages have not been

critical in their approach, leading to conclusions regarding the early medieval countryside based on an inadequate body of evidence. Rather, by delineating a finite, albeit arbitrary, historic 'core area' on OS First Editions maps, a more comprehensive understanding of the relationship between 'Middle Saxon' settlement remains and the later landscape will be reached. It is worth reemphasising here that explaining historic settlement is not the primary aim of this book, but it nevertheless remains pertinent that 'currently-occupied' is defined, given the frequency with which 'Middle Saxon' settlement deposits will be shown to be present within historic villages.

Finally, the utilisation by this book of sources other than archaeology has also been discussed. Whilst this research will adopt an archaeologically-orientated approach, using the material record as the 'primary text', in a proto-historic environment such as 'Middle Saxon' England it is fitting to engage with the range of alternative available data. Although the evidence contained in charters has particularly been used by researchers to reconstruct the 'Middle Saxon' countryside, such material is often uncritically projected across significant geographical areas and back several centuries. Such an approach assumes stability in the early medieval countryside that this book will illustrate probably did not exist. Utilising alternative sources to enhance the results derived from study of material culture, this research instead demonstrates the 'Middle Saxon' period as characterised by significant settlement transformation across all types of countryside. The changes apparent in the settlement and land use of rural communities, it will be shown, is reflective of fundamental changes across society. This theme of social change is explored most fully in the discussion (Chapter XIII), with the preceding chapters comprising a presentation and analysis of the archaeological evidence for 'Middle Saxon' settlement and landscape from the five counties in central and eastern England. The first of the counties, which occupies a central position both within the study area and amongst early medieval settlement research, is Northamptonshire.

Chapter III
Northamptonshire

The five counties of central and eastern England investigated by this book are, above all else, landscapes of extreme diversity and topographical complexity. Of these administrative units, Northamptonshire occupies a central position. Geographically, Northamptonshire is situated in the middle of the broad transect of counties that are the subject of this study, but the region has also proved intellectually central in progressing the discipline of early medieval settlement archaeology. This chapter will describe and analyse the evidence for settlement, dated between the seventh and ninth century, from the historic county of Northamptonshire. In particular, it will be shown that by going beyond investigation of the well-known and often celebrated type-sites, and using alternative forms of archaeological evidence, a far more nuanced picture of early medieval society in Northamptonshire may be reached. Contrary to previous academic models, which have invariably been based upon evidence from the landscape surrounding existing villages, this chapter will focus in particular on the vital contribution provided by excavations from villages in the county that are currently-occupied. Through this approach, the character of the 'Middle Saxon' countryside in Northamptonshire may be established, enabling the relationship between the changing settlement and social landscapes to be more comprehensively understood.

Following a brief introduction to Northamptonshire as a unit for study, this chapter will then outline the key physical divisions that characterise the county. A brief review of antecedent landscapes will be succeeded by an analysis of the way in which existing archaeological and historical research in the region has contributed to our understanding of the early medieval rural landscape. Detailed analysis of currently-occupied rural settlement research will then follow, including a series of case studies, divided by *pays*. The subsequent discussion section will demonstrate the way in which the emerging archaeological dataset from currently-occupied rural settlement excavation can transform our understanding of 'Middle Saxon' settlement in Northamptonshire. These changes can be associated with a significant period of development notable across the English countryside, characterised by a restructuring of the agricultural landscape and expansion and specialisation of economies and production (Chapter VIII; Rippon 2008, 265). Such developments, it will be argued, are indicative of fundamental changes to English society as a whole, which had significance not only during their own chronological timeframe, but which were also to have a lasting impact on the medieval and later landscape of Northamptonshire.

INTRODUCING NORTHAMPTONSHIRE

Northamptonshire was probably developed as a shire in the later ninth and early tenth centuries, emerging in the district occupied by the Danish army based at Northampton, previously part of Middle Anglia (Foard 1985, 193). Little is known of the form of government imposed by the Danish upon the territory surrounding Northampton after the conquest of 877, but the land unit appears to have been framed by the River Welland to the north and Watling Street to the south-west, with the eastern bounds of the county meeting those of the army centred on Huntingdon. This area was likely amalgamated later with the eight hundreds to the south-west of Watling Street to form the historic county, although the exact processes behind the formation of Northamptonshire remain unknown (Hart 1970, 12-13). Unlike some other areas studied in this book, such as Norfolk, where a regional identity can be argued to have persisted since the late prehistoric period (Chapter VII), the administrative and social cohesion of Northamptonshire can thus only reasonably be traced from the 'Late Saxon' period onward.

The development of Northamptonshire as an organisational entity from the late ninth century does not negate its suitability as a study area for 'Middle Saxon' settlement and landscape investigation, however. On the contrary, there are numerous factors that mark Northamptonshire as a particularly appropriate region in which to research the development of social and settlement hierarchies between the seventh and ninth centuries. Firstly, Northamptonshire boasts a particularly rich tradition of early medieval settlement research, and a number of key tenets of the discipline have been based on work undertaken within the county (see below). Targeted study of the region therefore allows some of the central ideas of early medieval settlement research to be analysed and interpreted, thus fulfilling one of the key objectives of this book (Chapter I, p19). Northamptonshire's history of enquiry has consistently demonstrated rich and complex early medieval settlement deposits, conditions which are also crucially characterised by an uninterrupted ceramic sequence (Parry 2006, 170-6). Despite being firmly located within the 'central province' of nucleated settlements and common fields that emerged as the prevailing landscape in the medieval period, Northamptonshire actually features a variety of dispersed and nucleated village forms (Roberts and Wrathmell 2002, 135-6; Jones and Page 2006). This eclectic mixture of later settlement and landscape types also presents an intriguing opportunity to assess the influence, if any, of 'Middle Saxon' communities upon later settlement character.

In addition to the archaeological evidence, the area that was later to emerge as Northamptonshire features a relatively well-documented early medieval political history. After absorption into Mercia during the seventh century, fervent royal patronage led to the establishment of important monastic centres in the region, such as Oundle, Pipewell, and most significantly *Medeshamstede* (later Peterborough Abbey). Relatively good survival of the charter material from *Medeshamstede*, certainly in comparison to minsters in other midland counties like Cambridgeshire (Chapter VI), provides an important insight into land use arrangements from the seventh century onwards, and represents a useful control for archaeological study (Kelly 2009). The value of *Medeshamstede'* documentary data adds to the motivations for investigating the historic extents of Northamptonshire (Figure 3.1). Whilst the historic and modern extents of Northamptonshire are largely coterminous, the one significant exception is the area known as the Soke of Peterborough. Traditionally governed separately from the rest of the county, the hundred was still regarded as part of Northamptonshire until its amalgamation into the county of Cambridgeshire in 1974. In addition to this strong historical association and the prevalence of surviving charter bounds from the pre-Conquest monastery, the Northamptonshire Sites and Monuments Record (NSMR) also holds all data relating to the Soke, and thus the area is included as part of this discussion.

THE PHYSICAL LANDSCAPE

Pays: A Framework for Research

For the purposes of this research all of the counties subject to study will be subdivided into landscape zones, known as *pays*. *Pays* emerged as a concept in historic landscape research during the 1960s and 1970s with the view that the countryside was comprised of various and unique landscape types. While distinctive communities occupying particular regions can be identified in all study areas, *pays* are usually defined in terms of physical characteristics, primarily geology and topography. The first archaeological researchers to utilise *pays* as a unit for study focussed particularly on the natural elements of the landscape: Alan Everitt's work on the evolving countryside of England, for instance, divided the country into 'natural regions' such as marshland, weald and woodland (Everitt 1979). Indeed, preceding units of secular and ecclesiastical administration, the distinct regional variation of *pays* was recognised as far back as the medieval period (Rippon 2000). Yet, researchers using *pays* as a framework for study must acknowledge the possibility of generalising about significant areas that often possess topographical and social idiosyncrasies at a local level. As Stephen Rippon (2008, 7) asserts, it is perhaps best to view *pays* as regional variations in landscape character that produce a series of unique districts. If the variety of such districts and the communities which inhabit them is recognised, *pays* remain an effective conceptual model, the value of which

continues to be utilised by archaeological researchers (e.g. Lake 2007; Williamson 2003; Rippon 2008).

Situated in the south-east Midlands, Northamptonshire extends from the edge of the Cotswold scarp at Banbury to the fens at Peterborough. The county forms a watershed between the River Severn and The Wash and is divided lengthways from Badby to Warmington by the River Nene. The northern boundary between Market Harborough and Easton on the Hill is framed by the River Welland (Hall 1995, ix). This extensive landscape can be divided into six landscape *pays*, loosely based upon frameworks developed by previous research (Lewis *et al.* 1997; Terrett 1971).

The use of Geographical Information Systems (GIS) by this research, however, allows the physical characteristics that influence the extents of the Northamptonshire *pays*, particularly the underlying geological makeup, to be plotted more accurately than earlier studies (Figure 3.1). It is simplest to introduce the six *pays* of Northamptonshire in geographical order, beginning in the extreme southwest of the county with the Wolds.

The Wolds

Located roughly between the towns of Daventry and Brackley, forming the south-western part of Northamptonshire are the Wolds. All of the topography of the Wolds is situated above the 150m contour, but the local geology creates a distinctively different landscape of steeper and more frequent valleys than the other extensive upland of the county, the Northampton Heights. Featuring less Boulder Clay, the Wolds are instead predominantly underlain by Oolitic Limestone and Upper and Middle Lias deposits. The Wolds are defined on the northern and eastern limits by tributaries of the River Nene, constituting a broad geological watershed. The southern and western limits of the *pays* are defined by the county boundary with Buckinghamshire. Domesday Book records a greater population in the Wolds than other upland areas such as the Northampton Heights, a density which remains evident in a modern landscape characterised by a significant concentration of villages and small, enclosed fields. Conditions in the Wolds are likely to have been broadly comparable during the early medieval period, and it is likely that the fertile and well-drained soils presented attractive conditions for occupation (Steane 1974, 26).

The Nene Valley

The Nene Valley *pays* is characterised by the low-lying fertile valleys of the River Nene and its tributaries. Defined by this study as the watershed of the vast river network below the 150m contour, the landscape is formed by easily eroded Oolitic Limestone, featuring gravels and alluvium in the valley basins and light, fertile soils on the peripheries (Lewis *et al.* 1997, 40; Terrett 1971, 389). The Nene Valley is by far the largest of Northamptonshire's *pays*, stretching almost the entire length of the county. The river system is framed on its northern and southern sides

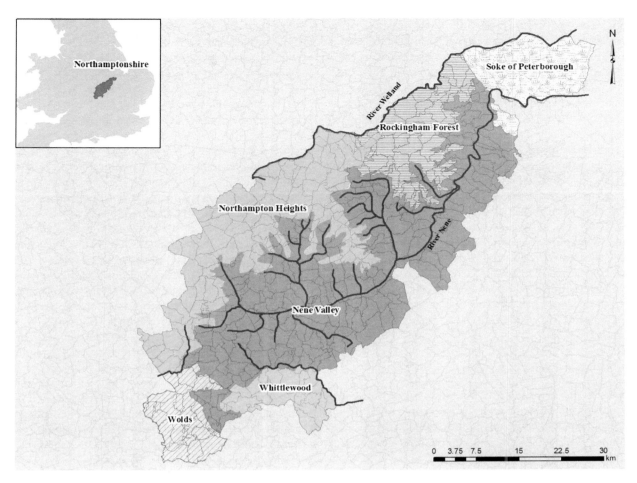

FIGURE 3.1: THE PAYS AND MAJOR RIVERS OF NORTHAMPTONSHIRE AND THE LOCATION OF THE COUNTY WITHIN SOUTHERN BRITAIN (INSET). SOURCE FOR MAPPING: HISTORIC PARISHES OF ENGLAND AND WALES ONLINE

by low dissected plateaus topped with Boulder Clay and heavy Oxford Clays. These Boulder Clay landscapes form watersheds between the Great Ouse River to the south and the River Welland to the north, of which the Rockingham Forest landscape is a part. The Nene Valley landscape is predominantly flat except along the valley sides where the tributaries have incised channels (Parry 2006, 1). Domesday Book suggests that the region was densely settled by at least the 'Late Saxon' period, and today the range of topographic environments and a relative lack of physical constraints for agriculture has made the Nene Valley a particular focus for archaeological investigation (Foard 1984), and indeed the Nene and its tributaries today remains a densely settled and heavily exploited arable landscape.

Whittlewood Forest

The character of Whittlewood Forest is largely derived from underlying Boulder Clay geology, which has created heavy soils susceptible to waterlogging, and a topography of low hills and shallow valleys. Similar to the landscape of Rockingham Forest (see below), the better-drained soils around the river valleys have historically been more intensively settled, although the evidence of limited exploitation of the Boulder Clay plateau during

the 'Middle Saxon' period demonstrates that such a model should not be too rigidly applied. Indeed, inconsistency in the depth of the clay soils has made some areas more suited to arable farming than others and the presence of alkaline chalk in the acidic Boulder Clay also helps to produce chemically neutral and fertile soils in some areas. The prevailing clay soils meant that Whittlewood was not the most attractive of Northamptonshire's *pays* for crop husbandry in the early medieval period, however, reflected in the low population density recorded in 1086, especially in the northern part of the forest (Jones and Page 2006, 32-6). Although demonstrating a geographical unity derived from a common geological profile, it is important to note that the area known as Whittlewood Forest was also defined by a legal status from the early post-Conquest period: as a royal forest, the area was subject to forest law, primarily developed to protect the crown's hunting landscape. Whittlewood today remains relatively sparsely populated, characterised by a mixture of tightly coalesced villages and smaller, more dispersed settlements.

The Northampton Heights

Located north-west of the River Nene, the Northampton Heights rise to over 150m OD, forming a wide arc of upland topography, extending to the south and west.

The landscape is characterised by extensive heavy Liassic Clays with sporadic Boulder Clay deposits. This geological profile produces a mixture of soils that are often heavy and prone to waterlogging, but are relatively fertile. A reasonably prosperous area at the time of Domesday, the Heights appear to have become increasingly well-settled throughout the early medieval period. Local geological variation is likely to have had a significant influence on settlement in the earliest medieval centuries, though probably represented less of a determinant from the 'Middle Saxon' period onward. Typified by arable regimes during the medieval period, the agricultural focus of the district has since shifted to pastoral farming (Lewis *et al.* 1997, 410). The medieval settlement pattern demonstrates that communities generally avoided the waterlogged and easily-flooded valley bottoms, with occupation instead focussing on the better-drained upland. Management of the river valleys from the post-medieval period led to more intensive occupation of these lowland zones, however, a process which intensified from the nineteenth century (Terrett 1971, 389).

Rockingham Forest

Similar to the royal forest of Whittlewood, Rockingham Forest is as much a legal entity as a topographical one, its extents being defined by the limit of the crown's peculiar hunting laws. Rockingham can also be defined by natural features, however, as the whole area of the royal forest is underlain by Boulder Clay, barring an outcrop of sandy limestone in the extreme north-east. The whole *pays* forms a plateau, sloping gently from north-west to south-east (Foard *et al.* 2009, 11). Whilst part of the same Boulder Clay formation that forms the watershed between the River Welland and River Nene, the sporadically wooded landscape of Rockingham forms a discrete *pays* in its own right. The plateau is dissected by numerous tributaries of the River Nene to the south, whilst to the north-west the scarp falls dramatically away to the Welland Valley and the county boundary. Rockingham was subject to sporadic cultivation throughout the medieval period, but land was often reverted to pastoral regimes, especially on impermeable Boulder Clay. Early medieval settlement of the forest appeared to have focussed around permeable geologies, as reflected in the distribution of communities in 1086. Although sparsely populated, Rockingham has been valued in the historic period for its alternative resources such as timber, iron ore and access to pannage (Foard *et al.* 2009, 54; Gover *et al.* 1933). Modern Rockingham remains thinly populated compared to other Northamptonshire *pays*, and following widespread deforestation today the 'forest' represents as much a culturally-defined landscape as one characterised by topography.

The Soke of Peterborough

Although the Soke of Peterborough is an administrative entity defined by a historic hundred, it is also a *pays* in the truest sense, characterised by an overarching topographical cohesion, being a low-lying fenland landscape with topography that in some areas drops as low as 2m OD. The area had been reclaimed during the Romano-British period, but after inundation in the post-Roman period, the fenland was not permanently reclaimed for agricultural use until the later medieval period (Lewis *et al.* 1997, 40). It appears increasingly unlikely that the area that was to become the Soke was perceived in the early medieval period as the fog-bound trackless bog, depicted in hagiographies such as Felix's *Life of Guthlac* (e.g. Roffe 2005). Although clearly eager to promote his ecclesiastical establishment, the twelfth-century Peterborough historian Hugh Candidus gave a detailed account of the productive landscape in which the abbey was located. The value of wetland landscapes to early medieval farming regimes, even before permanent reclamation, is also gradually being recognised by academic research (e.g. Rippon 2000a; 2004a; Kelly 2009, 4). Added to this was the importance for the early Church in taming 'wilderness' environments, demonstrated by foundation of many monastic institutions in liminal areas, including wetlands (Rippon 2009, 49). The Soke would certainly have presented challenging conditions for 'Middle Saxon' communities, requiring seasonal and specialised approaches in order to take advantage of natural resources. The lack of permanent reclamation within the Soke is demonstrated by the Domesday Survey, which indicates that the landscape was not extensively settled, despite the existence of some sizeable settlements located on islands within the wetlands or along the fen-edge (Terrett 1971, 389).

THE SOCIAL LANDSCAPE

The Human Dimension: Antecedent Landscapes

The six *pays* of Northamptonshire demonstrate the wide variety of physical environments within the study area: conditions that are likely to have influenced settlement and land-use between the seventh and ninth centuries. The historic landscape is not merely the product of the natural environment, however, but is also shaped by numerous social, economic and political influences. The potential significance of 'antecedent landscapes', being the way in which the landscape was utilised by previous communities, has been a particular focus of recent academic interest (e.g. Roberts and Wrathmell 2002, 72-7). The transition between Romano-British and 'Early Saxon' settlement and the extent to which 'continuity' of occupation between the periods can be demonstrated, has proved especially prominent within such discourse. Whilst the re-use or otherwise of Romano-British structures and field-systems has received the greatest attention, it is equally plausible that 'Middle Saxon' groups were influenced by the activity of earlier people. Indeed, some researchers have argued the case for a more enduring importance of antecedent features: Roberts and Wrathmell (2002), for instance, suggest that the 'central province' of England may have even influenced attitudes towards land use begun as early as the prehistoric period. Elsewhere, it has recently been suggested that the seventh-century palatial complex at Yeavering, Northumbria, was arranged along a 'sacred alignment', orientated around prehistoric features (Blair 2005, 56; Ulmschneider 2011, 160). Beyond the scale of the individual site, it is important to consider that broader trends of settlement and land-use patterns in Northamptonshire may have shaped activity in the period of study.

Late Prehistoric and Romano-British

In comparison with many other counties, Northamptonshire is fortunate to have a relatively abundant rich Iron Age archaeological record. The previous Bronze Age 'ritual landscape' of the Nene Valley was succeeded in the Iron Age by the construction of field systems and monumental defended sites. Seven hill forts, probably used for livestock control, have been identified in Northamptonshire but settlement organisation in the Iron Age was more typically characterised by a pattern of dispersed, open farmsteads (Kidd 2004, 49-56). From the middle of the first century the introduction of Roman governance began to change the pre-existing social and political structure of Northamptonshire. Under Roman administration a sophisticated settlement hierarchy emerged, with *civitates* founded within the previous Iron Age tribal territories. Such centres were likely supplemented by a lower tier of landscape organisation, the *pagi* and *vici* and their associated territories, although such subsidiary centres are likely to have grown organically (Lewis *et al.* 1997, 42). Although probably partly a consequence of the material durability that characterised the period, approximately a quarter of the entries in the Northamptonshire Historic Environment Record are assigned a Roman provenance, demonstrating an effective process of cultural 'Romanisation' across the county (Taylor and Flitcroft 2004, 63).

Numerous major towns such as Duston, Brackley and Irchester developed in the first century of Roman occupation, forming central places in the landscape (Figure 3.2). Much of the rural landscape of Northamptonshire in the Romano-British period was well-occupied, demonstrating widespread and often intensive settlement and agricultural management, related to expanded production, the development of a road network, and the formation of focal places such as markets. Landscape-orientated investigation in particular has provided insights into the workings of non-villa rural communities, demonstrating an increasingly broad range of settlement types, such as at Wollaston in the Nene Valley, where developer-funded research revealed an Iron Age and Romano-British landscape including a specialised farm featuring extensive vineyards (Meadows 1996). Agricultural exploitation was focussed on river valleys, areas that consequently became the focus of villas and other settlement forms. The River Nene Survey Project has shown that the fertile valleys were especially densely-settled, with the development of numerous villas and nucleated farmsteads (Meadows 2009). The heavier soils of the clay uplands were not as extensively farmed, but were still exploited intermittently for arable farming and, more commonly, for alternative resources such as timber and outlying pasture (Taylor and

Flitcroft 2004, 73-4). Fieldwalking has demonstrated that the sporadic settlement of the clay uplands was subject to significant contraction during the Late Roman period, with populations apparently moving to the more easily cultivable river valleys, marking the start of a trend that appears to have continued into the early medieval centuries (Brown and Foard 2004, 80; Jones and Page 2006, 85-7; Parry 2006, 3-9).

'Early Saxon'

Archaeological research in Northamptonshire is providing increasing evidence with which to characterise the period of transition between Roman Britain and 'Anglo-Saxon' England. A number of sites apparently demonstrate genuine continuity of use, such as at Brixworth where a room in a villa was fitted out with roof supports in the later fifth century (Woods 1970). The villa at Redlands Farm, Stanwick, also continued in use throughout the fifth century, occupation that was supplemented by three *Grubenhäuser* constructed less that 100m away (Keevill 1992a). There are also instances of deserted Romano-British sites being reused for burial purposes during the initial centuries of the early medieval period, such as the medieval inhumation that was recovered within the high-status settlement at Borough Hill, near Daventry (Jackson 1993/4a). It cannot be argued from the current archaeological evidence that reuse or continuity was typical, nor even common in transitional-period Northamptonshire, however, but it is possible that present understanding is skewed by the standards of past research. An inability to detect the ephemeral and fragmentary material that characterises the non-'Germanic' archaeology of the period, often coupled by a lack of chronological precision, means that the apparent break in settlement and land-use patterns may not have been as stark as initially appears.

Landscape-scale patterns of 'Early Saxon' activity in Northamptonshire in many ways appear to conform to established national models, such as the positioning of cemeteries outside of Roman urban centres, recognisable at places such as Duston (Brown and Foard 2004, 78-9). Fieldwalking surveys have proved particularly informative in developing models of post-Roman and 'Early Saxon' development on a landscape-scale, with artefact scatters demonstrating that 'Early-Middle Saxon' concentrations coincide with Romano-British material approximately twenty five percent of the time (Brown and Foard 2004, 80). It is uncertain in most cases though whether such distributions represent occupation or material derived from other processes, such as manuring, and only through excavation are detailed site sequences likely to be revealed. The social significance of the apparently strong correlation between Romano-British and 'Anglo-Saxon' material should also not be overstated, as suitable topographical areas for settlement are likely to have remained relatively constant throughout the first millennium AD, with the exception of the Soke of Peterborough.

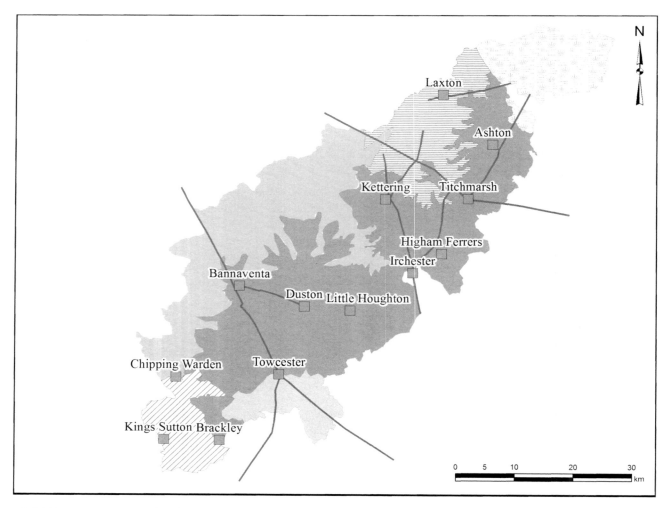

FIGURE 3.2: THE ROMAN ROADS (LINES) AND TOWNS (SQUARES), AGAINST THE PAYS OF NORTHAMPTONSHIRE. NOTE THE DENSITY OF MAJOR SETTLEMENTS IN THE NENE VALLEY, A PATTERN THAT CONTINUED IN THE EARLY MEDIEVAL PERIOD (AFTER TAYOR AND FLITCROFT 2004, FIG 3). SOURCE FOR MAPPING: HISTORIC PARISHES OF ENGLAND AND WALES ONLINE.

Attempts to identify post-Roman continuity are further complicated by the broad date ranges of early medieval ceramics (Lewis *et al.* 1997, 78). Most forms of organic-tempered early medieval pottery, the most commonly recovered ceramic in Northamptonshire, can only be given the broad chronology *c.*450-*c.*850, or 'Early-Middle Saxon' period (Northamptonshire Heritage 1996). Beyond the issue of early post-Roman continuity, the ambiguous chronology of early medieval ceramics has encouraged most previous studies of historic settlement in Northamptonshire to amalgamate the archaeology of the 'Early Saxon' and 'Middle Saxon' periods (e.g. Lewis *et al.* 1997). With an emphasis on currently-occupied rural settlement investigation, this chapter will demonstrate how the development of more sophisticated dating and excavation techniques can provide a far more chronologically-nuanced understanding of settlement change than previously realised. Before this is attempted, however, it is first necessary to review previous research traditions, in order to reveal the way in which they continue to shape current perceptions.

EXISTING PERSPECTIVES

Documentary Research Traditions

Before the traditions of early medieval archaeological research from Northamptonshire are analysed, it is first important to briefly assess scholarly approaches to the written material, and the way their changing interpretation likely impacts this study. Recent research has demonstrated the value of combining sources to provide new insights on the way the social and political environment influenced the landscape of the early medieval midlands (e.g. Bassett 2007; 2008). Indeed, in seeking to address the way in which social and political environments impacts settlement character, written sources provide a crucial insight. The earliest historical evidence for political organisation in post-Roman Northamptonshire relates to the sixth and seventh centuries and indicates a fragmentary socio-political situation. Documents portray these centuries as the period in which the principal 'Anglo-Saxon' kingdoms emerged, yet the written material gives little insight of the situation in the area that was to become the county of Northamptonshire. The ninth-century document known as the Tribal Hidage provides a list of tribal groups in the eastern and southern midlands that may be collectively identified as the Middle Angles. Two groups named in the Hidage are thought to have been located in the Northamptonshire region: the *North Gyrwe* in the Soke of Peterborough and the *Widderiggas*, near modern Wittering. These early, probably kin-based groups, make only a fleeting appearance in written texts, and their description in sources as subordinate geographical entities demonstrates that they had already been integrated into other kingdoms even by the date of first recording (Bassett ed. 1989).

The Anglo-Saxon Chronicle confirms the dependent political character of the Northamptonshire region in 653, when Peada is recorded as being made *princeps* of the Middle Angles by his father, the Mercian king Penda (*ASC* 653). This recorded Mercian overlordship represents a convenient historical starting-date for this research, although it is important to consider that early medieval settlement activity can rarely be associated with such specific events. Northamptonshire had been fully absorbed into Mercia by the ninth century at the very latest (Davies 1973, 20). Written sources for early medieval Northamptonshire are largely derived from monastic institutions, founded under Mercian royal patronage from the seventh century. By far the most significant religious foundation in Northamptonshire was located at *Medeshamstede*, later Peterborough Abbey, which developed as one of the most important monasteries of early medieval England.

Medeshamstede benefitted from strong royal backing from its foundation and the minster was a central focus during the period of the 'Mercian Supremacy', between the seventh and ninth centuries. Despite representing one of the best-documented institutions in the country from the twelfth century onwards, the historical evidence for pre-Viking *Medeshamstede* is relatively slight. The material consists of a memorandum of seventh century donations, two leases from the eighth and ninth centuries respectively, and early charters from four of the *Medeshamstede* 'colonies', none of which were located in Northamptonshire (Kelly 2009, 1). Reconstruction of the early history of the minster is largely reliant upon this material, key texts such as Bede's *Ecclesiastical History*, and references made in much later Peterborough historical compilations. Bede indicates that the minster of *Medeshamstede* was founded by Seaxwulf in 672 x 676 in the territory of the Gyrwe (*HE* IV, 6). It is not clear whether *Medeshamstede* possessed its own territory, rather it is more likely that it lay within the *provinciae* of Oundle, the only pre-Conquest reference in Northamptonshire detailing a unit of organisation greater than the Soke.

Medeshamstede was an especially important Mercian house in the later eighth and early ninth centuries, establishing satellite foundations in Northamptonshire at Weedon and

probably Brixworth (Kelly 2009, 67-9). While the control exerted over its known colonies in Kent, Leicestershire and Surrey is debated (e.g. Stenton 1933, 320-6 vs. Blair 2005, 83), there is little doubt that *Medeshamstede* and other Mercian monasteries had a significant influence in the developing landscape of Northamptonshire between the seventh and ninth centuries. Although the written documents related to landholding are disproportionately biased towards monastic activity, it must be borne in mind that the roots of minster establishments invariably lay in royal patronage, and the dynastic strategies of the secular elite (Yorke 2003, 243-8). Later documents, such as the tenth century will of Æthelgifu, which details estates in Northamptonshire (Crick 2007, 92-100), also demonstrates the existence of a progressively powerful landed-class with a vested interest in the rural landscape. Indeed, estates like Æthelgifu's, appear fully formed when first discernible in the written record, increasing the probability that the gentry were also influential in the management of the Northamptonshire countryside during the 'Middle Saxon' period.

The widely accepted historical narrative for the mid-ninth century onward witnesses drastic change to the political geography of Northamptonshire through increasing Danish activity, with the whole of the county east of Watling Street coming under Scandinavian control for a brief period in the early tenth century (Stenton 1971, 240-5). Whilst there are elements of Scandinavian influence in the place-names and local dialect of some parts of Northamptonshire, the archaeological evidence for Danish settlement is insubstantial. Scandinavian occupation was fleeting and by the middle of the tenth century the study area was under West Saxon control once more, and it is in the context of the three-tiered West Saxon administrative system that Northamptonshire was created (Lewis *et al.* 1997, 44-5). The complex network of hundreds and vills developed under the level of the shire established a new organisational landscape, within which the familiar manorial system of medieval society emerged (Brown and Foard 1998, 82-90).

Archaeological Research Traditions

The archaeological research traditions of Northamptonshire are in many ways reflective of broader national trends of early medieval settlement study. The focus of Northamptonshire as a productive area for investigation has led to the extrapolation of nationwide models, based on archaeological work undertaken in the county. More than any other aspect of academic research, village origins have come to dominate early medieval settlement discourse on both a regional and national scale, with researchers tending to focus on two facets of the phenomenon. Firstly, substantial effort has been made to identify the underlying causes of village development, an issue that has defied resolution. In a recent paper, Richard Jones (2010) asserts that the dearth of scholarly consensus is due to an inherent misunderstanding of the environments and processes by which villages formed. This argument, however, was based upon the assumption that the second facet of village origins has been resolved: the dating of village 'nucleation'. Phasing the development of the early medieval landscape has rightly been regarded as of central importance, as it informs the interpretation of the causal factors through which villages emerged. Contrary to Jones' declaration, however, the historiography of research in Northamptonshire demonstrates how elusive an agreed chronological sequence for early medieval settlement change still remains.

Until the 1970s, academic discourse regarding the development of the early medieval and later countryside was dominated by historians and historical geographers. Early twentieth-century paradigms which had viewed the origins of villages and common fields as early post-Roman in origin (e.g. Gray 1915), had been challenged by historians such as Joan Thirsk (1964), who argued that the 'Midland System' of settlement and landscape arrangement developed as late as the thirteenth century. A more lasting paradigm shift was to emerge during the 1970s, however, following the emergence of landscape archaeology, and in particular the development of large-scale, systematic fieldwalking surveys. Researchers increasingly recognised that the small, dispersed settlements of the fifth to ninth centuries identified through ceramics recovered in the ploughsoil, differed profoundly from the nucleated villages that apparently characterised much of Midland England by the end of the medieval period (Foard 1978; Hall and Martin 1979; Hall 1981). Throughout Northamptonshire a trend was recognised, almost without exception, for dispersed sites located outside of present village centres to produce ceramic concentrations consisting almost exclusively of organic-tempered pottery, with almost no evidence of ceramics dated later than c.850 (Jones and Page 2006, 87).

The dating of these scatters should have led to the development of interpretive frameworks which saw the abandonment of Northamptonshire's dispersed settlement pattern dated to between the seventh and ninth centuries: when 'Middle Saxon' pottery was in circulation, but before the widespread use of 'Late Saxon' wares (Rippon 2008, 11). Yet, in spite of the fieldwalking evidence suggesting reorganisation of the rural landscape *before* the 'Late Saxon' period, the majority of scholars have taken c.850 as the watershed date at which the process of village development began in earnest, not only in Northamptonshire, but across England's 'central province' of nucleated settlement (Roberts and Wrathmell 2002; Rippon 2008, 8). The wider context for this prevailing view of 'Late Saxon' landscape restructuring is generally taken as the fragmentation of large agricultural units, most commonly known in the literature as 'multiple estates' (Rippon 2008, 9). Historians in particular, such as Christopher Taylor (1981; 1983) and Christopher Dyer (2003), have persistently argued that the village landscape of midland England did not emerge until at least the tenth century, if not later. An inter-disciplinary project undertaken during the 1990s, headed by Dyer among

others, similarly concluded that villages and common fields emerged 'sometime after 850' as part of a protracted 'village moment' process (Lewis et al. 1997, 198). Based on the results of test-pitting within villages across Midland and Eastern England by the Higher Education Field Academy (HEFA), Carenza Lewis has reiterated the sentiment that, with the exception of some sites in Essex and South Suffolk, there appears to be little evidence for a relationship between 'Early' and 'Middle' Saxon sites and later villages (Lewis 2010, 103-4).

Archaeological evidence from Northamptonshire, particularly derived from fieldwalking, has therefore provided a critical contribution to scholarly discourse. Undoubtedly representing the principal region for which the paradigm of 'Late Saxon' landscape change has been argued, alternative research undertaken in the county has, however, produced some of the most forceful challenges to the popular model. As early as the 1980s some researchers alluded to an alternative, 'Middle Saxon' date for some aspects of landscape re-planning, with David Hall suggesting that the laying out of open fields was 'substantially completed during the eighth and ninth centuries' (Hall 1981, 36-7). A more significant dissenting voice, however, was that developed by Tony Brown and Glenn Foard in the late 1990s, based partly on material from landscape research, since comprehensively published, in and around the village of Raunds (Parry 2006; Audouy 2009; Chapman 2010). In a notable departure from previous explanation, the pair proposed a two-stage process which argued that villages and common fields were not developed contemporaneously (cf. Hall 1981; Lewis et al. 1997), but instead proposed that nucleation began as early as the seventh century, with shared field arrangements created later, and that this was then combined with a re-planning of existing villages around the tenth century. Fundamental to this book was the observation that dispersed settlement patterns associated with 'Early to Middle Saxon' pottery were abandoned before the introduction of 'Late Saxon' ceramics, suggesting an initial nucleation must have occurred before this mid-ninth century date (Brown and Foard 1998, 80-92).

The importance of pre-existing settlements in shaping the character of 'Late Saxon' Northamptonshire has also been forwarded by scholars involved with the Whittlewood Project (Jones and Page 2006). Beginning in the year 2000, the Whittlewood Project was a long-term multi-disciplinary research project that sought to detail the character and development of historic settlement and land use in the Whittlewood region. Presenting a mixture of nucleated and dispersed medieval settlement types, the Whittlewood landscape was viewed as a microcosm of the English countryside within which archaeological models could be developed and tested (Dyer 1999, 16; Jones and Page 2006). In a departure from the model proposed by Brown and Foard (1998), researchers concluded that the villages in the area were formed during the two centuries following c.850, combined with the commencement of common field farming. Crucially, however, the potential significance of 'pre-village nuclei' in shaping later occupation patterns was also recognised, although the character of such antecedent settlements and the processes by which they influenced later villages was not explored (Jones and Page 2006, 222). The identification of 'pre-village nuclei' by the Whittlewood investigators is of particular significance, as it is generally anticipated that village formation occurred later in well-wooded uplands (Rippon 2008, 11).

Studies such as these, questioning the accepted chronology for early medieval settlement development, are not restricted to Northamptonshire, however, but are part of a broader national research trend. Since Brown and Foard's (1998) initial challenge to the prevailing model, a significant quantity of research outside of Northamptonshire has since supported the general sequence of settlement change that the pair proposed. Open area excavation at Yarnton, Oxfordshire, for instance, located a dispersed and unbounded 'Early Saxon' settlement landscape, succeeded by more structured and permanent habitation around the eighth century, including 'village-like' characteristics, such as croft and toft-type arrangements (Chapter IV; Hey 2004). Village origins dating to the 'Middle Saxon' period have also been identified through excavation outside of the Midland counties, such as the pre-ninth century activity revealed by several interventions in Lechlade, Gloucestershire, but also by this book in eastern Cambridgeshire and Norfolk (Bateman et al. 2003; Reynolds 2006; Chapter VI and VII). The phasing of this emerging corpus of sites accentuates the potential significance of the seventh to ninth centuries as a period of transformation, witnessing fundamental and lasting developments to the rural landscape.

This rapidly growing body of research has not yet led to a paradigm shift in early medieval settlement studies, however, and arguments for widespread 'Middle Saxon' landscape reorganisation remain an undercurrent to more popular opinion. This continued chronological uncertainty has significantly impacted the other central theme of academic research: the underlying causes behind village origins. The break-up of 'multiple-estates', coincident with the beginnings of localised manorial organisation, has persisted as the most popular explanatory framework since its introduction, together with the 'Late Saxon' date for village origins in the late 1970s (e.g. Foard 1978). Northamptonshire has, however, been subject to a number of studies offering alternative rationales that also require consideration. The significance of some causal factors has been regularly reinstated by scholars, particularly the potential impact of changing demographic and physical conditions.

The majority of current scholars still agree with earlier models that posited general unabated population growth between the 'Middle Saxon' period and the fourteenth century (Williamson 2003, 12). Such a pattern was first firmly related to village origins by Joan Thirsk (1964) who saw intermingled strips and a crisis in land for grazing as the result of growing demographic pressure and laws of partible inheritance. As a consequence of such circumstances, Thirsk asserted, farmers were drawn into increased cooperation which affected the introduction of villages and common fields (Thirsk 1964). One of the most outspoken proponents of the 'great re-planning' model for the early medieval landscape of Northamptonshire, David Hall, similar cited 'increasing population' among other factors as a rationale for change (Hall 1981, 37). In their study of the midlands landscape, Christopher Dyer, Carenza Lewis and Patrick Mitchell-Fox also listed rising population among a number of factors that caused settlement nucleation and the emergence of the 'Midland System' (Lewis et al. 1997).

One of the most persistent views relating to population has been that areas of 'champion' countryside were the first to be settled by medieval communities. The concentration of population in such regions, it has been assumed, resulted in a greater degree of communal regulation resulting in nucleated villages and shared fields (Roberts 1973, 229; Everitt 1979, 85). Underlying such explanatory models, is the assumption that the central zone of England was characterised by superior conditions for settlement, bordered by landscapes that were less favourable and colonised later (Rippon 2008, 6-7). Recent research has challenged this preconception, however, demonstrating that regional variation of historic landscape character may have derived though various processes (Williamson 2003; Rippon 2008). For instance, Tom Williamson, researching a range of settlement and field systems across eastern England, argued that the variation recognisable was principally the result of environmental factors, particularly variations in soil character (Williamson 2003, 181-4).

The influence of soils upon agricultural arrangements has perhaps been the most commonly cited physical cause of village origins (e.g. Allison 1957), yet Williamson's explanatory model is notable due to its extrapolation of the dynamic relationship between the environment and society. Although physical conditions are implicit to many explanatory frameworks, researchers have not always succeeded in adequately discerning the processes by which they may impact settlement form. Most scholars, for instance, maintain that scattered 'Early Saxon' settlements were clustered mainly on lighter soils, moving to heavier but more agriculturally fertile river valleys during the 'Late Saxon' period. Yet, scholars have been guilty of failing to detail how human agency influenced such drastic upheaval, and the way in which these significant changes would have affected the social fabric of rural communities (e.g. Lewis et al. 1997). Williamson's is therefore a key insight, noting that 'social' factors were themselves moulded by the environment. The agency of demesne managers and the influence of medieval custom were, he suggests, 'the single most important articulating force in the organisation of early peasant communities', yet crucially states that these traditions were themselves shaped by underlying environmental considerations (Williamson 2003, 192).

Central to the majority of demographic and physical explanations for village origins outlined above is the dating of the early medieval settlement sequence, assuming the persistence of dispersed and unstructured occupation until at least the mid ninth century. The alternative chronology for village origins, forwarded by the likes of Brown and Foard (1998), has however led to a greater emphasis of social circumstance as a potential causal factor. Brown and Foard themselves suggest that the likely source of landscape upheaval was the transition from a tribute-based organisation, toward a society centred on service and rents: the economic basis of kinship (Brown and Foard 1998, 90). Such an outlook is part of a broader research trend that has stressed the importance of the 'long eighth century' in the development of social and settlement hierarchies, although academics have typically placed greater focus on more materially-prominent centres, such as *wics* and 'productive sites' (Wickham 2000; Moreland 2000). It has been suggested though, that archaeological evidence for transformation on apparently more prosaic rural settlement sites, gives weight to the idea that development of new elite centres was founded on more fundamental changes to agricultural means of production (Moreland 2000, 26-8).

A review of early medieval studies in Northamptonshire therefore reveals a long and impressive research tradition that has often reflected the overall progression of the discipline. Rightly or wrongly, results from investigations undertaken within Northamptonshire, perhaps more than any other county in England, have commonly been projected into regional and national interpretive frameworks. Early medieval landscape researchers have been preoccupied with the theme of village origins, and in particular the assigning of appropriate dates and causal factors to the emergence of 'nucleated' villages. These two facets are inextricably linked, with suggested rationales varying significantly, dependent on the socio-economic context provided by the adopted chronology. The most significant debate with regard to the date of village origins have been between proponents of a 'Middle Saxon' chronology, and those forwarding the more popular 'Late Saxon' interpretation. In general terms, scholars assuming the earlier phasing have tended to emphasise the significance of an increasingly stratified society, which stimulated new modes of agricultural production, and altered form, function and location (e.g. Brown and Foard 1998; Moreland 2000b). Whilst forwarding a series of different causal factors, the most persisting explanation assumed by academics of the 'Late Saxon' model is the breakdown of 'multiple estates', an interpretation that has not lost popular support since its introduction (e.g. Foard 1978; Dyer 2003, 30).

In attempting to discern the rural settlement character of 'Middle Saxon' Northamptonshire and its relationship to the social milieu, the history of archaeological research demonstrates the fundamental importance of developing an accurate chronological sequence for landscape change. It is somewhat ironic that academic understanding of village origins has been derived almost entirely from the

landscape surrounding villages with little attention paid to the archaeological material derived from the centres themselves. The growing body of material from, primarily development-led, currently-occupied rural settlement investigation investigation has until now been relatively neglected. This chapter will now review the limited commentaries made regarding currently-occupied rural settlement archaeology, and summarise current thinking regarding its significance to early medieval settlement studies. Following an analysis of the overall potential of 'Middle Saxon' occupation in currently-occupied villages, a series of detailed case studies will be presented. A discussion of the new insights provided by this approach, and the way in which they contribute to our perception of contemporary 'Middle Saxon' society will then conclude the piece.

'CORS': PERCEPTIONS AND POTENTIAL

Current Perceptions

The potential contribution of currently-occupied village investigation in Northamptonshire is gradually being realised by archaeological researchers, largely on the basis of recently-conducted fieldwork. A significant proportion of excavation has been related to development-led archaeological projects, following the introduction of statutory heritage protection in 1991. Although the main body of excavations within existing villages in Northamptonshire is the result of relatively recent research, there have been instances of earlier investigation. Limited excavation within the village of Newton-in-the-Willows in 1972, for example, yielded ceramics and metalwork datable to between the seventh and ninth centuries (Webster and Cherry 1973). Despite the absence of structural evidence, artefact concentrations appeared to demonstrate a 'Middle Saxon' origin for the settlement, although the rescue conditions under which investigation was conducted prevented more comprehensive analysis (Webster and Cherry 1973, 147). Researchers of the HEFA project have also investigated numerous villages across eastern and south-east England. Based on the results of this research, Carenza Lewis has reiterated her belief that villages and open fields developed in a broad mid ninth to twelfth century period (Lewis *et al.* 1997; 2007; 2010). There are, however, numerous difficulties with the methodological approach adopted by the HEFA scheme for the detection of early medieval settlement deposits, not least the inadequacy of test-pits for recognising typically ephemeral remains (see Chapter II). A more effective measure of the potential that occupied-village excavations in Northamptonshire have to enhance our understanding of early medieval settlements is revealed by analysis of the Archaeological Investigations Project (AIP).

Assessing Potential

The AIP records that, of the archaeological interventions undertaken in Northamptonshire that were archived between 1990 and 2009, twenty-nine were undertaken in

Interventions in 'CORS'	'CORS' interventions identifying archaeological deposits	'CORS' with 'Middle Saxon' artefactual material only	'CORS' with 'Middle Saxon' artefactual material and settlement structures from 'CORS'
29	23	5	8

Table 3.1: Of the archaeological interventions undertaken within 'CORS' in Northamptonshire, a significant quantity have located potential evidence for occupation dated between the seventh and ninth centuries.

locations which may be classified as currently-occupied rural settlements (Table 3.1) (see Chapter II). Twenty-three of these currently-occupied village excavations identified archaeological deposits of some kind, four of which recovered 'Middle Saxon' artefactual material only, and a further eight detected artefactual and structural evidence relating to settlement dated between the seventh and ninth centuries. The consistency with which 'Middle Saxon' settlement material has been located in Northamptonshire's still-occupied villages therefore stands at a remarkable thirteen out of twenty-three, or over fifty-six percent of investigations.

It must be remembered that the evidence derived from the AIP can only be realistically used as an approximate guide, and is not a completely comprehensive analysis, but if anything is likely only to represent a minimum indicator for the presence of 'Middle Saxon' occupation (see Chapter II). Detection of 'Middle Saxon' settlements deposits in over half of excavated rural villages in Northamptonshire is, therefore, extremely informative. The regular recovery of 'Middle Saxon' occupation deposits seriously challenges the popular model of 'Late Saxon' village origins, and promotes still further the need for a more detailed analysis of 'CORS' excavations in Northamptonshire. The following section thus comprises an analysis of some case studies of 'Middle Saxon' settlements revealed through excavation in Northamptonshire's currently-occupied rural settlements.

'CORS' AND 'MIDDLE SAXON' SETTLEMENTS

Introduction

Analysis of the AIP demonstrates a significant correlation between 'Middle Saxon' settlement remains and existing villages in Northamptonshire. In order to explore the significance of this association, however, more detailed analysis of the archaeological material and its relationship to the historic and modern landscape is required. This may be achieved through examining a series of case studies, exploring the character of seventh to ninth century occupation deposits recovered through currently-occupied rural settlement excavation, but also detailing the evidence from locations which later developed as towns (Figure 3.3). The sites will be presented geographically, according to the *pays* in which they are situated, an approach which will allow models regarding the significance of physical conditions in determining settlement character to be tested. It is immediately clear that two of the six *pays*,

Rockingham Forest and the Soke of Peterborough are not represented by currently-occupied rural settlement case studies. The causes and significance of this absence will be explored more fully, in the discussion which follows this section.

The Wolds

Situated in the south-westernmost corner of Northamptonshire, currently-occupied villages in the Wolds have been subject to comparatively little archaeological interventions compared to other *pays*. In spite of this deficiency, excavation on one site has recovered archaeological material relating to 'Middle Saxon' settlement. The diamond-shaped parish of Brackley St. Peter, bounded by the gravel terraces and alluvium of the Great Ouse to the south and east, is largely underlain by limestone and Boulder Clay over the 120m contour (RCHME Northampton IV 1982, 22). Sporadic excavation in the historic town core of Brackley presents intriguing evidence of its pre-Conquest development. Evaluation trenches at Edgerton House, immediately north of the churchyard of St. Peter's, recovered small quantities of organic-tempered pottery and Ipswich Ware, likely dated to the eighth or early ninth centuries (NHER: NN70854).

Further excavations in advance of a proposed extension to the church of St. Peter in the historic core of the town also produced an assemblage of 'Early-Mid Saxon pottery', possibly representing another occupation deposit (NHER: NN69533). Limited trial trenching in the churchyard found graves of mostly Saxo-Norman date, together with evidence of a Romano-British structure, potentially a bath suite or hypocaust. Whilst the lack of identified 'Middle Saxon' structural remains from Brackley is problematic, suggestion of a significant early centre is supported by the historical topography of the town. In spite of the 'Late Saxon' manorial focus and subsequent castle being located in the southern part of the town, by the medieval period the area around St. Peter's Church was known as 'Old Town' (Beresford and Joseph 1969; Clarke 1993; Foard and Ballinger 2000).

The suggestion that the location of the parish church represents the oldest settlement centre is supported by the curved churchyard, preserved by the pre-turnpike road network still evident in the Ordnance Survey First Edition (Figure 3.4). Early medieval churches are often associated with oval precincts, but similar enclosures may also have been associated with 'Middle Saxon' secular sites (see

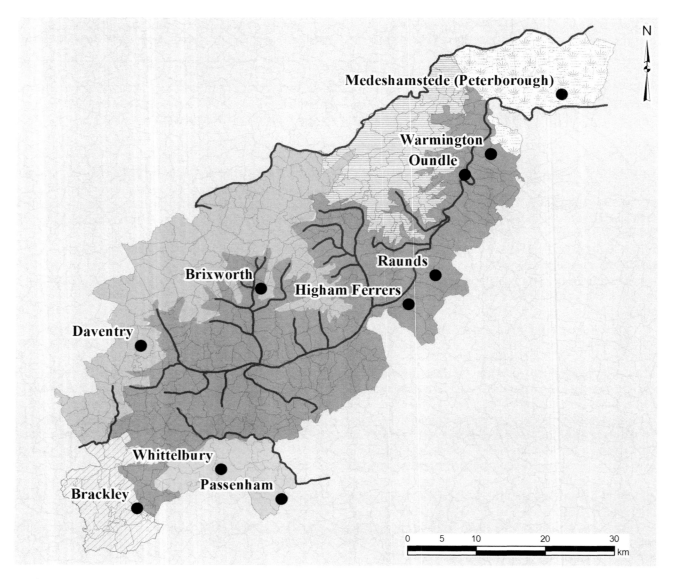

FIGURE 3.3: LOCATIONS OF PLACES MENTIONED IN THE TEXT. SEVERAL VILLAGES AND TOWNS IN THE COUNTY HAVE YIELDED EVIDENCE FOR 'MIDDLE SAXON' SETTLEMENT. SOURCE FOR MAPPING: HISTORIC PARISHES OF ENGLAND AND WALES ONLINE

below). John Clarke (1993) has previously asserted a likely seventh century date for the origins of Brackley, and whilst this is not supported by the current ceramic chronology of Ipswich Ware, the church dedication of St. Peter, commonly associated with Mercian influence under Offa, adds weight to the potential 'Middle Saxon' precedents of the town (Blinkhorn 1999). Further investigation, particularly in the area of the 'Old Town' is nevertheless required to push the argument for pre-ninth century origins beyond the circumstantial, but on current evidence it is possible that the historic street plan of Brackley developed after a short-range drift from a pre-existing 'Middle Saxon' focus.

The Nene Valley

The fertile valley of the River Nene and its major tributaries are recorded as the most densely settled *pays* of Northamptonshire by 1086, a regional concentration which has persisted into the present day (Parry 2006, 1-2).

This well-settled landscape provides ideal conditions for archaeological research in still-occupied villages, with high archaeological potential for 'Middle Saxon' settlement, combined with regular development-led excavations in advance of expansion and in-filling. As a consequence, the Nene Valley presents by far the most examples of villages which have produced evidence for pre-ninth century occupation. It is also within the Nene Valley *pays* that the influence of 'Middle Saxon' monastic foundations can most clearly be seen, such as the development of Oundle. Located on a spur on the bend of the River Nene, Oundle is situated on a combination of limestone and marls at a height of approximately 38m OD. The origins of the town as a monastic foundation of the Mercian Bishop Wilfrid (d.709) was cast into doubt by Foard (1985, 193), stressing that Bede described the minster as located only in the *provinciae* of Oundle. This challenge itself is now very questionable, however, following excavations in the town from the 1980s (Figure 3.5).

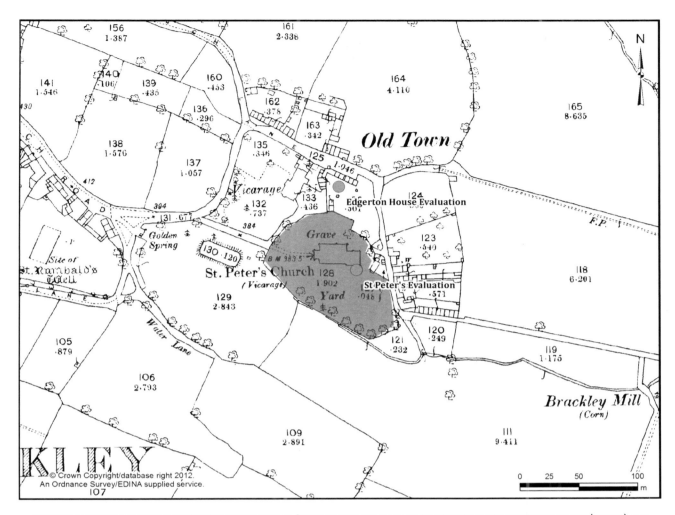

FIGURE 3.4: ORDNANCE SURVEY FIRST EDITION OF THE TOWN OF BRACKLEY, WITH THE LOCATION OF EXCAVATIONS MENTIONED IN THE TEXT (CIRCLES), AND PARTIAL OVAL OF ST PETER'S CHURCHYARD (SHADED). NOTE THAT THE 'MIDDLE SAXON' ACTIVITY IDENTIFIED AROUND THE CHURCH IS SLIGHTLY REMOVED FROM THE HISTORIC CORE OF THE TOWN, LOCATED AROUND 200M TO THE WEST, A RELATIONSHIP WHICH WILL EMERGE AS A PATTERN BY THIS RESEARCH, BOTH IN NORTHAMPTONSHIRE AND ELSEWHERE.

In 1985 excavation of an area immediately south of Black Pot Lane revealed early medieval settlement remains, located approximately 150m north of St Peter's Church. An excavated trench along the edge of Black Pot Lane exposed a V-shaped ditch (207), 2.8m wide and 1.4m deep. Two smaller linear ditches (201 and 204), likely cut by the larger ditch were also found, in addition to a buried 'Late Saxon' ploughsoil horizon to the south (Area E) (Johnson 1993/4). Perhaps significantly, the large V-shape ditch ran almost parallel to Black Pot Lane, exposing the possibility that early medieval structures influenced the historic street-plan. The ditch network was assigned a 'Late Saxon' origin by the excavators, despite the recovery of 'Early-Middle Saxon' organic-tempered wares and 'Middle Saxon' Ipswich Ware (Johnston 1993/4, 114). The presence of 'Late Saxon' ceramics certainly suggests that occupation extended beyond the ninth century, but the interpretation of all earlier material as residual does not appear sufficient, given that pre-ninth century pottery was found in every excavated structural feature (Johnston 1993/4, 114-6).

Considering the ideological weighting that the early English Church placed on the enclosure of sacred space (e.g. Biddle 1989, 23-4; Blair 2005, 250), it instead appears more plausible that the excavated ditches at Black Pot Lane represents the *vallum* of the historically-attested eighth-century monastic complex of St. Wilfrid. Indeed, pre-ninth century activity in the historic core of Oundle is further supported by the recovery of 'Early-Middle Saxon' organic-tempered wares from St. Peter's Church (Johnson 1993/4, 115). The cumulative results from these investigations therefore suggest that the origins of Oundle lie in its foundation as a monastic satellite of *Medeshamstede* (Stenton 1933; cf. Kelly 2009, 12-5). Unfortunately, the restricted nature of investigation prevents a comprehensive analysis of the likely economy or form of the 'Middle Saxon' minster, although the near-exact alignment of the excavated *vallum* with Black Pot Lane suggests that monastic activity may have been significant in shaping the structure of later settlement. The character of the archaeological material excavated in Oundle bears a striking resemblance to that identified

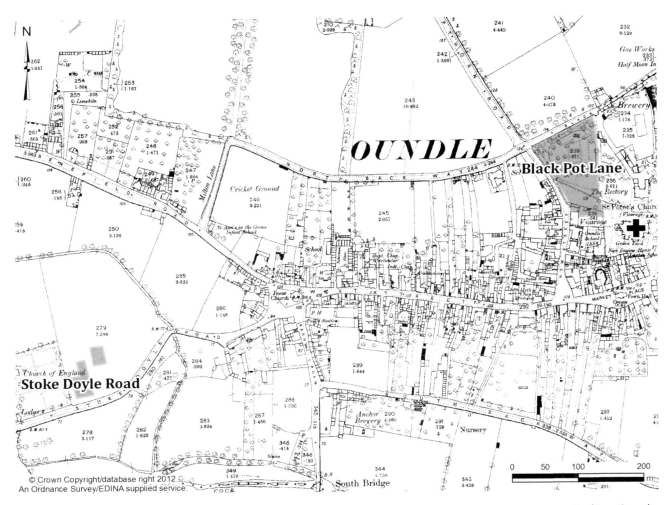

FIGURE 3.5: LOCATION OF ARCHAEOLOGICAL INTERVENTIONS IN OUNDLE THAT HAVE RECOVERED EARLY MEDIEVAL SETTLEMENT REMAINS. THE 'EARLY SAXON' OCCUPATION DETECTED SOUTH-WEST OF THE TOWN IS OF SIGNIFICANTLY DIFFERENT CHARACTER THAN THAT IDENTIFIED BY EXCAVATION AT BLACK POT LANE (AFTER JOHNSTON 1993/4, FIG 1).

at another of Northamptonshire's historically-attested ecclesiastical establishment at Brixworth, also located in the Nene Valley *pays*.

The village of Brixworth lies approximately 11km north of Northampton, in the centre of a triangular-shaped parish, underlain by a combination of Northampton sand and Boulder Clay (RCHME 1981, 26; Everson 1977, 55). Brixworth is renowned for its wealth of archaeological material from all periods, but is famed above all as the site of the remarkable Mercian church of All Saints'. First established by the clerics of *Medeshamstede c.*680, All Saints' is the largest standing early medieval building in England, which understandably remains an enduring focus for academic research (e.g. Gem 2009). Beyond the church, the parish was also the focus for the pioneering fieldwalking survey undertaken by David Hall and Paul Martin (1979) which proved so crucial in developing the new paradigm for 'Late Saxon' village origins. Subsequent targeted excavation of ceramic concentrations identified by the pair located 'Early-Middle Saxon' structural remains, ostensibly corroborating the 'Late Saxon' model for early medieval settlement change (Ford 1995).

The perceived distinction between 'Early and Middle Saxon' settlements and later nucleated villages noted by such research is brought into question though, following excavations in the vicarage garden of Brixworth village in 1972 (Figure 3.6) (Everson 1977). Situated to the north of the east-west orientated Church Street, rescue investigation in advance of housing development initially consisted of a single 10mx3m evaluation trench, which was followed by excavation of a more extensive 20mx15m area. These interventions revealed activity interpreted as part of the monastic precinct, the main features comprising a 3.4m wide ditch aligned north-south and eleven inhumation burials (Everson 1977, 67-73). Unfortunately, neither the ditch nor the burials produced ceramics, but organic-tempered pottery and Ipswich Ware were recovered in stratified horizons outside of the features. Radiocarbon dates from the fill of the ditch suggests that it may have originated as early as the latter part of the seventh century, with further analysis suggesting that the burials were broadly contemporary with, or slightly post-dated, the enclosure. It appears that by the 'Late Saxon' period the enclosure ditch, which almost certainly represents the *vallum*, was deliberately in-filled, marking the end of occupation (Everson 1977, 67).

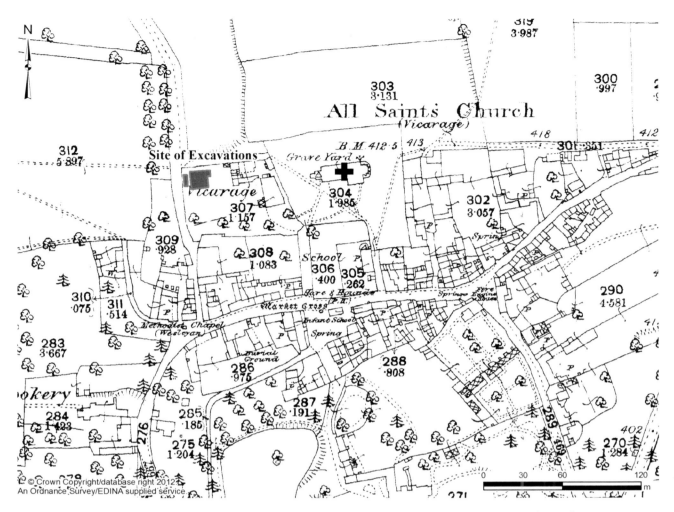

FIGURE 3.6: OS FIRST EDITION OF BRIXWORTH SHOWING ALL SAINTS CHURCH (CROSS) AND, TO THE WEST, THE EXCAVATED AREA (SHADED). AGAIN, NOTE THAT THE 'MIDDLE SAXON' FOCUS IS SLIGHTLY REMOVED FROM THE HISTORIC VILLAGE CORE (BASED ON EVERSON 1977, FIG 1)

It can be posited with a degree of confidence that the archaeological evidence from the vicarage garden at Brixworth is related to the documented 'Middle Saxon' minster, founded as a dependency of *Medeshamstede*. Identification of a substantial ditch, possibly cut as early as the seventh century, and several possible contemporary graves provides another glimpse of the likely key characteristics of early monastic establishments in the Northamptonshire landscape. The place-name of Brixworth is particularly interesting in this regard, combining the personal name *Beorhtel* or *Beorth* with OE *worth*, indicating an enclosure. *Beorth*, which may be translated as 'bright', appears to have been a very popular personal name, and in the case of Brixworth the element may preserve a noteworthy patron of the early church (Gover *et al.* 1933, 123; Everson 1977, 61; Crick 2011, *pers. comm.*).

The central importance of enclosure to minster communities is clearly demonstrated by identification of *vallum* at Brixworth and Oundle, surrounding the standing parish churches and 'Middle Saxon' focus at both sites. Monastic foundations are recognised by

scholars as a key tool of Mercian colonisation (e.g. Brown and Foard 2004, 89; Bassett 2007; 2008), and it is therefore unsurprising to find a degree of regularity in the form of *Medeshamstede's* likely early dependencies. Indeed, the importance of *vallum* as powerful social and ideological statements more generally has been recognised for some time: Charles Thomas noting their typical character as 'spiritual and legal, though hardly military defensible boundaries' (Thomas 1971, 32). Despite the clear significance of the *vallum* to early Mercian church foundations, archaeological investigation on other sites in Northamptonshire suggests that enclosures were not the preserve of 'Middle Saxon' ecclesiastics, but may also have been used by the secular elite (see below). Indeed, it appears that enclosure represents only one facet of a more general trend toward greater sophistication of spatial arrangements on rural settlement sites during the 'Middle Saxon' period, a pattern also confirmed by investigation in and around the village of Warmington.

The parish of Warmington, located in the north-eastern part of the Nene Valley *pays* only 3km north-east of Oundle, has been subject to a remarkable amount of archaeological

31

research. The local geology is somewhat typical of the Nene Valley, featuring gravels and alluvial deposits in the river valley, contrasted with Boulder Clay uplands (RCHME 1975). Early medieval settlement archaeology has been recovered through a series of development-led interventions in and around the modern village of Warmington, and the neighbouring hamlet of Eaglethorpe. Research has combined fieldwalking, environmental coring and excavation, the results from which allow a detailed reconstruction of early medieval landscape and settlement change. The first significant archaeological investigation carried out in Warmington parish took place between 1991 and 1993, in advance of construction of the Warmington Bypass, proposed to pass immediately northwest of Eaglethorpe.

Northamptonshire Archaeology carried out a comprehensive multi-disciplinary project of fieldwalking and geophysical survey, documentary research and evaluation trenching (Shaw 1993, 41). Four separate concentrations of organic-tempered 'Early-Mid Saxon' pottery were identified through fieldwalking, with a complete absence of 'Late Saxon' material conforming to the well-established phenomenon. 'Early-Middle Saxon' ceramics were exceptionally densely concentrated, with three scatters yielding seventy-seven, one hundred and four, and one hundred and ninety four sherds respectively. The fourth concentration, consisting of only twenty-six sherds, was interpreted as a likely area of manuring (Shaw 1993, 42-3). Taken in isolation, these results would almost certainly have been interpreted as further support for the 'Late Saxon' model for village origins, but at Eaglethorpe the picture from the landscape outside of the hamlet was supplemented by excavated data from within the currently-occupied rural settlement.

A total of fifteen evaluation trenches were excavated along the route of the proposed bypass, in the Mill End area of Eaglethorpe. Fourteen of the trenches were located in non-arable fields that could not be fieldwalked, while the other trench was intended to examine the site of the manor house and its accompanying 'Early-Middle Saxon' pottery scatter in Field WR13. For ease of interpretation, the trenches were grouped into three distinct areas: Area 1 was focussed immediately north-east of the hamlet and Area 2 was located in arable land to the south. Area 3 was situated closest to Eaglethorpe's core, with the aim of assessing deposits relating to the historic manor house. Areas 1 and 2 both produced evidence of 'Late Saxon' and medieval occupation, perhaps representing expansion from an existing focus, but no 'Early-Middle Saxon' material. The trenches of Area 3, however, identified a series of post-holes likely representing at least one hall-type structure, together with substantial quantities of organic-tempered ceramics, attributable to the 'Early-Middle Saxon' period (Shaw 1993, 43-6).

Excavation results from Eaglethorpe and its immediate environs therefore suggest that the origins of the hamlet may lie in the pre-ninth century period, although it is likely that 'Early-Middle Saxon' ceramic concentrations in the landscape around the hamlet represent a single *Wandersiedlung* or 'shifting settlement' typical of the period (e.g. Hamerow 1993) It is possible that the similarly-dated remains excavated within Eaglethorpe were also related to this preceding pattern, but it is equally likely that the 'Early-Middle Saxon' focus identified in the historic core represents the earliest origins of the later hamlet and challenges still further the development of archaeological models from fieldwalking evidence alone. Located less than 50m from apparent 'Late Saxon' occupation, it seems that early Eaglethorpe may have been subject to short-range shift sometime after the mid-ninth century, as identified on early medieval rural sites in Northamptonshire and elsewhere (e.g. Audouy and Chapman 2009; Hey 2004).

Indeed, the significance of 'Middle Saxon' settlement in shaping the location and form of later occupation has also been demonstrated by excavation within Eaglethorpe's neighbouring village of Warmington. Between 1996 and 1998, a programme of archaeological evaluation and excavation was undertaken within the village of Warmington, in advance of housing development on land south of Peterborough Road (Figure 3.7). Evaluation trenches identified a series of linear ditches and gullies fronting onto Chapel Street, in the southern part of the proposed development site. Further linear ditches in the north-eastern part of the site were broadly dated c.900-1200, although most likely used between c.1050 and 1100, according to the investigators. Following these initial results, a series of open area excavations uncovered part of an extensive settlement consisting of several phases of ditched enclosures, and numerous post-holes and pits. The post-holes almost certainly represent hall-type structures, although no individual buildings could be discerned (NHER: NN0791043).

Earliest occupation of the site consisted of a square enclosure measuring approximately 10m across, and a 60m long north-south aligned ditch with rounded terminals. To the west of the linear ditch, but on the same alignment, several post-holes and fenced boundaries were also detected (Figure 3.8). The zone between the ditch and enclosure appeared to have been subject to significant compaction, suggesting that it formed part of a droveway leading towards a fording point of the River Nene, located 200m to the north-west. This activity (Phase I) was crucially dated to before c.850, and most likely the eighth century, through the recovery of significant amounts of organic-tempered wares, and lack of 'Late Saxon' fabric. By the tenth century (Phase II) (Figure 3.8), the early enclosure system was modified in order to accentuate the droveway ditches and in the eleventh century (Phase III), a new system of enclosures suggests that the area was given over to a new form of stock management (NHER:NN102276; NHER: NN0791043). By this time, a contemporary focus had emerged to the north-east of the earlier settlement, adjacent to a moated site which developed as the medieval manorial centre (NHER: 102276).

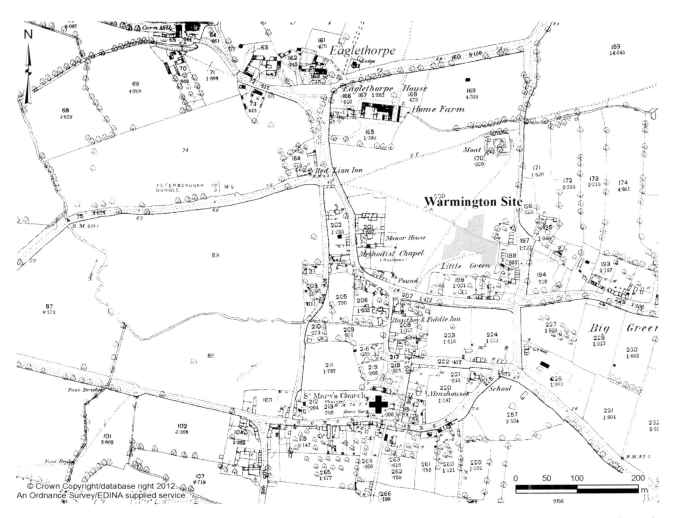

FIGURE 3.7: OS FIRST EDITION OF WARMINGTON (CENTRE) AND EAGLETHORPE (TOP), SHOWING THE SITE OF THE PETERBOROUGH ROAD EXCAVATION (SHADED) AND ST. MARY'S CHURCH (CROSS). INVESTIGATION AT THE SITE REVEALED A REMARKABLE SEQUENCE OF EARLY MEDIEVAL SETTLEMENT (NN0791043)

The Peterborough Road excavations demonstrate a remarkably long and complex sequence of early medieval settlement, located immediately adjacent to the historic core of Warmington. The form of the site, aligned with the later street pattern but entirely encompassed by it, suggests that the enclosure system, first developed in the eighth century, may have helped shape the succeeding tenurial arrangements of the later village. In a strikingly similar pattern to that recognised at Eaglethorpe and elsewhere, settlement development at Warmington appears to have been subject to short-range drift in the 'Late Saxon' or early post-Conquest period from an earlier 'Middle Saxon' focus. The introduction of semi-permanent ditches into the 'Middle Saxon' settlement at Warmington is also significant, differing drastically from the transient and shifting occupation often assumed to persist into the ninth century. Environmental and macrofaunal evidence from the site suggests a mixed farming economy typical of the period, although the network of enclosures does suggest a degree of specialised activity, and indeed, the presence of a droveway leading to the River Nene may be indicative of a site deliberately-positioned to control traffic over the crossing.

Livestock droving was an integral part of most early medieval estate economies and long-distance trade networks (Faith 1997, 109). Located 200m south-east from a fordable point of the River Nene, and between upland and lowland pastoral resources, Warmington would have occupied a key nodal point in the local landscape. Control of this arterial route may have resulted in the procurement of tolls and renders, at least during periods of seasonal transhumance. Warmington is recorded in the ownership of Peterborough Abbey by 1086, and although no contemporary records exist, it is not impossible that its initial establishment was also founded under the guidance of *Medeshamstede*. Domesday Book cannot be used as a reliable indicator of 'Middle Saxon' monastic ownership, however, and it is uncertain when the manor of Warmington may have come under the jurisdiction of Peterborough Abbey (see Chapter VI). Rather than attempting to associate the settlement sequences of Warmington and Eaglethorpe with particular elite activity, it is more appropriate to view their development as further evidence for the changing character of Northamptonshire's countryside beginning in the 'Middle Saxon' period. Among the first pieces of research to establish the significance of the seventh to ninth-century period, was the investigations undertaken

FIGURE 3.8: THE EXCAVATED SEQUENCE AT PETERBOROUGH ROAD, WARMINGTON (DERIVED FROM NN0791043).

as part of the Raunds Area Project, the evidence from which represents the last of the currently-occupied rural settlement case studies for the Nene Valley *pays*.

Established in 1985, the Raunds Area Project represents the longest-running landscape archaeology project ever undertaken in Northamptonshire, established with the aim of detailing a range of historic landscape elements through opportunistic 'rescue' excavations, set within a broader context of programmes of environmental research, field survey and documentary studies (Audouy 2009, 2-3). Through research from the landscape surrounding modern villages and investigation *within* settlements, both extant and deserted, the Raunds Area Project provides a unique insight into the development of part of the Nene Valley landscape throughout the medieval period. Of particular pertinence for this research, excavation at several locations within the modern village of Raunds yielded evidence for 'Middle Saxon' activity (Parry 2006). Investigation revealed a pre-ninth century occupation focus, slightly removed from the historic street-plan, leading the excavators to suggest a process of 'Late Saxon' short-range settlement drift. Of equal significance to understanding the early medieval landscape, limited excavation of the immediate agricultural hinterland revealed that the common fields were developed *after* initial settlement

restructuring around the eighth century (Audouy and Chapman 2009, 52).

The conclusions derived from the Raunds Area Project add to the picture from other currently-occupied rural settlement excavations in the Nene Valley which strongly suggest a 'two-stage' process of village formation; initial 'Middle Saxon' nucleation preceding a period of settlement restructuring and open field creation from the 'Late Saxon' period onward (Parry 2006). It is with a remarkable degree of consistency that archaeological investigation in village centres within the *pays* has recovered 'Middle Saxon' occupation. Whilst identification of early settlement at the documented minster centres of Oundle and Brixworth may have been anticipated, similar activity has been located at sites with no recorded high-status affiliations. Given the fragmentary and often unreliable character of documentary material though, such sources should not be relied upon to interpret excavated settlement remains. What can be said with far greater certainty is that the countryside of the Nene Valley was subject to widespread and fundamental changes in the 'Middle Saxon' period. Possibly from the seventh, and certainly by the eighth century, rural settlements demonstrate a far greater degree of structure and permanence than earlier forms and in some cases, structural elements of 'Middle Saxon' occupation can be

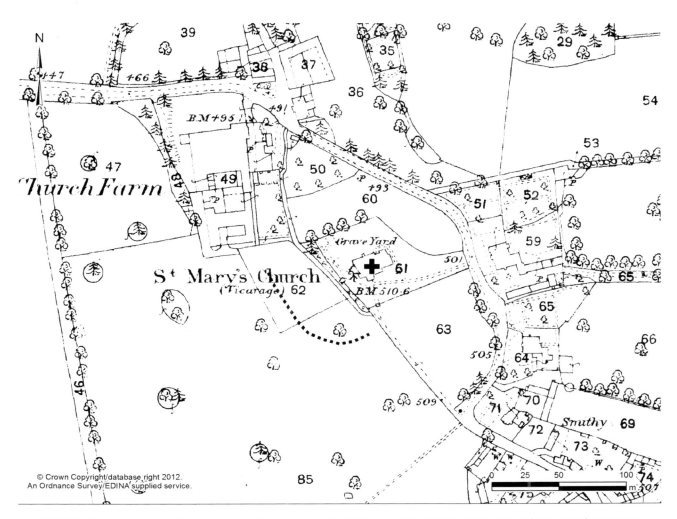

FIGURE 3.9: OS FIRST EDITION OF WHITTLEBURY WITH THE NEGATIVE ANOMALY DETECTED BY THE MAGNETOMETER SURVEY (DASHED LINE). THE FEATURE ALMOST CERTAINLY REPRESENTS THE DITCH OF THE HILLFORT, AND IT APPEARS THE ENCLOSURE WAS REUSED DURING THE 'MIDDLE SAXON' PERIOD. NOTE THE DISCRETE LOCATION OF THE CHURCH AMONGST THE DISPERSED SETTLEMENT PATTERN (AFTER WHITTLEWOOD PROJECT ARCHIVE, ARCHAEOLOGY DATA SERVICE).

seen to influence later village form. It should be considered, however, that this pattern is made evident by investigation within currently-occupied villages in the Nene Valley, which represents the most archaeologically rich and researched area of Northamptonshire. In order to discern whether this phenomenon is typical of Northamptonshire more generally, analysis of the remaining *pays* in the county is also required.

Whittlewood Forest

Whittlewood Forest is well known amongst early medieval landscape researchers as the focus of one of the most comprehensive studies of historic settlement in Northamptonshire: the Whittlewood Project (Jones and Page 2006). Of principal relevance to this book, are excavations undertaken within the still-occupied villages of Whittlebury and Passenham, the former as part of the Whittlewood Project, the latter as the result of a development-led investigation. The heavily-wooded parish of Whittlebury is situated almost entirely on Boulder Clay geology, forming part of a watershed between the rivers

Great Ouse and Tove in south-west Northamptonshire. The village lies at the highest point in the parish at 155m OD, a point from which a network of streams radiate (RCHME 1982, 167). Forming one of the twelve contiguous parishes examined by the Whittlewood Project, Whittlebury has been subject to detailed archaeological investigation, including fieldwalking in the northern part of the parish, earthwork recording, and test-pit excavation and geophysical survey in Whittlebury village (Jones and Page 2003, 46). Probably the most significant discovery of this research was the identification of a previously undetected hillfort in the north-west of Whittlebury village (Figure 3.9).

The monument enclosed an area of 3.5ha within which the later medieval parish church of St. Mary's was later located. Resistivity surveys revealed the footprints of at least twelve round houses but crucially investigation also yielded evidence of early medieval occupation within this earlier hillfort (Jones and Page 2003, 46-9). Test pit excavation in St Mary's churchyard recovered quantities of 'Early-Middle Saxon' ceramics, together with a single sherd of 'Middle Saxon' Ipswich Ware. Although no structural features were located, such ceramic finds suggests the presence of some form of 'Middle Saxon' activity in the hillfort (Jones and Pears 2003, 5-15). Indeed, in the wider context of the Whittlewood *pays*, the reuse of earlier landscape features may not be exclusive to Whittlebury, as it has been suggested that early medieval estate organisation of the area may have been based on Iron Age and Roman precedents, within which settlements located in close proximity to hillforts functioned as administrative centres (Jones and Page 2006, 64-5). The potential 'Middle Saxon' origins of Whittlebury are complemented by the archaeological evidence from another currently-occupied village in Whittlewood, at Passenham.

Located within the parish of Old Stratford, the village of Passenham is located on the gravels to the north of the River Great Ouse (RCHME 1982, 108). The reference to Passenham in the Anglo-Saxon Chronicle as the place where Edward the Elder overwintered his troops in 921 has stimulated previous scholarly interest, such as Brown and Roberts (1973) failed attempt to locate the postulated military encampment. More significantly, this reference supports a more extensive body of evidence that indicates Passenham's status as a 'Late Saxon' royal estate centre (Foard 1985, 198 and 218). It is likely that Passenham was one of three estate centres in the Whittlewood area, the organisational structure of which may have derived from an Iron Age and Romano-British territory centred on Whittlebury (Jones and Page 2006, 65). The most conspicuous archaeological evidence for early medieval activity at Passenham is the remains of an extensive cemetery, first identified in 1873 and somewhat optimistically associated with Edward's army (VCH Northants I 1902, 236). The recovery of funerary ornaments suggests an earlier provenance for at least some of the graves, although human remains recovered across the village suggests either a vast cemetery or several foci (RCHME 1982, 109-10; NHER 7739012). In addition to the likely early importance of Passenham suggested by documentary and mortuary data, archaeological investigation in the village has also produced evidence relating to early medieval settlement (NHER 7739012)

Evaluation trenching in Passenham at Manor Nurseries, located approximately 75m north of the parish church in 1996, ahead of proposed development, located a sequence of clearly-defined archaeological features. Excavation of a single 14.2m long trench, on what is now the periphery of the shrunken medieval village, revealed four ditches, aligned approximately north-east to south-west. Further features included four postholes, possibly representing a hall-structure, and a pit. Dating evidence was provided by Ipswich Ware, recovered in two ditches, and shelly-limestone ceramics recovered from the remaining features. Although the latter fabric is generally not precisely datable, its similarity with pottery recovered from Pennyland, Buckinghamshire, implies a 'Middle Saxon' origin (NHER 7739012; Knight 1993).

Archaeological investigation at Passenham, although extremely restricted, has nevertheless produced convincing evidence for 'Middle Saxon' occupation. Identification of a 'Middle Saxon' ditch sequence in an area slightly removed from the current village focus presents an increasingly familiar picture, developed from currently-occupied rural settlement excavation in Northamptonshire. The lack of further excavation cannot confirm whether the settlement was subject to the anticipated short-range drift during the 'Late Saxon' period, and further investigation is required in order to provide a clearer picture of Passenham's early medieval settlement development. The results from 'CORS' investigation at Whittlebury and Passenham nevertheless add further weight to the developing model of 'Middle Saxon' settlement and landscape change across Northamptonshire. The evidence from the Whittlewood *pays* is not as impressive as that from the Nene Valley, possibly due to the relative lack of excavation, but the limited research undertaken so far still suggests the establishment of semi-permanent settlements in the 'Middle Saxon' period, even in areas of wooded uplands. Excavation within still-occupied villages in the Northampton Heights, gives yet more support that the 'pre-village nuclei' detected by researchers of the Whittlewood project was not restricted to one particular landscape zone (Jones and Page 2006, 222).

Northampton Heights

The gently rolling uplands of the Northampton Heights feature one location which has yielded evidence with relevance to this research, at the market town of Daventry. The parish of Daventry is underlain by undulating Jurassic clays which typify the landscape of the Heights, drained by a series of small north-east flowing streams (RCHME 1981). The most impressive archaeological feature in the parish is the vast hillfort of Borough Hill, situated less than 2km east of Daventry itself. The monument is first recorded in the Badby Charter of 944 as the 'old burh' (S495), suggesting that the name derives from the earliest usage of *burh*, describing a defensible enclosure (Gover *et al.* 1933, 19; cf. Draper 2008). Fieldwalking in various locations across the parish, however, has somewhat surprisingly failed to identify 'Early-Mid Saxon' ceramic concentrations (Brown 1991, 11). The apparent dearth of early medieval activity from the landscape around Daventry is contrasted though, by the excavated evidence from the historic core of the town. Daventry has been subject to two substantial open area excavations that have yielded substantial evidence for early medieval settlement. In 1994, 3ha of land was investigated ahead of development adjacent to St. John's Square (Figure 3.10) (Soden 1994/5; NHER: NN43504).

Excavations revealed initial activity (Phase I) characterised by a series of ditches, post-holes and pits. One ditch (395), measuring a massive 7m across ran east-west across the site along the top of a natural ridge. Post-holes and groups of slots were also found in discrete clusters within the enclosure formed by the ditch, suggesting either zoning

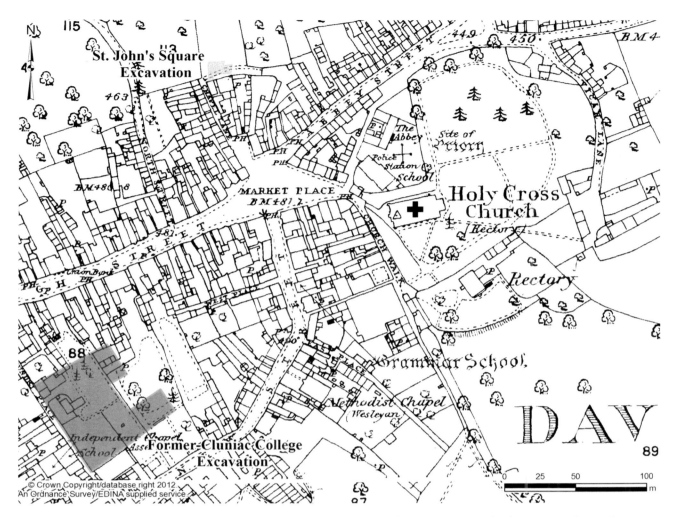

FIGURE 3.10: OS FIRST EDITION OF DAVENTRY, SHOWING THE LOCATIONS OF THE ST. JOHN'S SQUARE EXCAVATION (TOP), THE FORMER-CLUNIAC COLLEGE EXCAVATION, AND HOLY CROSS CHURCH (CROSS). EXCAVATIONS APPEAR TO SHOW A SHIFT IN OCCUPATION FOCUS FROM THE ST. JOHN'S SQUARE AREA FURTHER SOUTH AT SOME POINT IN THE 'MIDDLE SAXON' OR 'LATE SAXON' PERIOD.

of occupation, or the presence of a rampart-revetment or palisade (NHER: NN43504). The fill of the ditch yielded vast quantities of organic-tempered pottery, totalling a remarkable five hundred and ninety sherds. Although such ceramics are infamously difficult to date accurately, the excavators assigned them a sixth or possibly seventh century date (Soden 1994/5, 80-90). The presence of structures featuring foundation trenches, together with an absence of *Grubenhäuser* urges caution in accepting such an early date for activity, however, and given the construction techniques identified, a more cautious 'Middle Saxon' date, with activity perhaps peaking in the eighth century instead seems more appropriate (Hamerow 2011, 130-1).

If the 'Middle Saxon' date for the sherds recovered from the ditch at the St. John's Square site is accurate, it is even possible that it was not abandoned, as originally suggested by the excavators. The quantity of ceramic material recovered certainly suggests intensive, or more likely prolonged settlement, during the 'Middle Saxon' period which was superseded by a new arrangement of ditches

and enclosures *c*.900, together with the refurbishment of the ditch (NHER: NN43504). Remarkably, the Ordnance Survey First Edition map of Daventry reveals that the line of the ditch was preserved as part of the street-plan of the nineteenth century town: its northern extent being framed by a footpath, the ditch appears to form the northern edge of a sub-triangular enclosure to the north of the market place (Figure 3.11). It is possible that the 'Middle Saxon' enclosure ditch identified in the St. John's Square excavation was reused as a manorial centre in the 'Late Saxon' period, the lasting significance of which resulted in its fossilisation within the later street-plan.

The preservation of former manorial curia in subsequent settlement patterns has been speculated on other sites in Northamptonshire (e.g. Foard 1985, 207; Brown and Foard 2004, 94), and elsewhere in England. In Devon, for instance, sub-rectangular village cores at Thorverton and Silverton, both known as 'The Bury', may similarly preserve manorial or earlier enclosures, or filled-in market-places (Hoskins 1955, 51). 'Late Saxon' activity was also recognised in the other major excavation undertaken within

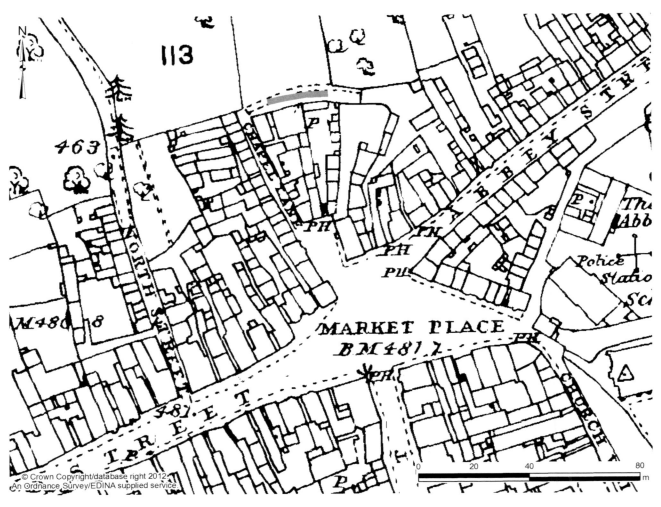

FIGURE 3.11: ORDNANCE SURVEY FIRST EDITION OF DAVENTRY. THE NORTHERN PART OF TRIANGULAR STREET PLAN IN THE CENTRE OF THE PICTURE IS FORMED BY THE 'MIDDLE SAXON' ENCLOSURE DITCH (SOLID LINE).

Daventry town centre, approximately 100m south-east of St John's Square. Investigations conducted at the site of a former-Cluniac college by Northamptonshire Archaeology in 2004 uncovered several inter-cutting pits containing 'Late Saxon' ceramics, suggesting an overall expansion and intensification of settlement in Daventry at this time (NHER: SNN105278). The early medieval occupation excavated within the historic core of Daventry underscores the significance of investigations within existing centres. If fieldwalking results from the landscape surrounding were the only evidence available, the origins of Daventry would probably have been assigned to the 'Late Saxon' period. Currently-occupied settlement excavation, however, provides a vastly different insight, suggesting that 'Middle Saxon' occupation was not only significant in its own right, but activity during this period may have influenced the subsequent growth of Daventry, the impact of which was still recognisable into the twentieth century, when the historic core of the town was redeveloped. Having detailed a series of case studies from a number of different *pays*, the evidence analyses here presents a series of key observations regarding the settlement, landscape and society of 'Middle Saxon' Northamptonshire.

SETTLEMENT, LANDSCAPE AND SOCIETY IN 'MIDDLE SAXON' NORTHAMPTONSHIRE

The growing body of archaeological data from currently-occupied settlement excavations provides a unique new insight into the developing early medieval countryside of Northamptonshire. By focussing on the results from exiting rural settlements, this research marks a significant departure from the majority of archaeological models of early medieval settlement in the county, which have invariably been developed from results of fieldwalking survey. The approach used by this book has proved particularly fruitful, encouraging a number of key observations which contribute to our understanding of early medieval settlement and society in Northamptonshire. The first and perhaps the most significant finding of this research, is the regularity with which 'Middle Saxon' settlement remains have been identified by 'CORS' excavation. Analysis of the AIP demonstrates that over fifty percent of investigations within Northamptonshire's currently-occupied villages have recovered some evidence which may be related to settlement dated between the seventh and ninth centuries. Whilst only useful as an approximate measure, these results strongly challenge the prevailing 'Late Saxon' model for village origins, suggesting a more complex process of settlement development in over half the sites excavated.

Only through more comprehensive study of particular sites has the somewhat tentative conclusion derived from the AIP data been able to be built-upon, however, illustrating in detail the conditions and evolving character of 'Middle Saxon' settlement in the county. The case studies presented here overwhelmingly support the model of a two-stage process of historic settlement development, first comprehensively forwarded by Brown and Foard (1998). When subject to extensive investigation, 'Middle Saxon' settlements within Northamptonshire's currently-occupied rural settlements consistently demonstrates a degree of organisational structure and permanence not generally anticipated for sites of the period. The excavated sequences at places such as Oundle, Brixworth and Warmington reflect long-lived settlements dating from as early as the seventh century, and not the small, dispersed settlements often assumed to persist well into the ninth century (Lewis *et al.* 1997, 198). In the case of Warmington, the enclosure system established by the 'Middle Saxon' period may have influenced the street and tenurial arrangement of the later village, the 'backfield' location of which suggests it was subject short-range settlement drift, probably in the 'Late Saxon' or early post-Conquest period.

The consistent pattern of 'Middle Saxon' settlements being identified slightly removed from the historic core of villages and towns in Northamptonshire strongly suggests that short-range settlement shift was a widespread phenomenon of historic settlement development. Only in very rare instances can this process be seen in significant detail, although excavations from Yarnton, Oxfordshire, provide a useful comparator (Chapter IV; Hey 2004). Dispersed and unstructured 'Early Saxon' settlement in the Yarnton area was superseded around the eighth century by more compact and semi-permanent occupation, which included the establishment of toft-like enclosure systems. Contemporary with this new settlement arrangement, the agricultural economy of the site intensified with greater arable production and the exploitation of the Thames floodplain as meadowland, following reclamation (Hey 2004, 46-8). Significantly, the eighth century changes notable at Yarnton did not lead to the permanent establishment of a village, as occupation continued to drift to the north and east. Probably only in the post-Conquest period did habitation at Yarnton eventually stabilise, with a restructured settlement focussed around the manor and church (Hey 2004, 87-8).

The early medieval settlement sequence at Yarnton is extremely significant, as the more restricted excavations undertaken within several of Northamptonshire's currently-occupied rural settlements have revealed an apparently comparable process. Sites such as Passenham and Brackley demonstrate a 'Middle Saxon' focus removed from the core of the later medieval village, and more

extensive excavation at sites such as Warmington reveal the likely semi-permanent and structured character of such settlements. It has been noted that several of the 'Middle Saxon' sites presented here have likely ecclesiastical links, with Oundle and Brixworth both characterised by similar enclosures, probably representing monastic *vallum*. Whilst the significance of enclosed space for the early English Church is undeniable (e.g. Biddle 1989, 23-4; Blair 2005, 250), it should not be assumed that such monuments were the preserve of the 'Middle Saxon' clerics. Excavation at Higham Ferrers in the Nene Valley, for instance, uncovered remarkable evidence for an extensive 'Middle Saxon' enclosure which has been associated with a royal rather than an ecclesiastical estate centre (Shaw 1991). Situated only 4km south-west of another key centre for early medieval settlement research at Raunds, investigation at Higham was undertaken in a landscape already subject to intensive multi-period investigation (Hardy *et al.* 2007, 1-3). The earliest post-Roman settlement activity identified at Higham consisted of *Grubenhäuser*, apparently occupied for around a century and abandoned by *c*.550. More notable settlement activity though, was that dated to the eighth and ninth century; excavation revealing a substantial horseshoe-shaped enclosure and structures (Figure 3.12).

The enclosure encompassed an area of 0.8ha, within which a handful of buildings were in use during the eighth century (Hardy *et al.* 2007, 30). In addition to these features, a further focus comprising a malting oven was identified 150m to the south-west, perhaps suggesting the deliberate zoning of 'Middle Saxon' settlement activity (Hardy *et al.* 2007, 194). It is likely that the enclosure at Higham functioned as a stock pen, perhaps used only seasonally, likely representing a significant centre for tribute accumulation within the regional landscape (Hardy *et al.* 2007, 30-5). Documentary material suggests that Higham was an *inland* belonging to an extensive estate centred on Irthlingborough, the royal status of which is evidenced by eighth century Mercian charter (Hardy *et al.* 2007, 201-4). Without this supporting written evidence, however, it is likely that Higham Ferrers would have been viewed as an ecclesiastical site, especially if partial investigation had located the enclosure ditch and failed to demonstrate the lack of internal buildings anticipated on a Church site of the period (Blair 2005, 198-202). Contrary to the model outlined by Faith (1997, 21), the development of *inlands* therefore appears to have been common to secular as well as religious institutions, underscoring the likely homogeneity of elite activity in the 'Middle Saxon' period. This uniformity is also emphasised by John Blair's (1996) reassessment of the excavated palace at Northampton, suggesting that the series of halls there were founded by ecclesiastical authorities.

Indeed, elite agency to particular early medieval sites and phenomenon is a persisting and, for the most part, unresolved theme of early medieval settlement research (Chapter VIII). Such discussions aside, what the cumulative analysis presented here does show is the undoubted central

FIGURE 3.12: RECONSTRUCTION OF THE 'MIDDLE SAXON' ENCLOSURE EXCAVATED AT HIGHAM FERRERS. THE FEATURE LIKELY ACTED AS A STOCK-PEN, AS PART OF A TRIBUTE CENTRE WITHIN A 'MIDDLE SAXON' ESTATE CENTRED ON NEARBY IRTHLINGBOROUGH (HARDY ET AL. 2007, FIG 3.3)

importance of the 'Middle Saxon' period in the settlement and social history of Northamptonshire. The detection of 'Middle Saxon' settlements in the topographically contrasted *pays* of the Wolds, Nene Valley, Whittlewood Forest and Northampton Heights suggests that environmental conditions were not the overwhelming causal factor behind their development. Indeed, Williamson's (2003) hypothesis that intractable clayland landscapes resulted in the greatest density of 'nucleated' villages is not supported by this study, with the greatest density of 'Middle Saxon' settlements identified in the fertile belt of the Nene Valley. Physical conditions no doubt influenced settlement in some circumstances, however, such as the anticipated absence of early settlement activity from the un-reclaimed Soke of Peterborough. Such conclusions are preliminary though, as 'Middle Saxon' colonisation of fen islands is detectable at places, such as Cambridgeshire (Chapter VI), and comparable but as-yet undetected sites may be present in Northamptonshire. The lack of activity detected in the Soke is also contrasted somewhat by the clearly industrious undertakings of *Medeshamstede's* clerics beyond their immediate hinterland.

Whilst physical conditions cannot be said to have been decisive in the development of Northamptonshire's 'Middle Saxon' settlement pattern, attempting to detect a single causal factor is perhaps unwise. Previous scholarly understanding has been impeded by the desire to assign a solitary crucial rationale to early medieval settlement development, and as Richard Jones has successfully demonstrated, settlement change is likely to have been affected by a series of complex processes (Jones 2010). What is clear, however, is that disparities in ecological

and functional variables often cited as stimuli for the increasingly hierarchical character of settlement seen in 'Middle Saxon' England lack real explanatory depth. Rather, a rapidly stratifying social hierarchy from the seventh century is more likely to have instigated fundamental change to the economy of rural communities, putting particular pressure on the modes of production on settlement sites (Moreland 2000, 83-4). It is likely that the changing character and intensified exploitation of Northamptonshire's countryside was at least partly the result of these more comprehensive changes to 'Middle Saxon' society, during a period which witnessed the more rigorous establishment of royal and ecclesiastical power (Chapter VIII).

CONCLUSION

This chapter has demonstrated how the 'Middle Saxon' period in Northamptonshire was a time of fundamental and lasting settlement change. Contrary to prevailing scholarly models that suggest little distinction between 'Middle Saxon' settlements and their 'Early Saxon' predecessors, this research has shown how crucial transformations to the lived experiences of rural communities began as early as the seventh century. The unique contribution of excavation within currently-occupied rural settlements has shown that 'Middle Saxon' settlements in Northamptonshire can regularly be revealed as being of more permanent, stable and specialised character than is commonly anticipated. These new settlement features are likely reflective of developing social and political conditions, particularly the stratifying social hierarchy which encouraged new approaches to the economic and productive infrastructure of the countryside. The influence of 'Middle Saxon' occupation in Northamptonshire is not merely reflective of its own chronological context, however, but the restructuring evident in the period had a lasting impact upon the later settlement landscape. Perhaps above all, the 'Middle Saxon' period in Northamptonshire can be seen as the period in which the location, form and above all the *identity* of rural settlements was firmly established, identities that continued to shape medieval and later communities.

Chapter IV
Oxfordshire

Following study of the midlands county of Northamptonshire, the focus of this research now moves south-westwards, to Oxfordshire. Whilst not generally considered part of the midlands Oxfordshire is nevertheless situated in a central position in southern England, and indeed is located within Roberts and Wrathmell's 'central province', that by the nineteenth century at least was characterised by tightly coalesced villages and enclosed former-open fields (Roberts and Wrathmell 2000, 31). Whilst few counties can claim to have been as pivotal as Northamptonshire in yielding evidence which forwards the discipline of early medieval settlement studies, the landscape of Oxfordshire has nevertheless been subject to a considerable amount of important research. Archaeological investigation is providing an increasingly coherent picture of the early medieval countryside, which can be supplemented by impressive documentary research relating to the area of the later county. This chapter will present the archaeological evidence for 'Middle Saxon' settlement and landscape from the historic county of Oxfordshire and, in employing a slightly alternative approach to that adopted for Northamptonshire, will nevertheless also emphasise the largely neglected archaeological material from currently-occupied rural settlements.

In contrast to Northamptonshire, though, where substantial 'Middle Saxon' settlement activity can be identified in most geographical *pays*, Oxfordshire is more imbalanced, with the vast majority of early medieval habitation sites identified thus far, located within the floodplain of the Thames Valley. The reasons for such a disparity is explored in greater detail below, but such research conditions means that investigation of Oxfordshire must adopt an alternative approach to the topographically-orientated analysis utilised by the other county-based chapters of this book. The archaeological material in this chapter will instead be presented according to status, divided between settlements that can likely be associated with royal or ecclesiastical agency and those where such direct elite impact cannot be clearly demonstrated as identified. Caution is required that such an approach does not perpetuate a dichotomy of 'high-status' versus 'low-status', given that nationwide archaeological research is gradually but convincingly demonstrating an ever-more diverse and complex 'Middle Saxon' settlement hierarchy (Ulmschneider 2011, 157). This chapter will therefore not underestimate the significant variety of activity that is covered by arbitrary divisions of status, whilst accepting them as a convenient framework for discussion. It will be shown in particular that the evidence for the network of minsters within the Thames Valley is not as wholly convincing as has been

suggested previously, and in places where documentary evidence is lacking, the archaeological evidence alone offers little to distinguish between sites of secular and ecclesiastical character.

After first introducing Oxfordshire as a study area, this chapter will then detail the primary topographical zones of the county. Although *pays* are not being used to structure discussion of this chapter, the differing geographical conditions across the county nevertheless influenced the form of early medieval settlement. Defining *pays* also allows the degree of previous archaeological investigation in differing areas to be assessed, so that the influence of varying research traditions upon scholarly interpretation can be considered. Following introduction of Oxfordshire's *pays*, a brief overview of the pre-'Middle Saxon' archaeology from the county will be made, underlining the constant role of the Thames as a gateway for early people. This will be succeeded by an analysis of previous early medieval settlement research undertaken in Oxfordshire: a county which in some ways can be seen as the birthplace of the discipline. Analysis of the 'Middle Saxon' settlement archaeology of the county, with an emphasis on the evidence from currently-occupied rural settlements will then precede the final discussion, which underlines the way in which such material presented may transform our understanding of contemporary society in the period.

INTRODUCING OXFORDSHIRE

The administrative territory of Oxfordshire is first mentioned in the first decades of the tenth century, recorded in the Anglo-Saxon Chronicle as *Oxnaford scire* under the year 911 (*ASC* 911). Whilst the kingdom of Wessex had been divided into shires from at least the ninth century, the areas north of the Thames were subject to similar development only much later. The Thames had formed the frontier between Wessex and Mercia until as late as the tenth century, and it was probably not until the early eleventh century that Oxfordshire and the surrounding counties were formally 'shired', possibly as part of a single event of administrative structuring (Whybra 1990, 4-12). It is important to note that for the purposes of this study that the modern boundaries of Oxfordshire, rather than the historic extents of the county, will be utilised. The motivations for the use of modern Oxfordshire as a unit for research are manifold. Primarily, as the historic county probably only gained its form after the West Saxon re-conquest of the south midlands in the late tenth century, the 'Late Saxon' territory has little relevance for a study that has an earlier chronological focus. Furthermore, the most significant recent adaptations made to form the modern county has been the incorporation of extensive areas south of the river that originally belonged to historic Berkshire. Removing the Thames as the southern boundary of this study therefore goes someway to lessen the somewhat artificial administrative geography of historic Oxfordshire, and instead creates a study area that possesses an overriding unity as the basin of the Upper Thames (Figure 4.1). Finally, and perhaps most significantly, the Oxfordshire Historic Environment Record (OHER) holds records relating to the historic county, and thus the area was partly chosen as a matter of research practicality.

THE *PAYS* OF OXFORDSHIRE

Going beyond Oxfordshire's unifying featuring as the basin of the Upper Thames, it becomes increasingly clear that the modern county represents something of a transitional territory, encompassing landscapes of greatly different character. With an absence of physical boundaries, barring the notable exceptions of the Rivers Thames and Cherwell, Oxfordshire exhibits a series of topographical areas that are instead seen as characteristic of neighbouring counties. The limestone hills of the Cotswolds for instance, lie partially within Oxfordshire, but are chiefly located further north and west, in the county of Gloucestershire. As a region of transition, Oxfordshire has similarly been used as a watershed by early medieval social and political groupings, forming part of the Thames region repeatedly utilised as a frontier between developing polities (see below). In addition to influencing the form of political boundaries, it is likely that underlying physical conditions also impacted the character of early medieval settlement in the region. Of perhaps more significance in Oxfordshire, however, is the clear disparity in archaeological research undertaken in the differing topographical zones which significantly influence our understanding of the 'Middle Saxon' countryside. In very basic terms, the landscape zones of Oxfordshire are characterised by a series of limestone hills and clay vales but are most suitably divisible into four distinct *pays* (Figure 4.2) (Jessup 1975, 13; Darkes 2010, 6).

North Oxfordshire Upland

The North Oxfordshire Upland occupies the northernmost portion of the county and is characterised by iron-rich soils, largely underlain by a series of Lias Mudstone deposits, all of which are situated at heights over 150m OD (Figure 4.2). Sometimes referred to as the Redlands, after the rust-coloured local stone and plough soil, the southern limit of the *pays* extends from west to east between the villages of Hook Norton and Deddington, from which a southern projection of the upland follows the course of the River Cherwell. Historically the region has been subject to surface mining for ore and quarrying for the golden brown Middle Lias deposits known locally as 'Marlstone', used extensively in the vernacular buildings of the local villages (Jessup 1975, 15). Outcrops of Lower Jurassic Lias Clay, the oldest strata in the county, have also been

quarried for brickmaking around Banbury and Deddington (Powell 2010, 8). Domesday Book records arable land heavily concentrated along the Cherwell Valley, and the land around Banbury arguably represents the highest quality arable land anywhere in the county. Whereas the quality of the soils in the river valleys resulted in the highest Domesday populations in the county, far fewer plough teams were present further east in the *pays*, where the heavy soil made cultivation more difficult. Similarly, highly valued meadow resources appear to have been prevalent along the fringes of the River Cherwell, but sparser elsewhere (Page 2010, 34).

Cotswolds

The Oolitic Limestone of the Cotswolds is perhaps the most distinctive of all of Oxfordshire's *pays*, the gently undulating landscape ranging between 100m and 240m OD, only significantly interrupted by the broad valleys of the Rivers Evenlode and Windrush (Figure 4.2) (Darkes 2010, 6). Although this landscape appears largely uniform, the quality of the limestone is extremely variable. The Great Oolite Group outcropping at Taynton and Burford is of particularly good quality, providing stone for buildings across the region (Powell 2010, 8). Significant settlements include Chipping Norton in the north, and Bicester and Witney fringe the *pays* to the south. During the Romano-British period a series of substantial villas were established along the newly established road network, such as at North Leigh and Stonesfield. In a similar land use pattern to that recognisable in the North Oxfordshire Upland, the density of arable farming and meadowland by 1086 appears largely dependent on proximity to river valleys. Settlements such as Shipton-under-Wychwood and Charlbury beside the River Evenlode were associated with high numbers of plough teams indicative of an arable-orientated farming economy, but away from the river networks, farming regimes were probably more mixed in character. In these areas, such as Wychwood Forest, arable farming was unsurprisingly lacking (Page 2010, 34).

Thames Valley

The Thames Valley comprises the most varied geographical elements of any of the Oxfordshire *pays*, but is chiefly distinguishable as the floodplain of the River Thames. Characterised by land mostly below the 60m contour on geology of Oxford and Gault Clays, this predominantly flat landscape contains most of the county's floodlands, including the only truly marshy area of the region at Otmoor. These clay deposits provided brick-clay for the developing city of Oxford in the nineteenth century, and these areas are still subject to intensive quarrying. The only significant exception to the flatness of the Thames Valley *pays* is a small escarpment known as the Oxford Heights. Surrounding the city of Oxford, this gentle upland is formed by a combination of sandstone and limestone, in addition to areas of clay. The formation extends from Cumnor Hill, 5km to the south-west of Oxford, in a north-easterly direction to Brill in Buckinghamshire (Darkes

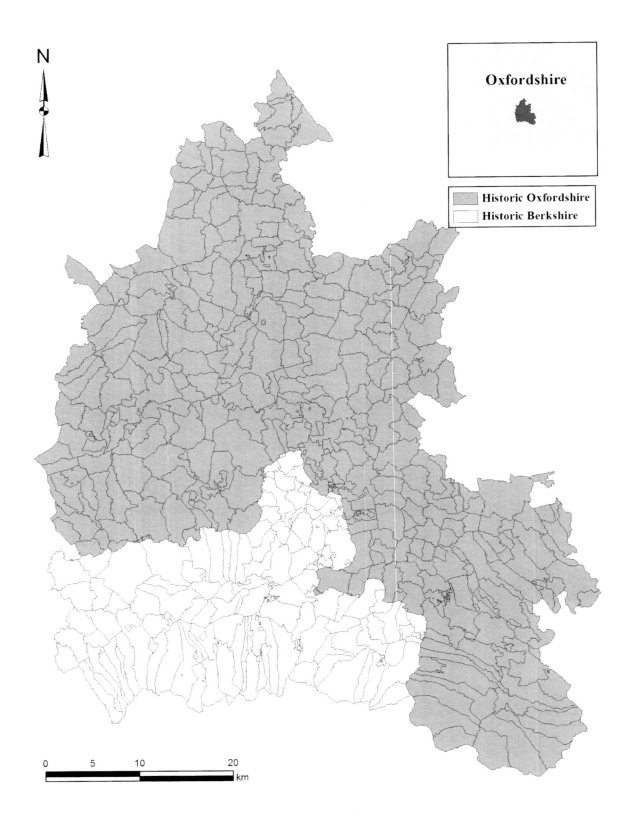

FIGURE 4.1: THE STUDY AREA, WHICH IS REPRESENTED BY THE MODERN EXTENTS OF THE COUNTY OF OXFORDSHIRE (HEREAFTER 'OXFORDSHIRE'), AND ITS LOCATION WITHIN SOUTHERN BRITAIN (INSET). ADOPTING PARISHES WHICH WERE PREVIOUSLY PART OF HISTORIC BERKSHIRE PROVIDES A MORE COHERENT TOPOGRAPHIC AREA FOR RESEARCH. SOURCE FOR MAPPING: HISTORIC PARISHES OF ENGLAND AND WALES ONLINE.

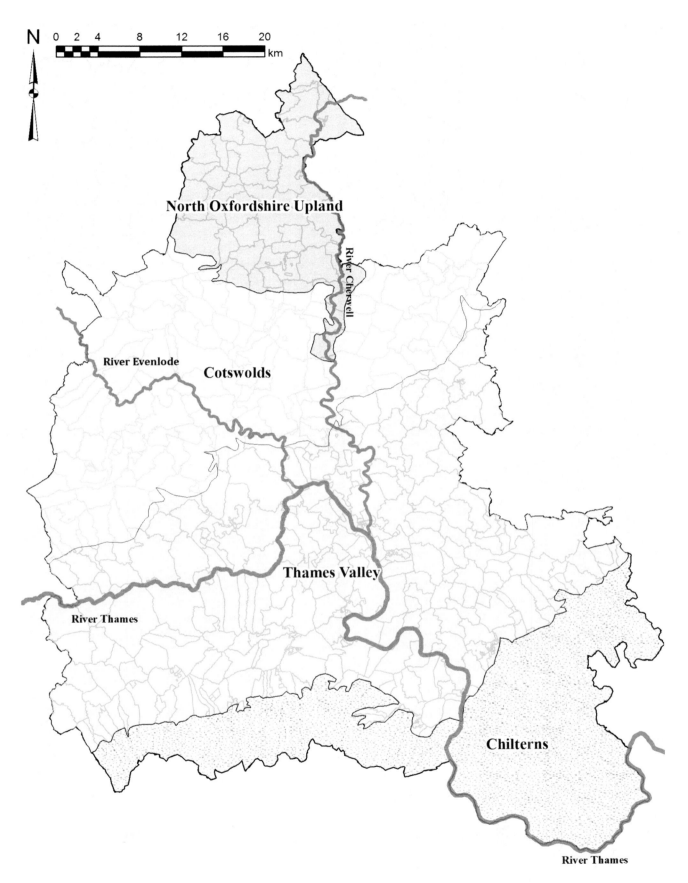

FIGURE 4.2: The pays and major rivers of Oxfordshire. The county is characterised by a series of hills and clay vales, separated by the expansive drainage basin of the Thames Valley. Source for mapping: Historic Parishes of England and Wales Online

2010, 6; Powell 2010, 8). The Thames Valley appears to have been well populated during the Romano-British period, with a combination of villas and more 'normal' farmstead types (Booth 2010, 16).

A substantial number of early medieval sites, particularly of the fifth to seventh centuries, have also been identified in the Thames Valley *pays*. This apparent concentration may be reflective of differing research conditions, with many sites coming to light as a result of quarrying in gravel areas. The same landscapes also provide good crop mark visibility on aerial photographs (Blair 1994, 22; Dodd 2010, 18). The viability of the Thames as an artery for transport and trade before the eleventh century is hard to reconstruct, though increased alluviation detectable in the ninth century suggests that waterways were clearer in the seventh and eighth centuries (Blair 2007). By 1086 areas of dense cultivation are recorded in the southernmost part of the *pays* at the base of the Chiltern escarpment, part of the plain between the rivers Thame and Thames. In sharp contrast, very low lying areas with particularly heavy clay soils featured few plough teams, such as the land around Otmoor. The varying ground conditions of the Thames' numerous clay terraces have been crucial in shaping historic settlement and land use. In particular, a rise of the permanent water table from the late Iron Age flooded much of the first terrace, resulting in a zone of productive pastoral husbandry but one that was more difficult for arable farming: a situation which persisted throughout the early medieval period (Miles *et al* 2007, 373-6; Page 2010, 34).

Chilterns

The southern portion of the county is formed by the chalk scarps of the Chiltern Hills. The main part of the escarpment is formed by Middle Chalk, a deposit that lacks flint inclusions but at certain levels gives rise to a series of springs which have formed important foci for settlement. The Upper Chalk, the flints from which are used as building material, caps the upland and also forms the dip slope towards the Thames (Powell 2010, 8). Several Roman villas have been identified on the Chilterns, but settlement in general during the Romano-British period appears to have been less intensive than in most other areas of Oxfordshire. Substantial woodlands are recorded in the Upper Chalk by the end of the Anglo-Saxon period, suggesting that the flint-rich soils were more difficult for arable cultivation (Page 2010, 34). The intractable soils of the Chilterns would have made the area of Middle Chalk around the spring line, and the adjacent, fertile lowlands even more valuable for early medieval communities. These conditions are reflected in the thin strip arrangement of many Chiltern parishes, orientated approximately north to south so that as many townships as possible were able to exploit the range of available resources. The trend towards greater settlement density on the Middle Chalk continues today, with the most significant towns and villages clustering around the base of the escarpment rather than the upland.

THE RIVER THAMES: GATEWAY AND FRONTIER

Introduction

The River Thames floodplain, occupying a central position in Oxfordshire, has been pivotal in shaping past human activity in the region. During the Late Iron Age the Upper Thames Valley was a borderland between three groups: the *Dobunni* in the west, the *Atrebates* in the south and the *Catuvellauni* in the east. Abandonment of earlier hillforts, which perhaps acted as centres for emergent chiefdoms along the Thames watershed, coincided with the emergence of archaeologically more visible tribal societies, who developed more varied and sophisticated settlements such as the oppida detected at Silchester in nearby Hampshire (Clarke *et al.* 2007). The Iron Age in the Upper Thames Valley also saw the continuation of conditions that had apparently emerged during the Bronze Age as a highly productive region whose populations were also invested in long-distance trade. By the late prehistoric period, a divergent relationship between the Upper Thames as a productive zone, contrasted by the economically more developed Thames estuary had been firmly established. A similar economic situation was to re-emerge in the early medieval period, but after the Roman invasion of AD 43 the gateway character of Oxfordshire declined and its peripheral role reasserted, as most of the region is located at some distance away from the major towns of the region such as Cirencester, Gloucestershire and Silchester (Miles *et al.* 2007, 376-80).

A network of roads linking these centres attracted settlement such as Sansom's Platt and Asthall, but communities also emerged away from the road infrastructure, such as Chipping Norton in the Cotswolds (Figure 4.3). Generally speaking, current understanding of Romano-British settlement in Oxfordshire suggests a mixture of heavily 'Romanized' sites such as villas and the walled towns of Dorchester-on-Thames (hereafter Dorchester) and Alchester, combined with farmsteads of more prosaic character (Booth 2010, 16).

Early Medieval Transition: The Fifth and Sixth Centuries

The Thames floodplain is also the area in which changes to the agrarian landscape brought about by Roman administration can most clearly be seen, as alluvial deposits and floodwater on the first terrace were drained and managed on a large scale for the development of hay meadows (Williamson 2003, 164). Accordingly, it is in this *pays* that the breakdown of Roman infrastructure during the fifth century is also most apparent, and all early post-Roman sites excavated in the area thus far demonstrate abandonment of drainage systems and a retreat from settlement and exploitation of the first terrace (Miles *et al.* 2007, 400). The schism of agricultural regimes in the region was not absolute, however, and evidence of continued settlement activity has been identified at some sites. Barton Court Farm, the site of which now underlies the north-eastern suburbs of modern Abingdon,

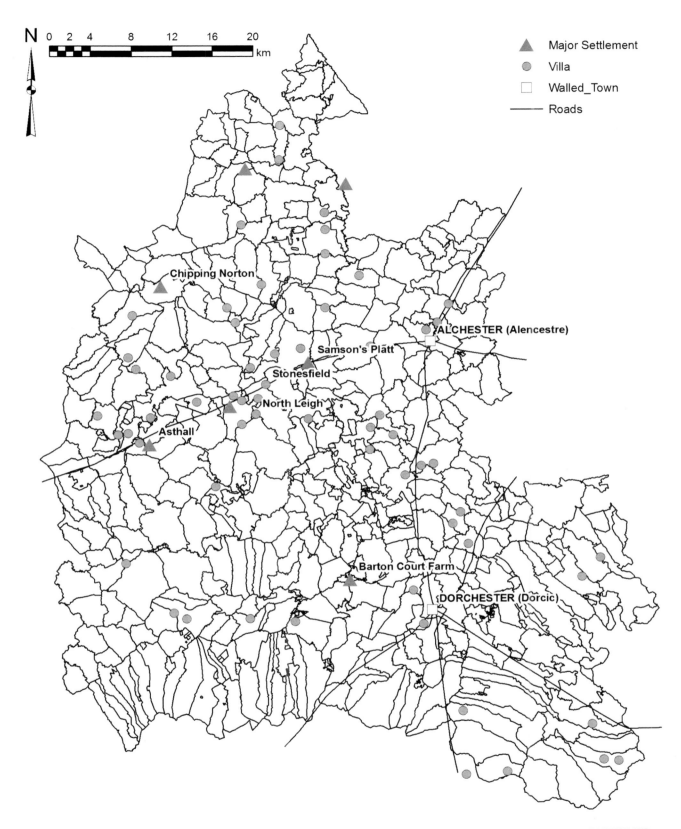

FIGURE 4.3: THE KEY ROADS AND SETTLEMENTS OF ROMAN OXFORDSHIRE. COMMUNICATIONS WERE CENTRAL IN SHAPING THE SETTLEMENT PATTERN BUT COMMUNITIES ALSO EMERGED AWAY FROM MAJOR ROADS. THE LABELLED SITES ARE THOSE MENTIONED IN THE TEXT (AFTER BOOTH 2010, FIG 1). SOURCE FOR MAPPING: HISTORIC PARISHES OF ENGLAND AND WALES ONLINE.

is among the most famous examples of site that reveals the progression from a Romano-British farmstead to an early medieval settlement. Although the buildings of the earlier farmstead were abandoned by the fifth century, a linear feature was reused to form an enclosure around which several Grubenhäuser were established (Miles 1986).

Of equal significance is the environmental data which suggests that the agrarian regime in the immediate vicinity of Barton Court Farm was maintained, demonstrating that the breakdown of Roman governance did not necessarily determine wholesale agricultural disruption (Miles 1986). There is little to suggest that the inhabitants of fifth century Barton Court Farm had any connection with its former occupants though, a pattern also evident in the re-used villa of Shakenoak, North Leigh, located at the interface between the Cotswolds and Thames Valley *pays* (Brodribb *et al.* 2005). Attempting to argue for continuity in settlement and cemetery sites in the early post-Roman period are further inhibited by a more inherent problem encountered by early medieval settlement studies nationwide. Archaeological research is clearly demonstrating that the removal of Roman economic, military and administrative support had a disproportionate impact on the material record, rendering many communities archaeologically invisible (Hills 2011, 9). Perhaps the earliest evidence of this marked shift in material culture that so characterised the earliest phases of the early medieval period in England comes from Dorchester, where Germanic-style objects have been associated with the final phases of the Roman town.

Dorchester and its environs formed the primary case study for the now celebrated paper by Dunning and Hawkes (1961) who asserted the presence of continental *foederati* soldiers in Late Roman Britain, based upon the distribution of Germanic-style graves containing Roman official belt fittings (Figure 4.4). It is now thought likely that items from such graves were not buried until the 430s or 440s, however, so the interpretation that the individuals represent mercenaries hired in the dying stages of Roman administration is not entirely straightforward (Dickinson 1991, 65; Hamerow 2000, 24). Whilst the scale and character of migration in the Oxfordshire region remains hotly disputed, there can be little doubt that there was a demographic influx of at least some Germanic peoples into the region at this time (Brugmann 2011, 30). Although the graves furnished with Germanic-style items are the most well-known and intensively studied archaeological material, Oxfordshire is remarkable in featuring cemeteries that could indicate large-scale indigenous survival. At Queenford Farm, just outside Dorchester, five radiocarbon dates from a large Romano-British cemetery demonstrate continued use into the fifth and sixth centuries (Chambers 1987). The Romano-British cemetery at Frilford, located 5km west of Abingdon, also appears to have been consistently utilised well into the fifth century (Meaney 1964, 46).

Examples of the continued use of cemeteries into the early medieval period in Oxfordshire remain few, however, and it is notable that most burial grounds featuring Germanic grave-goods were established at *de novo* sites (Hamerow 2000, 25). It is the evidence from these newly-founded cemeteries that most strongly indicates that the River Thames again emerged as a gateway territory from the fifth century, acting as a corridor for at least some population movement and settlement. It is perhaps during the sixth century that the presence of Germanic material culture becomes more clearly prominent in the archaeological record of Oxfordshire though, with almost twice as many cemeteries established than in the preceding century (Blair 1994, 14). The geographical distribution of burial grounds across the county can also be seen to change at around this time, with more cemeteries established outside of the Thames Valley watershed. Burials suggest expansion onto the Oxfordshire Heights at Headington and Wheatley, onto the Cotswolds at Lyneham Camp, and, for the first time, cemeteries also appear in the Chilterns (Dodd 2010, 18). John Blair (1994, 14) suggests these cemeteries can be used to plot two persisting British frontiers in Oxfordshire: one in the Middle Thames along the scarp of the Chilterns and the other in the western Cotswolds.

The use of furnished burial rites to trace the progression of population movements and demarcate likely tribal and cultural territories is a contentious approach but fortunately, the chronological remit of this study precludes the centuries around which these debates are centred, beginning as it does in the middle of the seventh century. Scholarly interest from this period has instead been characterised by discourses of amalgamation and absorption, with the Anglo-Saxon Chronicle charting the development of kingdoms in gradually more plausible terms. Explanatory models generated from burial archaeology continue to influence settlement and landscape studies with a later chronological focus, however, partly a product of the comparative dearth of occupation sites in large areas of Oxfordshire, as demonstrated by a review of settlement research in the county.

EARLY MEDIEVAL SETTLEMENT RESEARCH IN OXFORDSHIRE

Archaeological Research

Modern Oxfordshire can in many ways be described as the home of Anglo-Saxon settlement study, hosting the pioneer work of E.T Leeds at Sutton Courtenay in the 1920s (Leeds 1923; 1927; 1947). The excavations at Sutton Courtenay (historically part of Berkshire) were the first to appropriately identify early medieval settlement remains in controlled conditions anywhere in England (Figure 4.5). Although Leeds' work introduced unprecedented levels of rigour and analysis, the investigations at Sutton Courtenay were actually part of a more antiquated tradition of early medieval settlement study. As early as the 1850s Stephen Stone had plotted 'Anglo-Saxon' soilmarks from the back of his horse, and possibly located the remains of *Grubenhäuser* during investigation of artefact scatters at Ducklington, near Witney (Stone 1859b). It was the work

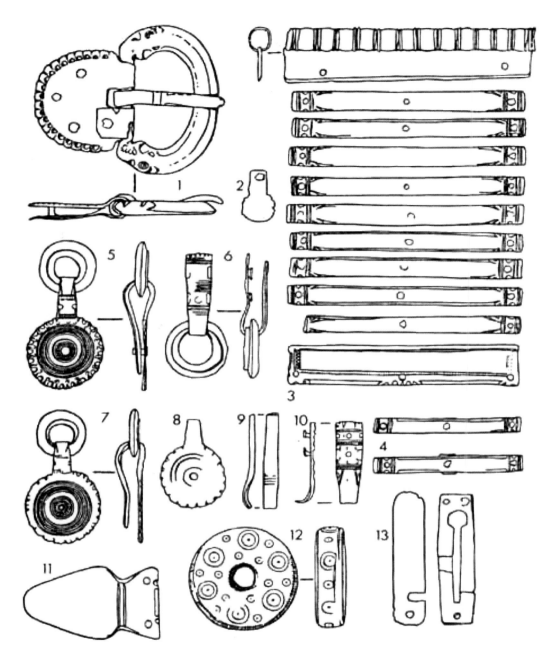

FIGURE 4.4: ROMAN BELT FITTING FOUND IN 1874 AT DYKE HILLS, IMMEDIATELY SOUTH OF DORCHESTER ON THAMES. THE ASSOCIATION OF SUCH ARTEFACTS WITH 'GERMANIC' STYLE OBJECTS IN GRAVES HAS BEEN TRADITIONALLY SEEN AS INDICATING THE PRESENCE OF CONTINENTAL FOEDERATI SOLDIERS (KIRK AND LEEDS 1952-3, FIGURE 27).

at Sutton Courtenay, however, that can be seen as marking the beginning of a more methodological excavation of early medieval settlements in Oxfordshire.

Since this early work many investigations of early medieval settlements have taken place in the county, the vast majority of which have been undertaken in the Thames Valley *pays*. Rescue excavations and more recently commercial interventions, have taken place with great regularity in the central floodplain, largely in advance of industrial gravel extraction. Whilst the concentration of archaeological work in a single *pays* continues to distort our perception of early medieval settlement and land use in Oxfordshire,

some genuine county-wide trends can nevertheless be outlined. With the exception of Oxford, where excavations have exposed occupation on top of banked alluvial clay datable to between the mid eighth and mid ninth centuries, no early medieval settlements have been located on the first gravel terrace of the River Thames, despite numerous interventions (Dodd 2003, 14-6). In stark contrast, numerous fifth to seventh century occupation sites have been identified on the second gravel terrace of the River Thames, such as New Wintles Farm near Eynsham (Clayton 1973) and Barrow Hills near Abingdon (Chambers 2007). Significantly, it is upon this second terrace that the series of important Thames-side minsters were later established,

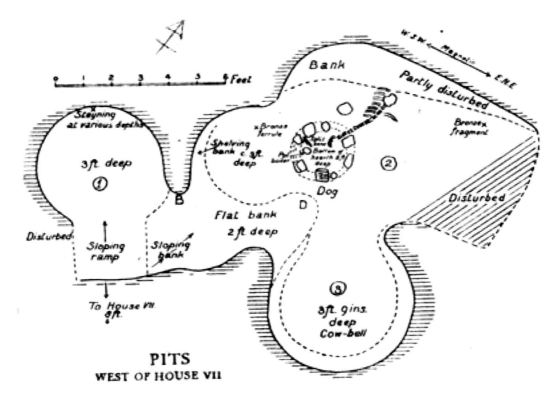

FIGURE 4.5: E.T. LEEDS' PLAN OF A 'THREE-ROOMED' HOUSE AT SUTTON COURTENAY. THE FEATURES PROBABLY IN FACT REPRESENT THREE GRUBENHÄUSER (LEEDS 1923).

profoundly affecting settlement and agriculture in the region from the seventh century. It is thus likely that this terrace of the River Thames did indeed represent a 'core area' of substantial and numerous settlements, at least between the fifth and seventh centuries. Indeed, the heavy concentration of –ēg (island) place-name elements in the Upper Thames supports the premise that raised sites were established around the peripheries of the floodplain at this time (Blair 1994, 22-3).

Less thorough archaeological investigation undertaken in Oxfordshire's other *pays* has unsurprisingly produced a more fragmentary picture, but the available evidence similarly suggests that rivers were fundamental in shaping patterns of occupation. Fieldwalking has identified possible 'Early-Mid' Saxon occupation sites in the North Oxfordshire Upland such as at Banbury and Cropredy (OHER 15847), the latter found in close association with a probable early medieval enclosure (see below). In spite of the clear relationship between rivers and early medieval settlement, occupation sites have also been found away from the network of major tributaries. 'Early-Mid' Saxon sites have been excavated at Black Bourton (Gilbert 2008) and at Kirtlington (OHER 16989), both located in the Thames Valley *pays* but away from substantial rivers. This somewhat sporadic archaeological investigation from other parts of Oxfordshire therefore suggests at least low intensity settlement outside of the 'core area' of the Thames and its major tributaries until at least the seventh century, cautioning that the wealth of archaeological material produced from the central *pays* cannot immediately be viewed as either unique, nor even typical of the county.

Early medieval settlement research in the Oxfordshire region has particularly benefited from research by scholars based at the University of Oxford: in addition to E.T. Leeds, several doyens of early medieval archaeology based at the institution have dedicated at least some scholarship to their immediate environs (Hawkes 1986). In addition, the work of John Blair and Helena Hamerow, represent made significant contributions to our understanding, both of early medieval Oxfordshire (e.g. Blair 1994; Hamerow 1992), and England more generally (e.g. Hamerow 2002; Blair 2005). The developing academic research agenda is increasingly linked to commercial archaeology schemes, especially given the reduction of research-orientated excavations by universities. This is exemplified by the series of large-scale commercial projects undertaken over the past decade or so that have identified 'Middle Saxon' settlement remains. This corpus marks a significant addition to our knowledge of the developing early medieval landscape and includes the excavation of the rural settlement at Yarnton (Hey 2004) and the minster church site at Eynsham (Hardy *et al.* 2007). The sequence at Yarnton in particular represents a unique insight into the progression from a dispersed, loosely arranged community into a more structured settlement, marking the origin of the later medieval village (Hey 2004, 49-52) (see below).

It is therefore clear that Oxfordshire possesses an impressive tradition of early medieval settlement research, being a particularly notable focus for pioneering excavations in the first half of the twentieth century. Despite this inheritance, Oxfordshire is has not generally received as much scholarly interest as many other parts of the 'central province', and the county is rarely included in discussion regarding early medieval settlements. This chapter will demonstrate how archaeological evidence from Oxfordshire can contribute to central debates and in particular how the material data for early medieval settlement can enhance our understanding of 'Middle Saxon' social conditions. Key to understanding a period where archaeology reveals fundamental restructuring of the rural landscape is the political context in which such important changes took place. Before the archaeological evidence is assessed in greater detail, it is therefore necessary to delineate the social and political background of the region during the period, which is mainly derived from the surviving historical material. The main political narrative which forms the context for this study is the changing fortunes of the increasingly powerful polities of Wessex and Mercia, as Oxfordshire once again featured as a frontier zone in central southern England.

The Historic Context

Development of high status complexes such as Drayton/ Sutton Courtenay and Long Wittenham are the first clear indicators in terms of settlement, of the elite groups that dominated the political history of seventh to ninth century Oxfordshire. The presentation in the Anglo-Saxon Chronicle of the inevitable rise of large and stable polities is almost certainly misleading, despite its continued prominence in current scholarship. The underlying purpose of the Chronicle was to legitimise the ninth century kings of Wessex and their predecessors, illustrating how King Alfred's ancestors first consolidated and then colonised from their Hampshire home. Historians have since challenged this narrative, however, and suggested instead that the Upper Thames was the likely origin of Cerdic and his people. This hypothesis is far more consistent with the archaeological evidence, stressing the Upper Thames region as the cultural centre of the *Gewisse* (Yorke 1997, 4-5). Delineating the political history of Oxfordshire in this period is therefore extremely difficult given the unreliability of the Chronicle and the sporadic coverage of Bede's *Historia Ecclesiastica*. The earliest definable territories are perhaps instead indicated by the presence of '-ingas' names, representing 'followers of' compounds usually prefixed with a personal name. Traditionally interpreted as preserving the location of migratory enclaves, '-ingas' place-names are now generally believed to have been coined later, perhaps during the sixth century, and viewed as representing emergent groups once they had become powerful enough to require territorial definition (Gelling 2011, 994-7). Examples in Oxfordshire include Goring, which may preserve the name of the early *Gāringas* group, and the more elusive *Færpingas*, who were possibly a people based close to Charlbury (Blair 1989, 100-3).

The defining of territories in such a way suggests the process of social stratification was well under-way by at least the start of the seventh century, and probably earlier. In addition to high-status settlement complexes such as

Long Wittenham, the increasingly polarity of wealth and status in society is clearly manifest in the establishment of short-lived but significant furnished burial rites. In Oxfordshire, the most conspicuous element of these new rites is the collection of monumental barrow burials along the southern Cotswold fringe. Burials have been identified at Cuddeston and Lyneham Camp but most famously at Asthall where the remains of a cremated man were buried alongside a horse and a range of wealthy grave goods (Leeds 1924) (Figure 4.6). Documented migration has again been cited as the dynamic behind these monuments, attributed to West Saxon expansion, firstly by Leeds (1940, 29), and later Dickinson (1973, 249). Hawkes (1986, 93-4) preferred the interpretation that the barrows were colonial traits belonging to the aristocracy of the *Hwicce*, based on the 'Anglian' style of the grave goods, but the distinctive suite may equally represent adoption of fashions by a pre-existing elite who felt threatened by the growing power of their northern neighbours (Blair 1994, 48).

Perhaps the more remarkable feature of the early seventh century Upper Thames barrow burials is their regular association with 'Kentish' style ornaments, most conspicuously demonstrated by the princely burial of Taplow in nearby Buckinghamshire (Tyler 2000), hinting at the political and commercial power being exercised by Kent at the time, and perhaps a common Frankish link. Although the authority of the Kentish kings was to wane significantly by the end of the century, the continued influence of Canterbury is reflected by the aggression of the Mercian kings Æthelbald, Offa and Coenwulf. Offa's permanent acquisition of large estates at Cookham (S1258) and Eynsham (S1436), both of which were previously under the jurisdiction of Canterbury, in particular demonstrates the desire of the Mercian kings to link their heartland with London and the economically developed south-east (Brooks 1984; Hardy and Blair 2003, 9; Giandrea 2007, 139; Brooks and Kelly forthcoming 11-20). The earliest stages of Mercian overlordship in Oxfordshire likely came under the early rule of Penda (?626-56) whose expansive approach led to either the annexation or integration of the *Hwicce* (Brooks 1989, 160). The diocese of the bishops of Worcester, established in the seventh century, is thought to best represent the extents of the *Hwiccan* kingdom, and suggests that the majority of its territory was located in Gloucestershire. The Wychwood toponym in north-west Oxfordshire is generally taken to represent an outlying woodland resource of this territory, yet it is equally possible that the boundary of the later diocese was not entirely precise and that parts of north-west Oxfordshire fell within the kingdom (Hooke 1985, 12-6).

Irrespective of the exact extents of the *Hwiccan* kingdom, the overlordship exerted by Penda gave access to the River Severn, but more crucially for this study, also provided a platform with which to launch attacks into the territory of the *Gewisse* who by then exerted control over most of Oxfordshire. The *Gewissan* federation was certainly significant after the death of Cealwin, with Bede suggesting a mobile and increasingly expansionist attitude

FIGURE: 4.6: THE ASTHALL BARROW UNDER EXCAVATION BETWEEN 1923-4. THE PRINCELY BURIAL CONTAINED A CREMATION AND GRAVE GOODS, PROBABLY DATING TO THE EARLY SEVENTH CENTURY (ASHMOLEAN MUSEUM WEBPAGE).

from the 620s. The exact success of Penda's expansion into Oxfordshire is hard to assess, but a measure may be provided by the apparent tribute held in the region by his son Wulfhere from early in his reign (Blair 1994, 39-44). The death of Penda in *c*.655/6 provides a convenient historical marker for the beginning of this research: although the political environment of the first decade of this study was probably somewhat fluid, and it appears that Penda's death represented a mere hiatus in Mercian colonialism. As early as the 660s Wulfhere had the authority to appoint a sub-king in Surrey, and sell the bishopric of London. By the end of the seventh century, Mercian supremacy in the Thames valley is demonstrated by the *Gewisse's* abandonment of the Dorchester bishopric, marking a move towards Hampshire where they were to emerge as the better-known West Saxons (Yorke 1990, 136-7).

In Oxfordshire, Mercian overlordship was to continue throughout most of the seventh century, though from the 680s the resurgent West Saxon kings, who had already annexed Kent and parts of Berkshire, began to threaten the Upper Thames. Cynewulf of Wessex was certainly in control of the Upper Thames during the 750s, possibly as a result of Cuthred's victory at *Beorhford* in 752 and it was only in 779 that Offa was able to regain the *villa regalis* at Benson (*ASC I*; Yorke 1990, 141). It was probably the result of the Benson victory that allowed Offa to consolidate lands around the Thames, including Cookham, and establish a stable corridor along the length of the river (cf. Wormald 1983, 117). Offa's successor Coenwulf further consolidated these acquisitions by acquiring the

huge monastic estate centred on Eynsham, and Mercia continued to exert overlordship in the region until the 820s. According to the Chronicle, Wessex 'conquered everything south of the Humber', albeit briefly, in 829 but these military efforts irreversibly changed power relations between the two major kingdoms (*ASC II*). From the first quarter of the ninth century and partly as a result of increased Scandinavian influence, the English kingdoms adopted an approach of mutual interest with Wessex acting as the senior partner (Blair 1994, 56).

It is this political climate in which the chronological remit of this research ends, ushering in a new era in which a common English identity was eventually created. The transitory nature of Oxfordshire both as geographical entity and political territory provides unique conditions for scholarly investigation. Indeed, this study of the developing settlement and landscape environment of seventh to ninth century Oxfordshire must consider these broader narratives as potential dynamics for change. This chapter will now describe and analyse the archaeological evidence for 'Middle Saxon' settlement and land use from the modern county of Oxfordshire. Following an analysis of the 'Middle Saxon' remains investigated within historic village centres in Oxfordshire, this chapter will discuss the archaeology of elite settlements, followed by an investigation of the corpus from more prosaic rural sites. It will be shown how this cumulative evidence can provide a new insight into the landscape of early medieval Oxfordshire and the reflexive relationship between settlement, society and elite authority.

Interventions in CORS	CORS interventions identifying archaeological deposits	CORS with 'Middle Saxon' artefactual material only	CORS with 'Middle Saxon' artefactual material and settlement structures from CORS
54	49	8	6

Table 4.1: Although Oxfordshire is not considered part of the 'village landscape', a significant minority of CORS excavations have recovered occupation material dated between the seventh and ninth centuries.

'CORS' RESEARCH IN OXFORDSHIRE

Although Oxfordshire has been interpreted as part of the 'village landscape' of midland England (Roberts and Wrathmell 2002, 31), compared to other counties there has been relatively little academic interest in currently-occupied rural settlement research. No villages in the county have been subject to study by the University of Cambridge's HEFA scheme, and the potential of 'CORS' investigation realised by research projects such as Shapwick, Somerset, has not been replicated in Oxfordshire (Lewis 2010; Gerard 2007). Despite this different pattern of scholarly activity, development led interventions in particular have recovered 'Middle Saxon' evidence from currently-occupied rural settlement excavation, as illustrated in the table below (Table 4.1).

Of the forty-nine occupied village excavations in Oxfordshire that have located archaeological deposits, eight (16%) have recovered 'Middle Saxon' artefactual material only, and six (12%) have identified artefactual and structural remains. Fourteen currently-occupied rural excavations have therefore found 'Middle Saxon' material of some description, a quarter of the total interventions that have located archaeological deposits. With the significant exception of Yarnton, where an extensive open area excavation has located a near complete early medieval settlement sequence in and around the historic village centre, it is notable that the 'Middle Saxon' evidence located by this investigations in Oxfordshire has not been as extensive as that located by research in other counties studied by this book. Combined with other sources of archaeological evidence from the county, however, this somewhat fragmentary evidence can be used to gain a greater insight into the early medieval landscape of Oxfordshire. Archaeological evidence both from sites associated with elite groups, and those that do not have such high-status links, is showing that key changes to the rural landscape of Oxfordshire took place during the 'Middle Saxon' period. This transformation, which can be seen most clearly from the eighth century, is likely to have been the result of significant changes in the way society was organised, and the landscape perceived.

ELITE COMMUNITIES

Introduction

The prominent tradition of early medieval archaeological research in Oxfordshire has produced a significant body of material relating to settlements of 'special' status. From the seventh century, the rise of a network of high-status sites, identified primarily through the historical record, has been seen as exerting profound influence upon the rural landscape of the region. The Thames Valley *pays* provided the focus for the largest and most important centres of the region, the choice of densely settled areas possibly perhaps reflecting the pastoral remit of church sites in particular (e.g. Brooks 1984, 87-90) (Figure 4.7).

As discussed in Chapter I, the development of written sources is inherently linked to the rise of the Augustinian Church, and the process of conversion. Our written sources relating to early elite centres are therefore of ecclesiastical character, a factor which is likely to have coloured existing interpretation of early medieval settlement character. The historical data relating to early minsters in Oxfordshire has been thoroughly reviewed by John Blair (1994, 56-77), and whilst the detail of his analysis will not be replicated here, this research treats his subsequent interpretation of the archaeological material with great caution. Developing a national model for identifying minsters, Blair has argued that early church sites can be identified through a number of distinctive attributes (Blair 2005, 204-15). This approach has received significant criticism, however, and it is increasingly apparent that in places where relevant documentary evidence is lacking, distinguishing between sites of secular and religious character based on archaeology alone is rarely possible (e.g. Pestell 2004, 4-50; Gittos 2011, 827-8; see also detailed discussion in Chapter VIII).

Where reliable 'Middle Saxon' written sources to identify a centre are lacking, it is therefore necessary to take a more cautious approach and describe such settlements as simply 'high-status' or 'elite'. Such an approach represents a marked departure from that of Blair, who has deemed it more appropriate to back-project the status of particular places from later documentary evidence (e.g. Blair 1994, 65). This interpretation in no way undermines the clear influence of the early religious communities upon the 'Middle Saxon' countryside, but instead implies that patterns of elite activity may not have been as clear-cut as has previously been postulated. In terms of written sources relating to the early Church in Oxfordshire, Bede's history has again proved extremely influential. Writing almost one-hundred years later, Bede asserts that the process of church foundation was begun in Oxfordshire with the establishment of the See at Dorchester in the 630s. As if to emphasise the inadequacy of using documentary sources

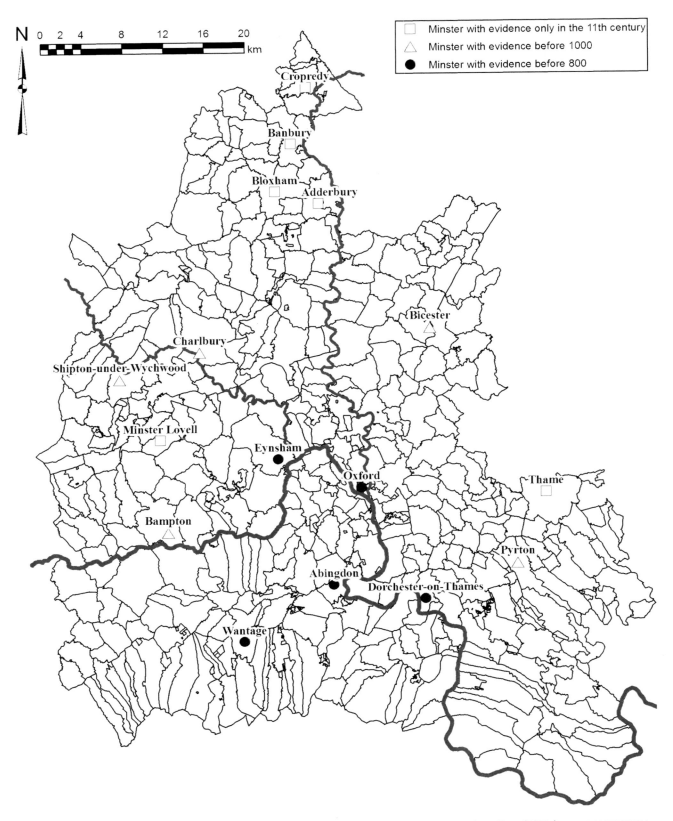

FIGURE 4.7: LOCATION OF HIGH-STATUS CENTRES MENTIONED IN THE TEXT, AGAINST THE PAYS OF OXFORDSHIRE. JOHN BLAIR (2010A) IDENTIFIES NEARLY ALL OF THE SITES AS EARLY MINSTERS, BUT WHILST ALL WERE IMPORTANT CHURCH CENTRES BY THE END OF THE EARLY MEDIEVAL PERIOD, THIS CHAPTER WILL SHOW THAT THE EXTENT OF 'MIDDLE SAXON' MINSTER FOUNDATION MAY HAVE BEEN OVERSTATED. SOURCE FOR MAPPING: HISTORIC PARISHES OF ENGLAND AND WALES ONLINE.

alone though, high-status settlement which preceded the documented establishment of the See has been detected in the landscape around the modern centres of Abingdon, Dorchester and Sutton Courtenay.

Drayton/Sutton Courtenay

At the site of Drayton/Sutton Courtenay, the early findings of Leeds have been enhanced by subsequent investigation that has transformed our knowledge of the scale, character and significance of the settlement. Identification of large timber buildings on aerial photographs, and metal-detector finds of early medieval coins and metalwork were among the first indicators that the site straddling the parish boundary was actually a high-status complex (Benson and Miles 1974; Hamerow 1999, 32-6). The majority of the settlement is located on the second gravel terrace of the River Thames, conforming to the model that it was this zone that formed a core area for habitation throughout the early medieval period (Hamerow *et al.* 2007, 113). More recently, a series of fieldwalking projects, geophysical survey and small-scale excavation hastened by recovery of the metal-detected finds have yielded further information regarding the organisation and extent of activity, as well as the construction-type of one of the timber buildings (Hamerow *et al.* 2007). The cumulative results produced by these, albeit limited, investigations allow some limited conclusions to be drawn about the early medieval Drayton/ Sutton Courtenay landscape.

The earliest Anglo-Saxon features discovered by Leeds comprised over thirty *Grubenhäuser* and two probable post-built structures, the latter of which went unrecognised at the time. These *Grubenhäuser* remain the earliest features to have been excavated from the site, with finds dated between the fifth to at least the seventh centuries, though some of the plain chaff-tempered wares may have been produced as late as the eighth century. Cumulative investigations have since shown that the features dug by Leeds form part of a complex that spreads across a 10ha area, with the known limits stretching approximately 750m north to south. It appears unlikely that all of the structures were in use contemporaneously, and it is more likely that the extensive distribution of features is indicative of a settlement that periodically shifted, a phenomenon most clearly demonstrated at Mucking, Essex (Hamerow 1991; Hamerow *et al.* 2007, 184; cf. Powlesland 1997). A variety of early medieval dress fittings recovered by metal-detectorists suggests that the early settlement was serviced by a contemporary cemetery, immediately south-east of Leeds' excavations. Further metalwork finds suggest that it was towards the end of the sixth century that the site began to acquire special significance. A fragment of gold disc brooch, copper alloy mounts and a disc-shaped escutcheon illustrate not only continued interment on the site into the seventh century, but also the burial of at least one high-status individual (Hamerow *et al.* 2007, 183-6). The most striking evidence of the special status of the Drayton/Sutton Courtenay complex, however, is the group

of large timber-built structures located towards the centre of the complex.

Limited excavation of one such feature indicated double-plank construction, which recovered pottery suggests was established at some point during the seventh century. The halls are therefore likely to have been established during a period when at least some *Grubenhäuser* remained in use, and burial was taking place nearby (Hamerow *et al.* 2007, 187). Significantly, the size of the halls suggests a degree of monumentality, and their loose axial alignment is a characteristic noted at similar high-status early medieval settlements such as Yeavering, Northumberland and Cowdery's Down, Hampshire (Hope-Taylor 1977; Millett 1983; Hamerow *et al.* 2007, 187). Unlike these sites, however, the Drayton/Sutton Courtenay community does not seem to have been totally abandoned after the seventh century. The recovery of fourteen *sceattas*, dating between *c.* 700-*c.*730, illustrates the emergence of the site as a recognised meeting place where trade was being carried out (Hamerow *et al.* 2007, 187). Trading activities at the site are likely to have been enhanced by its previous incarnation as a high-status settlement, forming a focus for communication networks but also likely etching a social memory as a central place, perhaps for several generations.

The continued significance of the Drayton/Sutton Courtenay settlement is confirmed by the role of 'Sutton' as a royal estate centre during the ninth century, recorded by charter dated 868, and remaining in royal hands by 1086 (S338a; Hamerow *et al.* 2007, 190). Given the piecemeal character of investigation and the broad site phasing, it is not possible to confirm uninterrupted high-status practice at Drayton/Sutton Courtenay but it is likely nevertheless that the lasting importance of the site encouraged its continued reuse throughout the early medieval period, even if there were substantial interruptions in activity. Although prehistoric monuments did not obviously determine the arrangement of the monumental halls as they apparently did at places like Yeavering, Northumberland (Bradley 1987; Hamerow *et al.* 2007, 191), it is possible too that the prehistoric importance of the site did act as an attraction to early medieval people. What is perhaps most remarkable about the area in which the Drayton/Sutton Courtenay settlement is located is that the monumental complex does not appear to have been entirely unique, as a similar site with great halls has been identified at Long Wittenham, 5km to the east (Hawkes 1986, 89). Taken together, the two sites underline the importance of this part of the Thames Valley as a high-status landscape from at least the sixth century, possible representing the main focus of royal power in the region. Indeed, the continued significance of this part of the Thames Valley is underlined by the development of the Roman town of Dorchester from the seventh century.

Dorchester-upon-Thames

Whilst the exact nature of the immediate post-Roman activity in and around Dorchester is unclear, written evidence suggests that it was one of two key centres, together with Benson, that emerged at the heart of the *Gewissan* territory during the sixth century. It is possible that from the seventh century, Dorchester replaced the monumental 'palaces' at Drayton/Sutton Courtenay as the focus of elite authority in the area although Blair (1994, 39) has challenged the assumption that Dorchester emerged as a centre of royal power, asserting instead that the reuse of the old Roman town was instead specifically associated with the growing authority of the early Church. The intimacy with which secular and religious authorities conducted their activities during this period makes such a distinction difficult to corroborate, and whilst in the case of Dorchester the written material can reliably taken as evidence for the presence of a religious community, the archaeological investigations undertaken in the town have identified little that could be termed as particular to a religious centre alone. Again, scholars have tended to rely on Bede to provide us with a more detailed account of Dorchester's early development, following foundation of the See. The *HE* tells us that Birinus was installed as bishop of the *civitas* in the late 630s, spreading the influence of the Italo-Gallic Christianity of Kent to the *Gewisse* under the probable direction of the Northumbrian kings (*HE* III, 7). During a period in which archaeological evidence more clearly indicates the increasing stratification of society, Dorchester would have been a place of recognisable and antiquated importance, which an emergent military power naturally adopted, *together* with the new authority of the Roman Church (Blair 1994, 39-41).

Excavations across the town have corroborated the picture of Dorchester as an important 'Middle Saxon' centre, with investigations consistently identifying evidence for early medieval settlement activity (Figure 4.8). In 1962 excavations within an allotment plot within the town identified a single *Grubenhäus*, and although the mid sixth century dating attributed to it was based only on the decoration on ceramics, the alignment of the structure with the Roman high street hints that property plots may have been maintained, or at the very least that the road continued to be used into the early medieval period (Frere 1962). Slightly later occupation has also been located by excavations in the north-western part of Dorchester's Roman circuit, where a series of timber halls, later rebuilt on a large scale and in stone, were probably in use between the seventh and ninth centuries (Rowley and Brown 1981). Further evidence of pre-Viking domestic occupation has also been found in the south-west corner of Dorchester and further extramural settlement has been located to the north-west (May 1977; Morrison 2009, 47-53).

The cumulative results from such interventions suggest a relatively dense settlement within the old Roman town, but archaeological deposits that are most likely to be associated with the 'Middle Saxon' minster were also found during excavations in the Cloister Garden of the Abbey church, immediately north of the current abbey (Keevill 2003). Investigations revealed two *Grubenhäuser* and two timber-framed buildings, in addition to a pit, a

well, and four sherds of a single very high-quality vessel, possibly imported from the eastern Mediterranean. Other ceramics recovered could only be given an 'Early-Middle Saxon' date but the degree of correlation between fabric types and the stratigraphic sequence suggested to the excavators that occupation began in the seventh century, and could possibly be related to the historically recorded appointment of Birinus (Keevill 2003, 355-8). The pre-Conquest church itself remains elusive though, and whilst it seems likely that it remains underneath the buildings of the present Abbey, the 'Middle Saxon' archaeology recovered from Dorchester usefully demonstrates the ambiguity of the material record.

Without the documentary sources relating to Dorchester's earliest medieval development, there is little in the material record that would distinguish the later town as the site of a religious community. Indeed, even the identification of a church, if indeed it is located beneath the present Abbey, would not confirm 'Middle Saxon' Dorchester as an exclusively ecclesiastical settlement, as the secular elite also established churches within their centres (Pestell 2004, 45). The archaeological evidence retrieved from across Dorchester, particularly the use of stone-built structures (cf. Morris 2010, 183-6), therefore suggests a measure of elite continuity throughout the documented Mercian overlordship, between the recorded presence of a Mercian See in the 670s and its later re-appearance as a West Saxon bishopric and later minster (Rowley and Brown 1981). The presence of a settlement focus around the current parish church is likely significant, and has also been noted at Benson, although the relative lack of archaeological work from Dorchester's most likely comparator means that it is difficult to extrapolate the relationship between the dual power centres in the pre-*c*.650 period (Pine and Ford 2003). Far more substantial evidence relating to an elite community of likely ecclesiastical character has been identified by excavation in the town of Eynsham, also located within the Thames Valley *pays*.

Eynsham

Aside from the Roman town of Dorchester, the centre in the Thames Valley which can most confidently be identified as a minster through the written sources is Eynsham, for which a significant quantity of early medieval archaeological evidence has also been detected. The first recognition of pre-Conquest remains at Eynsham by systematic investigation were made in 1971, when part of a cemetery was excavated in Nursery Field, to the east of the present St. Leonard's Church (Gray and Clayton 1978). 'Early-Mid Saxon' deposits were similarly identified during interventions close to St. Leonard's Church in 1975 and 1992, but failed to identify evidence of early medieval structures (Chambers 1976; OHER: PRN 9506). The most extensive and revealing archaeological investigations at Eynsham to date was a major programme of rescue excavations undertaken in advance of the extension to the cemetery of St. Leonard's Church (Figure 4.9) (Hardy *et al.* 2003), prompted by earlier evaluation

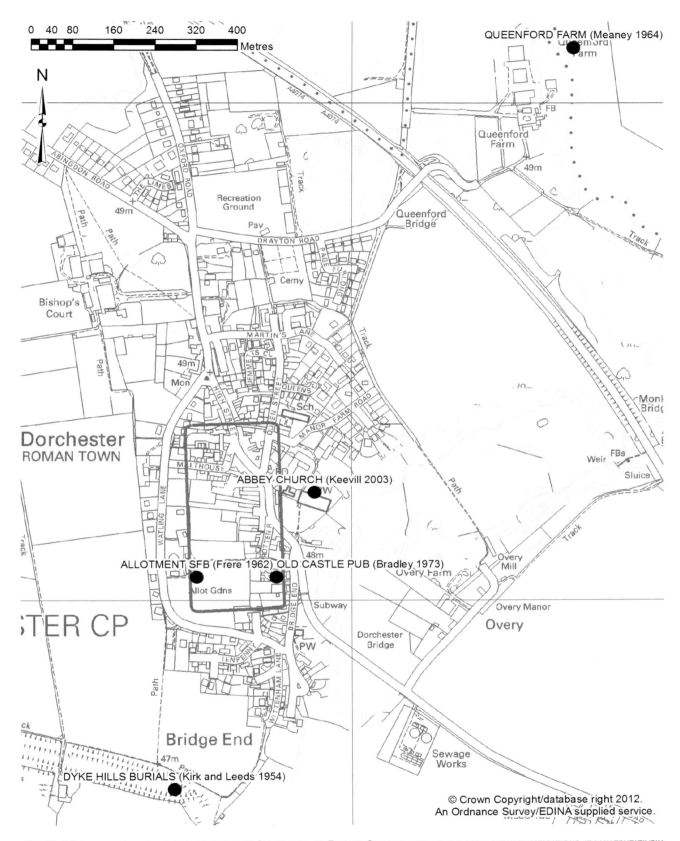

FIGURE: 4.8: LOCATION OF EXCAVATIONS UNDERTAKEN IN DORCHESTER-ON-THAMES. COLLATING THE RESULTS FROM SUCH INVESTIGATIONS, IT MAY TENTATIVELY SUGGESTED THAT THE TOWN CONTINUED AS AN ELITE FOCUS FROM THE EARLY SEVENTH CENTURY. THE SOLID RECTANGULAR FEATURE MARKS THE LINE OF THE ROMAN CIRCUIT (EDITED BY THE AUTHOR FROM AN ORDNANCE SURVEY/EDINA SUPPLIED SERVICE, 2012).

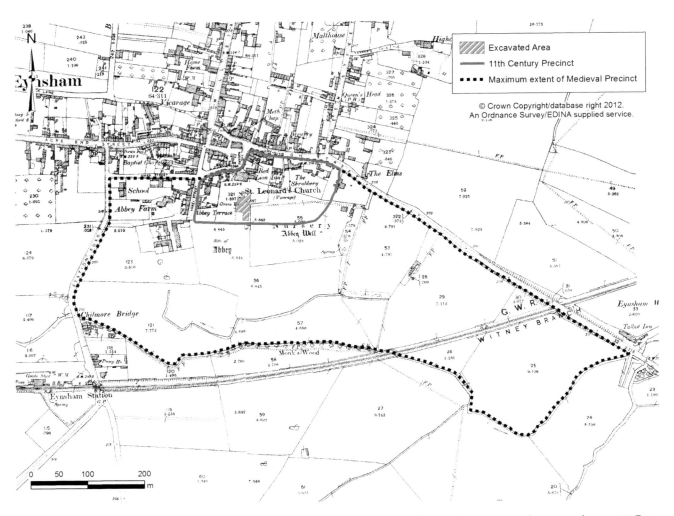

FIGURE: 4.9: OD FIRST EDITION REVISION OF EYNSHAM SHOWING THE PLAN OF THE LATE SAXON (SOLID LINE) AND MEDIEVAL (DOTTED LINE) PRECINCTS. THE AREA OF THE MOST EXTENSIVE ARCHAEOLOGICAL EXCAVATION TO DATE, WHICH IDENTIFIED 'MIDDLE SAXON' ACTIVITY IS HACHURED (AFTER HARDY ET AL. 2003, FIG 1.2).

which had revealed significant early medieval deposits including the first structural evidence for the documented pre-Conquest minster.

The earliest early medieval features identified were five *Grubenhäuser*, and a small number of associated features, dated by ceramics and radiocarbon dating to the sixth or early seventh century (Hardy *et al.* 2003, 28). The scale and character of activity at Eynsham changed markedly around the late seventh century, however, with occupation represented by a series of hearths, burnt areas and pits as well as numerous structures of posthole, beamslot and stakehole construction (Phase 2B). Although the stratigraphic distinction between phases is not entirely secure, it is likely that there was a second stage of 'Middle Saxon' occupation, dated by Ipswich Ware to between the late or mid eighth century, and until the late ninth century. This latter phase (Phase 2C) comprised a pit group, boundary features and two probable posthole buildings (Hardy *et al.* 2003, 27-8). These features represent the first evidence for formal organisation at the site, the end of the phase coinciding with the first written evidence for a minster at Eynsham, dating to the middle of the

ninth century. In addition to the recorded grant of a three hundred hide estate which probably represents Eynsham by the Archbishop of Canterbury to Coenwulf in *c*.821 (see above), a more reliable grant dated 864 explicitly mentions the minster church (Hardy and Blair 2003, 7).

Development of a more rigid organisational structure at Eynsham, which broadly coincides with the first documented reference to the site, cannot be taken as a ninth-century foundation for the minster, however. The character of occupation before this date is difficult to determine through archaeological evidence alone, and whilst it is possible that a religious community occupied the site from the early seventh century, it is equally likely that the earliest detected activity at Eynsham was not associated with the early Church. Based on written sources only, a case for a minster at Eynsham before its first recording in the ninth century can be made, however. Following the almost feverish endowment of minsters indicated by surviving charters dated *c*.670-730, the English church experienced almost two centuries of cooling enthusiasm from secular patrons. By the early ninth century, churchmen under increasing economic pressure were attempting to prevent minsters from permanently alienating their lands. Religious centres, later identifiable as mother churches, losing estates in the ninth century are thus likely to represent earlier minsters that were previously liberally endowed by earlier generations (Cubitt 1995, 194-8).

It is possible that a similar process occurred at Eynsham, with alienation of lands in its extensive minster estate first documented in the ninth century. The existence of a 'Middle Saxon' minster at Eynsham is not supported by its location, however, as has previously been claimed. Whilst it might appear that Eynsham 'fills a gap' between other possible 'Middle Saxon' minsters in the Thames Valley (Hardy and Blair 2003, 7), such a model is based on the premise that later documented sites can be positively identified as earlier ecclesiastical centres. The view that a network of near-contemporary minsters was developed in the Thames Valley in the seventh and eighth centuries, though, relies upon associating archaeological evidence with much later written references, and questionable traditions. The medieval churches of Aylesbury and Thame, for instance, possess particularly shadowy origin stories (Blair 1994, 46-7), and the similarly dubious written records relating to Oxford means that the 'Middle Saxon' material located in the county town is difficult to relate to ecclesiastical agency alone.

Oxford

Until recently, archaeological evidence for seventh to ninth century activity in Oxford was restricted to the northern bank of the Thames, not extending far beyond the immediate environment of the Thames crossing. Modern investigation away from this zone of high early medieval potential, however, has now identified pre-*burh* activity at places such as Oxford Castle, where a total of twenty-three redeposited 'Early-Mid Saxon' pot sherds were recovered, with pit digging and evidence of possible structures also found (Poore *et al.* 2009, 1-2). Further afield, 'Early-Middle Saxon' activity has been detected at the Oxford Science Park, located approximately 4km south of the medieval town, and at Barrow Hills, Radley (OHER: 16299; Chambers 2007). Taken together, the evidence both within the medieval town and further afield demonstrate that this part of the Thames Valley was probably a well-populated agricultural landscape during the 'Middle Saxon' period.

Whilst data has therefore been found to suggest that settlement extended away from the second gravel terrace, the most convincing evidence for a seventh century high-status site in the Oxford region has come from excavations close to the Thames crossing itself, the supposed location of the 'Oxen ford' (Figure 4.10). Deep tunnelling at the southern end of St Aldate's Church in the centre of the city recovered six timbers, one of which was radiocarbon dated to c.660-900. This dating, though broad, strongly suggests a pre-*burh* river crossing at Oxford (Dodd 2003, 15-9). 'Middle Saxon' in the area is also supported by the

retrieval of a seventh century radiocarbon date for burial 402 at Christ Church (Boyle 2001), and the recovery of 'Early to Middle Saxon' pottery immediately south of St Ebbe's Church (Moore 2004).

It has previously been suggested that 'Middle Saxon' evidence found near to the river crossing at Oxford provides material support that 'St Frideswide's' minster was established on the site before or during the 690s, and that the Frideswide legend may actually preserve the garbled details of genuine people, places and events (Blair 1994, 52-4). The tradition holds that a Mercian sub-king founded a monastery at Oxford during the early eighth century at the behest of his saintly daughter Frideswide, who became the first abbess (Campbell 1986, 218-9; Blair 1987, 72-5). This interpretation again relies on the back-projection of later sources, which in this case is represented by an extremely dubious origin tradition. It is equally possible that the somewhat sporadic evidence for 'Middle Saxon' activity around the 'Oxen ford' was the result of secular authorities, developing a centre which obtained a minster only later. Whilst the agency behind Oxford's earliest development are thus open to conjecture, what can be said with greater certainty is that its origins do not lie in its development as an Alfredian *burh*, as recently reasserted by Haslam (2010). Rather it is likely that the earliest ninth century defences were developed around an existing focus, of likely high-status character. The piecemeal character of investigation in Oxford does not allow the pre-*burh* complex to be reconstructed, more substantial research in Bampton provides a useful comparator.

Bampton

Located in West Oxfordshire, a number of strategically-located archaeological interventions within the modern town of Bampton from the 1980s have revealed a significantly longer-lived centre than that first recorded by charter in 1069 (Blair 1998, 124-6). From the seventh century, the area that was later to become the periphery of the town was developed as a cemetery featuring furnished burials, adjacent to a chapel dedicated to St Andrew. Within Bampton itself, pre-Viking burials, dated primarily by radiocarbon analysis, have been excavated within the churchyard of St Mary's, which was originally located within a large oval enclosure (Blair 1998, 128).

Although no contemporary features were identified, excavation of two plots 200m to the south of St Mary's Church also recovered pottery sherds of 'Middle Saxon' North French Blackware. The sherds, found in a residual context, indicate the likely presence of a high-status centre at Bampton from at least c.800, and confirm the influence of trade up the Thames into this part of Oxfordshire (Mayes *et al.* 2000, 288). By the end of the early medieval period, it is possible that a royal centre had probably been constructed across the Shill Brook on the site of the later castle. It has been theorised that Bampton represents a case where a secular residence was attached to a previously autonomous minster in a pattern that becomes clearly

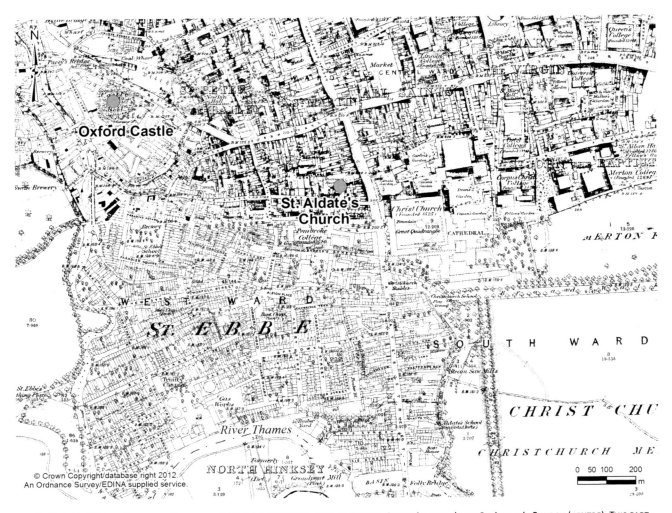

FIGURE 4.10: OS FIRST EDITION OF OXFORD SHOWING THE EXCAVATED SITES OF OXFORD CASTLE (TOP LEFT) AND ST. ALDATE'S CHURCH (CENTRE). THIS PART OF THE THAMES VALLEY IS LIKELY TO HAVE BEEN WELL-POPULATED IN THE 'MIDDLE SAXON' PERIOD, BUT THE 'OXEN FORD' WAS CLEARLY DEVELOPED BEFORE ESTABLISHMENT OF THE BURH.

recognisable by the Conquest (Blair 2010b, 30). Once more, however, the archaeological evidence can only be taken as indicating 'Middle Saxon' activity of likely elite character. For instance, whilst there is no doubt that enclosed space was important to minster communities, such monuments were equally utilised on secular sites, such as that at Higham Ferrers, likely attached to the nearby *villa regalis* at Irthlingborough (Chapter III).

Abingdon

Located approximately 10km south-west of Oxford, Abingdon is a place for which far less is now known than had previously been believed. The early charters that had been transcribed in the *Abingdon Chronicles* are now widely accepted as representing the archive of the lost minster at Bradfield (Kelly 2001 xxxv-liii), and earliest evidence for a settlement at Abingdon is instead represented by place-names and archaeology. It has been postulated that if a pre-Viking settlement was located at Abingdon that it is likely to have been situated within the extensive estate of *Earmundesleah*, possibly founded by a certain Æbbe, whose influence is preserved in the place

name of Abingdon or 'people of Æbbe's hill' (Gelling 1974, 432-3). This interpretation is problematic, however, as Abingdon lies on the floodplain of the Thames and not in an elevated position, and whilst it has been forwarded that the term was ascribed to the surrounding territory (Watts 2004), the place-name evidence alone adds little to our understanding of the early medieval landscape. Indeed, the existence of any 'Middle Saxon' site at Abingdon is supported by only slight archaeological evidence. Blair (1994, 65) has conjectured that an earlier minster focus at Abingdon is likely to have been situated not at the site of the later Abbey, but in the area of the Church of St. Helen, which itself is located within part of an earlier Iron Age hillfort (Figure 4.11). The only evidence for pre-Conquest activity from Abingdon, however, is the find of an elaborate 'Black Cross' relic recovered from the Church of St. Helen area, illustrated in a Chronicle of the Abbey. This find provides only the slightest backing for a 'Middle Saxon' presence, however, and certainly cannot be taken as evidence for a minster.

The relatively well-settled countryside of the Thames Valley appears to be an exception when compared to the

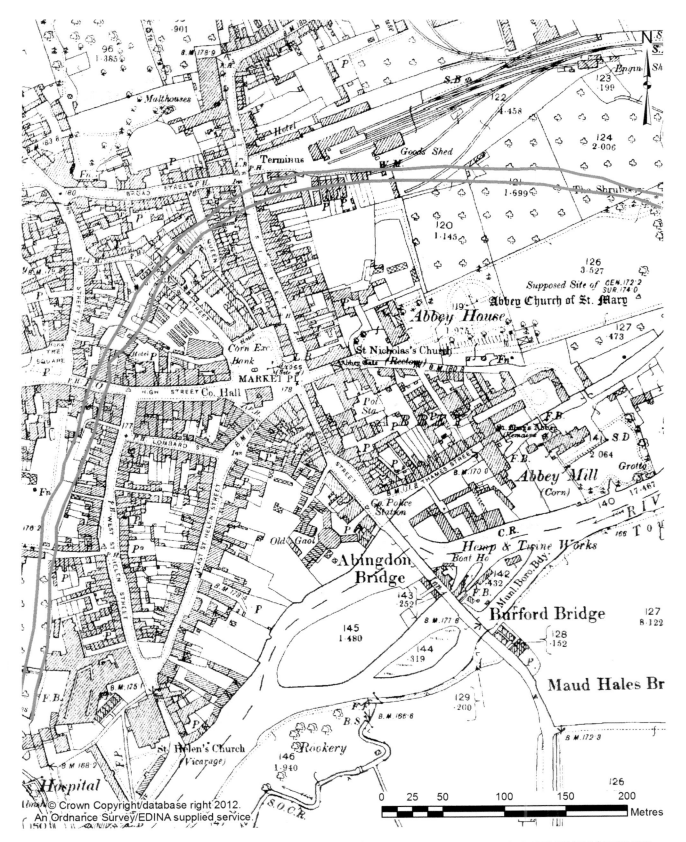

FIGURE 4.11: OS FIRST EDITION REVISION MAP OF ABINGDON, WITH THE CONJECTURED LOCATION OF RAMPARTS BELONGING TO THE IRON AGE HILLFORT (DOUBLE LINE). REUSE OF EARLIER ENCLOSURES BY EARLY MONASTIC COMMUNITIES APPEARS TO HAVE BEEN RELATIVELY COMMONPLACE, WITH SUCH SITES PROBABLY AMONGST THE EARLIEST USE OF BURH PLACE-NAMES (AFTER THOMAS 2010, FIG 2.).

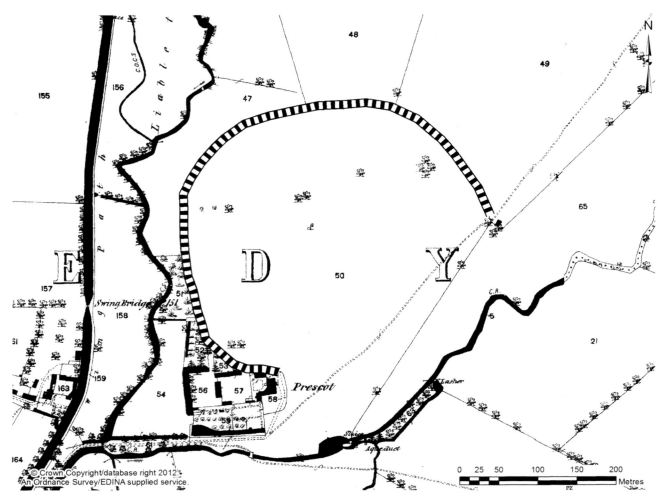

FIGURE 4.12: THE CIRCULAR FIELD BOUNDARIES NORTH OF PRESCOTE MANOR, NEAR CROPREDY. IT HAS BEEN SUGGESTED THAT THE HEDGEROW ALIGNMENT PRESERVES A CHURCH ENCLOSURE, AN IDEA SUPPORTED BY THE FIELD-NAME 'ANKERS FIELD'. RECENT FIELDWORK HAS ALSO IDENTIFIED EARTHWORKS OF A DESERTED SETTLEMENT OF UNKNOWN DATE (WASS AND DEALTRY 2011).

rest of Oxfordshire's landscape. Away from the fertile central *pays*, the written evidence for 'Middle Saxon' centres is even worse, such as Pyrton, where a pre-Conquest minster is only recognisable through a single charter reference (S 104). Our understanding of pre-Viking minsters in the Cotswolds is marginally clearer. Dispersed groups of burials at Shipton-under-Wychwood hint at a more extensive or shifted earlier churchyard and nearby Charlbury is mentioned by Bede as the place where the relics of seventh century Diuma were held (Blair 1994, 66-7; 2010a, 26). The pre-Conquest landscape of the North Oxfordshire Upland is particularly enigmatic, however, with Adderbury, Bloxham, Cropredy and Banbury all recorded as minsters in 1100, but with virtually no evidence to suggest their earlier existence. Early medieval activity has been identified at Banbury (Stevens 2004; Blair 2010a, 26), and at Prescote, a small hamlet immediately north-west of Cropredy, where an enclosure may represent a significant early medieval centre (Blair 1994, 75-7; Wass and Dealtry 2011) (Figure 4.12). An ecclesiastical significance here is supported by the presence of the names 'Ankers-field' and 'Ankers-meadow', perhaps referring

to the former presence of an anchorite's cell. There has been no archaeological investigation which allows further exploration of this possibility, however, and to-date there has been confirmation of early medieval activity in the area. The Chilterns *pays* is similarly lacking in evidence for possible early medieval settlements, barring the notable exception of Wantage.

Wantage

In addition to archaeological evidence for pre-Viking occupation in the area of the town, Wantage was almost certainly the centre of a royal estate by the ninth century (Forster *et al.* 1975, 163). Wantage is celebrated as the likely birthplace of Alfred, Asser noting that he was born at the *villa regalis* there in 849 (*Asser* 1, 154; Hindley, 2006, 206). Wantage was also the site of a minster by at least the tenth century, with a minster church documented in the will of Wynflæd (Whitelock 1930, 12). Two archaeological excavations undertaken in the town, however, indicate that the Wantage may have been a significant centre long before its first written recording (Figure 4.13).

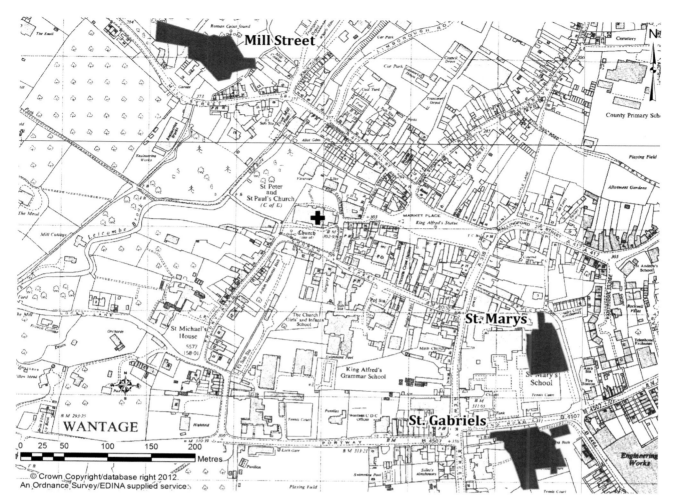

FIGURE: 4.13: LOCATION OF EXCAVATIONS IN WANTAGE THAT HAVE UNCOVERED EARLY MEDIEVAL SETTLEMENT ACTIVITY. AN 'EARLY SAXON' FOCUS IDENTIFIED TO THE WEST OF THE CURRENT TOWN WAS SUCCEEDED IN THE EIGHTH CENTURY BY SETTLEMENT SOUTH-WEST OF THE PRESENT PARISH CHURCH OF ST. PAUL'S (CROSS).

The first extensive investigation to locate evidence for pre-Viking occupation was undertaken between 1993 and 1994 at Mill Street in the historic core of the town, approximately 250m north-west of the medieval church of St Peter and St Paul. Excavation was conducted by Cotswold Archaeology following recovery of Romano-British deposits during an earlier evaluation by Wessex Archaeology (Holbrook and Thomas 1996). Romano-British remains were encountered, including field boundaries, a small timber granary and a probable domestic structure. This sequence, dated to the second century was succeeded by a stone-built square structure dated to the fourth century, interpreted by the excavators as a tower granary. In the fifth and sixth centuries the stone from the structure was robbed and a series of ditched enclosures orientated on a new alignment were dug and sealed by a dumped silt horizon, evidence which may relate to the development of agricultural plots (Holbrook and Thomas 1996, 65-8).

More recent excavation by Thames Valley Archaeological Services identified further early medieval settlement features at the site of St Mary's School in the southern part of Wantage (NHER: 17005). Approximately 250m south-east of the parish church, two open areas were excavated

in 2008; the St Mary's school site and approximately 250m further south, a second area termed St Gabriel's. Investigation at the St Mary's School site, located several phases of settlement activity, reliably datable to the eighth or early ninth century by the recovery of Ipswich Ware and North French Blackware (NHER: 17005, 26-8). Most ceramics were retrieved from a context which also included a number of post-holes possibly indicating a structure, pits, a truncated ditch and a crouched burial (NHER: 17005, 30-1) (Figure 4.14). The character of ceramic finds strongly suggests high status activity at Wantage, as across the county, North French Blackware is only known from the likely early minsters of Bampton and Oxford. The ceramics found in the county-town were associated with radiocarbon dates centring on the mid-eighth century, and outside of Oxfordshire, the distribution of North French Blackware and Low Countries Blackware is restricted to the Lower Thames Valley (Mellor 2003, Table 6.7). The presence of Ipswich Ware at Wantage similarly advocates elite occupation between c.725-850. The pottery type is generally rare west of London, and in Oxfordshire has only been found on a handful of likely minsters or other sites of special status (Mayes et al. 2000; Blinkhorn 2002).

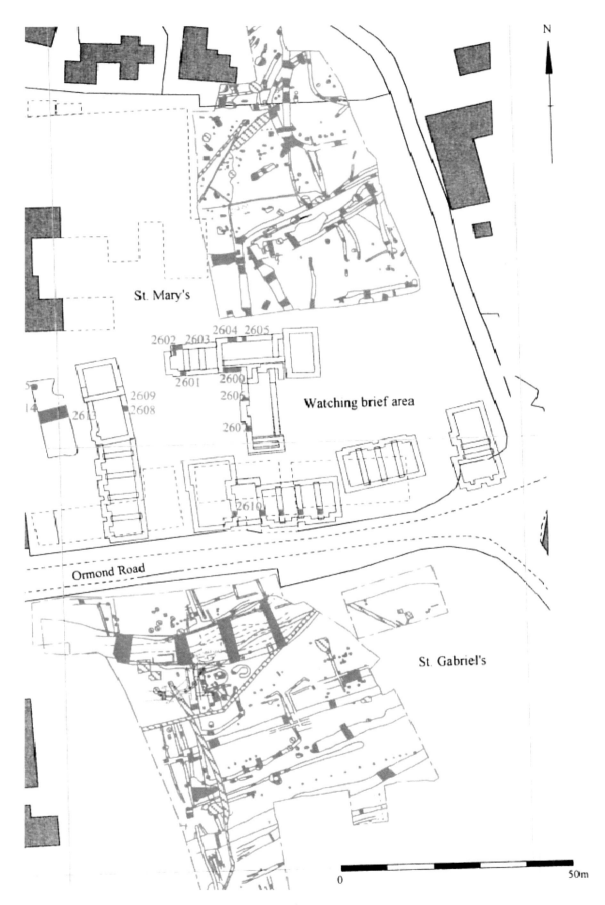

FIGURE: 4.14: PLAN OF EXCAVATED FEATURES AT THE ST. MARY'S SCHOOL SITE, WANTAGE. EIGHTH CENTURY OCCUPATION WAS LOCATED AT THE SCHOOL SITE, BUT NOT AT ST GABRIEL' DURING THE SAME PROJECT, SUGGESTING THAT THE FORMER INVESTIGATION IDENTIFIED THE SOUTHERNMOST EXTENSION OF A SETTLEMENT FOCUS LOCATED FURTHER NORTH, POSSIBLY IN THE AREA OF THE PRESENT PARISH CHURCH.

The first signs of post-Romano-British occupation in Wantage, probably dating to the fifth and sixth centuries were located by the excavation on Mill Street. This site may have remained occupied in the seventh century but was certainly abandoned by the eighth, indicating a shift of settlement focus in the area possibly towards the recognisable historic core around the church of St Peter and Paul. The south-westerly extent of this centre is perhaps indicated by results from the St Mary's School excavation, as only the northern section encountered settlement activity pre-dating the eleventh century. The high-status character of the ceramics at the site strongly suggests elite activity commencing during the eighth century (NHER: 17005, 30). It is therefore distinctly possible that the St Mary's School site represents the southern edge of occupation associated with the *villa regalis*, though the moderate density of features precludes interpretation as the primary settlement focus. The archaeological evidence reasonably pushes back the earliest habitation in Wantage some fifty years, and occupation could have conceivably begun as early as *c.* 725, if the current interpretation of Ipswich Ware is accepted (Blinkhorn 1999).

Arguing the case for uninterrupted occupation between the Mill Street and St Mary's School site at Wantage is dubious, given the broad date ranges provided by the pottery recovered from both sites. What can be said with greater certainty, however, is that high status occupation around the core of the historic town commenced during the eighth century, possibly over a century before the first documented reference to Wantage as the site of a *villa regalis* (*Asser* 1, 154). It is somewhat ironic that the first reference to Wantage relates to it as King Alfred's birthplace, an individual widely credited with development of the network of *burhs* (Biddle 1975; Haslam 2005), and to whose lifetime many of the earliest origins of England's medieval rural settlement framework have been attributed (e.g. Lewis *et al* 2001; Dyer 2003). The archaeological evidence presented here instead suggests that Alfred was born in a centre that had been inhabited for a century or more, and was probably already the site of an elite centre of some description, but again distinguishing between 'secular' or 'religious' character again is not possible.

Summary

The archaeological evidence from Oxfordshire outlined above is helping to create a gradually more coherent picture of elite social life during the 'Middle Saxon' period. The prevalence of the Church shaping the 'Middle Saxon' settlement hierarchy has been a particular prominent theme of past research, but in many cases it can be demonstrated that the influence of religious groups has been overstated. Only Dorchester possesses pre-ninth century documentary evidence relating to the ecclesiastical community, and elsewhere in the county, minster centres have been postulated largely on the basis of back-projection of later written sources. At present, there is a very real danger of identifying all 'Middle Saxon' settlements as minsters, and scholars need to be critical of their sources, especially when identifying archaeological evidence with later documents. In particular, the view that a network of near-contemporary minsters were established in the Thames Valley from the late seventh century is not supported by the exiting evidence, but instead is the result of plotting sites of likely various date upon the same map. The preconception that minster foundation in the Thames Valley was a singular 'Middle Saxon' movement therefore probably obscures the true palimpsest-character of Oxfordshire's early medieval settlement landscape.

Rather than perpetuating the distinction between 'secular' and 'religious', this research instead be emphasises that the archaeological evidence relating to 'Middle Saxon' Oxfordshire demonstrates extremely similar patterns of activity across the entire social elite. Indeed, the intimate relationship of 'Middle Saxon' elite society is demonstrated by the patronage of Oxfordshire's minsters, the fragmentary documentary evidence from which suggests that they were invariably founded by members of the Mercian royal house (Yorke 2003, 243-8). Beginning in the late seventh century, establishment of church centres was a key colonial tool of Mercian house and 'church sites' are as likely to have been occupied by members of the royal entourage and secular elite as those that we back-project as nominally 'churchmen'. The Church was certainly among the key mediums for material expression in the 'Middle Saxon' period, but elite interest in the landscape undoubtedly preceded the arrival of the minsters. Rather it is the monumental hall complexes of Drayton/Sutton Courtenay and Long Wittenham, which may reasonably be termed 'royal' centres, which represent the first settlement indicators of an increasingly ranked and stratified society in the Oxfordshire region from the late sixth century.

Comparable with similar sites of the period from across England, such as Yeavering, Northumberland and Bremilham, Wiltshire, the peak of occupation of the halls at Drayton/Sutton Courtenay appears to have been *c.*600-650 (Hope-Taylor 1977; Hinchliffe 1986; Chapter V). Together with the 'princely burials' of the Upper Thames region, the elaborate residential centres illustrate an increased interest in the formal articulation of the landscape by the emerging social elite, beginning in the early seventh century. These changes are not unique to Oxfordshire but are part of a pattern detectable across much of early medieval England, where diverse phenomena that included 'princely' burials, ritual centres arranged around axial points, and the arrangement of burials within cemeteries in ordered rows, reflect a new formal articulation of the landscape (Carver 1998, 52-9). The establishment of ecclesiastical infrastructure from the latter part of the seventh century was not therefore unique to Christian institutions but part of a more protracted process of monument-building that had been exercised for almost a century previously (Blair 2005, 52).

The arrival of the Church as a focus for consumption did see a rising concern with the reuse of the past, however, apparent in Oxfordshire by the establishment of the bishopric in the Roman town of Dorchester during the 630s. Yet, recycling the imperial past was not the sole motivation behind the choice of the town as the centre of the diocese, as together with Benson, as Dorchester is likely to have already been one of the key centres for the *Gewisse* in the sixth century. The development of the ecclesiastical centre of Dorchester remains an exception when compared to the rest of the Upper Thames region though, being the only 'Middle Saxon' minster centre which possesses contemporary documents, and thus does not rely on back-projection of later sources. The broader national picture derived from charters does suggest prolific church foundation from the late seventh century, and there is no reason to doubt that the same process occurred across the countryside of Oxfordshire. As has been demonstrated though, care is required when identifying specific sites and this research preserved a more conservative interpretation of the primary archaeological material, viewing the stratifying 'Middle Saxon' settlement hierarchy as part of increasing investment in the landscape which occurred across society. This growing consumption did not occur in a vacuum, however, and the following section demonstrates that outside of elite centres, the pattern of rural settlement and the character of individual communities also radically changed through the period. These developments, it will be argued, are reflective of fundamental changes to the structuring of society, and whilst church communities were possibly the first to adopt new attitudes to permanent settlement, even on sites that cannot be explicitly associated with minsters, a similar trend towards stratification of the landscape in the 'Middle Saxon' period can be demonstrated.

RURAL COMMMUNITIES

Introduction

Outside of archaeological investigation into high-status settlements and landscapes, aspects of the countryside of early medieval Oxfordshire that are not necessarily the product of elite activity have also been well-served by previous research (Figure 4.15). Even although archaeological material is gradually providing a more coherent picture of the character and development of elite sites in Oxfordshire, one of the most significant difficulties for researchers attempting to trace the developing pattern of early medieval settlements has been the relative lack of fieldwalking surveys compared to other midland counties. There have been notable exceptions, though, the results from which provide a specific insight into the evolving pattern of settlement in the landscape. Fieldwalking at North Stoke 3km south of Wallingford by Steve Ford and Annette Hazel (1989) for instance, initially identified thirty-three sherds of 'Early-Mid Saxon' pottery on the second gravel terrace of the Thames. Further targeted fieldwalking centred upon a ceramic concentration recovered almost eight-hundred further sherds, almost certainly indicating the site of a former settlement (Ford and Hazel 1989, 18-20). Significantly, the site is situated 100m south of the current village of North Stoke, possibly

demonstrating the occurrence of short-range settlement drift.

A similar process may have also taken place at Purwell Farm, 1km north of Cassington on the gravel terraces of the River Cherwell. Approximately 10km north-west of Oxford, an 'Early Saxon' cemetery and settlement were at first recognised through surface artefacts, on farmland north of Cassington village (Leeds and Riley 1942, 62-3; Dawson 1961-2, 1). Subsequent excavation revealed evidence for an extensive inhumation cemetery located 400m from a contemporary settlement which included several pottery kilns. Significantly, the settlement is situated around 90m north-east of the present Purwell Farm, again perhaps suggesting a drift in focus after the seventh century (Arthur and Jope 1962-3, 1-5). Fieldwalking surveys producing such insightful results have been few and far between in Oxfordshire, however, and it is the results from excavations that provide the majority of material relating to early medieval settlement in the county.

For instance, archaeological evidence for settlement in Cassington parish is not restricted to Purwell Farm as excavation has recovered further deposits to the south of the village. Identification of several *Grubenhäuser* and early medieval burials were made in advance of gravel extraction and the construction of the A40 (Leeds 1940), the density of which perhaps demonstrates an unusually intensive occupation (Hoskins 1959, 42; Dickinson 1976, 66-7). Scholarly understanding of the landscape surrounding Cassington and the neighbouring village of Yarnton has been transformed, however, by intrusive investigations beginning in the late 1980s. The presence of an early medieval settlement was first noted during archaeological evaluation in 1990, leading to an English Heritage grant to fund an initial 2.5ha of open area excavation. The obvious archaeological potential of the area resulted in further intrusive investigation over the next six years, ranging from single evaluation trenches to open area excavation (Hey 2004, 3-4). These interventions revealed an extensive early medieval settlement, the earliest phases of which were located on the edge of an Iron Age and Romano-British occupation site. Fifth to seventh century settlements in the wider region appear to have been closely associated with cemeteries, and a similar pattern was recognised in the Yarnton and Cassington landscape where occupation began in the late fifth or early sixth century (Hey 2004, 39).

Yarnton

The earliest post-Roman activity in the Yarnton landscape was characterised by what is generally regarded as typical 'Early Saxon' settlement: dispersed farmsteads exhibiting occupation which perhaps lasted a generation, as the focus of settlement gradually shifted across the landscape over time. Excavation in the landscape around Yarnton and its neighbouring villages, however, demonstrated a marked shift in settlement activity from the first decades of the

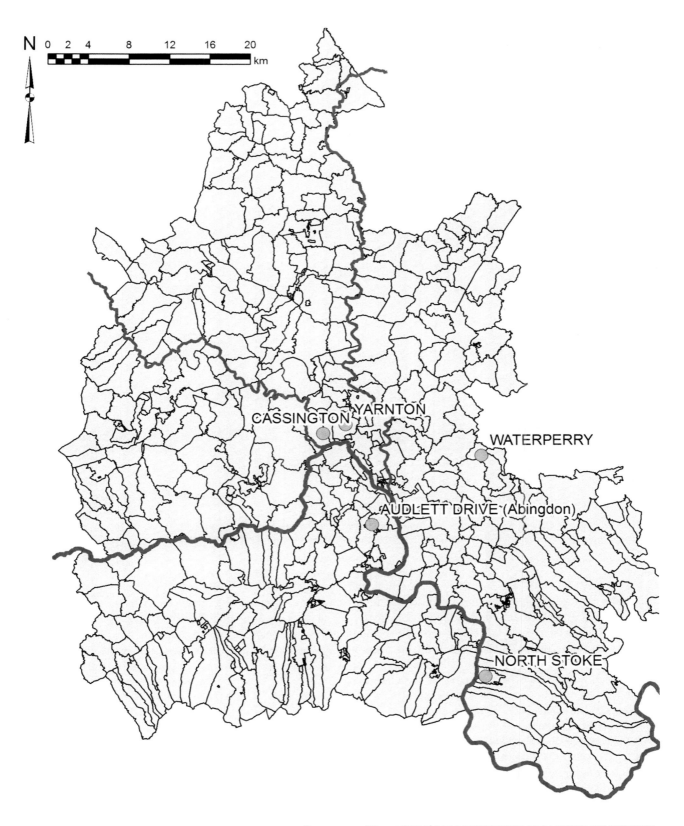

FIGURE 4.15: LOCATIONS OF RURAL SITES MENTIONED IN THE TEXT IN OXFORDSHIRE. 'MIDDLE SAXON' OCCUPATION REMAINS HAVE LARGELY BEEN RECOVERED FROM THE THAMES VALLEY. SOURCE FOR MAPPING: HISTORIC PARISHES OF ENGLAND AND WALES ONLINE.

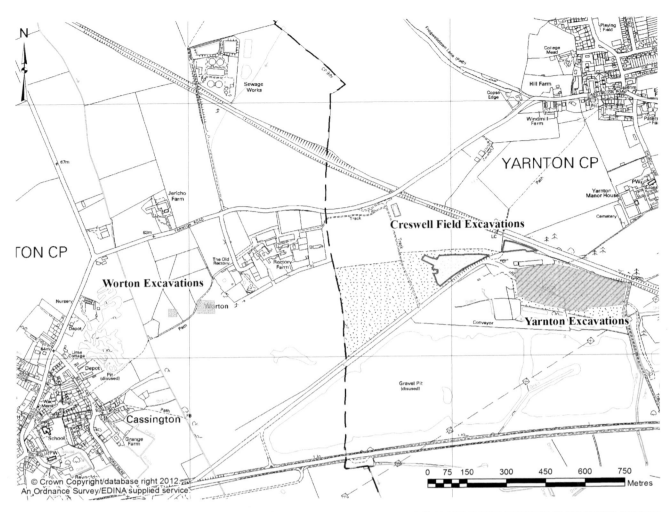

FIGURE 4.16: PLAN OF AREAS INVESTIGATED BY THE YARNTON-CASSINGTON INVESTIGATION PROJECT. THE MULTI-FACETED CHARACTER OF THE PROJECT REVEALED
ACTIVITY SPANNING THE ENTIRE EARLY MEDIEVAL PERIOD (AFTER HEY 2004).

eighth century. This 'Middle Saxon' phase, dated by the excavators to the eighth and ninth centuries, and was detected in three main concentrations around the currently-occupied villages: at Cresswell Field, Worton and Yarnton (Figure 4.16) (Hey 2004, 43). The 'Middle Saxon' features at Cresswell Field, approximately 500m west of the Yarnton site, were unexpectedly discovered intruding into earlier Iron Age occupation deposits. Fenced enclosures and four *Grubenhäuser* were found in association with a timber hall, all of which were probably in use between the seventh and ninth centuries. At Worton, roughly 1km west from the Creswell Field, excavation located a single post-in-trench building, a feature which had previously been recognised as a rectangular anomaly on aerial photographs (Hey 2004, 45).

By far the most extensive remains from this period were located at the 3ha Yarnton site, however, where occupation probably began in the late seventh or early eighth century. Located approximately 300m south-west of the medieval parish church of Yarnton, excavation recovered four or five timber halls, nine other post-built structures, ten *Grubenhäuser* and numerous pits and wells, all lying within a series of fenced and ditched enclosures and paddocks

(Hey 2004, 42-3) (Figure 4.17). These features represent a fundamental change in the character of settlement in the area, as greater emphasis was placed on creating deeper, ditched enclosures and existing buildings were re-instated, rather than built in new areas. These changes likely reflect an increasingly formal organisation of the habitation space, but may also have been encouraged by restricted availability of land (Hey 2004, 46-8). The 'Middle Saxon' enclosures partly resemble the toft-like arrangement also identified in the 'Late Saxon' phase, a phenomenon that is paralleled at other places investigated by this research, such as at Cottenham in Cambridgeshire. Only the periphery of the tenth-century township, featuring a small smithy, was observed in the north-eastern part of the excavated area, suggesting that the settlement continued to shift after the 'Middle Saxon' period, despite the increasingly structured and permanent approach to habitation. It is most likely that the settlement eventually became stabilised in the post-Conquest period, with its focus around the church and manor on either side of Church Lane (Hey 2004, 87-8).

Perhaps as significant as the change in settlement form detectable in the 'Middle Saxon' phases at Yarnton is the environmental evidence, which suggests the adoption

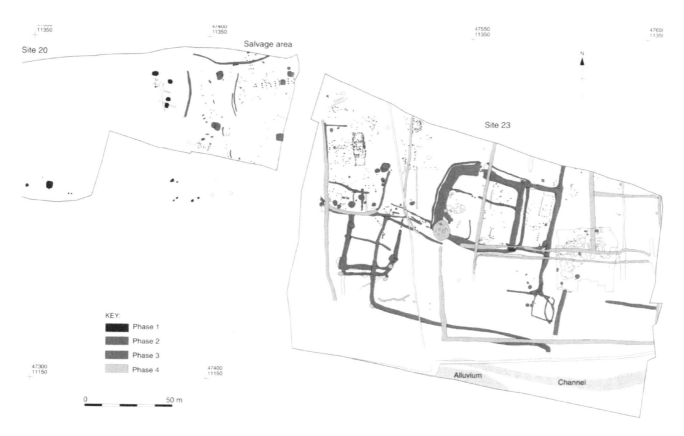

FIGURE 4.17: EARLY MEDIEVAL FEATURES IDENTIFIED AT YARNTON. THE EIGHTH CENTURY PHASE (PHASE 3) OF OCCUPATION WAS MARKED BY A MOVE TOWARDS A MORE STRUCTURED SETTLEMENT CHARACTER, WHICH COINCIDED WITH INTENSIFICATION AND DIVERSIFICATION OF THE AGRICULTURAL ECONOMY (HEY 2004, FIG 5.5).

of a more sophisticated farming regime during the same period. The exploitation of a wider range of crops was coupled with diversification of animal species, and a series of new structures such as a granary and fowl house built were in order to serve the requirements of the new farming regime. The 'Middle Saxon' period at Yarnton is thus best summarised as showing 'radical differences in size of the settlement area, in the degree of organisation within it, in building type and in the variety of structural remains' (Hey 2004, 45). The developing character of the agricultural economy and settlement organisation at Yarnton illustrates fundamental transformation of rural life, which probably began around the eighth century. Whilst the settlement sequence cannot be directly associated with the form of the later medieval village, the 'Middle Saxon' period was defined by a step-change in the countryside surrounding Yarnton. Whilst toft arrangements were introduced into the settlement as early as the eighth century, it was only following settlement shift and restructuring, probably occurring in the tenth century that the historic form of Yarnton was developed.

The excavated evidence from Yarnton's therefore demonstrates again a probably two-stage process of village development, already demonstrated at Northamptonshire on sites such as Raunds, Daventry and Brixworth. Although it may be tempting to see the Yarnton sequence as indicative of a continually shifting settlement until its eventual stabilisation from the 'Late Saxon' period, it is notable that crucial 'village-like' elements emerged around the eighth century. The development of deep enclosures that formed trackways and toft-like property boundaries express fundamental changes to perceptions of property and land ownership (Hey 2004, 88-91). In the light of evidence from sites such as Yarnton, the 'Middle Saxon' countryside can no longer be viewed as a stable, unchanging environment but a landscape which experienced significant change, underpinned by broader developments that occurred across society (Hey 2004, 87; Rippon 2008, 263; Chapter III). These key insights aside, the archaeological evidence from Yarnton cannot be viewed as totally representative of all rural settlement sites in Oxfordshire. Settlement at Creswell Field, excavated during the same project, presented a more loosely structured layout to Yarnton and the site appears to have been abandoned when the hall building went out of use at the end of the eighth century. It is possible that the occupants of Creswell Field re-settled to the Yarnton site at this time, the increased population perhaps providing another stimulus for the stratification of settlement space. The apparent mobility of the Yarnton settlement, demonstrating a tendency to relocate focus even after the introduction of semi-permanent ditches, is somewhat contrasted in Oxfordshire by the excavations in the village of Waterperry which apparently showed stability from a far earlier period.

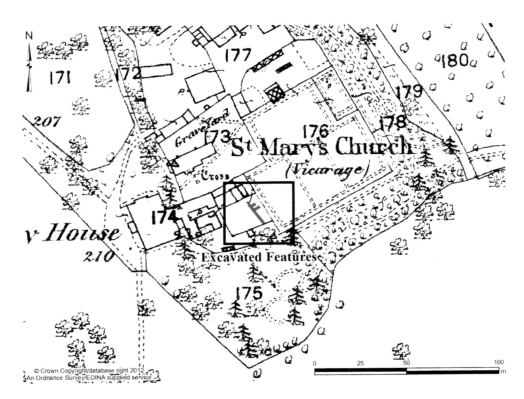

FIGURE 4.18: THE ORIENTATION OF THE 'MIDDLE SAXON' FEATURES AT WATERPERRY. THE DITCHES ARE ALIGNED PERPENDICULAR TO THE HISTORIC STREET-PLAN, SUGGESTING THAT FUNDAMENTAL STRUCTURAL ELEMENTS OF THE VILLAGE CAME INTO EXISTENCE AT AROUND THIS TIME (AFTER WEAVER AND HULL 2000, FIG 3).

Waterperry

The historic core of the modern Waterperry is today dominated by Waterperry House and Garden, and the church of St. Mary. Excavation adjacent to the parish church in 1972 first indicated the potential for early medieval remains through ceramic finds (Hassall 1972), although elements of the church fabric often suggested as 'Saxon' in origin (e.g. Weaver and Hull 2000, 333), have been firmly re-dated to the post-Conquest period (Blair 1994, 181). Further excavation of five trenches in the grounds of Waterperry House 15m south of St. Mary's in 1998 identified a series of ditches, pits, postholes and walls dated between the 'Early Saxon' to the medieval periods. Initial early medieval occupation, given an 'Early-Middle Saxon' phase on the basis of ceramics was represented by three pits and a ditch (Weaver and Hull 2000, 333-5). The succeeding phase, dated to the 'Middle to Late Saxon' period, again by pottery finds, was characterised by two ditches, a pit or ditch terminal, a single gully and two postholes. Although the lack of diagnostic ceramics makes phasing this sequence difficult, a small quantity of decorated pottery suggested to the investigators an approximate seventh century date for the second phase (Figure 4.18) (Weaver and Hull 2000, 335).

Significantly, the two ditches of this period were orientated differently to the earlier phase, perpendicular to the historic street plan and may therefore represent an embryonic tenement arrangement (Figure 4.19). The excavators implied that the early significance of Waterperry is also represented by the 'substantial settlement belonging to Robert D'Oley recorded in Domesday Book' (Weaver and Hull 2000, 343). The ten hide holding estate for Waterperry, however, is not untypical of an aristocratic holding, granted through royal patronage or through alienation of monastic lands in a well-recognised process of estate fragmentation which intensified during the ninth century (Sims-Williams 1990, 155; e.g. Rippon 2008, 95). Investigations at Waterperry nevertheless re-iterate the significance of the 'Middle Saxon' period in shaping the rural settlement character of Oxfordshire, reflecting the rapidly increasing articulation of the landscape evident through the eighth century.

Summary

The combined evidence from archaeological investigation into the rural landscape of early medieval Oxfordshire suggests a stratification of the settlement hierarchy between the seventh and ninth centuries. Central to the changing character of rural communities was the increased structural arrangement of sites, most clearly observable through the establishment of more substantial and regular enclosures, which are likely to represent private tenement plots. Environmental data from the more substantial excavations at Yarnton also indicate contemporary transformation of the agricultural economy, with diversification of farming regimes and exploitation of new aspects of the landscape. Dating these developments with accuracy remains problematic due to the broad phasing of early medieval ceramics, coupled with the lack of alternative dating

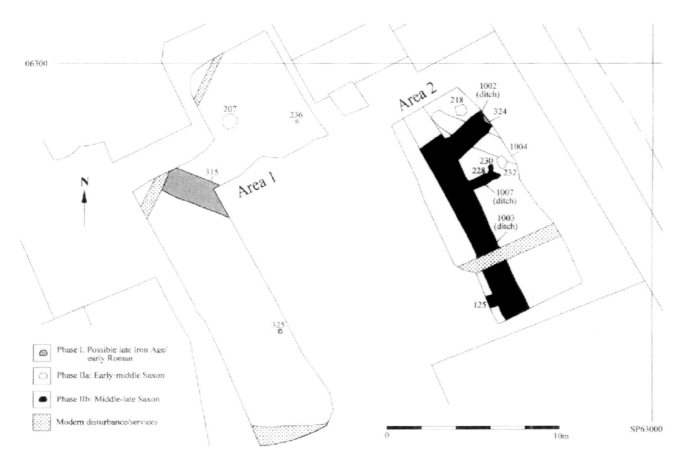

FIGURE 4.19: IRON AGE TO 'LATE SAXON' FEATURES IDENTIFIED AT WATERPERRY HOUSE. THE 'MIDDLE SAXON' OCCUPATION ON THE SITE, MOST LIKELY DATED TO THE EIGHTH CENTURY, MAY RELATE TO THE DEVELOPMENT OF AN EARLY PERMANENT SETTLEMENT (WEAVER AND HULL 2000, FIG 3

material from many sites. Indeed, radiocarbon dating at Yarnton demonstrates that settlements in Oxfordshire previously identified as 'Early Saxon', on the basis of structural features and pottery may have been occupied into the eighth and ninth centuries (Blinkhorn 2004, 268-271).

The scale of excavations at Yarnton also supports the model of a two-stage process of historic village development, first recognised by Brown and Foard in Northamptonshire (Brown and Foard 1998; Chapter III). This model suggests that a 'Middle Saxon' 'nucleation' phase, characterised by more permanent habitation and greater organisation of settlement space, was followed by a 'Late Saxon' or early post-Conquest readjustment, resulting in the creation of the historic villages. Such a sequence is quite clear at Yarnton, but the restricted extent of currently-occupied village excavations elsewhere in Oxfordshire makes it difficult to say with certainty whether this was a county-wide trend. What can be said with greater confidence, though, is that comparable to Northamptonshire, even on sites that were probably not centres of elite activity, the 'Middle Saxon' period in Oxfordshire was a time of fundamental transformation that impacted the character and functioning of communities across the countryside. As stated previously, the structuring of evidence into 'high-status' versus 'low-status' almost definitely masks a far more nuanced picture of a rapidly stratifying and

sophisticated settlement hierarchy. Whilst this division has been useful for the purposes of this chapter, research of the five counties serves only to emphasise the variety of site-types that were developed in the countryside of 'Middle Saxon' England.

CONCLUSION

This chapter has demonstrated the significance of the 'Middle Saxon' period as a time of substantial social change in the area that was later to become Oxfordshire. The cumulative archaeological material, produced through the rich research tradition of the county, suggests that the 'Middle Saxon' countryside was subject to crucial changes to the way in which it was settled and exploited. Archaeologically speaking, the most prominent communities are those occupied by high-status groups. The assumption that most of these centres were the sites of ecclesiastical communities is difficult to corroborate based on archaeological material alone, and the back-projection of status should be treated with caution. One only needs to look at the conclusions of the excavators at the site of Flixborough, Lincolnshire, to see the tendency that some early medieval elite centres may have had to undergo changes in ownership or administration (Loveluck 1998; 2007). Assigning sites to a peculiar elite group without reliable and contemporary documentary material is therefore a risky exercise, especially when the close relationship between the 'Middle Saxon' secular elite and the Church is considered. Indeed, the scholarly preoccupation with labelling elite centres as either 'ecclesiastical' or 'secular' appears increasingly inappropriate, certainly in terms of the archaeological evidence, and it could even be questioned whether such a distinction was made in the minds of contemporary populations (see Chapter VIII). Rather, the development of Oxfordshire's minster network from the seventh century should be viewed as part of a more protracted interest in elite landscape investment that can be seen from around the year 600, when a nationwide trend towards monument building and a more ordered approach to space is notable.

In Oxfordshire, the earliest significant site that is attributable to the process of landscape change is the monumental hall complex of Drayton/Sutton Courtenay, which probably experienced a peak in occupation c.625. From the late seventh century, however, more significant and lasting change was introduced by the systematic development of settlement centres. Accompanying such developments was a changing agricultural economy, with greater concern with agricultural intensification and specialisation. In some cases, such as Waterperry and Yarnton, eighth century transformations to the farming economy and structural organisation of settlements can be seen to pre-empt the later medieval village landscape of Oxfordshire. The excavations at Yarnton are especially significant, as they seem to reveal the complete process of two-stage village development, increasingly recognised by academic research. The results from the Yarnton investigations are even more remarkable given the relative dearth of currently-occupied rural settlement research undertaken in Oxfordshire that has identified substantial

'Middle Saxon' remains. Analysis of the AIP shows that around a quarter of currently-occupied village excavations have identified some form of 'Middle Saxon' activity, yet the material from Oxfordshire is more fragmentary than the results from other counties studied by this book. Sheer circumstance of investigation is the most likely explanation for such a discrepancy, but the material that has been recovered from Oxfordshire is rarely integrated into scholarly discourse.

This research, however, has sought to counter this prevailing trench, and has demonstrated that the process of 'Middle Saxon' settlement and landscape change detectable in Northamptonshire was also underway in the countryside of Oxfordshire. The sequences revealed at sites such as Yarnton, and to a lesser extent Waterperry and Wantage reveal a fundamental transformation in the character and economic orientation of rural communities from the seventh century onward. It is highly likely that increasingly powerful landowners were central to these changes, but the degree to which lords could exert control over rural communities should not be seen as the singular explanation, and the ability of peasant groups to change their circumstances should not be wholly disregarded. Either through lordly intervention, or through more subtle practices such as social emulation or communal organisation, individuals inhabiting rural settlements therefore began to experience the rural landscape in a different way. Although the Thames floodplain remained the most populated area, increasingly sophisticated groups also began to take advantage of a range of landscapes, as the more recognisable countryside of Oxfordshire began to take shape.

Chapter V
Wiltshire

Continuing the journey south and west, this book now directs its emphasis to the county of Wiltshire. After Oxfordshire, Wiltshire represents the second county investigated by this research that can be described as truly transitional in its geographical character, bridging a divide between the chalkland and clayland landscapes of central-southern England. Also comparable to Oxfordshire is Wiltshire's regular omission from early medieval settlement scholarship, although unlike its north-easterly neighbour most of the county was not located within the landscape of medieval nucleated villages and common fields. Rather, Roberts and Wrathmell's (2000) analysis divided Wiltshire almost equally between the village landscape of the central province in the west, and the eastern half of the county which more regularly features the dispersed farmsteads and irregularly enclosed fields of the south-eastern province. Whilst one might be given to think that this mixture of regional landscape diversity offers an attractive area for research, Wiltshire has generally not been deployed as a case study by early medieval settlement archaeologists. Instead, documentary material has proved a far more popular basis for pre-Conquest landscape research in Wiltshire, partly as a result of good coverage of boundary clauses in charters relating to the county.

Wiltshire certainly possesses the least impressive profile of excavated archaeological data of the five counties studied by this book, yet this chapter will demonstrate that the material evidence that has been recovered can shed significant new light on the 'Middle Saxon' countryside. Crucially, the evidence from Wiltshire alongside that from Norfolk, offers a perspective outside the scholarly focus of the English midlands, and acts as a useful comparator for assessing the impact of the antecedent 'Middle Saxon' countryside upon historic landscape variation. With this in mind, this chapter will investigate the seventh to ninth-century settlement archaeology of Wiltshire through geographical *pays*, an approach adopted in all but one of the county-based studies of this book. After briefly introducing Wiltshire, the different topographical *pays* of the county will be outlined, followed by a discussion of the region's archaeological and historical research traditions. A detailed analysis of Wiltshire's 'Middle Saxon' settlement archaeology forms the main body of this piece, which closes with a discussion of the significance of the material presented. Particular emphasis will be placed on whether the evidence from Wiltshire provides an alternative model of development to the narrative produced by archaeologically better-researched counties such as Northamptonshire. It is also apparent that a large proportion of the 'Middle Saxon' settlement material

in Wiltshire is derived from existing towns, rather than more moderately-sized rural settlements, hinting at the possibility that important 'Middle Saxon' foci were targeted for development by the later kings of Wessex.

INTRODUCING WILTSHIRE

Wiltshire is first explicitly referenced in The Anglo-Saxon Chronicle entry for 878, though it is likely that both *Wiltunscir* and '*Wilsæte*' were used throughout the ninth century to denote the area we now recognise as the historic county (*ASC* 878). The '*sæte*' suffix refers to the people of a region and has generally been viewed by scholars as the term of greater antiquity, yet in Wessex the first reference to the '*scir(s')* predates the citation of '*sæte(s)*' by over a hundred years (Draper 2006, 59). The mention of *Hamtunscir* in 757 suggests that central-southern England was organised into taxable units by at least the eighth century, with eponymous centres providing regional foci for tribute. It is probable that the people of *Hamtunscir* directed their renders to *Hamwih* (modern Southampton), with Wilton fulfilling a similar role for Wiltshire. In the Wessex region, central settlements such as *Hamwih* and Wilton would have represented locales not merely for royal accumulation, but also foci for early 'shire' identity. Ascribing origins for this administrative framework has proven especially difficult, but as Barbara Yorke has highlighted, the lack of evidence for a Roman inheritance at such places likely indicates their 'Middle Saxon' origins (Yorke 1995, 87).

The historic and modern boundaries of Wiltshire are almost entirely contiguous, with only detached portions of some parishes in the extreme north and east of the county having been ceded to Berkshire during the nineteenth century. The Wiltshire Sites and Monuments Record (WSMR) holds information relating to the extents of the historic county, and for convenience this chapter utilises the same geographical extents as a unit for study. From as early as the sixteenth century, authors such as John Speed and William Camden noted the broad topographical division of Wiltshire, between the chalk downland landscapes of the south and east, and the clay soils that proliferate in the north and west. This distinction was reemphasised by John Aubrey in the seventeenth century, who detailed the 'tillage, shepherds and hard labour' of the chalk in the south of the county, and the 'dirty claey country' of the pastorally-based communities to the north (Underdown 1985, 73). Unsurprisingly, these conditions have resulted in different patterns of historic settlement and land use. By the later medieval period, the chalk downland was a landscape characterised by compact villages surrounded by open fields, although these villages were of markedly different character from the agglomerated villages of the 'champion' midlands (Lewis 1994, 176). Such an approach to community organisation was nevertheless contrasted sharply with the claylands where the medieval settlement pattern was more dispersed. In such areas, communities typically inhabited a combination of isolated farmsteads or small, loosely arranged villages (Rackham 1986, 17; Lewis 1994, 172).

THE *PAYS* OF WILTSHIRE

Since the accounts of early antiquaries, the broad distinction of Wiltshire's landscape has attracted repeated scholarly comment, yet when the topography of the county is studied in greater detail it is immediately apparent that the binary division between the locally-termed 'Chalk and Cheese' masks far more complex topographical conditions. The geography of Wiltshire is more meaningfully divided into smaller landscape zones or *pays*, each possessing distinctive physical traits which may potentially have shaped the character of early medieval settlement and land use (Figure 5.1). As a region of transition comparable to Oxfordshire (Chapter IV), Wiltshire acted as a watershed landscape for early medieval communities. The northern portion of the county formed part of the wider Thames Valley region that was repeatedly utilised as a frontier between developing polities, particularly the kingdoms of Wessex and Mercia in the 'Middle Saxon' period. In order to assess the influence of the physical environment upon the social and settlement landscape, this research has divided the topography of Wiltshire into seven *pays*. The mapping of these *pays* broadly follows models previously outlined by Lewis (1994) and Draper (2006), but recognises more acutely local geological and topographical variations.

Wiltshire Cotswolds

The Oolitic Limestone plateau of the Cotswolds extends in an approximate north-south direction along the north-western fringes of Wiltshire. Stretching between the modern towns of Bradford-on-Avon and Malmesbury, the geological profile of Jurassic Great Oolite with clay outcrops creates a topography of deeply incised 'V' shaped valleys in the limestone, drained by the upper limits of the Bristol Avon in the north and the River Bybrook in the south. The limestone bedrock helps to form generally light soils, making the region clearly distinguishable from the Northern Clay Vale which borders it to the south (VCH Wiltshire I 1957, 14). Above the river basins, the landscape is characterised by flat-topped hills ranging in height between 80m and 180m OD. This well-drained, relatively fertile landscape is today dominated by arable agriculture, with the exception of limited woodlands located mainly on the steep-sided valley slopes (Draper 2006, 4).

The historic settlement character of the Cotswolds well-illustrates the shortcomings of the simplistic 'Chalk-Cheese' division of the Wiltshire landscape: traditionally incorporated into the 'woodland' settlement type of the 'Cheese' zone of northern Wiltshire, the Cotswolds is in fact the only *pays* in Wiltshire to have featured frequent tightly-coalesced villages in the medieval period (Lewis 1994, 172). Accordingly, the Domesday Survey records a high density of plough teams and meadowland, indicating a well-established arable economy. Further north in the Cotswolds, recent archaeological excavations near Cheltenham, Gloucestershire, have revealed an extensive early medieval community suggesting that the wider region was subject to intensive and permanent settlement from as early as the sixth century (Cotswolds Archaeology Website 2011).

Northern Clay Vale

Also located in north-western Wiltshire is an area of low-lying claylands, known as the Northern Clay Vale. The geology is dominated by Oxford and Kimmeridge Clays, interrupted by gravels and sands in the river valleys. This low-lying, often marshy landscape is drained by the western limit of the Upper Thames Valley in the north and by the Bristol Avon and its tributaries in the south. The upland areas of clay divide the two major river networks, forming a watershed that extends to the northeast of Malmesbury (Draper 2006, 5; Lewis 1994, 172-3). In the medieval period much of this *pays* was relatively well-wooded. This coverage, coupled with the propensity for the heavy clay soils to become waterlogged, has resulted today in a largely pastoral farming economy. Remains of ridge and furrow nevertheless suggest that at least some of the area was previously subject to arable agriculture, a notion supported by the high density of Domesday plough teams recorded for many clayland townships (Darby and Finn 1967). Despite the mixed farming regimes in use by the 'Late Saxon' period, the medieval settlement landscape of the *pays* was overwhelmingly dispersed, often featuring sporadic, loosely clustered farmsteads (Lewis 1994, 177).

Greensand Belt

Extending in an almost continuous line from Mere, Somerset, in the south-west to Highworth on the Hampshire border in the north-east, the Greensand Belt spans the eastern watershed of the Bristol Avon and the southern watershed of the River Thames. Although consisting of chiefly Upper and Lower Greensand, this *pays* also comprises large quantities of Corallian Limestones and Sandstones, Gault Clay, and Kimmeridge Clay. This mixed geological profile forms an elevated band of low hills, ranging from approximately 100m OD in Gault Clay and Greensand areas, to a height of 180m OD on the Corallian Limestone. The variable geology of the *pays* has resulted in mixed historic agricultural regimes, with large tracts of woodland in the lower clayland vales contrasting with areas of arable and pasture on the better-drained soils of the sandstone and limestone districts. The interface of the Greensand Belt and chalk escarpment of the Marlborough Downs and Salisbury Plain is punctuated by springs that formed a focus for past settlement (Lewis 1994, 173). The long, thin arrangement of parishes in these zones, such as

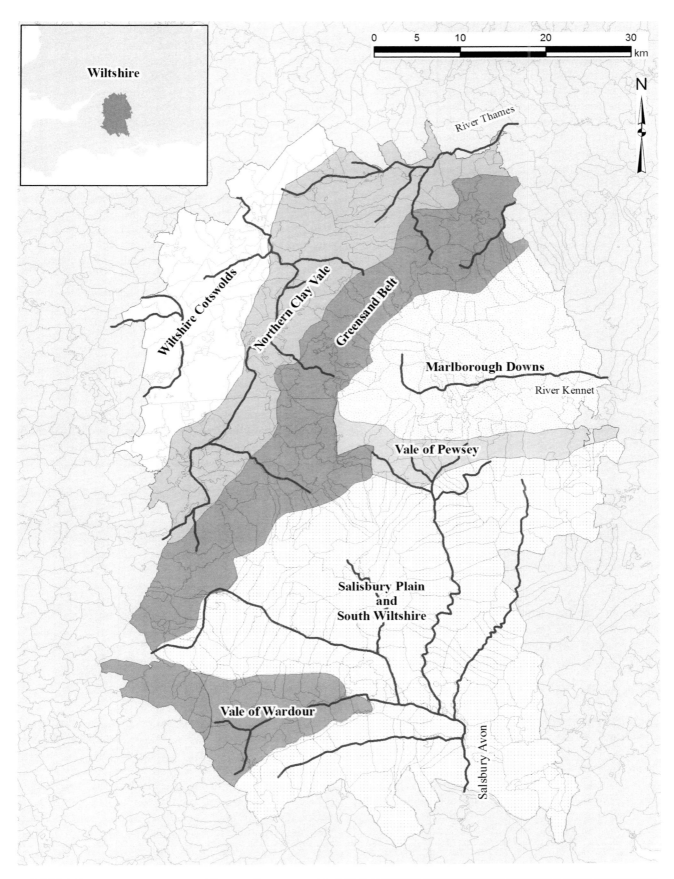

FIGURE 5.1: THE PAYS AND MAJOR RIVERS OF WILTSHIRE. THE DISTINCTIVE CHALKLAND LANDSCAPES OF THE COUNTY ARE REPRESENTED BY THE MARLBOROUGH DOWNS AND SALISBURY PLAIN AND SOUTH WILTSHIRE PAYS. SOURCE FOR MAPPING: HISTORIC PARISHES OF ENGLAND AND WALES ONLINE

Wanborough and Liddington in the north, and Urchfont and the Lavingtons in the south, reflect attempts by medieval people to incorporate a range of resources under the jurisdiction of each township. The medieval settlement pattern of the Greensand Belt was generally dispersed, but featured a wide variety of arrangements including interrupted rows, common-edge villages and farmsteads. Accordingly, Domesday Book records a mixed farming economy, with a relatively high number of plough teams combined with extensive areas of meadow (Darby and Finn 1967).

Marlborough Downs

Wiltshire's northernmost outcrop of chalk, the Marlborough Downs stretches from the Avebury and Overton Downs, eastwards to Barton Down and Marlborough Common, with a northerly extension along the Og valley. The River Kennet and its tributaries drain the *pays*, following its course eastward where it flows into the Thames (VCH Wiltshire I 1957, 7). Alluvial deposits characterise the valleys of the river networks but the upland landscape is dominated by undulating chalk, divisible into two distinct topographical areas: the 'summit' area to the north and west of Marlborough where the Downs reach elevations as high as 280m OD, and the lower chalk plateau where the hilltops are more commonly around 150-200m OD in height. The chalk summits are capped with a layer of clay with flints, much of which are covered by woodland and in the medieval period lay within the Royal Forest of Savernake. Away from the highest uplands, some areas of the light freely-draining soils are used for arable cultivation but their tendency to rapidly lose their fertility means that much of the landscape is given over to sheep-pasture (Draper 2006, 5). The Marlborough Downs displayed a mixture of settlement form in the medieval period, with a riverine distribution in the west contrasting with a less structured arrangement to the east, particularly in the more low-lying chalkland areas. By 1086, the Domesday Survey reflects the preponderance of arable farming in valley locations, with the chalk uplands likely utilised for pastoral agriculture (Darby and Finn 1967).

Vale of Pewsey

The Vale of Pewsey is a low-lying band of Upper Greensand, extending from Devizes to Burbage. Dividing the chalk expanses of the Marlborough Downs and Salisbury Plain, the *pays* varies in height between 100 and 150m OD. The steep chalk escarpments that surround the Vale rise to nearly 300m OD at Milk Hill, the highest point in Wiltshire and to the south the Vale is drained by the Salisbury Avon. The fertile soils have been used for a combination of arable, pasture and woodland, ensuring a densely settled landscape in the historic period. Medieval settlement in the *pays* was characterised by a mixture of dispersed and more coalesced villages. Intriguingly, linear settlements were more commonly arranged across rivers, rather than along them as was the case in *pays* such as Salisbury Plain (Draper 2006, 5). Such an organisation is more closely comparable

to the fertile river valleys of the midlands, such as Raunds in the Nene Valley of Northamptonshire, than the medieval settlement pattern found elsewhere in Wiltshire (e.g. Parry 2006). The rich and varied resources of the Vale made it a relatively prosperous area by the Conquest, with the high proportion of plough teams recorded in Domesday Book demonstrating a leaning towards arable agriculture (Darby and Finn 1967).

Salisbury Plain and South Wiltshire

Following the lead of Draper (2006), this study amalgamates Salisbury Plain and the landscape of south Wiltshire into a single *pays*, creating an area with an overriding unity of chalk geology. The downland of Salisbury Plain is one of the most distinctive landscapes in Wiltshire, and an area that features substantial well-preserved prehistoric remains. Apart from the valleys of rivers such as the Salisbury Avon, most of the Upper Chalk comprises relatively poor soils for cultivation (McOmish *et al.* 2002, 8). Some of the earliest evidence for early medieval activity in the county comes from archaeological remains found on the Plain; such as the burials at Winterbourne Gunner, which demonstrate the use of 'Germanic'-style funerary rites from as early as the fifth century (Eagles 2001, 206). The well-drained upland of Salisbury Plain is bisected unequally by the Salisbury Avon and its tributaries, which flow south to converge with four other watercourses near Salisbury (Draper 2006, 5). These rivers create fertile zones of alluvium and gravel within the gently undulating chalk landscape, which proved attractive for medieval communities. The settlements which focussed on the valleys typically coalesced in proto-nucleated arrangements, contrasting with the uplands that appear to have remained sparsely occupied throughout the period (Lewis 1994, 176; McOmish *et al.* 2002, 109). Large quantities of meadow recorded by Domesday demonstrates that the fertile valleys were intensively exploited by the 'Late Saxon' period, although the low number of plough teams and extensive areas of pasture suggest that most medieval centres operated livestock-centred regimes (Darby and Finn 1967).

Vale of Wardour

The Vale of Wardour is formed by a complex geological profile of sandstone, clay and limestone that produces a contrasting landscape to the chalk which encompasses it in three directions. The Vale features steep-sided valley slopes with extensive woodland, particularly on the clay parishes to the west of the *pays*, interrupted by small and irregular fields (Lewis 1994, 172). Low-lying hills vary in height between 120-200m OD, rising above a network of streams, many of which originate from springs (Draper 2006, 6). The varied woodland and farming resources, in addition to the presence of good quality Portland Stone, used for building, has made the Vale of Wardour an attractive area for historic settlement. A dispersed medieval settlement pattern characterised the area, with coalesced settlements largely absent, although the economic potential of the Vale was substantial enough for the foundation of a monastery at Tisbury as early as the seventh century. Fieldwalking survey in the *pays* has recovered little evidence for early medieval settlement, although a significant quantity of material relating to prehistoric activity has been identified (Gingell 1983; Pitt 2003, 61-3).

EARLY MEDIEVAL WILTSHIRE

Introduction

The contrasting geological and topographical conditions of the Wiltshire *pays* have made the shire an attractive area of historic settlement and land use, and in the early medieval period the area emerged at the core of the powerful kingdom of Wessex, a coherent polity likely developed during the seventh century, out of the movement of the *Gewisse* from their earlier focus around the Oxfordshire Thames (Chapter IV; Yorke 1997, 4-5). The territory of Wessex was firmly consolidated by the ninth century and in the third quarter of the tenth century Edgar (959-75) was somewhat justifiably described as 'King of the English' (Stenton 1943, 250; Yorke 1995, 94-6). The success of Wessex as a political entity allowed the establishment of a relatively stable framework of ecclesiastical landholding in Wiltshire, a product of which is the survival of charters recording land grants to West Saxon religious communities (Aston and Lewis 1994, 2).

The charters, largely dated to the tenth century, provide a detailed account of the pre-Conquest landscape of the county, and have been pivotal in most previous reconstructions of Wiltshire's early medieval countryside (see below). The scholarly focus on such written material, however, has been somewhat at the expensive of the archaeological evidence for the county, which remains relatively neglected. Most studies of early medieval settlement in Wiltshire quite rightly use a combination of the available written and material evidence, yet the strength of the charter data and the perceived dearth of archaeological evidence has often led to a reliance on documentary sources (e.g. Lewis 1994). This chapter will demonstrate that by studying the archaeological evidence in greater detail, a more comprehensive understanding of changing early medieval settlement may be gained. Previous research though, has been successful in generating a broad social and historical context for this study, a brief overview of which is given below beginning with the 'Early Saxon' period.

'Early Saxon' Wiltshire

During the two centuries following the end of Roman administration, radical cultural change is evident in the archaeological record of Wiltshire. Current explanatory narratives continue to present migration as the fundamental causal factor behind the emergence of 'Germanic' funerary rites and construction techniques (e.g. Eagles 2001). Although the introduction of this dominant new material culture can be understood through other dynamics such as indigenous change and transmission of ideas (Scull 1992), it is almost certain that Wiltshire experienced an influx of at least some continental migrants in the fifth and sixth centuries. Cultural influence in the county appears to have come from two primary directions; along the Upper Thames Valley to the north, and up from the network of river valleys of Hampshire to the south (Eagles 1994, 14). The earliest datable 'Germanic' style objects come from a series of probable fifth century cemeteries in the Salisbury area. The cemeteries at Charlton in the Avon Valley, Harnham to the south of Salisbury, and Petersfinger to the southeast of the town, all possess graves of possible fifth-century origin (Leeds and Shortt 1953). At Winterbourne Gunner an individual buried with Frankish-influenced objects may also date from the late fifth century, though the chronology derived from grave-goods and ceramics is approximate (Eagles 1994, 13-14; Musty and Stratton 1964). Of the fifth century burial sites in Wiltshire, the furthest westward so far discovered is that at Market Lavington where excavations in 1990 revealed an apparently contiguous and contemporary settlement and cemetery complex that remained in use into the seventh century (Williams and Newman 1998).

Settlement evidence from the 'Early Saxon' period in Wiltshire is much less extensive, though, with only a handful of sites excavated to date. In addition to the site at Market Lavington (Williams and Newman 1998), the only other occupation site with 'Early Saxon' activity subject to substantial excavation was located at Collingbourne Ducis (see below) (Pine 2001). These exceptions aside, attempts to characterise settlements of the fifth and sixth century in Wiltshire are frustrated by the same problems as those of the 'Middle Saxon' period, particularly the broad chronological phasing attributable to local ceramics. Very general conclusions regarding 'Early Saxon' occupation may be made, however, and whereas once it was assumed that early settlements were located in hilltop locations on well-drained but infertile soils, the body of archaeological evidence relating to valley bottom sites now stresses the importance of rivers as foci for activity during the period (Arnold and Wardle 1981; Draper 2006, 96). The pattern of early 'Germanic' cultural influence in Wiltshire detectable through burial and settlement sites is also significant. Extremely little 'Germanic' material is recognised west of an approximately line between Teffont, Warminster and the northern and western limits of the Greensand Belt *pays* (Figure 5.2) (Eagles 2001, 219). This stark difference does not appear to be a product of an inequality in previous archaeological research, but instead suggests an absence of 'Anglo-Saxon' cultural influence in these areas before the start of the seventh century, after which a more characteristically 'Germanic' material presence became more prolific.

The nature of the 'Anglo-Saxon' *adventus* in Wiltshire provided by the Anglo-Saxon Chronicle is even less reliable than the archaeological record though, as it is not until at least the seventh century that accounts are likely to incorporate contemporary information. The events

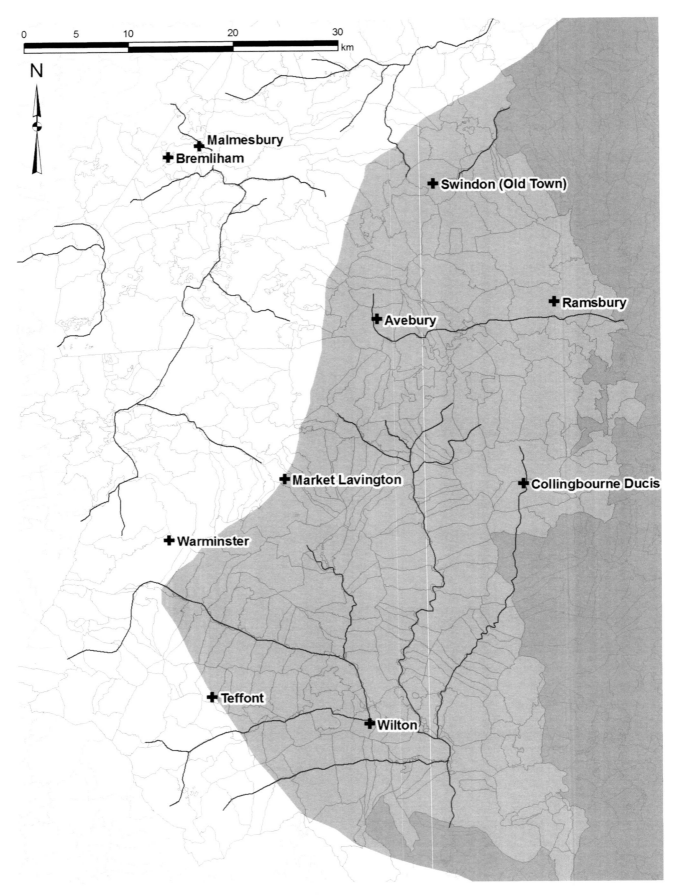

FIGURE 5.2: LOCATIONS MENTIONED IN THE TEXT, TOGETHER WITH THE AREA THAT APPROXIMATELY REPRESENTS THE REGION FROM WHICH SEVENTH-CENTURY 'GERMANIC' MATERIAL CULTURE HAS BEEN IDENTIFIED (SHADED). BASED PRIMARILY ON GRAVE-GOODS, THERE APPEARS TO BE A CESSATION OF 'GERMANIC' STYLE OBJECTS TO THE WEST OF TEFFONT, MARKET LAVINGTON AND THE CLAY LOWLAND PAYS (AFTER EAGLES 1994). SOURCE FOR MAPPING: HISTORIC PARISHES OF ENGLAND AND WALES ONLINE.

of the fifth and sixth centuries may not be completely fabricated, yet it is hard to elucidate any historical truth from writing that is frequently semi-mythical in character (Yorke 1995, 34). It is therefore somewhat surprising, that the Chronicle somewhat corroborates the archaeological evidence for an influx of 'Germanic' culture, entering Wiltshire from the south along the Salisbury Avon. The evidence from burials recovered from the Salisbury area predates the mid sixth century dates given by the Chronicle for the battle between the Britons and Saxons at Old Sarum, but suggests nevertheless that by c.600 parts of Wiltshire were directly affected by groups who identified themselves through 'Germanic' goods (Draper 2006, 38). In north Wiltshire, it is probable that the obscure entry recording a battle at *Wodensbeorg* in c.592, identified as the Neolithic long barrow of Adam's Grave in Alton parish, is a later fictional addition (*ASC* 592; Gover *et al.* 1939, 318). North Wiltshire was a highly contested military frontier in later periods and, with neither of the combatants identified and an almost identical conflict recorded for the year 716, it is likely that the earlier account was used to provide a historical explanation for the later political climate (Reynolds and Langlands 2006, 15-17). The combined archaeological and documentary evidence for 'Early Saxon' Wiltshire, whilst fragmentary, does therefore suggest some migration of new peoples into Wiltshire during the fifth and sixth centuries, although it is extremely difficult to discern the nature of interaction between native and incoming groups. Irrespective of their ethnic background, by the middle of the seventh century documentary sources reveal a group calling themselves the *Gewisse*, who probably migrated from an original focus in the Upper Thames Valley, beginning to firmly establish their authority in the Wiltshire landscape.

Settlement and Landscape in 'Middle Saxon' Wiltshire: Documentary Material

Although when used in isolation the Anglo-Saxon Chronicle is an inadequate source to explain the dynamics by which the *Gewissan* federation came to assume political control of Wiltshire, these details, when combined with the early charters of Glastonbury and Malmesbury, are sufficient to suggest that control was exercised at least nominally over much of the region by the accession of Ine in 688 (Yorke 1995, 60; Kelly 2006). The term 'West Saxon' or '*Occidentales Saxones*', deployed interchangeably with '*Gewisse*' by Bede, appears to have only been used from the seventh century, perhaps in order to distinguish themselves following Cædwalla's (685/6-688) conquest of the 'South Saxons' of Sussex (Yorke 1990). During the same period, expansion and consolidation of groups using 'Germanic' material culture is also evident in Wiltshire. 'Germanic' style funerary rites in particular, apparently restricted to the eastern half of Wiltshire during the fifth and sixth centuries, began to be adopted in the western portion of the county from the early 600s. Included in this corpus are new forms of elaborate burial, such as the richly furnished barrow burial at Swallowcliffe, in south-west Wiltshire (Speake 1989). It is likely that conspicuous

statements of 'Germanic' identity represent an attempt by a newly powerful group to assert their authority, although the use of barrows may equally hint at the assumed legitimacy of a shared pagan past (Eagles 2001, 219; Carver 1998).

Whilst the southern half of Wiltshire seems to have lain at the political heartland of the *Gewisse* by the 'Middle Saxon period', documentary evidence suggests that the area north of Salisbury Plain remained contested until the start of the ninth century. The continued southern expansion of Mercia, following the mid-seventh century annexation of the *Hwicce*, resulted in the *Gewissan* abandonment of the bishopric at Dorchester-upon-Thames by the 660s. These developments created a hotly disputed political frontier between the *Gewisse* and the Mercians, stretching from north Somerset, through north Wiltshire, and into Berkshire. It is possible that around this time the great earthwork monument known as Wansdyke was constructed, with dating evidence retrieved over the last ten years suggesting that it is a 'Middle Saxon' construction (Reynolds and Langlands 2006). The importance of the region is reflected by the grants of land to Malmesbury Abbey by both royal houses from the later seventh century, with a number of estates such as Tockenham and Puton passing between West Saxon and Mercian control throughout the eighth century (Kelly 2005, 3-6). If the later account of William of Malmesbury is to be believed, Aldhelm of Sherbourne even had to obtain special privileges for the minsters at Malmesbury, Bradford-on-Avon and Frome, for fear that the continuing conflict could jeopardise the future of the establishments (Haslam 1984, 114).

It was only West Saxon victory at the battle of Kempsford, Gloucestershire, in 802 that marked the decisive detachment of northern Wiltshire from Mercian overlordship, although it seems that north Wiltshire continued to be perceived as a contested zone until 825 when the Mercian hegemony was ended by another defeat at the battle of *Ellandun*, probably located near the village of Wroughton, 3km south of Swindon (Stenton 1943, 229). For this study, the most significant feature of the unstable political environment of north Wiltshire throughout the 'Middle Saxon' period was the use of minsters as instruments of expansion and consolidation by the royal houses of Wessex and Mercia. The granting of land to churches through charter has resulted in a potentially valuable resource for scholars attempting to understand the character of Wiltshire's early medieval landscape. In the northern part of the county, Malmesbury Abbey possesses the best-preserved corpus, but the archive at Shaftesbury Abbey, Dorset also includes a notable body of charters detailing lands across mostly southern Wiltshire (Costen 1994, 97; Kelly 1996).

It should be noted that none of the diplomas relating to Wiltshire survive in their original form, and we are mostly dependent on versions copied into post-Conquest cartularies. There are a total of sixty identifiable estates in the county, some of which are described in boundary clauses surviving in charters of donation, or as detached bounds (Costen 1994, 97). The Shaftesbury archive in particular possesses a high proportion of probably authentic charters, including a remarkably early example, detailing disputed land claimed by Tisbury minster (Kelly 1996, xx). The document apparently outlines the revision (S 1256) of an earlier text, originally issued in the 670s (S 1164) in order to negotiate a settlement between King Cynewulf and Bishop Cyneheard of claims to land at Fontmell Brook, Dorset. Although the grant only survives in a fifteenth century cartulary, the core of the text is almost certainly datable to the 750s, and adapted from a largely authentic seventh-century original (Kelly 1996, 4-10; Foot 2000, ii).

Excluding the recognisable later alterations, Coenred's original charter is the earliest diploma relating to Wiltshire and one of the very earliest in England, providing a unique insight into perceptions of land ownership in the seventh century (Kelly 1996, 6). In spite of such examples, it is only from the tenth century that charters survive in numbers significant enough to allow more comprehensive reconstruction of contemporary landscape organisation, yet the tendency of earlier grants to describe topographical units that bear a close resemblance with the more rigorous economic regimes of the 'Late Saxon' period, has convinced some scholars to seek earlier origins for the recorded landscapes (Reynolds and Langland 2006, 30). Combined with other sources such as Domesday Book and place-name evidence, in addition to texts such as writs, wills and leases, which become increasingly prevalent in the period, charters have frequently been used to reconstruct pre-tenth century arrangements in Wiltshire (Aston and Lewis 1994, 2). Della Hooke (1994, 86, 90), for example, has reconstructed several valley-based 'archaic hundreds' in the county that she claims may reflect division of resources originating as early as the fifth century. The reliability of this approach of back-projection is far from secure, however, and there is particular uncertainty whether charter estates can be viewed as typical of contemporary land-use arrangements.

This fundamental problem is illustrated by the disparity between the size of estates described by charter, and those recorded in Domesday Book: in 1086, the average size of holdings in Wiltshire was just over eight hides, whereas the average size of tenth-century charter estates was over seventeen hides. The difference must partly have been the product of estate fragmentation in the intervening century, as larger, earlier units were broken up as the process of 'Late Saxon' manorialisation grew apace. It is unlikely, however, that increase in secular landholding can be held completely to account for the difference in the size of estates, and it is probable that the substantial extents of charter territories actually reflects their unique development as social and economic arrangements (Costen 1994, 97). The use of charters as the central source in the reconstruction of the 'Middle Saxon' landscape of Wiltshire is therefore questionable, and is further compounded by the regional bias in their survival. Far greater numbers of grants survive from the Cotswolds and chalkland *pays* of the county but as this chapter will demonstrate, archaeological evidence

suggests that few areas were left unsettled by the end of the early medieval period (Lewis 1994, 186-7).

Perhaps the most fundamental and as yet unresolved research issue regarding charters, is whether the mass granting out of land during the middle decades of the tenth century was made with reference to freshly described units, or whether such documents in fact fossilise component parts of earlier estate structures (Reynolds and Langland 2006, 30-1). Although some scholars have seen parallels between 'Middle Saxon' and tenth century charters as evidence for continuity of economic regimes (e.g. Reynolds and Langlands 2006, 30), the lack of reliable pre-tenth century charters from which comparisons can be drawn remains problematic. Only six charters from the Shaftesbury archive, for example, claim origins before the tenth century but even this slight corpus is of mixed reliability, with evidence for numerous interpolations and re-workings of the original text in subsequent periods (Kelly 1996, xvi-xviii).

The archive of charters from Malmesbury Abbey has an even worse reputation, and only a handful of early texts can be regarded as reasonably faithful copies of original documents (Kelly 2005). Despite the efforts of several scholars, most notably Patrick Wormald (1985), Heather Edwards (1988), and more recently Susan Kelly (2005), many charters in the Malmesbury archive remain exceptionally difficult to provenance and interpret. Whilst several are unequivocal fabrications, more problematic are texts that have positive features but include details that illicit suspicion (Kelly 2005, 51). The earliest likely reliable grants from the corpus date to 758 (S 260) and 796 (S149) respectively, but the majority of the later eighth and ninth-century charters are less trustworthy. Analysis of such texts is particularly restricted by the lack of relevant and reliable copies preserved in other archives, and the modest value that the Abbey apparently placed on the integrity of its pre-Conquest documents. The concerted modification of earlier texts was part of a protracted campaign by Malmesbury against encroachment of its lands which reached its zenith in the early twelfth century (Kelly 2005, 51- 64).

The charter archives of Shaftesbury and Malmesbury, which contain the most abundant material relating to early medieval landholding in Wiltshire, are therefore best understood as a collection of ancient documents that have been adapted and modified. Unfortunately, the insufficient volume of reliable 'Middle Saxon' charters renders reconstruction of substantial areas of landscape unfeasible, and the approach of back-projection lacks legitimacy when considered more carefully (see Chapter II). Perhaps the most significant doubt cast over the use of later documents, is the dynamic character of the early medieval landscape, most clearly manifest by estate fragmentation in the 'Late Saxon' period. There is little to suggest that organisation of the 'Middle Saxon' countryside was any less susceptible to change, and scholars should not assume that estates remained static from their inception until their first recording. The propensity of early charters to describe arrangements similar to those documented in the 'Late Saxon' period does not necessarily justify 'Middle Saxon' or even 'Early Saxon' origins as some have claimed (e.g. Hooke 1994, 86, 90; Reynolds and Langland 2006, 30), and certainly does not negate the potential for estates to change their economic and settlement structure over time.

The evidence from charters should not be disregarded wholesale though, and the details from grants represent useful comparative material for this research. Indeed, survival of the small corpus of 'Middle Saxon' charters suggests that by the seventh century, at least parts of Wiltshire's countryside was exploited in a similarly sophisticated manner to that already outlined in Northamptonshire and Oxfordshire. As this chapter will demonstrate, however, the most effective way to gain a more comprehensive insight into the 'Middle Saxon' settlement of Wiltshire is not by focussing upon the back-projection of later documents, but through multi-disciplinary research, of which archaeological material makes a key contribution. The tendency of early medieval settlement research in Wiltshire to concentrate on documentary studies over material data is partly due to the assumed paucity of archaeological evidence, which many believe does not allow the character of settlement development or hierarchy to be discerned (e.g. Bonney 1979; Goodier 1984; Hooke 1994). As the following analysis of existing research illustrates though, the cumulative archaeological material in the county provides a unique insight into the character of 'Middle Saxon' settlement and landscape, and demonstrates how material remains can help us to better understand contemporary society.

MIDDLE SAXON WILTSHIRE: EXISTING PERSPECTIVES

Whilst this chapter will demonstrate that cumulative research can present new understandings of early medieval settlement in Wiltshire, it is immediately apparent that the quantity of archaeological investigation from the county is comparatively slight, especially when compared to the extensively-studied counties of the midlands (Chapter III; Draper 2006, 103; Lewis 1994, 187). The Wiltshire Sites and Monuments Record classes a total of 142 records as 'Saxon Settlements', but the majority of this sample have been identified on the basis of historical or place-name data. Archaeological evidence is less well represented, with the WSMR featuring approximately fifty sites with material remains considered indicative of occupation. This corpus is certainly slight, yet a more significant problem for researching 'Middle Saxon' settlement in Wiltshire is the character of the early medieval ceramic sequence. Archaeological research has shown that many communities in the Wessex region used grass-tempered pottery, only broadly datable to the 'Early-Middle Saxon' period; in neighbouring Dorset, for instance, two 'Middle Saxon' iron production centres excavated at Gillingham (Heaton 1992) and Worget (Hinton 1992) were dated on the basis of radiocarbon and dendrochronology analyses,

as both sites failed to produce ceramics earlier than the twelfth century.

When pottery is recovered from sites in Wiltshire, assemblages are dominated by the locally-produced organic-tempered wares which can usually only be ascribed an approximate fifth to ninth century provenance (Haslam 1980, 30-1). The longevity of vessel form makes typological sequencing of such wares difficult, and the household-scale of production has left archaeologists with few production centres whose study could potentially refine the existing chronology more closely (Williams and Newman 1998, 85-7). The prevalence of organic-tempered wares in early medieval settlement assemblages is not unusual, and has already been shown as the dominant ceramic on rural sites in Northamptonshire and Oxfordshire (Chapter III and IV). A more significant problem for research in Wiltshire is the lack of more typically diagnostic material, represented either by foreign imports, or from production centres in eastern England such as Ipswich (Lewis and Aston 1994, 8). Indeed, the singular prevalence of highly-friable organic-tempered wares may partly be responsible for the lack of early medieval settlements identified by the few large-scale fieldwalking surveys that have been undertaken in the county (Draper 2006, 96).

The character of the early medieval ceramic sequence may not be entirely responsible for the lack of 'Middle Saxon' settlements recorded by fieldwalking in Wiltshire, however. Most fieldwalking projects in the county have not sought to define the pattern of post-Roman settlement, as traditionally scholarly efforts have been more concentrated on identifying prehistoric and Romano-British archaeology (e.g. Bradley 1994; Fulford et al. 2006). The imprecise chronological sequence of early medieval pottery in the county is nevertheless a principal obstacle for study, and is surely at least partly responsible for the underrepresentation of archaeology in research of historic settlement and landscape (e.g. Eagles 2001; Lewis 1994). In spite of such difficulties, there is emerging from Wiltshire an increasing corpus of settlement archaeology which can be dated between the seventh and ninth centuries. That the significance of this material is yet to be recognised by scholarly research is partly due to the unusual contexts from which it derives. Similar to other counties of this research which feature significant archaeological remains from currently-occupied settlements, in Wiltshire a large percentage of 'Middle Saxon' evidence is derived from existing towns.

By 1086, Wiltshire had more boroughs than any other county, although these were small especially in comparison with towns in midland and eastern England. Many of these were already key centres of administrative and economic activity by the tenth century, possibly featuring truly urban physical and social characteristics (Haslam 1984, 87-9). Ten places in Wiltshire are described with characteristics typical of a town in 1086, and Haslam (1984, 87) forwards a further four possible locations not listed by Domesday

Book that could be viewed as likely urban centres of 'Late Saxon' origin. Tenth century and later development should not colour our interpretation of preceding periods, however, and the increasing corpus of archaeological evidence relating to 'Middle Saxon settlement both from towns and from other contexts in Wiltshire is increasingly informative. Cumulative archaeological investigation, especially that from unpublished excavations held by the WSMR, means it now possible to chart significant developments in the character and range of settlements in the county between the seventh and ninth centuries. Dividing the archaeological material into geographical *pays*, this chapter will now show the consistency with which the landscape of Wiltshire appears to have been adapted during the 'Middle Saxon' period. Progressing from north to south, the landscape of the Wiltshire Cotswolds possesses amongst the most impressive evidence for high-status settlement anywhere in the county (Figure 5.3).

WILTSHIRE: THE ARCHAEOLOGY OF MIDDLE SAXON SETTLEMENT AND LANDSCAPE

Wiltshire Cotswolds

Located in the far north-west of the county, the limestone landscape of the Wiltshire Cotswolds is an agriculturally fertile zone that has proved attractive to communities throughout the historic period. Numerous high-status Romano-British villas have been detected in the *pays*, such as the examples excavated near Bradford-on-Avon and Malmesbury (Hart *et al.* 2005), and by 1086 the area was recorded as a densely populated upland with large numbers of plough teams, suggesting a focus on arable farming. Documentary sources suggest that the Cotswolds was also desirable during the 'Middle Saxon' period, forming part of a highly disputed political region to the north of Salisbury Plain. For Mercia in particular, control of north Wiltshire meant access to the Thames and London, which represented a vital outlet for an otherwise land-locked kingdom (Maddicott 2005, 7-10). Although a handful of early charters from Malmesbury Abbey indicate the value that the West Saxon and Mercian royal houses placed on the Cotswolds, archaeological evidence for elite settlement in the period is equally revealing. The town of Malmesbury itself occupies a steep-sided triangular promontory on the north bank of the Sherston and Tetbury branches of the Bristol Avon (Figure 5.4). Although a document of much later origin, at least some of the details of the Abbey's foundation, recorded in the *Eulogium Historiarum*, are supported by archaeological evidence from the town. The account in the *Eulogium* describes how an Irish monk named *Maeldulph* or *Malidub* came to a fortified *castellum* called *Caer Bladon*, the later site of Malmesbury, in the early to mid-seventh century (Haslam 1984, 111; Yorke 1995, 162-3).

Existence of a British 'city' on the site of the later Abbey has previously found support amongst scholars, despite the fictional character of the *Eulogium*. Peter Fowler, for instance, had argued that an extant earthwork

at Malmesbury could have been used as a military or tribal centre from the fifth century (Fowler 1971). The topographical situation of the town has also suggested to some a likely hillfort location, surrounded by steep slopes on three sides above the confluence of two rivers (English Heritage EUS Malmesbury 2004, 7-8). Archaeological indicators for a pre-medieval centre at Malmesbury have been uncovered as early as the early nineteenth century. In 1805, J.M. Moffat noted a vitrified matter uncovered during digging works, which he suspected formed a 'vitrified bank or *vallum*' and later interpreted by Haslam (1984, 112) as representing a burnt timber-framed limestone slab wall (Moffat 1805, 101). Haslam (1976, 35) similarly assumed an early date for a bank identified along the edge of Nun's Walk in the eastern part of the town, partially sealed beneath the town wall. Measured survey of the monument confirmed its proportions and form, with the investigators also suggesting a possible Iron Age or 'Saxon' origin (WSMR: ST98NW200). More recent archaeological investigation, however, also in the Nun's Walk area of the town, has produced far more compelling evidence for a substantial pre-medieval settlement at Malmesbury. Excavations as part of a restoration programme in two locations along the line of the medieval town wall recovered evidence that the defences originated as a hillfort (Figure 5.5). A combination of ceramic and radiocarbon analysis demonstrated that a substantial earthwork was first constructed in the early Iron Age, upon which the later town wall was constructed (Longman 2006; Collard and Havard 2011). Although excavation has been limited to the eastern part of the town, it is likely that the prehistoric monument enclosed the whole promontory in order to make the site defendable.

The excavated evidence from Nun's walk enhances the idea amongst some academics that foundation myths such as that recorded in the *Eulogium* may conceal genuine traditions regarding early monasticism (e.g. Yorke 1995, 162). Although the presence of a pre-existing centre has been confirmed through excavation, archaeological evidence for the early church has been less forthcoming. The lack of early medieval material from the Nun's Walk excavations is not unexpected, as it apparently represents an area of later medieval settlement expansion. Rather, the 'Middle Saxon' ecclesiastical focus is thought to have been centred in the area of the later Abbey, although material evidence is sparse (WSMR, 2007:038). Excavations adjacent to the market cross, 50m to the south of the Abbey precinct recovered 'Late Saxon' graves and a similarly-dated boundary ditch, possibly associated with the Alfredian *burh*, but no structural or artefactual evidence for 'Middle Saxon' activity (English Heritage EUS Malmesbury 2004, 10). It has been implied that the southern part of the promontory was the focus of the extramural settlement of the 'Middle Saxon' minster (WSMR, 2007:038), and it is in this area that the most significant archaeological evidence for pre-*burh* settlement has been located.

In 2006 an archaeological watching brief of a high-voltage cable, the route of which ran through much of the

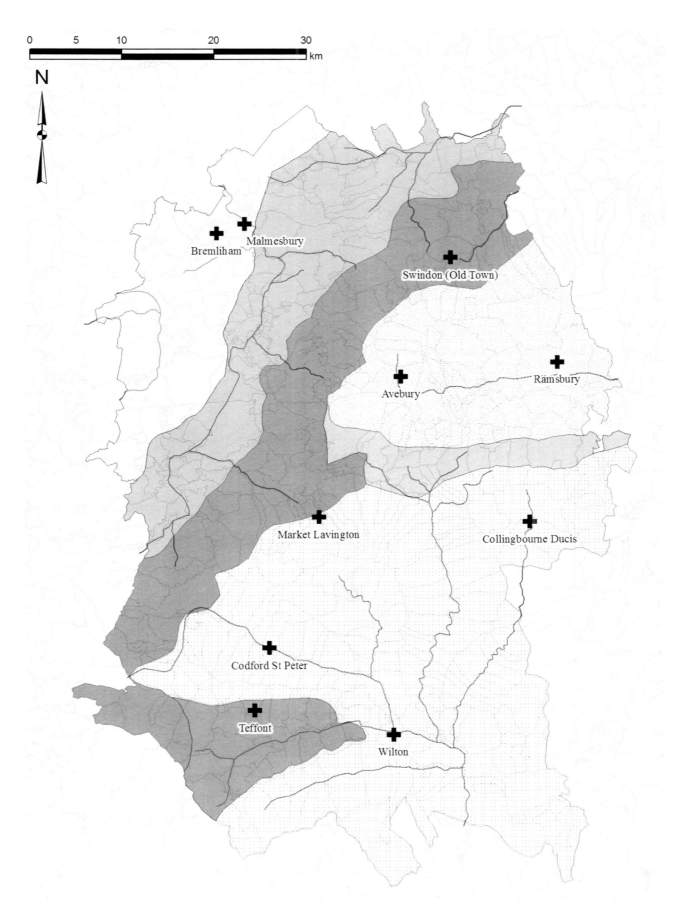

FIGURE 5.3: KEY SITES MENTIONED IN THE TEXT AGAINST THE PAYS OF WILTSHIRE. THE LACK OF 'MIDDLE SAXON' EVIDENCE FROM SOME PAYS IS UNLIKELY TO REPRESENT AN ACTUAL LACK OF ACTIVITY IN THE PERIOD, BUT IS INSTEAD INDICATIVE OF A LACK OF ARCHAEOLOGICAL INVESTIGATION IN SUCH AREAS. SOURCE FOR MAPPING: HISTORIC PARISHES OF ENGLAND AND WALES ONLINE.

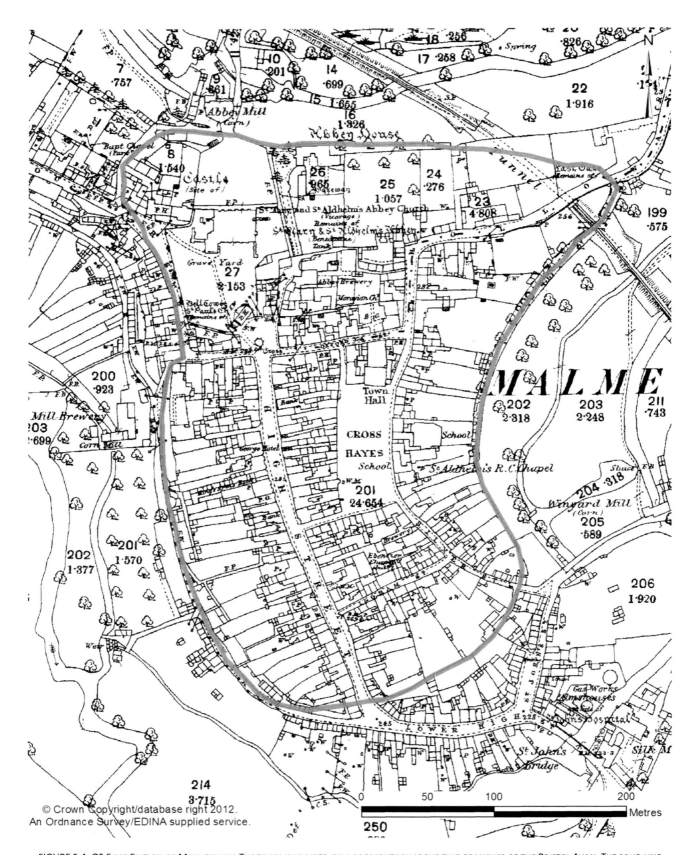

FIGURE 5.4: OS FIRST EDITION OF MALMESBURY. THE TOWN IS LOCATED ON A PROMONTORY ABOVE TWO BRANCHES OF THE BRISTOL AVON. THE SOLID LINE DENOTES THE LOCATION OF THE MEDIEVAL TOWN WALL, EXCAVATION OF WHICH HAS REVEALED THAT IT IS LOCATED ON THE EARTHWORK BANK OF AN IRON AGE HILLFORT.

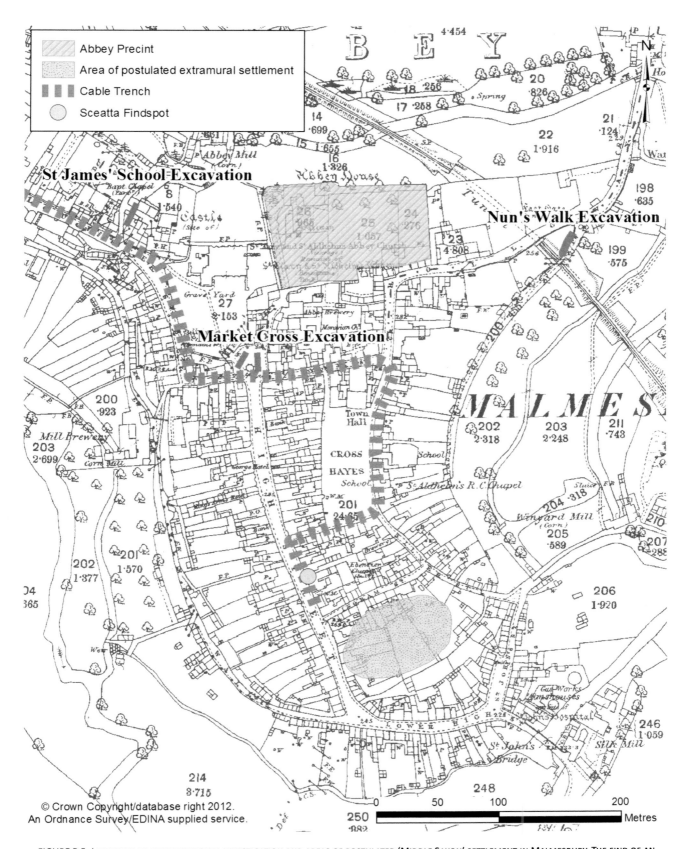

FIGURE 5.5: LOCATIONS OF ARCHAEOLOGICAL INVESTIGATION AND AREAS OF POSTULATED 'MIDDLE SAXON' SETTLEMENT IN MALMESBURY. THE FIND OF AN EIGHTH-CENTURY SCEATTA NEAR THE SOUTH OF THE CABLE ROUTE SUPPORTS THE IDEA THAT 'MIDDLE SAXON' EXTRAMURAL SETTLEMENT WAS LOCATED IN THIS AREA.

medieval town, recovered a cobbled path horizon which yielded a small assemblage of 'Early-Middle Saxon' finds, mostly comprising ceramics (WSMR, 2007:038). The remains were recovered at the southern end of the route, approximately 50m north of the postulated area of 'Middle Saxon' extramural settlement. The most significant find in the collection of artefacts was a Series H type 49 sceatta, probably minted under the reign of Cynewulf (757-786) (WSMR, 2007:038). Not only does this refine the broad ceramic dating and give a probable eighth-century date for the assemblage and the cobbled path, but it is also significant that this type of coinage is rarely found outside of Hampshire (Metcalf 1988, 20-8). A late eighth century date suggests links with the West Saxon heartland during a period of significant political upheaval in north Wiltshire, which saw a power struggle between Offa of Mercia and Cynewulf of Wessex. The identification of a pathway also supports the presence of a 'Middle Saxon' settlement focus outside of the ecclesiastical precinct at Malmesbury, suggesting that the minster may have served as a focus for more extensive occupation (Figure 5.5).

The only other structural evidence that may possibly date between the seventh and ninth centuries was excavated at St. Joseph's School, 75m west of the Abbey precinct (Figure 5.5) (WSMR 2002:052). A bank and ditch orientated north-south could only be given a 'Early-Mid Saxon' date on the basis of pottery finds, but the excavators deemed that the feature was probably associated with the 'Middle Saxon' church community (*WSMR* 2002:052). Despite these two examples of excavated evidence, there remains somewhat of a dearth of 'Middle Saxon' deposits from Malmesbury. This deficiency is unlikely to represent a genuine absence of activity between the seventh and ninth centuries, however, but is instead probably a product of the scale and character of archaeological investigation undertaken. Current archaeological understanding of early medieval Malmesbury is derived almost entirely from development-led mitigation projects of limited extent, many of which consist only of archaeological watching briefs (English Heritage EUS Malmesbury 2004, 5).

It is likely that even activity associated with the high-status 'Middle Saxon' minster occupied only a limited extent of the present town, probably underneath the site of the current Abbey church. Archaeologists are yet to excavate the Abbey precinct and, given its continued use as a consecrated burial ground, are unlikely to do so in the future. The likelihood remains therefore, that excavation in Malmesbury has yet to concentrate on the nucleus of 'Middle Saxon' settlement. Identification of the 'Middle Saxon' pathway nevertheless provides an archaeological indicator for pre-*burh* occupation in the town, and suggests that the Malmesbury was already a central place by the eighth century. Perhaps the most remarkable aspect of this part of the Wiltshire Cotswolds is that Malmesbury does not appear to have been the only elite centre within a restricted geographical area, and investigations in the hinterland of the town indicate that another high-status focus may have been situated nearby. Approximately 2.5km south-west of Malmesbury, aerial photographs provided the first indicator of what appeared to be several timber structures at Cowage Farm, Bremilham. Following initial detection in 1975, further archaeological investigation, including geophysical survey and limited excavation established more comprehensively the extent and character of the complex (Figure 5.6) (Hinchliffe 1986, 242-5).

The two most substantial features located by the research at Cowage Farm were an east-west aligned structure, with what appears to be a semi-circular annexe on its east end (Structure A), and a north-south orientated structure with ancillary buildings at its northern and southern ends (Structure B). Structure B appears to be the central hall of the settlement and Structure A, located within a rectangular ditched enclosure and with its apsidal-like annexe, probably represents the remains of a church (Figure 5.7). Both structures were subject to excavation in 1983, revealing post-pit construction techniques characteristic of other elite settlement complexes, such as Cowdery's Down, Hampshire (Millet and James 1983). A number of the smaller structures were also sectioned, demonstrating that post-in-trench construction was also in use. A single radiocarbon date from the charcoal fill of one of these smaller features (Structure C) produced a date range between the mid sixth and mid seventh centuries (Hinchliffe 1986, 250-253).

The combined investigation of Cowage Farm has clearly demonstrated the existence of a substantial high-status settlement, probably in use during the sixth and seventh centuries. The form and date of the complex is comparable to sites such as Yeavering, Northumberland (Hope-Taylor 1977) and Drayton/Sutton Courtenay, Oxfordshire (Hamerow *et al.* 2007; Chapter IV). In the Wessex region, similar elite centres have also been excavated at Chalton and Cowdery's Down, both in Hampshire (Addyman 1972; Millet and James 1983). Bremilham distinguishes itself from these other sites in Wessex, however, by possessing a probable church structure, the form of which is very similar to the seventh century stone and timber church at St Paul-in-the-Bail, Lincoln (Gilmour 1979; Hinchliffe 1986, 252-3). Indeed, John Blair (2005, 213-4) views Bremilham as a monastic demesne or 'grange', partly based on its close proximity to Malmesbury. The distinctive appearance of the site, he suggests, is indicative of a semi-monastic cell with agrarian functions that would have lain within the Malmesbury estate. The functioning of such 'Middle Saxon' monastic *inlands* first described in detail by Faith (1995, 15-8) is steadily being supplemented by archaeological material, such as the site excavated at West Fen Road which probably serviced Ely Abbey, Cambridgeshire (Chapter VI; Mortimer *et al.* 2005).

It seems probable that the 'Middle Saxon' monastic territory of Malmesbury lay within the estate of Brokenborough, an area recorded in two tenth century charters (S 629 and 1577), which also probably equated to the demesne lands of the *burh* (Kelly 2005, 230-1). Kelly (2005, 231) has argued that the 'hundred-hide of Brokenborough' was

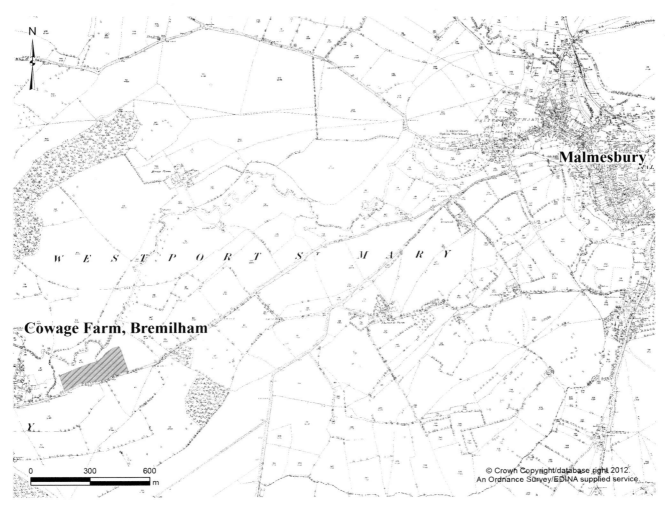

FIGURE: 5.6: THE LOCATION OF COWAGE FARM, BREMILHAM IN RELATION TO THE TOWN OF MALMESBURY. THE CLOSE GEOGRAPHICAL RELATIONSHIP OF THE TWO SITES SUGGESTS THAT BREMILHAM MAY HAVE BEEN A 'GRANGE' TYPE FARM ON MALMESBURY'S INLAND ESTATE (FAITH 1995, 15-8 BLAIR 2005, 213).

land associated with a *villa regalis* to which the minster was later attached. Her hypothesis contradicts that of Blair, and implicitly suggests that Bremilham was a royal vill, perhaps one of several, within the extensive 'Middle Saxon' estate which was later transferred to the church. In this respect, the character of the Bremilham settlement is part of a larger research issue, and underlines the likelihood that monastic sites were not consistently and obviously distinct from secular centres (Chapter VIII). Irrespective of the interpretation adopted, Bremilham is doubtless a remarkable site and a centre whose intrigue is accentuated by its close proximity to the early minster at Malmesbury.

The evidence for high status centres at both Bremilham and Malmesbury underlines the value of the Wiltshire Cotswolds to the 'Middle Saxon' social elite, although the later development of the two sites is notably contrasting. Whereas the minster at Malmesbury appears to have acted as a focus for settlement and was subsequently developed as a 'Late Saxon' *burh*, it is possible that the complex at Bremilham was already out of use by the end of the seventh century. Such a sequence is strikingly similar to that identified by this research in Oxfordshire, where occupation of the 'palatial' site of Drayton/Sutton

Courtenay appears to have waned by the seventh century, coinciding with more concerted development of the nearby fortified centre at Dorchester (Chapter IV). This change in high-status settlement types is perhaps indicative of the increasing investment in the Church by the secular elite, changes which are particularly detectable in the proliferation of charters from the late seventh century (Maddicott 2005, 7-10). The importance of enclosed space to the early Church is reflected by the reuse of the existing earthworks at Malmesbury, a defensive circuit that was utilised again in the 'Late Saxon' and medieval periods. The potential of early ecclesiastical centres providing a focus for 'Middle Saxon' and later settlement that can be seen in the Cotswolds at Malmesbury can also be demonstrated in the Greensand *pays* of Wiltshire.

Greensand Belt

The mixed geology of greensands, limestone, sandstones, and clays that comprise the 'Greensand Belt' forms a watershed between the Northern Clay Vale and the chalk landscapes of the Marlborough Downs and Salisbury Plain. The medieval settlement in this region is usually classified as dispersed in character by scholars (e.g. Lewis 1994,

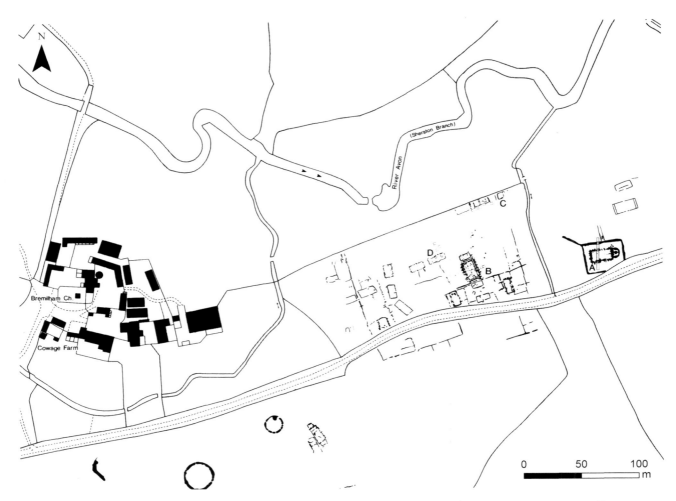

FIGURE 5.7: PLAN OF FEATURES AT COWAGE FARM, BREMILHAM BASED ON AERIAL PHOTOGRAPHS AND THE RESULTS OF GEOPHYSICAL SURVEY. THE FORM OF STRUCTURE A, LOCATED IN THE EASTERN PART OF THE COMPLEX, STRONGLY SUGGESTS A CHURCH BUILDING. AFTER HINCHLIFFE 1986, FIG 1.

173), especially in the eastern part of the *pays* (Roberts and Wrathmell 2000). Archaeological investigation in the historic core of Swindon demonstrates that at least some settlements in such dispersed regions possess origins dating to the 'Middle Saxon' period. Swindon is located at the eastern end of an east-west orientated ridge formed by limestone-capped clay deposits, which rises to around 40m above the clayland immediately north. The River Ray curves to the south of this ridge, and it in this area that the historic settlement developed, now known as 'Old Swindon' or 'Old Town'. Nineteenth-century growth stimulated by canal and rail development led to the absorption of previously distinct medieval villages, such as Moredon and Penhill.

Swindon itself did not possess town status until the thirteenth century when a market is recorded, but the presence of an early medieval settlement is supported by the taxation of the manor of '*Swinedune*' in the Domesday Survey. Land in the manor was held by five different lords in 1086, the most substantial being the ten hides of 'High Swindon', probably centred in the area of 'Old Town' (WSMR, 1993:032). Several small excavations in the 'Old Town' district of Swindon have consistently recovered evidence for even earlier settlement, however (Figure

5.8). In 1975 excavations at Swindon House, to the east of the historic market square, identified a *Grubenhäus*, rebuilt in the same location at least once. The first structure appeared to have been constructed on an even earlier Romano-British building (WSMR, 1975:001). During the same project, excavation at the rear of the Masonic Lodge, 15m south of Swindon House, also detected early medieval settlement deposits. Again demonstrating at least two phases of occupation, the excavators interpreted the structure as another *Grubenhäus* (WSMR, 1975:001, 5), although the identification of numerous postholes suggests that the feature is more likely a hall.

On the basis of recovered pottery, the excavators concluded that the structures were first occupied in the sixth century, with habitation perhaps persisting until the eighth or even early ninth centuries (WSMR, 1975:001, 4-6), although the wide date-range for locally-produced early medieval ceramics makes this interpretation somewhat speculative. The final phase of the Masonic Hall structure did, however, exhibit timber-slot construction, supporting the idea that at least this area of occupation was in use during the 'Middle Saxon' period (Ulmschneider 2011, 157-9). Early medieval settlement archaeology has also been excavated on the site of Lloyds Bank, 100m north of Swindon House where

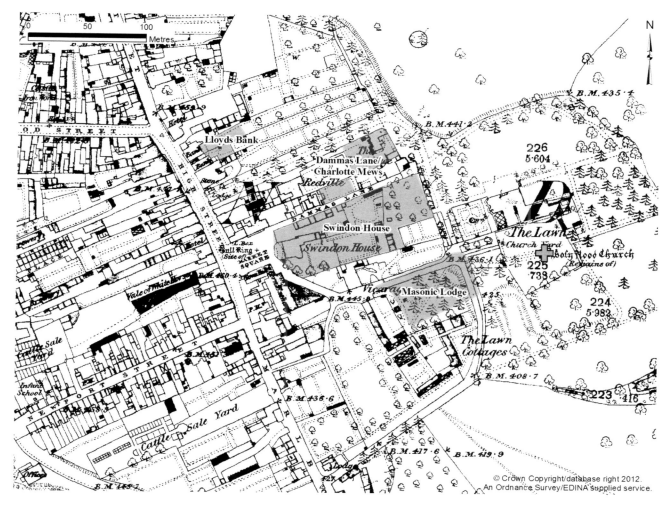

FIGURE 5.8: AREAS OF EXCAVATED AREAS IN SWINDON MENTIONED IN THE TEXT. THE CHURCH OF THE HOLY ROOD, LOCATED IN 'THE LAWN' TO THE EAST OF THE TOWN CENTRE, IS MARKED WITH A CROSS.

two *Grubenhäuser* were dug (Figure 5.8) (WSMR 1977: 049). Two small investigations between Dammas Lane and Charlotte Mews failed to detect structural features but did recover some finds relating to domestic activity of likely 'Middle Saxon' date (Butterworth and Seager Smith 1997).

It has previously been suggested that 'Middle Saxon' settlement in Swindon was concentrated in the area later occupied by a house known as The Lawn, roughly 100m east of the market square (WSMR, 1993:032). The grounds of the house feature the Church of the Holy Rood, first recorded in 1154, although only the chancel of the building remains standing. The chancel of the church was converted to form a chapel in 1852 for the Goddard Family, but before this date had served as the only parish church in Swindon since its establishment (*WSMR: SU18SE471*). The Ordnance Survey First Edition depicts the largely ruined church surrounded by a complex series of earthworks (Figure 5.8). These features may have been created by landscape gardening, but the consistent recovery of medieval ceramics from the area of the church makes it more likely that the earthworks represent earlier settlement remains (WSMR: SU18SE455). It is possible

that the church formed a similar role at an earlier date, although further excavation is required to determine whether the 'Middle Saxon' remains found closer to the medieval core extend further east.

The archaeological evidence for 'Middle Saxon' settlement from Swindon is not as comprehensive as many sites in Wiltshire, but nevertheless suggests that the ridge of high ground was occupied from as early as the sixth century. Although the Church of the Holy Rood is only first recorded in the twelfth century and features no indicators of earlier or exceptional status, its role as the parish church for Swindon and its position surrounded by probable medieval earthworks suggests that it formed a focal point for early settlement. Whether this activity represents a direct successor to that excavated close to the market square is not possible to say, but 'Middle Saxon' antecedents for the later town cannot be discounted. There is a chance that 'Middle Saxon' occupation was subject to short-range drift towards the area of the parish church in the 'Late Saxon' or medieval periods, in a two stage process of settlement nucleation. A similar process has already been demonstrated by this book, in locations such as Warmington, Northamptonshire and Yarnton,

Oxfordshire (Chapter III and IV), but further excavation is certainly required in order to supplement the somewhat slight evidence. The possibility of a 'Middle Saxon' origin for Swindon is nevertheless consistent with the archaeological evidence from other regions in Wiltshire, such as the Marlborough Downs which also possesses settlements with apparently similarly early antecedents.

The Marlborough Downs

The Marlborough Downs is the most northerly of Wiltshire's chalk landscapes, the historic settlement pattern of which has largely been shaped by the regional river network. Later medieval occupation was most dense in valley locations where farmsteads were tightly coalesced, but outside of these areas some dispersed villages and hamlets did occupy the quickly-draining uplands (Draper 2006, 5). Rivers appear to have also been influential in the pre-Conquest period; substantial 'Middle Saxon' remains have been identified at two sites adjacent to the most substantial watercourse of the *pays*, the River Kennet. Located on the northern bank of the Kennet, the village of Ramsbury lies approximately 8km to the east of Marlborough. The geology of the Ramsbury area is typical of a downland river valley, with Upper Chalk on the high ground and river gravels and alluvium in the basin of the Kennet itself. Ramsbury village is situated on a thin layer of gravelly sediment that is underlain by bedrock of Upper Chalk (English Heritage EUS Ramsbury 2004, 3).

Modern Ramsbury is a relatively small village, despite being subject to an Extensive Urban Survey by English Heritage, and the first mention of a market centre here is during the thirteenth century (EH EUS Ramsbury 2004, 6; Haslam 1984, 97). The chief interest of Ramsbury in the historic period lies in its choice, together with Wells and Crediton, as the seat of one of the newly created Bishoprics of the West Saxons in 909 (Brooks 1984, 278-9). The development of Ramsbury as an ecclesiastical centre from the tenth century is also evidenced archaeologically; alterations to the present parish church of the Holy Cross in the late nineteenth century identified 'Late Saxon' carved stone fragments incorporated into the fabric of the church, strengthening the existing theory that the church lies on the site of a predecessor of at least tenth-century date (Haslam 1980, 1). Archaeological investigation has demonstrated, though, that it is unlikely that the see was created at a *de novo* site in the tenth century, and it seems instead that Ramsbury was already an important centre by the 'Middle Saxon' period.

Identification of cross shaft fragments in the parish church, one of which dates to *c*.800, is the most recent hint of a potential 'Middle Saxon' centre at Ramsbury before the establishment of the see (Bailey 1996, 22; English Heritage EUS Ramsbury 2004, 3-5), but the most significant remains were found during excavations in the 1970s (Haslam 1980). Following demolition of nineteenth century houses along the northern edge of Ramsbury High Street, a team led by Jeremy Haslam undertook excavation as part of research into the early urban sites of Wiltshire (Figure 5.9). Investigation revealed an iron smelting and smithing site, comprising a series of four bowl furnaces, a number of forges or hearths, and a timber-framed shelter, all of which demonstrated three clear phases of use. It is unlikely that excavation uncovered the entire working area of industrial activity, as accumulation of debris in the north-west corner of the site suggested that further deposits lay beyond the investigated area. A combination of artefactual and radiocarbon dating suggested that the complex was in use during the eighth and early ninth centuries, with the final phase of activity sealed by a 'Late Saxon' occupation layer and subsequent medieval activity (Haslam 1980, 45-55).

The iron ore processed at Ramsbury seems to have been imported a significant distance, probably from a source at Seend, near Melksham, some thirty kilometres from the site (Haslam 1980, 56-7). Provision of raw material over such significant distances represents control of a sophisticated transport infrastructure and a degree of organisation not always associated with 'Middle Saxon' communities. The site at Ramsbury is not alone in illustrating an increasingly sophisticated approach toward economic specialisation in the Wessex region from the eighth century, however. Archaeomagnetic dating of probable corn drying ovens at Gillingham produced a date centring on the eighth century (Heaton 1992) and dendrochronology from a possible mill structure filled with slag and furnace residues at Worgret suggest they were deposited *c*.664-709 (Hinton 1992). Identification of furnace sites is therefore almost becoming a pattern in the region, and complements the national picture of the 'Middle Saxon' period as a time of fundamental social and economic change, reflected in technological and infrastructural developments (Chapter VIII; Hinton 1994, 35).

The recognition of specialised industrial processing suggests that Ramsbury was an important centre from at least the eighth century, and as the excavators have convincingly argued, probably the site of a *villa regalis* served by a minster church (Haslam 1980, 64). Both Ramsbury and Great Bedwyn, located 8km to the south, preserve characteristics of estate and minster foci in their later administrative organisation, situated at the centre of large estates with various dependant chapels. The entry for Ramsbury in Domesday Book, for instance, outlines ownership of a huge 90 hide estate, representing the second largest non-royal holding in Wiltshire at the time (English Heritage EUS Ramsbury 2004, 5).

The OE -*burh* element in Ramsbury also supports the case for a 'Middle Saxon' elite site. Although the usage and meaning of the element changed significantly over time, the work of Simon Draper has shown the consistency with which 'Middle Saxon' -*burh* names can be associated with pre-Viking church centres (Draper 2011, 99-103). Although not recorded in the Burghal Hidage, the foundation of the tenth-century see at Ramsbury demonstrates its continued social and administrative importance into the 'Late

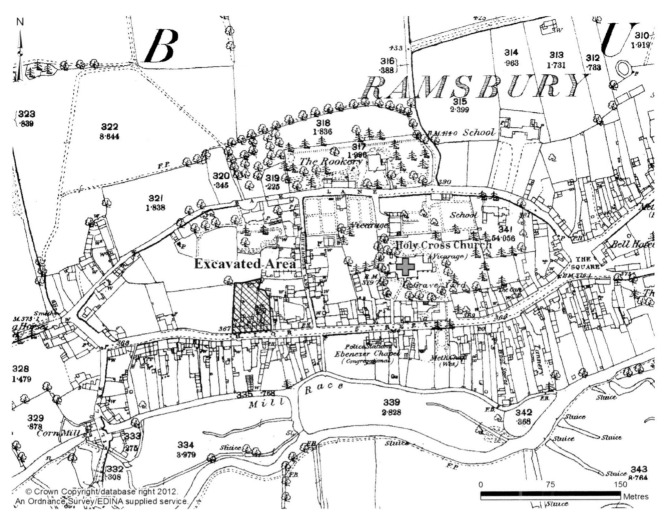

FIGURE 5.9: OS First Edition of Ramsbury, showing the excavated area in which the 'Middle Saxon' industrial centre was found, situated 150m west of the Holy Cross Church. Late eighth-century carving has been identified in the church, supporting the possibility that Ramsbury was the site of a high-status 'Middle Saxon' centre.

Saxon' period. This lasting significance was clearly based on earlier foundations, however, as the archaeological material indicates the presence of a significant centre by the eighth century. Indeed, the elliptical street-plan of Ramsbury is comparable with other important 'Middle Saxon' centres with minster churches and *burh* suffixes in the Wessex region. In addition to Kentbury in Berkshire, the village of Avebury also located in the Marlborough Downs presents evidence of a street pattern which perhaps preserves a much earlier arrangement (Figure 5.10) (Pollard and Reynolds 2002, 102).

Located on the western edge of the *pays* roughly 10km west of Marlborough, Avebury stands at the headwaters of the River Kennet in one of the most fertile valleys in northern Wiltshire. The village is famous for its great Neolithic henge, situated in a remarkably well-preserved prehistoric landscape that includes Silbury Hill and West Kennet Long barrow, 1.5km to the south-east (Malone 1989, 12-13). Celebrated for its prehistoric monuments, the early medieval heritage of Avebury is also unique: it is the only place in Wiltshire for which both excavated and standing

structural evidence for early medieval settlement has been recognised. Several archaeological fieldwork projects in and around the village have identified evidence for pre-Conquest activity, usefully synthesised and published by Joshua Pollard and Andrew Reynolds (2002).

Amongst the first archaeological interventions in the village were a series of limited excavations in the area now occupied by the visitors' car park, beginning in the 1970s, which produced evidence for a dispersed pattern of 'Early Saxon' settlement (Figure 5.11) (WSMR: 1976:13). At some point in the eighth or early ninth century, however, the location and character of settlement in the area underwent a distinct change. Excavations at the site of a local school and in agricultural land known as Butler's Field to the west of the present village, demonstrate a shift in occupation northwards in the late eighth or early ninth centuries (Figure 5.11) (WSMR: 1993:47). Investigations at the 'School Site' revealed a series of three curvilinear enclosures within which two buildings were identified. Initial occupation in this area was dated by radiocarbon analysis to between the late eighth and early ninth centuries

91

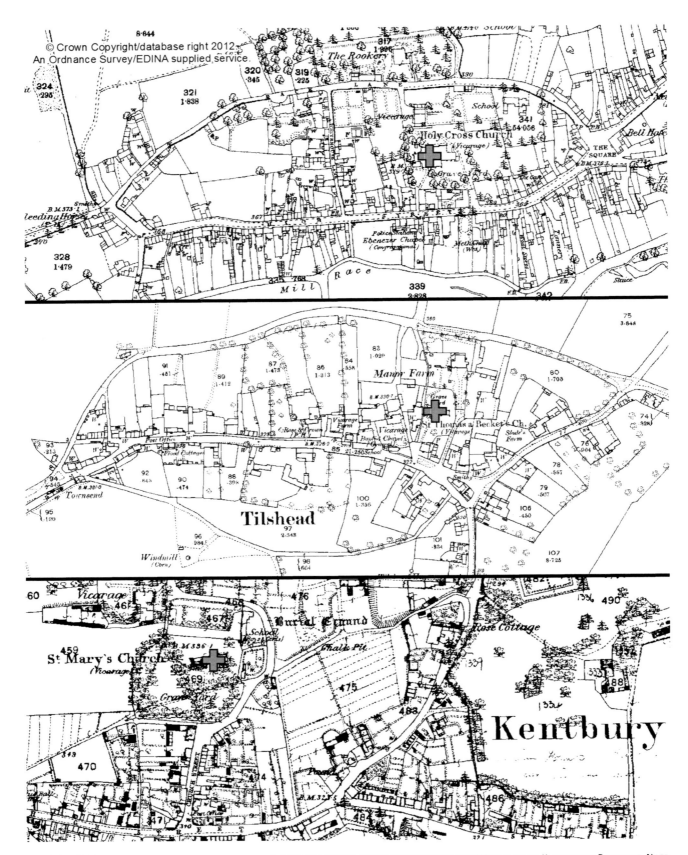

FIGURE 5.10: ELLIPTICAL STREET-PLANS OF BURH PLACES IN THE WESSEX REGION: RAMSBURY AND TILSHEAD IN WILTSHIRE AND KENTBURY IN BERKSHIRE. NOTE THE LOCATION OF THE PARISH CHURCHES IN OR ADJACENT TO THE ENCLOSURE FORMED BY THE STREET-PLAN. ALTHOUGH 'MIDDLE SAXON' MATERIAL HAS ONLY BEEN FOUND AT RAMSBURY, THE TOPOGRAPHY IN PARTICULAR SUGGEST THAT TILSHEAD AND KENTBURY MAY ALSO HAVE BEEN SIGNIFICANT DURING THE EARLY MEDIEVAL PERIOD (AFTER REYNOLDS AND POLLARD 2002, FIGURE 89).

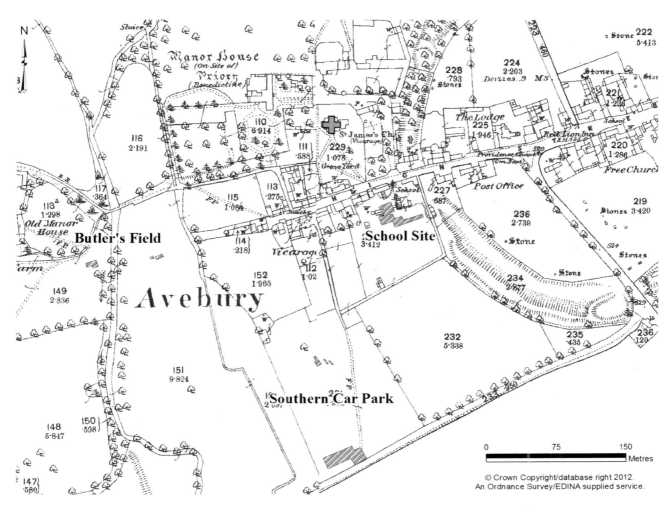

FIGURE 5.11: OS FIRST EDITION OF AVEBURY WITH EXCAVATED AREAS (SHADED) AND PARISH CHURCH OF ST JAMES' (CROSS). THE 'EARLY SAXON' OCCUPATION IN THE SOUTHERN CAR PARK WAS SUCCEEDED IN THE EIGHTH OR NINTH CENTURY BY RELOCATION FURTHER NORTH. 'MIDDLE SAXON' SETTLEMENT WAS IN TURN SUPERSEDED BY A RESTRUCTURING IN THE 'LATE SAXON' PERIOD TO FORM THE HISTORIC VILLAGE PLAN.

(WSMR: 1969:9). The extent of the 'Middle Saxon' enclosure arrangement beyond the 'School Site' was confirmed by a Royal Commission (RCHME) measured survey, which detected a series of complex earthworks surrounding Avebury village. Underlying, and therefore preceding, the present rectilinear tenement arrangement which possibly represents the remains of *burh* defences (see below), the RCHME survey noted an alternative series of earthworks which broadly correspond to the boundary ditches excavated at the School Site (RCHME Field Investigation, Avebury: 01-SEP-1991).

The evidence from the School Site and measured survey indicate that 'Middle Saxon' activity at Avebury was likely characterised by a large settlement structured around a series of large enclosures, with an elliptical street plan at its core (Pollard and Reynolds 2002, 198). The results from the Butler's Field excavations, although less impressive, suggest that the area of settlement also extended west of the area occupied by the medieval village. No structural evidence was found in Butler's Filed, but domestic artefacts and deposits attributed a broad *c*.800-1200 by radiocarbon dating were recovered (WSMR: 1993:47). Pollard and Reynolds (2002, 204-5) have suggested that in

the 'Late Saxon' period Avebury was developed as a *burh*, with a sub-rectangular enclosure surrounding regular plots of land perpendicular to the street. Draper (2006, 2011) has challenged the place-name interpretation on which this model is based, however, and instead suggests that OE -*burh* is not specific to fortification but instead refers to any type of enclosed settlement. Irrespective of the meaning of the place-name, 'Late Saxon' Avebury certainly appears to have undergone settlement reorganisation. Not only have differing enclosure networks been demonstrated by the RCHME survey, but the location of the excavated 'Middle Saxon' settlement material is clearly slightly removed from the current, and presumably 'Late Saxon', village focus.

From an 'Early Saxon' pattern of dispersed settlement, distinct from the location of the prehistoric monument, occupation at Avebury in the eighth and early ninth centuries shifted towards the line of a likely *herepað*, the route of which passed through the henge (Figure 5.12) (Pollard and Reynolds 2002, 187-91). This 'Middle Saxon activity' did not mark the end of settlement migration, or formalisation of the historic tenement pattern, however. Rather, the evidence from Avebury again demonstrates a 'two-stage' process of village creation,

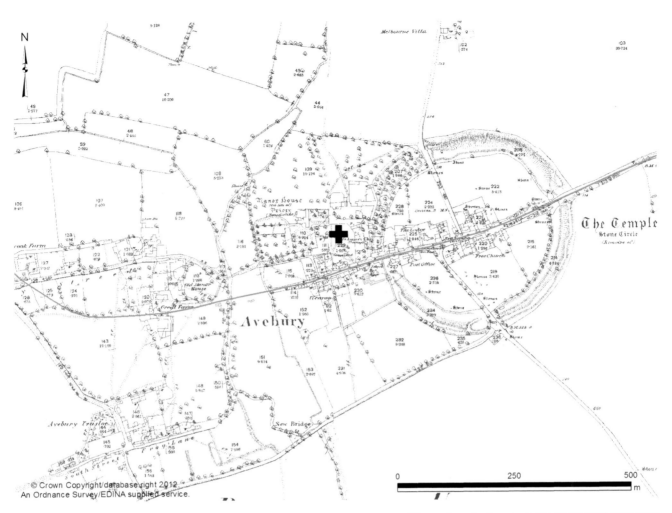

FIGURE 5.12: THE VILLAGE OF AVEBURY WITH LOCATIONS OF EXCAVATIONS THAT HAVE IDENTIFIED 'MIDDLE SAXON' SETTLEMENT REMAINS (SHADED), THE PARISH CHURCH OF ST JAMES (CROSS) AND THE LIKELY ROUTE OF THE LONG-DISTANCE HEREPAÐ (SOLID LINE). THE ROUTE, WHICH RUNS BETWEEN YATESBURY AND A ROMAN ROAD RUNNING NORTH OF MILDENHALL, HAS BEEN RECONSTRUCTED BY ANDREW REYNOLDS USING VARIOUS SOURCES OF EVIDENCE (REYNOLDS 1995; REYNOLDS AND POLLARD 2002, 224-6). NOTE HOW 'MIDDLE SAXON' SETTLEMENT IS LOCATED ALONG THE SOUTHERN EDGE OF THE HEREPAÐ, BUT IT WAS ONLY LATER THAT THE FINAL VILLAGE FORM OF AVEBURY, ARRANGED ON BOTH SIDES OF THE THOROUGHFARE, WAS CREATED.

with crystallisation of the property and street arrangement only occurring in the 'Late Saxon' period following initial 'Middle Saxon' 'nucleation' around what would later become part of a medieval long-distance routeway. The most enigmatic question regarding the eighth-century landscape restructuring around Avebury, remains whether development was influenced by the presence of an ecclesiastical community (Pollard and Reynolds 2002, 202). Domesday Book records a church along with two hides, which evidence, together with identifiable tenth century fabric, suggests that the parish church of St James was a minster by at least the 'Late Saxon' period, although no evidence for an earlier centre has yet been identified (Blair 1985, 108).

Without further excavation in and around Avebury village, the question of whether 'Middle Saxon' occupation was influenced by a new church will remain unanswered. Whether an early minster was located at Avebury or not, it is nevertheless clear that the period around the eighth century marked a watershed moment in the development of

local settlement and landscape character. 'Middle Saxon' settlement was marked by a previously unprecedented approach to habitation, characterised by semi-permanent and structured occupation, around an important long-distance route. Such changes represent the first part of a two-stage process of early medieval settlement development at Avebury, as at some point during the 'Late Saxon' period the existing village underwent a restructuring of tenement plots arranged more coherently around the historic herepað. It is during this period that 'village elements' can be viewed more acutely, with the herepað emerging as the High Street, together with the church, and probably a manor.

The evidence from Avebury therefore indicates again the extent and significance of settlement and landscape change in the Marlborough Downs around the eighth century. Given the significance that is usually placed on the creation of defended burh places in the 'Late Saxon' period, the evidence presented here unquestionably indicates that the importance of antecedent centres has been overlooked. The excavated evidence from Ramsbury has led Haslam (1980, 64) to suggest that the origins of 'Late Saxon' urban centres in the Wessex region should not automatically be attributed to royal foundation of newly-founded sites. Rather, he points out that the growth of some towns may have occurred through gradual development of functions, perhaps under royal patronage, that may have already characterised extant centres, as illustrated at Ramsbury and Avebury (Haslam 1980, 64; Haslam 1984, 97-8). At Ramsbury, as also seen at Malmesbury, the presence of a high-status institution could also have been of value in providing a stimulus for settlement from the 'Middle Saxon' period onward. It is possible that a church afforded a similar focus at Avebury, where the approach to habitation around fixed tenement plots from the eighth century can be seen most clearly.

Where centres like Ramsbury and Great Bedwyn differ from Malmesbury though, in that they were not developed as *burhs* in the 'Late Saxon' period. Rather, in the Marlborough Downs *pays*, the hillfort of Chisbury, 1.5km north of Great Bedwyn, and probably Marlborough were developed as part of the network of central places by the kings of Wessex. Draper has somewhat unconvincingly argued that Chisbury was an existing 'Middle Saxon' centre, although his similar assertion for Marlborough is more persuasive (Draper 2006). The 'Kingsbury' street name in the eastern part of Marlborough is also found in two other of Wiltshire's early medieval towns, at Calne and Wilton, with early medieval finds made at the latter supporting the likelihood of an earlier centre (see below) (Draper 2006, 150). Avebury, too, may have been intended as a defensible economic and social centre which did not develop as successfully as nearby Marlborough, although this understanding is largely based on a disputed place-name interpretation (Reynolds and Pollard 2002, 204-5; cf. Draper 2006, 152-4). The clear pattern recognisable both from the Cotswolds and the Marlborough Downs, of significant 'Late Saxon' and medieval centres featuring 'Middle Saxon' antecedents, is also replicated in southern Wiltshire, where the seventh to ninth century period can also be seen as one of fundamental and lasting change.

Salisbury Plain and South Wiltshire

Separated from the Marlborough Downs by the fertile Vale of Pewsey, Salisbury Plain and South Wiltshire comprises a vast downland, although with variations in the consistency and character of underlying chalk. Two locations in the *pays* have been subject to substantial archaeological investigation that have identified 'Middle Saxon' settlement remains, at Collingbourne Ducis and Market Lavington, but piecemeal evidence has also been found elsewhere. Together this material contributes to our understanding of 'Middle Saxon' southern Wiltshire, and emphasises that the landscape of the southern part of the county was also subject to considerable changes between the seventh and ninth centuries. The modern village of Collingbourne Ducis is located alongside the River Bourne in the north-eastern part of Salisbury Plain, approximately

12km south-east of Pewsey. Excavation at a site located to the east of the High Street in the late 1990s revealed evidence for 'Middle Saxon' settlement (Figure 5.13) (Pine 2001). Occupation on Cadley Road was focussed at the interface between the chalk bedrock and river gravels. The main features identified across the 80m x 25m excavated area included ten *Grubenhäuser*, a possible post-built structure and isolated pits and postholes. Finds were mostly restricted to the *Grubenhäuser*, but included an eclectic range of quotidian objects, the most elaborate of which was a bone pin made from walrus ivory. Crucially, a series of four radiocarbon dates were recovered from the site, demonstrating that most of the excavated features dated between the eighth and tenth centuries. One slightly earlier structure was dated between the seventh and ninth centuries, suggesting that more extensive preceding settlement may have been located to the north and west (Pine 2001, 110-114).

It is significant that the migration of early medieval settlement around Collingbourne Ducis appears to have been limited to the stretch of the Bourne valley in which the modern village is also situated (Pine 2001, 115). The restricted area in which early medieval activity was focussed is also demonstrated by the close proximity of settlement to a contemporary cemetery. Sixth and seventh century burials have been identified approximately150m north-east of the excavated settlement by two separate interventions: in 1974 and 2007 (Figure 5.13) (Gingell 1978; Pine 2001). The absence of 'Middle Saxon' or later property boundaries at Collingbourne Ducis is disappointing, providing little insight on how changing tenurial arrangements influenced the formation of the medieval and later village. The location of 'Middle Saxon' settlement slightly removed from the focus of the subsequent focus nevertheless highlights the possibility of a two-stage process of village creation, but without further investigation any conclusions remain provisional.

Collingbourne Ducis has been identified as a probable minster and royal estate centre on the basis of the archaeological deposits identified and some slight documentary material, yet the case for a 'Middle Saxon' high-status settlement is not as straightforward as has often been asserted. The earliest written reference to Collingbourne Ducis is often cited as the charter of 903 (S.370), which details the granting of fifty hides of land at Collingbourne to New Minster, Winchester. The charter is almost certainly a later forgery, however, and may have been created as late as the fourteenth century (Rumble 2001, 231). The first reliable written reference to the area is therefore found in Domesday Book, where the manor of 'Collingbourne' is listed under royal ownership, hinting that it may have formed part of an earlier estate. It appears unlikely that Collingbourne was a 'Middle Saxon' estate centre, however, as Domesday Book also records that the derelict church was held by Gerald, a priest of the minster at Wilton in 1086, making it more probable Collingbourne was the site of a 'new' or 'secondary' minster (Pitt 1999, 60; 2003; Blair 2005).

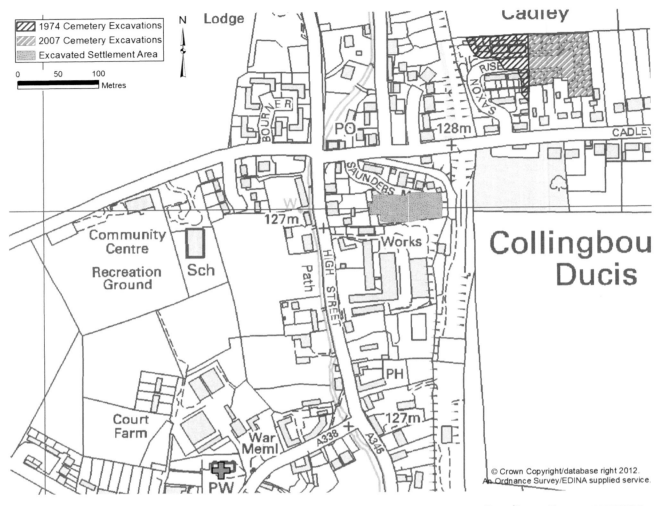

FIGURE 5.13: OS FIRST EDITION SHOWING THE EXCAVATED SETTLEMENT AND CEMETERY AREAS AT COLLINGBOURNE DUCIS/CADLEY. NOTE CLOSE PROXIMITY BETWEEN 'MIDDLE SAXON' CEMETERY AND SETTLEMENT, AND THE PARISH CHURCH LOCATED TO THE SOUTH-WEST. THE RE-FOCUSSING OF COLLINGBOURNE'S OCCUPATION CENTRE PROBABLY CAME IN THE 'LATE SAXON' PERIOD WHEN A DEPENDENT OR 'SECONDARY' MINSTER WAS ESTABLISHED.

Jonathan Pitt (1999) has demonstrated that in Wiltshire during the tenth century, existing minster territories were reshaped into a system of hundredal mother-parishes. Within this overarching framework, new parishes were carved out by major landlords wishing to found private churches, further diversifying the character of landscape organisation and church endowment throughout the tenth and eleventh centuries (Pitt 1999, 58-70). The church recorded at Collingbourne thus probably represents a thegnly establishment founded during the 'Late Saxon' period, with documentation in 1086 as a dependency of Wilton underlining its secondary status. Patronage of churches in Wiltshire throughout the tenth and eleventh centuries reflects the unique conditions of the Wessex region during the period, as the concentration of royal landholding and the power of the minster at Winchester in particular created an environment in which religious houses and dependencies continued to be established when most of the country was subject to a widespread contraction of investment (Blair 2005, 301). The power of an increasingly extensive secular elite is also reflected in the growth of manorial complexes; previously the preserve of bishops and kings, by the tenth century the ownership of

a *burh-geat* was also one of the trappings associated with thegnly status (Whitelock 1979, 468-71). Whilst the church and manor house (known as Court Farm) at Collingbourne Ducis are located within a series of irregular enclosures in the centre of the village, the OS First edition shows the majority of historic tenements arranged perpendicular to the High Street. The 'Late Saxon' private church was thus established within an existing 'Middle Saxon' focus, but the same lordly influence is likely to have been responsible for the restructuring of settlement around this time, which resulted in the form of the medieval and later village.

The OS First edition also makes it clear that Collingbourne Ducis is only one of several settlement foci within a small area of the Bourne Valley, with the hamlets of Cadley and Sunton situated within 500m north of the parish church (Figure 5.14). Simon Draper (2011, 103) has shown how manorial enclosures within areas of polyfocal settlement in Wiltshire are often associated with 'Burton' or 'Bourton' place-names. In the chalk downlands of Salisbury Plain and South Wiltshire in particular, the term appears to have been used to denote the hamlet within a wider grouping where the manorial *curia* was located. The *burh* place-name

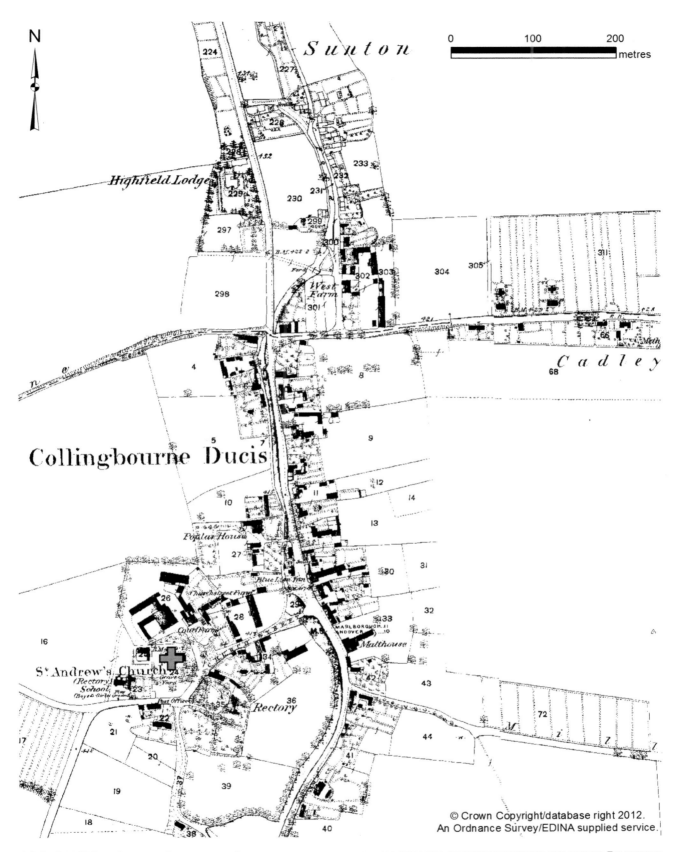

FIGURE 5.14 OS FIRST EDITION OF COLLINGBOURNE DUCIS, DEMONSTRATING THE DISPERSED CHARACTER OF THE HISTORIC SETTLEMENT PATTERN. THE MODERN VILLAGE ACTUALLY COMPRISES THE HISTORIC CENTRES OF CADLEY, SUNTON AND COLLINGBOURNE.

element is lacking at Collingbourne Ducis, but is present elsewhere on the plain at Shrewton and Codford St Peter. At Shrewton, 15km to the south-west of Collingbourne Ducis, Bourton comprises one of eight distinct hamlets which comprise the current village. The parish church in the village of Codford St Peter, located a further 12km to the south-west, situated within an irregular churchyard called 'The Bury', also suggests the fossilisation of an earlier enclosure (Figure 5.15) (Draper 2006, 99).

It has also been argued that the enclosure in the village of Bourton, located within Bishops Canning parish in the Vale of Pewsey, also preserves an earlier enclosure (Draper 2006, 144; 2011, 103). Bourton is situated 500m north-west of the parish church and episcopal estate centre of Bishops Cannings (Figure 5.15). The potential of 'Burton' enclosures forming foci for settlement outside of the Salisbury and South Wiltshire *pays* is supported by the presence of a church and manorial settlement at the village of Burton, within Nettleton parish in the Cotswolds (Draper 2011, 103). The establishment of polyfocal settlement centres by the medieval period, especially in the chalklands of southern Wiltshire, is probably due to the limited access to river valleys. Rivers not only provided access to water within an otherwise fast-draining landscape, but were also essential in giving access to resources such as meadowland. At Collingbourne Ducis, the restricted character of occupation is a good indicator that physical conditions were similarly important in shaping 'Middle Saxon' settlement and land use, a hypothesis supported by the results from the other significant excavation on Salisbury Plain with relevance to this book, at Market Lavington.

Market Lavington is situated under the northwest scarp of the chalk massif of Salisbury Plain, approximately seven kilometres south of Devizes. The village is actually located upon a small ridge of Upper Greensand, overlooking the Gault Clay lowlands of the Vale of Pewsey to the north, but the parish also extends onto the Upper Chalk (Williams and Newman 2006, 1). The interface between the chalk and greensand has proved an attractive zone for settlement throughout the historic period, offering access to a mixed resource base and numerous freshwater springs. Market Lavington is first recorded as *Laventone* in Domesday Book, but the OE –*ingas*, 'people of', element in the place-name hints at possible earlier significance (Gover 1939, 240). The centre was split into the two manors of Market Lavington and West Lavington in the late eleventh or early twelfth century, and located at the meeting point of two historic routeways, both prospered throughout the medieval period. Today, Market Lavington and West Lavington are almost contiguous, but clearly originated as separate foci and maintain something of their distinctive identities.

For the purposes of this study, Market Lavington's significance lies in the results of excavations undertaken during the 1990s. Investigation at Grove Farm, immediately north of the graveyard of the parish church

of St. Mary, identified one of the most substantial early medieval settlement sites found in Wiltshire. Initial geophysical survey and evaluation trenches demonstrated the high archaeological potential of the site, and identified the remains of a Romano-British building and a number of early medieval ditched features. These investigations provided the basis for more extensive excavation of three further areas (Areas A, B and C) which revealed more conclusively the existence of an early medieval settlement, together with a broadly contemporary cemetery on the site of an earlier Romano-British structure (Figure 5.16). The evidence for settlement comprised three *Grubenhäuser* and partial evidence for a post-built structure, probably a hall. Only one structural feature, a linear ditch (13748) likely representing the remains of a timber structure, was assigned a tentative 'Middle Saxon' date on the basis of ceramic phasing, and it appears instead that the occupation of the site was concentrated between the fifth and seventh centuries.

The cemetery appears to have been broadly contemporary with the settlement, but was probably utilised most intensively during the fifth and sixth centuries. It is therefore probable that the excavated settlement at Grove Farm outlived the use of the cemetery, although the recovery of unstratified seventh century grave-goods suggests that subsequent burials are located to the north and west. Following a dearth of activity during the eighth and ninth centuries, the excavated area was again occupied in the tenth century, when boundary ditches were constructed to form a series plots. An earlier boundary ditch, which may have remained in use during the eighth and ninth centuries, was also reused in this 'Late Saxon' phase (Williams and Newman 2006, 12-22). The feature possibly formed a northern boundary for settlement throughout the early medieval period, and was supplemented by a north-south ditch in the tenth century.

The excavations at Grove Farm present early medieval settlement archaeology of unparalleled detail from a currently-occupied rural settlement in Wiltshire. Activity was delineated to the north by a boundary ditch, but the lack of further demarcation in other directions suggests that excavation explored only a small percentage of the complex. The distribution of excavated features also strongly implies that further activity is present particularly to the south of the site, toward the area of the medieval parish church. The dearth of eighth and ninth century settlement deposits is significant though, and suggests that the focus of occupation moved away from the excavated area during this period. In a similar pattern to that recognised at sites elsewhere in Wiltshire such as Collingbourne Ducis and Avebury, it is probable that 'Middle Saxon' settlement at Market Lavington shifted towards the area of the later village. From this core, the tenement arrangement is likely to have undergone a restructuring in the tenth century. Occupation at this time was also expanded from its southerly focus, indicated in the excavated area by the presence of 'Late Saxon' boundary ditches. The tenth century settlement arrangement appears

FIGURE 5.15: EXAMPLES OF 'BURY' LOCATIONS WITHIN POLYFOCAL SETTLEMENT PATTERNS IN WILTSHIRE. BOURTON FARM IN SHREWTON (TOP), THE CHURCH ENCLOSURE KNOWN AS 'THE BURY' AT CODFORD ST PETER (MIDDLE), AND THE POSTULATED ENCLOSURE AT BOURTON, NEAR BISHOPS CANNING (BOTTOM) (AFTER DRAPER 2011, FIG 5.5).

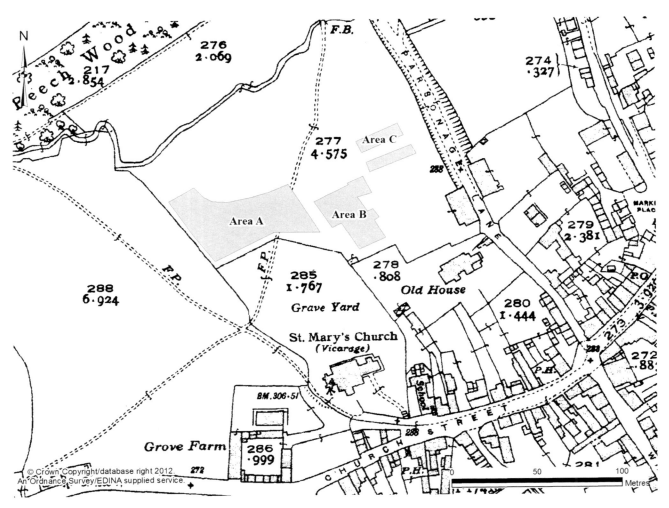

FIGURE 5.16: AREAS OF EXCAVATION AT MARKET LAVINGTON

decisive in developing the form of the historic village, as the excavated ditches clearly demonstrate a close correlation with the later street and property plan (Figure 5.17). It is tempting to suggest that the foundation of a church in its present location provided a focus for 'Middle Saxon' settlement, although there is currently no evidence for an ecclesiastical centre at Market Lavington during the early medieval period.

Whilst excavation of 'Middle Saxon' remains at Market Lavington was slight, the early medieval settlement sequence apparently conforms to an increasingly well-established pattern of development: a two-stage process of settlement change, demonstrated in this chapter at Avebury and Collingbourne Ducis. The three examples of this phenomenon in Wiltshire all come from chalkland landscapes, where physical conditions appear to have restricted the extent of occupation throughout the early medieval period. At Avebury and Collingbourne Ducis, habitation was concentrated around the local river network, and was probably also the case in other polyfocal settlement landscapes, such as Shrewton. At Market Lavington though, it was likely the proximity

to the springline that was decisive. Although the two-stage development in Wiltshire has only been identified in chalk downland *pays*, that it was not the preserve of such landscapes has already been demonstrated by this book. Similar processes were taking place, for example, at Warmington in the Nene Valley of Northamptonshire and in the Thames floodplain at Yarnton, Oxfordshire. Rather than geology, the consistent theme emerging from this corpus is their close proximity to water, particularly rivers and their floodplains. Whilst such an observation does not provide an explanation for 'Middle Saxon' settlement change, it serves as a reminder of the influence that physical conditions continued to have upon the character of occupation throughout the early medieval period.

A further notable aspect of the archaeological material from Market Lavington, is the absence from other sources suggesting the presence of an early medieval settlement in the area. This clearly highlights the potential of 'Middle Saxon' settlement archaeology in Wiltshire at places that have not been recognised as such by other forms of research. There are other examples in Wiltshire, however, where the opposite is true: where sources other than archaeology hint

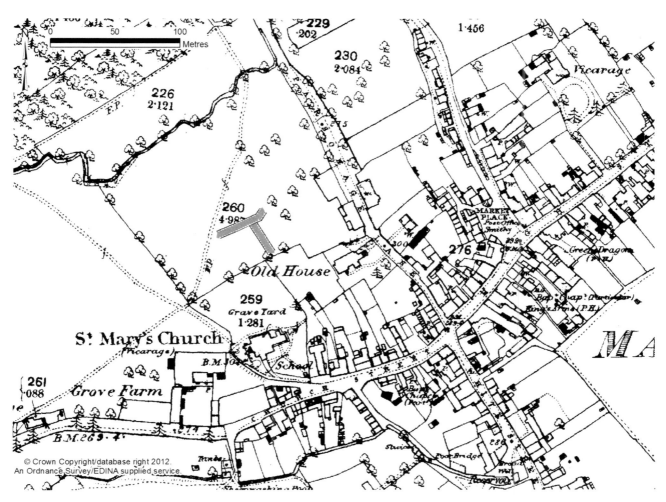

FIGURE 5.17: OS FIRST EDITION OF THE MARKET LAVINGTON, WITH 'LATE SAXON' DITCHES MARKED AS BROAD SOLID LINES. NOTE HOW THE ALIGNMENT OF THE EXCAVATED FEATURES BROADLY CORRESPONDS WITH THE ORIENTATION OF THE NINETEENTH CENTURY PATTERN OF PROPERTY BOUNDARIES AND STREETS. THE BOUNDARY DITCHES LIKELY REFLECT THE EXPANSION AND RESTRUCTURING OF AN EARLIER 'MIDDLE SAXON' FOCUS, LOCATED TO THE SOUTH OF THE EXCAVATED SITE.

at important 'Middle Saxon' sites, but which have not been confirmed through excavation. The previous county-town of Wilton, situated at the confluences of the River Wyle and Nadder on the southern edge of Salisbury Plain, provides a good case in point. The presence of Wilton in the county name is often cited as reflecting its early importance, as the centre possibly represented a tribute focus for the people of *Wiltunscire* (Yorke 1995, 87). Della Hooke (1994, 87-8; 1996, 85) has also reconstructed the estate pattern of the Wylye Valley in which Wilton is located and claims that it may have originated in the immediate post-Roman period. Although the use of 'Late Saxon' charters to reconstruct much earlier territorial arrangements is somewhat dubious, Hooke's work also emphasises the likely significance of Wilton and the Wylye Valley from at least the 'Middle Saxon' period.

In addition, later medieval sources from Wilton also attest to a new church foundation made by King Alfred. The earliest surviving pre-Conquest references to a religious house at Wilton date only from the tenth century, however, and it therefore appears most likely that the documents relating to an Alfredian foundation are a forgery, with

development of a house for religious women only occurring in the 'Late Saxon' period only (Foot 2000, 221-9). Indeed, the significance of Wilton from the eighth century, hinted at by research such as Hooke's (1996), also lacks backing from the archaeological record. One of the few significant finds from the modern town is a fifth-century hanging bowl, recovered from the market centre known as the Kingsbury. Even though Draper (2011, 101-2) has suggested that this name, together with the town topography, is indicative of a 'Middle Saxon' high-status centre, there is currently a striking dearth of archaeological material for a place which other sources hint may have been an important eighth-century and earlier site (Figure 5.18).

This situation at Wilton is paralleled in the Vale of Wardour, where archaeological evidence relating to the minster at Tisbury is similarly lacking. Contemporary documents relating to Tisbury minster are much earlier than those from Wilton, with a documented reference to the Abbot of Tisbury from the seventh century indicating that it was probably the second earliest monastic foundation in Wiltshire, after Malmesbury (S 239; Crowley 1987, 195;

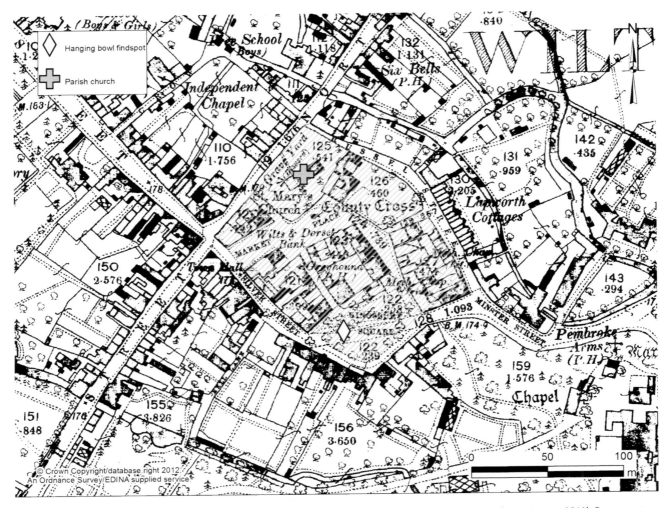

FIGURE 5.18: OS First Edition illustrating the topography of Wilton, with the area of a possible shaded (after Draper 2011). Despite the 'Kingsbury Square' name in the south-west part of the enclosure, the recovery of an 'Early Saxon' hanging bowl remains one of the few archaeological indicators for the importance of pre-Viking Wilton.

Kelly 1996, 107-14). The medieval settlement pattern in the parish, consistent with much of the Vale of Wardour, was one of isolated farmsteads, located in the narrow valley basins (Lewis 1994, 189). This wood-pasture landscape makes it difficult to carry out fieldwork, and is particularly poorly suited to fieldwalking, conditions which may partly account for the complete lack of archaeological evidence for the 'Middle Saxon' minster.

Wilton and Tisbury both provide useful cautionary case studies, and demonstrate the need for an interdisciplinary approach when researching the early medieval settlement and landscape of Wiltshire. Although this chapter has concentrated largely on the archaeological material from the county, other sources have contributed to provide a more comprehensive understanding of changing settlement conditions in the 'Middle Saxon' period. In the following discussion section which summarises the key deductions of the cumulative data outlined above, it is clear that despite some developments unique to Wiltshire, the 'Middle Saxon' period was a time of fundamental social and settlement change, reflecting conditions comparable to those already made apparent in other parts of England by this research.

SETTLEMENT AND SOCIETY IN 'MIDDLE SAXON' WILTSHIRE

For a county that is usually viewed as possessing little evidence for early medieval occupation (e.g. Lewis 1994), this chapter has underlined something of the scale and significance of 'Middle Saxon' settlement archaeology from Wiltshire. The relative neglect of archaeology in early medieval settlement studies in the county is partly due to the difficulties of interpreting the material evidence, in particular the lack of diagnostic and closely datable ceramics. Perhaps more crucially, however, the wealth of documentary material relating to pre-Conquest Wiltshire has traditionally drawn most scholarly focus. Such study has been productive, undoubtedly improving our comprehension of the early medieval landscape of Wiltshire (e.g. Pitt 2003). The significance of the archaeological material should not be undermined though, especially the contribution of material data in providing insights into the landscape of 'pre-*burh*' Wiltshire.

One of the most fundamental challenges when researching Wiltshire's early medieval settlement archaeology is the various contexts from which much of the material is

Interventions in 'CORS'	'CORS' interventions identifying archaeological deposits	'CORS' with 'Middle Saxon' artefactual material only	'CORS' with 'Middle Saxon' artefactual material and settlement structures from 'CORS'
17	12	3	3

Table 5.1: Only seventeen 'CORS' excavations have been undertaken in Wiltshire, although of this figure six investigations identified some form of 'Middle Saxon' activity. Collingbourne Ducis and Market Lavington represent two of the three excavations that identified structural remains for 'Middle Saxon' occupation.

derived. It is particularly notable that rather than featuring a large amount of evidence from currently-occupied rural settlements, a significant quantity of archaeological evidence in Wiltshire also comes from current urban contexts. As Table 5.1 illustrates, few currently-occupied villages in Wiltshire have been subject to excavation, especially in comparison with other counties investigated by this book. This is largely the result of the relative lack of development of rural places, as urban centres such as Swindon and Salisbury have experienced far more population growth and settlement expansion, and thus have been subject to more investigation. The outcome from these research conditions is that early medieval settlement history of Wiltshire has typically concentrated on the origins and development of 'Late Saxon' urban centres, particularly the much-celebrated system of *burhs*. This 'urban-centric' approach perpetuates the view that the 'Late Saxon' period marked the beginning of a time when the landscape of England was irreversibly transformed, a time during which most academics also attribute the roots of historic villages and fields (e.g. Lewis *et al.* 2001; Dyer 2003).

Whilst the lack of excavation in currently-occupied rural settlements clearly impinges on the breadth and detail of evidence available to the archaeologist, one of the notable positives from the lack of rural development is the preservation of historic village topographies. This chapter has illustrated interesting and potentially significant elements of currently-occupied village plans, demonstrating the excellent preservation of many Wiltshire village plans. The lack of archaeological investigation remains problematic, however, as intriguing topographical arrangements have rarely been subject to excavation which could potentially determine their date and sequence of development. Archaeological research of 'CORS' in Wiltshire therefore represents something of a double-edged sword, with the dearth of evidence from excavation somewhat softened by the preservation of village plans of possible historic significance. The archaeological research that has been undertaken in Wiltshire does, however, allow for some significant observations to be made regarding the central importance of the 'Middle Saxon' landscape.

One of the chief deductions of the presented evidence is that several places of recognised 'Late Saxon' and medieval importance in Wiltshire actually originated as centres in the 'Middle Saxon' period. The tenth-century see at Ramsbury was clearly established at an existing, high-status focus that boasted specialised industrial processing by the eighth century (Haslam 1980). At Avebury too, 'Late Saxon' settlement was characterised by a restructuring of earlier occupation (Reynolds and Pollard 2002). The interpretation of place-name evidence is of crucial importance here, as sites such as Avebury and Ramsbury contain the -*burh* suffix, yet are not viewed as part of the system of defensible places recorded in the tenth century Burghal Hidage. Although Reynolds and Pollard (2002, 204) have asserted that Avebury contains the element due to its role as an undocumented 'Late Saxon' fortified centre, Draper (2008) convincingly argues that the term refers to enclosures of various type and date, and should not be definitively associated with the network of tenth century defended sites. Irrespective of this interpretation, this chapter has made it clear that, as Haslam (1980, 64) has previously asserted, many 'Late Saxon' urban and other centres were clearly not wholly the result of royal establishment on *new* sites.

The countryside of 'Middle Saxon' Wiltshire also appears to have been a place of increasing industrial specialisation, most clearly illustrated by the excavated remains for metal processing at Ramsbury. Two similar industrial facilities, also first in use during the eighth century, have been excavated in Dorset suggesting expansion of the economic infrastructure of the Wessex region more generally at this time (e.g. Maddicott 1989). The import of raw materials for use at the Ramsbury site from at least thirty kilometres away, indicates the existence of a coordinated resource procurement and transport network. Unfortunately, the environmental remains from most settlements excavated in Wiltshire does not allow for assessment of whether such changes were associated with coterminous agricultural specialisation, but such economic developments are notable at rural sites elsewhere in England around the eighth century. At Yarnton in Oxfordshire, for instance, the eighth century marks a period of increased landscape exploitation, as the gravel terraces of the Thames were drained and used as water meadows, and the breadth of farming produce was diversified (Hey 2004, 46-8).

Despite the lack of environmental evidence, the changing structural character of settlements in the 'Middle Saxon' suggests that similar process were underway. At Avebury, shifting and dispersed 'Early Saxon' occupation was replaced around the eighth century by more permanent habitation, probably focussed upon the long-distance *herepað*. More lasting change appears to have been made in the 'Late Saxon' period, however, when settlement was restructured. Around the tenth century, a new arrangement of enclosures was introduced at Avebury, perpendicular to the *herepað* which later developed into the High Street. This two-stage process of village development, featuring a 'Middle Saxon' 'nucleation' phase succeeded by a 'Late Saxon' restructuring, is detectable elsewhere in Wiltshire. At Collingbourne Ducis and Market Lavington, earlier more ephemeral settlement was followed by a shift towards what would later become the medieval village. Only in the succeeding centuries, however, do recognisable village elements come more clearly into focus, as churches and manors become more clearly detectable amongst new tenurial arrangements.

The potential of churches performing a focal role for settlement in the period before the tenth century is illustrated by the excavated evidence from Malmesbury in the Cotswolds. Here, the likely early church developed within the circuit of an Iron Age hillfort, which also appears to have attracted settlement outside of its immediate precinct by the eighth century. The identification of a 'Middle Saxon' floor surface suggests that this activity was not sporadic or piecemeal, but likely arranged around its own network of paths and routeways. A church was also likely present at Ramsbury in the Marlborough Downs and possibly at Swindon on the Greensand Belt, but archaeological evidence for other 'Middle Saxon' ecclesiastical foci is disappointingly lacking. The potential for further significant 'Middle Saxon' church centres is highlighted by Wilton and Tisbury. Documentary and other sources hint that both places were important from at least the seventh century, although the archaeological evidence so far recovered is extremely slight.

The examples of Wilton and Tisbury make it clear that even where there are apparent gaps of 'Middle Saxon' settlement archaeology in Wiltshire, these are just as likely the result of research conditions as actual absence of activity in the period. Three *pays* in Wiltshire have produced little in the way of significant 'Middle Saxon' occupation remains; The Northern Clay Vale, The Vale of Pewsey and the Vale of Wardour. It is unlikely that the shared 'non-chalk' geological profile of these areas resulted in a lack of 'Middle Saxon' occupation, and if anything the preceding chapters have shown it is often lowland environments such as these in which we often see increased exploitation in the period (Chapter III and IV). Rather, the lack of archaeological investigation in such zones probably accounts for the paucity of activity detected in them, although the important minsters documented at Bishops Canning in the Vale of Pewsey and Tisbury in the Vale of Wardour emphasise the likelihood that such landscapes were equally settled and exploited.

There is also little to suggest an 'east-west' divide in the 'Middle Saxon' settlement of Wiltshire, as has been advocated by Roberts and Wrathmell (2000) in their study of the medieval landscape of England. This is probably because, whilst fundamental settlement and landscape changes were clearly underway around the eighth century, it was only in the succeeding centuries that the elements and arrangement of medieval villages as we now recognise them were more firmly crystallised. Explaining later medieval settlement form is not the primary aim of this book, however, and what is notable from the evidence presented here is that the 'Middle Saxon' landscape of Wiltshire underwent similar changes as those detected in Northamptonshire and Oxfordshire. Behind the increased industrial activity, the 'nucleation' and restructuring of settlement arrangements, and the development of occupation around new foci, were fundamental changes to the fabric of society. The rising power of an increasingly powerful elite class is likely to have been decisive, during a period in the social structure below the very upper elite goes largely undocumented. Whilst the charters and manorial enclosures of the 'Late Saxon' period are usually highlighted as evidence of a new thegnly class, the changing character of lordship is also likely a factor behind the changes apparent in the 'Middle Saxon' landscape.

CONCLUSION

This chapter has demonstrated the changing character of 'Middle Saxon' settlement in Wiltshire, indicative of developments in the social, political and economic makeup of communities, that impacted the wider rural landscape. Crucially, this chapter provides a narrative from outside of the intensively-researched midlands of England, and shows the value of archaeological evidence from Wiltshire that is generally neglected by scholarly study. It seems that even outside the 'champion' landscape of central England, comparable changes of settlement and land use were taking place between the seventh and ninth centuries. 'Middle Saxon' restructuring does not appear to have been decisive in shaping medieval settlement, as it was more often than not 'Late Saxon' reorganisation that determined the form of later villages. Rather, the results presented here provides more significant insights into the immediate 'Middle Saxon' historic context, suggesting that transformations in the expressions of lordship began to impact upon the Wiltshire countryside in the shape of changing settlement structure and unprecedented exploitation of the landscape. Although invisible to other sources, archaeology shows the increasing influence of elite lordship, suggesting origins of a gradually powerful thegnly class below the better-documented influence of royal authority.

Chapter VI
Cambridgeshire

For the penultimate county-based chapter of this book, the focus of research moves again to the east midlands, and to the county of Cambridgeshire. The topography of Cambridgeshire is most commonly divided in two, with the silt and peat fens that characterise north-west Norfolk and the Soke of Peterborough also extending across the northern half of the county, whilst further south, undulating terrain is formed by a combination of Boulder Clay, limestone and chalk geology. This bipartite division of the Cambridgeshire landscape is over simplistic, however, and this chapter will demonstrate how slight topographical variations have been critical in shaping historic settlement and land use across the county. During the early medieval period, the area that is now Cambridgeshire formed something of a frontier zone, with the fens in particular forming a natural barrier between the Mercians, East Angles, and to a lesser extent, the Anglians. This transitional character is perhaps most obviously manifest by the foundation of minsters by Mercian and East Anglian royal houses on either side of the wetlands, but in southern Cambridgeshire too there is evidence that the River Cam was used as a political boundary from the prehistoric period (Smith 1980, 36; Keynes 2003, 10-12).

Cambridgeshire is also a transitional district in terms of its medieval settlement character, featuring a mixture of village and field forms which have been the subject of significant scholarly interest. Roberts and Wrathmell's 'central province' extends only across the western portion of the county, with eastern Cambridgeshire more commonly characterised by small hamlets and isolated farmsteads dispersed across the countryside (Roberts and Wrathmell 2002). This mixture of historic settlement form has led to Cambridgeshire's regular use as a study area for early medieval landscape research. A number of studies have focussed solely on the archaeological evidence from Cambridgeshire (e.g. Oosthuizen 2006), but more frequently the county is integrated into works with a broader geographical remit (e.g. Williamson 2003). In spite of such research, early medieval settlement studies in Cambridgeshire remains contested ground, with continued debate regarding the processes and chronology of pre-Conquest landscape change. Scholars have particularly disagreed on the origins of 'nucleated' villages and common fields, and in a situation typical of national historic landscape research, the 'Middle Saxon' archaeology of the county has most commonly been deployed in order to explain later settlement forms. As such, the intrinsic potential of Cambridgeshire's 'Middle Saxon' settlement and landscape archaeology to inform us of contemporary social, economic and political conditions has for the most part been neglected.

This chapter will redress this imbalance in research by using Cambridgeshire's rich 'Middle Saxon' settlement archaeology, especially that derived from currently-occupied rural settlement excavations, to better understand the communities that inhabited them. It will be demonstrated that, paralleled with the counties already presented, the landscape of Cambridgeshire underwent a restructuring during the 'Middle Saxon' period, as the internal arrangement of settlements in particular underwent drastic development. This piece will first briefly introduce the historic county of Cambridgeshire as an area for study, after which its topographical *pays* will be defined. The 'Middle Saxon' settlement and landscape archaeology of the county will then be analysed, with discussion divided into topographical *pays*. It will be demonstrated that although Cambridgeshire does not feature a significant quantity of 'Middle Saxon' evidence from landscape-orientated projects, excavations within existing villages in the county have revealed especially important data for this study. This chapter will then close with a discussion of 'Middle Saxon' settlement archaeology in the county, and the way in which it improves our understanding of early medieval societies both in the region, and across the country.

INTRODUCING CAMBRIDGESHIRE

For the purposes of this research, the modern county of Cambridgeshire, as opposed to the historic extents, will be the subject of study, represents an area which includes the early medieval county of Huntingdonshire and the Isle of Ely. Despite being included within modern Cambridgeshire, the Soke of Peterborough does not form part of this chapter as it has historically been associated with Northamptonshire. As a consequence, the Northamptonshire Sites and Monuments Record holds all records relating to the Soke, and the area has therefore been investigated as part of the chapter on Northamptonshire (Chapter III). The Cambridgeshire Historic Environment Record (CHER), however, does hold data relating to Huntingdonshire and the Isle of Ely and these areas are consequently included within the current chapter. The combined study area of Cambridgeshire, Huntingdonshire and the Isle of Ely (hereafter simply Cambridgeshire) is often rather basically divided in half, between the 'uplands' of the southern part of the county and the 'lowland' fens of the north. Although south Cambridgeshire is an 'upland' area in comparison to the fens, maximum heights rarely exceed 120m OD and most of the area is considerably lower. The fens, however, are virtually flat with the whole region lying less than 10m OD, and some areas are actually situated below sea level (Taylor 1973, 23).

On closer inspection, however, the topography of Cambridgeshire is more varied than it first appears. Whereas there is no doubt that the fens are relentlessly flat, it is not an entirely homogenous landscape, but rather is formed by peat deposits to the south and silts further north. The peat of the Cambridgeshire fens in particular includes more durable geologies forming low islands, which have been crucial in shaping patterns of past human activity. Similarly the 'uplands' of southern Cambridgeshire do not possess a completely uniform geological profile, and comprise Boulder Clay, limestone and chalk which has resulted in subtle variations in soil makeup. Rather than a bipartite approach, this research has therefore divided modern Cambridgeshire into four distinct *pays*; topographical zones which will provide the framework for discussion of 'Middle Saxon' settlement and landscape archaeology of the county (Figure 6.1).

THE *PAYS* OF CAMBRIDGESHIRE

Siltlands

Occupying the northern extent of the county, the Siltlands are the smallest of the Cambridgeshire *pays*. The Siltlands are the product of regular tidal inundation from the North Sea, which resulted in the deposition of a complex series of silts and clays, extending around the Wash basin from Lincolnshire into Norfolk (Hall and Coles 1994, 1-3). Akin to other areas of the fens in eastern England, slight variations in topography have been crucial in shaping historic settlement character in the Siltlands. The former existence of tidal creeks has resulted in the development of low silt islands, known locally as roddons, which represented key areas of dry, cultivable land for early medieval communities. In Cambridgeshire, Wisbech emerged as an important centre by the end of the early medieval period, but settlement in the Siltlands does not appear to have been dense, especially when compared to similar landscapes around the Wash, such as the Marshland of Norfolk (Silvester 1988, 158). Documentary sources from the 'Late Saxon' period onward reveal the impact of industrious minsters exploiting the Siltlands for its mixture of natural resources. Indeed, by the end of the early medieval period, all of the Siltlands and most of the Peat Fen fell within the two hundreds of Ely Abbey, although the low population density and plough teams recorded in Domesday Book demonstrate that the far north of the county was not particularly settled even by the eleventh century (Darby 1952, 310-2). By contrast, the more varied geological profile of the Peat Fen had attracted a number of important settlement centres by the end of the pre-Conquest period.

The Peat Fen and its Islands

Bordering the Siltlands to the south, the Cambridgeshire Peat Fen and its Islands extends in a broad arc from the north-west to the south-east of the county. The peat beds were formed from the stilling of freshwater estuaries, following the earlier deposition of sands and gravels which now forms the bedrock of the *pays*. Following the receding of brackish water during the late Bronze Age, peat accumulated across the Cambridgeshire lowlands, except in the slightly raised Siltlands to the north. Peat growth remained uninterrupted until the area was drained in the seventeenth century, except in areas of freshwater pools or alluvial deposition (Hall 1996a, 6-7). Whilst for the most part an uncultivable landscape throughout the entire medieval period, accumulation of clays in particular led to the creation of islands in some areas. Reaching heights of up to 36m in Haddenham parish, most of the Cambridgeshire fen-islands are much more muted, ranging between 1m and 5m OD. By the 'Late Saxon' period, a number of the 'fen islands' had attracted significant settlements, most notably the minster located on the island of Ely, which supported a substantial population. Elsewhere, the islands featured more moderate communities by 1086, typically operating mixed farming regimes that were supplemented by thriving fishing and salt-working industries. Similar economies were operated by the numerous vills that had developed around the fen-edge by the end of the early medieval period, such as Fordham and Cottenham, whose Domesday entries clearly demonstrate the importance of fen resources (Darby 1952, 312-4).

Boulder Clay Plateau

Occupying south-west Cambridgeshire, the Boulder Clay Plateau is a gently undulating scarp and vale topography forming a subdued level plain, mostly situated around 50m OD but dropping to as low as 5m OD along the fen-edge. The *pays* is divided frequently by river valleys, most notably the broad valleys of the River Great Ouse and River Cam. The Boulder Clay Plateau, which is bordered by the Peat Fen to the north-east and the Cambridgeshire Heights to the south-west, is as the name suggests, formed by Boulder Clay but also features occasional outcrops of limestone and greensand. The resultant calcareous soils are very fertile, reflected in the dense population of the townships recorded in Domesday, even in comparison to other 'champion' districts elsewhere in central England (Darby 1952, 312; Williamson 2003, 72). Indeed, the *pays* delineates almost exactly the eastern extent of Robert and Wrathmell's 'central province' of nucleated settlements and common fields, and is a landscape which was for the most part dominated by villages and large hamlets by the end of the medieval period (Roberts and Wrathmell 2000, 31). In most places these nucleated settlements were farming regular two or three field systems by the thirteenth century, although the western third of the *pays* commonly had more divisions. Not all medieval occupation in the Ouse-Cam watershed was of 'nucleated' character, however, and abundant small hamlets and single farmsteads formed important 'daughter' settlements for larger centres (Taylor 1973, 77-80). A typical example of this kind of settlement pattern is the higher ground surrounding the Bourn Valley, where recent work indicates that key elements of the landscape may have begun to emerge before *c.* AD850 (Oosthuizen 2006).

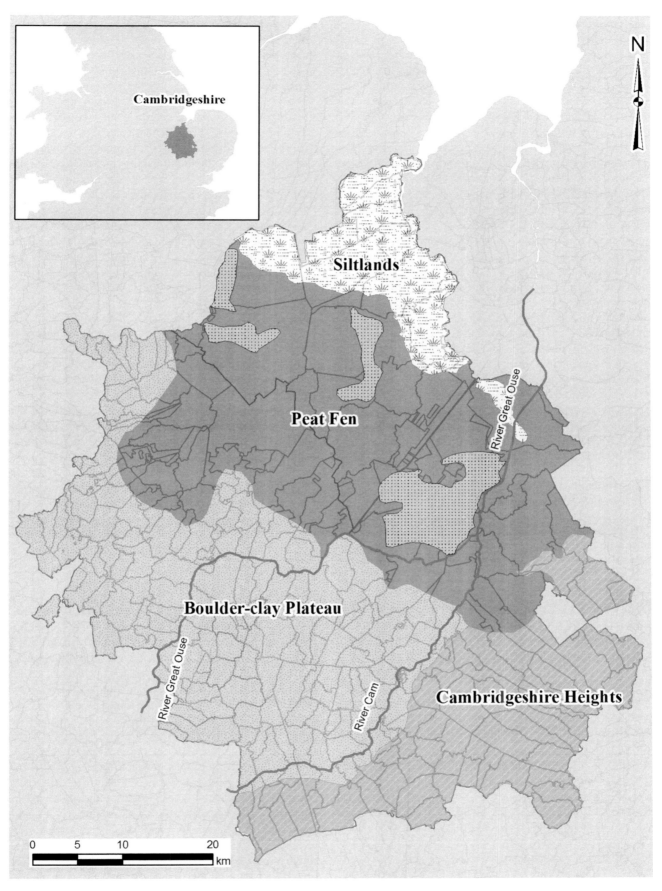

FIGURE 6.1: THE PAYS AND MAJOR RIVERS OF CAMBRIDGESHIRE. THE MAJOR FEN-ISLANDS ARE REPRESENTED BY THE STIPPLED SHADING. THE DIVISION OF THE COUNTY INTO FOUR TOPOGRAPHICAL ZONES BETTER-SUITS CAMBRIDGESHIRE'S TOPOGRAPHICAL VARIATION THAN A BIPARTITE APPROACH. SOURCE FOR MAPPING: HISTORIC PARISHES OF ENGLAND AND WALES ONLINE

The Cambridgeshire Heights

The Cambridgeshire Heights *pays* is formed by a belt of chalk and greensand which produces acid sands that gently rise southward from the valley of the River Cam. Framing the south of the county, the Cambridgeshire Heights vary in height from around 40m OD near the Cam Valley in the north, up to 120m in some isolated spots further south (Darby 1952, 312-3). The *pays* actually forms part of a more extensive area of upland known as the East Anglian Heights, a north-eastern continuation of the Chiltern escarpment. By 1086 settlements appears to have been fairly evenly distributed over the upland, though some parts of the chalk belt in particular remained sparsely populated. The Cambridgeshire Heights has been open, treeless landscape since prehistoric times and by the time of Domesday the area carried little woodland. 'Sheep-corn husbandry' characterised the economy of the *pays* until well into the post-medieval period, with large flocks of sheep systematically grazed on the downland acting as 'mobile muckspreaders' for the nutrient deficient soils (Darby 1952, 313; Williamson 2003, 79). The medieval field systems of the Cambridgeshire Heights was characterised by regular two or three field arrangements, although many exceptions where more numerous parcels were in use are apparent (Postgate 1964; Williamson 2003, 80).

EARLY MEDIEVAL CAMBRIDGESHIRE: A FRONTIER LANDSCAPE

The topographical variety of Cambridgeshire is likely to have played a significant role in the development of the region as a politically-disputed landscape during the 'Middle Saxon' period. Cambridgeshire was created as a territorial unit in 917 by Edward the Elder, who formed a new administrative framework straddling the Cam Valley following the West Saxon re-conquest of the eastern Danelaw (Oosthuizen 2001, 52). Perhaps deliberately, tenth century Cambridgeshire was developed from a far more ancient border territory between the major polities of Mercia and East Anglia. The distribution of coinage and hillforts located on the high ground surrounding the Cam, may indicate a frontier zone of greater antiquity, possibly forming the border between the Iceni to the east, the Trinovantes in the south-east, and the Catuvellauni to the west and south (Oosthuizen 1998b, 89). The reassertion of the British name *Granta* for the River Cam throughout the early medieval period may also suggest the persistence of this area as a disputed landscape until its reorganisation in the tenth century (Smith 1980, 36-7).

It was not only the River Cam that represented a cultural boundary, however. The frontier character of the Cambridgeshire region more generally during the 'Middle Saxon' period is demonstrated by the establishment of early religious houses on either side of the Fens by the Mercians and East Angles. Mercian kings founded a network of minsters along the western fen-edge between Peterborough and Crowland from the middle of the seventh century, whereas East Anglian claims to the lowlands were forwarded by the development of Ely and Soham (Keynes 2003, 10-12). The Cambridgeshire fenland therefore geographically and ideologically separated, and in some means protected, the political territories of the East Angles, Mercians, and to a lesser extent the Anglians (Roffe 2005, 284-6). Greater Mercian influence began to be felt in the region as early as the eighth century, however, when Cambridgeshire itself came under control of the kingdom. Whilst East Anglian influence in the county is likely to have extended well into the ninth century, the political dispute between English dynasties was abruptly extinguished by Scandinavian raiding and settlement from *c*.870. Although the Viking incursion provides a convenient cut-off date for the purposes of this research, unfortunately the integration of Cambridgeshire into the Danelaw likely impacted the survival of documentary evidence relating to the former political and ecclesiastical administration of this part of eastern England (Oosthuizen 2001, 50; Crick 2007, 17).

It is not only during the early medieval period that Cambridgeshire displays the characteristics of a zone of a transitional zone, however. Reconstructing the medieval landscape of England using nineteenth century OS maps, Roberts and Wrathmell (2001; 2002) reasserted a well-recognised national pattern of settlement types and fieldscapes (e.g. Gray 1915). The pair demonstrated that a zone of tightly coalesced or 'nucleated' settlements and open fields was most densely concentrated in a broad 'central province' of England, stretching the length of the country from Somerset to Yorkshire (Roberts and Wrathmell 2000, fig 1.1). Outside of this zone, it was suggested, patterns of settlement were generally more dispersed and townships had operated alternative agricultural regimes. This division of settlement types has since been studied in greater detail in Cambridgeshire by Christopher Taylor (2002). Whilst this nationally-orientated pattern, which was almost certainly established by at least the end of the medieval period, must be treated with caution when being projected onto a regional scale, Roberts and Wrathmell's research assessed that the 'central province' extended across the western part of modern Cambridgeshire (Figure 6.2). In simple terms then, according to Roberts and Wrathmell, rural Cambridgeshire by the end of the medieval period was a landscape of contrasts, between the 'nucleated' villages and common fields in the west, and the dispersed settlement forms in the eastern part of the county. Although explaining these later settlement and field patterns is not amongst the primary aims of this book, research into village origins in Cambridgeshire has led to debate regarding the significance of the 'Middle Saxon' period as formative in the overall development of the rural landscape. The following review of existing research demonstrates that whilst there is a general scholarly consensus regarding the character of the 'Early Saxon' countryside, the development of rural Cambridgeshire from the seventh century remains a source of contention.

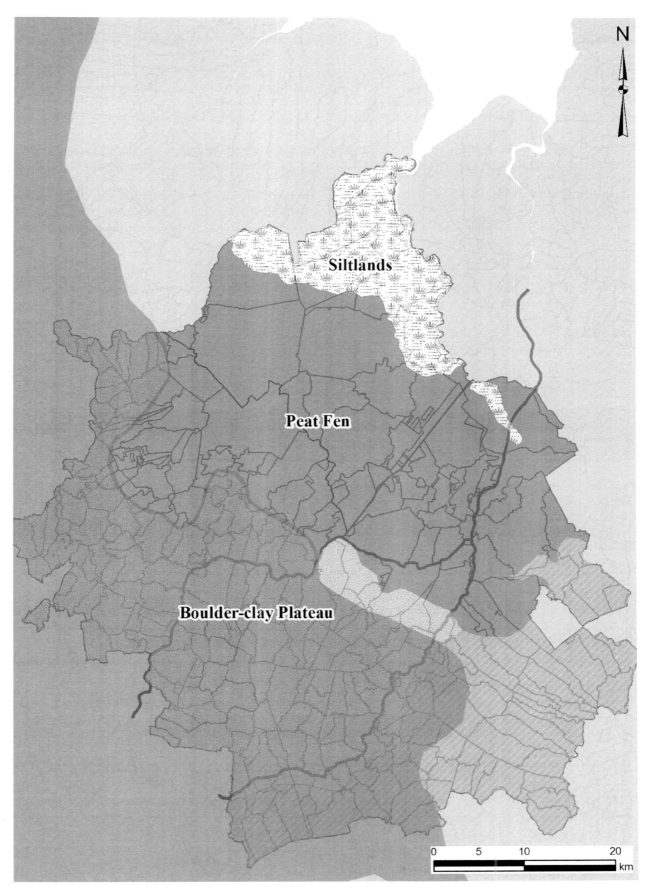

Siltlands

Peat Fen

Boulder-clay Plateau

N

0   5   10   20
km

FIGURE 6.2: THE EXTENT OF ROBERTS AND WRATHMELL'S 'CENTRAL PROVINCE' IN CAMBRIDGESHIRE (SHADED) (FROM EH ATLAS OF RURAL SETTLEMENT ONLINE 2011). THE LIMIT OF THE 'CENTRAL PROVINCE' IS CLEARLY DEFINED BY THE PEAT FEN IN THE NORTHERN PART OF THE COUNTY, BUT NOT SO FURTHER SOUTH, WHERE IT WAS DEEMED THAT THE CAMBRIDGESHIRE HEIGHTS IN PARTICULAR FEATURED A MIXTURE OF MEDIEVAL SETTLEMENT FORM. SOURCE FOR MAPPING: HISTORIC PARISHES OF ENGLAND AND WALES ONLINE.

EARLY MEDIEVAL SETTLEMENT RESEARCH IN CAMBRIDGEHIRE

Introduction

Situated at the interface between differing zones of medieval settlement character and farming regimes, the inclusion of Cambridgeshire has been integral to many investigations into the origins and causes of the divergent pattern. Numerous studies have focused upon the landscape of Cambridgeshire in detail (e.g. Postgate 1964; Taylor 1973; Oosthuizen 2006), but more commonly the county has been integrated into research with a broader geographical remit (e.g. Williamson 2003; Martin and Satchell 2008; Rippon 2008; Lewis 2010). Site-specific investigation in the county has been notably furthered by the work of the Cambridge branch of the Royal Commission on the Historical Monuments of England (RCHME), more recently English Heritage (RCHME Cambridgeshire 1968). Later medieval settlements have featured particularly heavily in RCHME surveys, from which productive lines of academic research have also been pursued (e.g. Oosthuizen 1997).

Significantly, though, Cambridgeshire has not been the focus of the kind of concerted landscape research project that has proved so vital in forwarding our understanding of early medieval settlement change, such as undertaken in Whittlewood, Northamptonshire (Jones and Page 2006). The most extensive landscape-orientated investigation carried out in Cambridgeshire to date was archaeological research as part of the Fenland Project (Hall and Coles 1994; Hall 1996a). Combined with palaeoenvironmetal investigation and radiocarbon dating, the primary survey method employed by the project involved the fieldwalking of as much of the fenlands of eastern England as possible within the six years allotted to the project. All of Cambridgeshire's Siltland parishes were subject to at least partial investigation, and a vast majority of the Peat Fen *pays* (Hall and Coles 1994, xii). Several of the Cambridgeshire Heights and Boulder Clay Plateau parishes that fringe the wetlands were also subject to fieldwalking, as many of them extended into areas of Peat Fen (Figure 6.3). Fewer early medieval sites were identified in Cambridgeshire than the other counties researched by the Fenland Project, although this is partly a consequence of the limited quantity of silt fen that falls within the county: types of landscape which proved especially attractive for pre-Conquest settlement elsewhere around the Wash (Chapter VII; Hall and Coles 1996, 128). The Fenland Project is particularly useful though, when used in combinations with the 'Early Saxon' settlement data emerging from excavation.

'Early Saxon' Settlement in Cambridgeshire: Prevailing Views

The key observation for this research made by the Fenland Project is that although the Cambridgeshire fenlands were not densely occupied in the early medieval period, fen-islands did form crucial foci for 'Middle Saxon' settlement

(Hall and Coles 1994, 122; Mortimer *et al.* 2005; Mudd and Webster 2011). The character of these communities will be explored in greater detail below, but it is clear that early church groups were particularly responsible for the exploitation of wetland landscapes at this time (see below). In the centuries preceding *c.*700, however, evidence for activity on the fen-islands identified by the Fenland Project is largely restricted to funerary material. The fen-edge also appears to have formed a focus for activity well before the seventh century, but again domestic deposits are poorly represented in these areas in comparison to grave-goods. Fieldwalking in the Siltlands recovered very little 'Early Saxon' material, although some grave-goods have previously been identified in the Wisbech area (Hall and Coles 1994, 126-90).

Outside of the fenland basin, more limited fieldwalking surveys have also contributed to form a basic understanding of 'Early Saxon' settlement in southern Cambridgeshire. In simple terms, it appears that the dispersed Romano-British settlement pattern in the county persisted into the first centuries of the early medieval period (Taylor 1989, 218). Indeed, fieldwalking has shown that the repeated use of settlement sites during both Romano-British and 'Early Saxon' periods was most frequent in the 'upland' *pays* of the county. At Hinxton Quarry, located in the southernmost part of the Cambridgeshire Heights, for instance, two *Grubenhäuser* situated close to the River Cam formed part of a community that reoccupied a pre-existing fourth century enclosure system (CHER: 11306B). Elsewhere, in the central Boulder Clay Plateau, excavation on the outskirts of Godmanchester revealed a Romano-British farmstead that perhaps experienced uninterrupted occupation until the eighth century (Gibson and Murray 2003).

Current research of 'Early Saxon' settlement in Cambridgeshire therefore suggests with a certain degree of confidence that there was a distinction between activity in wetland areas and the remainder of the county. Whilst it no longer appears that the fenlands were completely abandoned in the fifth century, only sporadic funerary finds on fen-islands indicate activity of some sort, although it appears unlikely to have been either permanent or extensive. Further south, however, it seems that the 'upland' landscapes remained relatively well-populated, albeit in a dispersed pattern, after the immediate withdrawal of Roman administration (Dodwell *et al.* 2004; Oosthuizen 2006). Although scholars have generally agreed on this model of 'Early Saxon' settlement in Cambridgeshire, there is far greater uncertainty regarding the processes and chronology by which these conditions were superseded. Researchers are divided between those who believe that villages and open fields were a product of the 'Late Saxon' period, and those who believe 'Middle Saxon' developments were crucial in laying the foundations of the later medieval landscape. Although this book does not chiefly seek to understand the character of late medieval villages and fields, transformation of the 'Middle Saxon' countryside has already emerged as a consistent theme

FIGURE 6.3: FIELDWALKING COVERAGE OF THE FENLAND PROJECT IN CAMBRIDGESHIRE (SHADED). VERY LITTLE FIELDWALKING SURVEY HAS BEEN UNDERTAKEN IN CAMBRIDGESHIRE OUTSIDE OF THE LOWLANDS, AND THEREFORE ARCHAEOLOGISTS ARE MORE RELIANT ON EXCAVATED DATA FOR INSIGHTS INTO THE EARLY MEDIEVAL LANDSCAPE IN SUCH AREAS (AFTER HALL AND COLES 1994, FIG. 2).

in the preceding chapters. Indeed, as this chapter will demonstrate, the restructuring of the landscape that occurred from the seventh century provides unique insights into the lived experience of rural communities in Cambridgeshire, as well as revealing broader themes of social, economic and political change. The majority of academic research into the early medieval landscape of Cambridgeshire has, however, sought to explain the occurrence of 'nucleated' villages in some parts of the county, and equally the creation of the fields that surrounded them.

'Middle Saxon' Settlement in Cambridgeshire: Divergent Narratives

Whilst the divergent village forms of medieval Cambridgeshire have been the focus of academic investigation, a research tradition peculiar to the county is that almost equal scholarly effort has been invested into the study of historic fields and land use patterns. Indeed, the varied character of agricultural regimes, combined with good preservation of relict field systems, has seen Cambridgeshire used as a region for study since the earliest systematic research (e.g. Tate 1944). The first studies of field systems were almost solely directed towards characterisation and categorisation, and it was only during the 1970s and 1980s through the development of landscape-scale survey such as fieldwalking, that attempts to provide a chronological sequence for land use arrangements were made (e.g. Taylor 1981; Hall 1982). From these early works, the prevailing view emerged that the common fields of the 'central province' were first laid out between the ninth and twelfth centuries (e.g. Hooke 1988), with most scholars accepting that their development coincided with the movement of populations to coalesced settlements in a protracted 'village moment' process (Lewis et al. 1997, 198). Based on research in Cambridgeshire, however, Susan Oosthuizen has challenged the prevailing model, on both grounds of chronological precision, and the assumption that open field planning and settlement 'nucleation' were coterminous (Oosthuizen 2006; 2009).

Based on archaeological and regressive-map research in the Bourn Valley, a tributary of the River Cam south-west of Cambridge in the Boulder Clay Plateau, Oosthuizen (2006) has outlined an alternative model for common field development. Suggesting that common fields did not necessarily emerge in the same way throughout central England, Oosthuizen posits that a two-phase process was behind their development in some instances. The first phase of this sequence, she asserts, involved the development of a 'proto-common field', often incorporating existing prehistoric or Romano-British features. Crucially, Oosthuizen dates this first process to between the eighth and ninth centuries, after which the existing field arrangement was extended to incorporate most of the medieval vill at a later date. The operation of a less extensive 'proto-common' field system would have been viable within the functioning of an early medieval estate, but it was only after fragmentation of such administrative structures that the newly independent townships expanded the regime across more of their territory (Oosthuizen 2006, 140-4). In more recent research, Oosthuizen (2009; 2010) has challenged more explicitly the assumption that 'nucleated' villages and common fields were created as part of the same process. Whilst there is undoubtedly a relationship between the two, she suggests, this does not preclude the possibility that their development was not wholly contemporary and the probability remains that fields were held in common before the foundation of coalesced villages (Oosthuizen 2010, 131).

Oosthuizen's study of common field origins contradicts the overwhelming majority of existing research, which suggests that 'nucleated' villages were formed together with new agricultural arrangements from the 'Late Saxon' period (e.g. Taylor 1981 and 2000; Hall 1988; Williamson 2003). Although Oosthuizen encourages that village and common field origins should not necessarily be seen as homogenous, her two-stage model bears striking parallels to the early medieval settlement sequence already demonstrated by this book. As has been shown in the preceding chapters, 'Middle Saxon' settlement remains have consistently been identified within the environs of later rural villages, supporting the idea first outlined by Brown and Foard (1998) for a two-stage process of village development, in some instances. The increasing evidence for a stratifying 'Middle Saxon' landscape in Cambridgeshire stands in stark contrast, however, to the conclusions drawn by other early medieval settlement scholars.

In Cambridgeshire, the work of Carenza Lewis in particular has consistently argued for a tenth century and later date for village and common field origins (Lewis et al. 1997; 2007; 2010). Combining her research aims with those of the Cambridge Higher Education Field Academies (HEFA) project, Lewis has directed her most recent efforts into delineating early medieval landscape development through the investigation of currently-occupied villages in central and eastern England (Lewis 2007; 2010). First piloted in 2005, the primary methodology of the HEFA scheme is the excavation of test-pits within private gardens or small plots of undeveloped land in and around existing rural villages. The investigations, carried out by teams including young volunteers from the local community, consists of 1m square test pits excavated to a maximum depth of 1.2m. Although archaeological features have sometimes been encountered, more regularly it is the recovery of artefactual remains, particularly pottery, which has been effective in identifying likely occupation. A total of ten villages have been excavated in Cambridgeshire which, Lewis claims, allows their chronological and geographical development to be reconstructed (Figure 6.4) (Lewis 2010, 101-3). As mentioned in Chapter II, according to Lewis, one of the overwhelming conclusions of the investigations by HEFA in Cambridgeshire and elsewhere is that there is little evidence for the co-location of 'Early Saxon' and 'Middle Saxon' settlements and later occupied villages (Lewis 2010, 103-4).

Research by two historic landscape archaeologists, Oosthuizen and Lewis, both of whom are based at the same university department, has therefore come to divergent conclusions regarding the character of settlement and landscape in pre-Conquest Cambridgeshire. Based on excavation of test-pits in ten modern Cambridgeshire villages, the work of Carenza Lewis and the HEFA project ostensibly indicates little relationship between 'Middle Saxon' settlements and later occupied sites. This assessment corresponds to the popular view of the early medieval landscape, which implies a lack of change

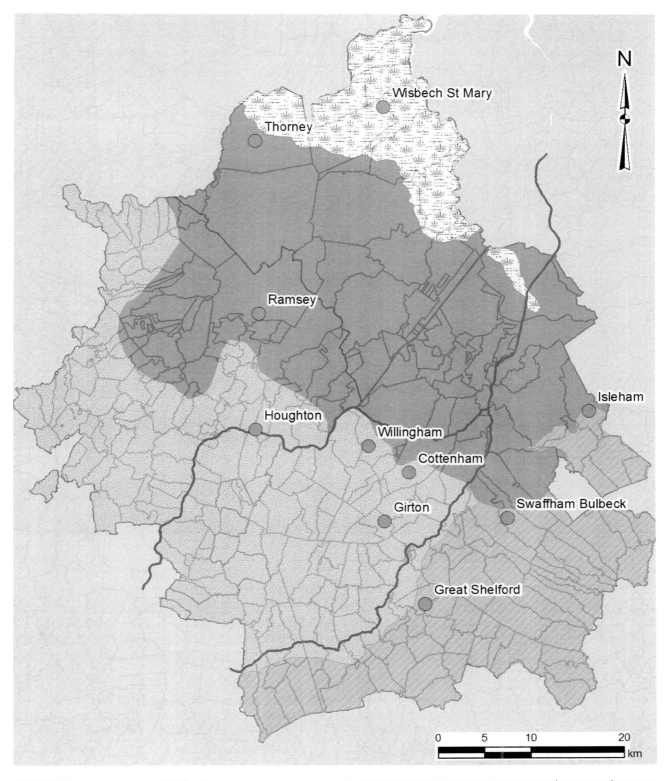

FIGURE 6.4: LOCATION OF THE TEN 'CORS' IN CAMBRIDGESHIRE INVESTIGATED BY THE HEFA PROJECT. THE SCHEME HAS FOUND LITTLE 'CO-LOCATION' BETWEEN 'MIDDLE SAXON' SETTLEMENT ARCHAEOLOGY AND LATER VILLAGES (LEWIS 2010, 103).

until at least the ninth century when communities were reorganised to form recognisable 'nucleated' settlements. However, utilising an alternative methodology centred around retrogressive-map analysis, complemented by archaeological and historical evidence, the work of Susan Oosthuizen has asserted that the countryside of the county was subject to more formal organisation from the 'Middle Saxon' period onwards. Whilst keen to eschew the relationship between 'nucleated' villages and common fields, her model complements the settlement-orientated investigation of this book, which has already demonstrated a 'Middle Saxon' restructuring of the rural landscape, especially in Northamptonshire and Oxfordshire (Chapters III and IV).

Although it is not the main purpose of this book to investigate the origins of historic villages and common fields, there can be little doubt that the model proposed by Oosthuizen, and indeed the contrary findings of Lewis, have relevance for this research. The most pressing issue derived from the divergent narratives outlined above, is the uncertainty surrounding 'Middle Saxon' settlement change in Cambridgeshire. In the preceding chapters it has been shown that from the seventh century, rural settlements underwent significant developments including the introduction of property boundaries and specialisation of agricultural regimes, and it has been demonstrated that the transformation of such communities is most likely the product of deep-rooted social change, which resulted in new expressions of power and exploitation of the landscape. Whilst similar arguments have already been made for Cambridgeshire by Oosthuizen, her work centred on development of the region's field systems, rather than the settlements themselves.

This chapter will demonstrate how evidence derived from currently occupied villages in particular suggests that similar process of 'Middle Saxon' settlement change did indeed occur across the landscape of Cambridgeshire. Dividing the archaeological evidence for 'Middle Saxon' settlement in the county by geographical *pays*, it is increasingly clear that the resources of the Peat Fen and its Islands were perceived as especially valuable to early medieval communities who sought to transform the islands and fen-edge in order to more effectively exploit them. The agency of early ecclesiastical groups appears to have been decisive in this regard, as the industrious clerics of minsters such as Ely took advantage of the varied topographical conditions of the Cambridgeshire countryside. More broadly though, the archaeological evidence suggests that landscape change in 'Middle Saxon' Cambridgeshire was due to broader social changes, which was not restricted only to religious groups. Such insights are all the more significant, as it will be shown how 'Middle Saxon' occupation deposits cannot viably be used as a determinant to explain later medieval settlement form, which has preoccupied some previous researchers. Although Cambridgeshire boasts relatively little archaeological evidence derived from landscape-orientated research, a number of currently-occupied village excavations have identified 'Middle Saxon' sites of significant extent and complexity. These sites, and their potential to inform us of social conditions in 'Middle Saxon' Cambridgeshire more generally, form the majority of the following analysis.

CAMBRIDGESHIRE: MIDDLE SAXON SETTLEMENT AND LANDSCAPE

Introduction

Perhaps more than any other county studied by this book, the understanding of early medieval Cambridgeshire has been forwarded by development-led excavations within currently-occupied villages. The introduction of statutory heritage protection in the early 1990s has since led to a number of archaeological mitigation projects within present-village cores. The expansion of towns such as Huntington and Cambridge has stimulated development, not just within the centres themselves, but also in the rural hinterland around them. As a consequence, a number of rural settlements in Cambridgeshire have been subject to development, which in turn has often led to archaeological excavation within villages (Figure 6.5). These investigations have located significant evidence relating to 'Middle Saxon' occupation and, together with the material from other archaeological research, contribute to a more comprehensive understanding of settlement in seventh to ninth-century Cambridgeshire.

The Siltlands

The lowland landscape of the Siltlands is the most poorly represented of the Cambridgeshire *pays* in terms of 'Middle Saxon' settlement archaeology. Accidental finds and the fieldwalking surveys undertaken by the Fenland Project suggest 'Early Saxon' activity in the region, particularly on the low island of Wisbech. Two bronze brooches were discovered at Wisbech in 1858, and burial urns were also recovered during construction of the Wisbech museum (Phillips 1939). Only two 'Middle Saxon' sites of note have been identified in the Siltlands, however, both located near the centre of Tydd St. Giles. Fieldwalking by David Hall during the Fenland Project recovered two concentrations of artefacts deemed indicative of occupation, with Ipswich Ware finds suggesting that they were occupied during the eighth or ninth centuries (Hall 1996b, 182). The overall dearth of 'Middle Saxon' activity across the Cambridgeshire Siltlands though, led to no sites in the county being investigated as part of the subsequent excavation campaign, based on the findings of Fenland Project fieldwalking (Crowson *et al.* 2005). The limited extent of the Cambridgeshire Siltlands, however, is probably a decisive factor in the dearth of 'Middle Saxon' material identified thus far. Indeed, fieldwalking by the Fenland Project in Lincolnshire and Norfolk demonstrated that the silt landscapes of eastern England were generally more heavily exploited from the seventh century than the peat. Indeed, documentary sources indicated that the Cambridgeshire silt villages, such as Elm and Wisbech, were founded well before the Conquest, and it is possible that the evidence for 'Middle Saxon' activity in the *pays* has yet to be fully appreciated (Hall and Coles 1994, 124; Hall 1996, 180-2).

The Boulder Clay Plateau

More extensive evidence for 'Middle Saxon' settlement in Cambridgeshire has been detected in the gently undulating landscape of the Boulder Clay Plateau. Settlement appears to have been particularly concentrated in the northern part of the *pays*, bordering the Peat Fen. Communities located in this area of interface were ideally situated to take advantage of natural resources in both *pays*, and indeed the 'Late Saxon' parishes of the region display

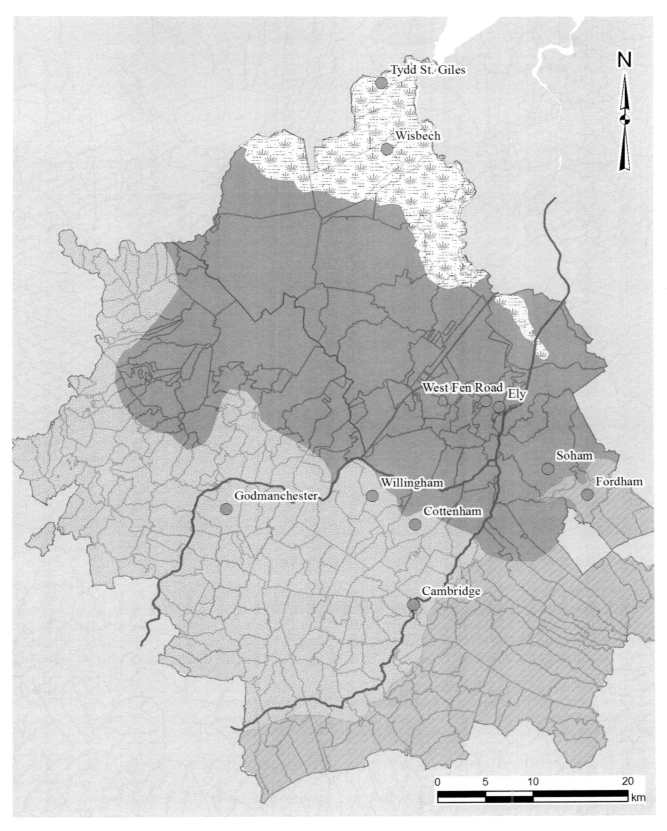

FIGURE 6.5: LOCATIONS OF PLACES MENTIONED IN THE TEXT. THE LACK OF FIELDWALKING SURVEY OUTSIDE OF THE FENLANDS MEANS THAT THE EVIDENCE FROM EXCAVATIONS IS CENTRAL TO RECONSTRUCTING THE 'MIDDLE SAXON' SETTLEMENT LANDSCAPE OF CAMBRIDGESHIRE. SOURCE FOR MAPPING: HISTORIC PARISHES OF ENGLAND AND WALES ONLINE.

arrangements designed to provide rights over both types of countryside. One such parish is Cottenham, which from the eleventh century was amongst the largest villages in the county (Mortimer 2000, 5-6). Liable to flooding due to its fen-edge location, the village of Cottenham is sited approximately 9km to the north of Cambridge. The village has been the focus of several archaeological interventions and was also included in J.R. Ravensdale's (1974) historical analysis of fen-edge communities in Cambridgeshire. The current settlement has an elongated core, extending over 1.5km along a crooked High Street, which may have gained its present form by the thirteenth century (Figure 6.6). Ravensdale has suggested that the route follows the western and northern boundaries of the earliest settlement in the village, but such a hypothesis was not supported by excavation by Cambridge Archaeological Unit (CAU) at the junction of High Street and Telegraph Street in 1997, however, as no evidence of activity before the twelfth century was identified (CHER: CB15525). Despite the identification of some Late Saxon features, a series of ditches excavated to the south of Denmark Road in 1996 were also overwhelmingly dated to the post-Conquest period (CHER: CB15526).

These archaeological mitigation projects in Cottenham therefore produced almost exclusively tenth-century and later evidence, apparently detailing a sequence of village development from the 'Late Saxon' period regarded by many scholars as typical for Cambridgeshire (e.g. Lewis 2010). This model was to be significantly revised, however, following the excavation of land at Lordship Lane, north of High Street (CHER: CB15522; Mortimer 2000). Located in the north-west of Cottenham, alongside the Scheduled Monument of Crowlands Moat, a site extending over ten hectares was excavated by CAU in advance of housing development (Figure 6.7 and 6.8). Earlier evaluation trenches had demonstrated the presence of early medieval activity, but the complexity and extent of archaeological features was far more significant than first anticipated. Five main phases of development were identified on the site, with Phase I characterised by 'Early-Middle Saxon' activity (Mortimer 2000, 5-7). A lack of Ipswich Ware ceramics was taken as evidence that Phase I occupation commenced around the seventh century, when a substantial enclosure was constructed (Blinkhorn 1999). The extent of the feature, which delineated the densest area of activity, was identified to the north, west and south with a maximum known diameter of 170m from west to east (Figure 6.8).

The excavators deemed it likely that further enclosure ditches continued out of the excavated area, probably extending along a low ridge formed by outcropping greensand. In addition to the ditch network, a series of pits and wells were also associated with Phase I of the site sequence, although further evidence probably lay beneath two standing buildings at the centre of the site. Within the north-western edge of the enclosure, two post-built structures (Structures 1 and 2) with associated fence-lines were identified amongst a dense scatter of posts and

post-trenches, which probably represented the remains of buildings (Mortimer 2000, 8). A third, poorly-defined post-built structure (Structure 3) located within a small internal ditched enclosure and a single *Grubenhäus* were also associated with this seventh-century phase of habitation. The greatest concentration of material from Phase I was located in the northern part of the excavation (Area C), in areas of the site that remained relatively undisturbed by subsequent development. The northern part of the site was not totally abandoned after the initial phase, however, but it later appears to have changed use to an area of paddocks behind the later settlement focus (Mortimer 2000, 10).

At some point in the eighth century, however, the settlement at Cottenham underwent a drastic reorganisation. During this second phase of the site sequence, the large north-south ditch of the earlier enclosure was used as an 'axis of expansion' for a new settlement arrangement (Figure 6.9) (Mortimer 2000, 8-10). This new approach to habitation involved the development of a radial enclosure pattern through the construction of a series of new ditches, deeper and wider than any of the Phase I features. Unfortunately the radial enclosures appear to have been orientated around a focus located to the south, which remained unexcavated. Excavation nevertheless located three small structures associated with the new enclosure system (Structures 5-7), all of which were of beam-slot construction, generally regarded as a 'Middle Saxon' building technique (Hamerow 2002, 47; 2011). Significantly, it appears that each of the excavated enclosures possessed a single building, although it is unlikely that they represent the primary domestic accommodation for inhabitants of the settlement. Rather, the beam-slot structures were probably outbuildings located at the back of more substantial domestic residences, located to the south of the excavated area (Mortimer 2000, 10-11).

Phase II was dated largely on the basis of the ceramic assemblage, which mostly comprised organic-tempered wares, only broadly datable to the 'Early-Middle Saxon' period. Crucially, however, small quantities of Ipswich Ware were also found in the Phase II horizons, providing a more refined eighth or early ninth-century date for the establishment of the new settlement arrangement (Blinkhorn 1999; Chapter VII). Ceramic finds suggested that the Phase II enclosure network continued in use into the 'Late Saxon' period, when it was abandoned. The excavated area probably remained in use as a backyard, perhaps only sporadically, until the thirteenth century, after which it probably reverted to pasture until its redevelopment in the modern period (Mortimer 2000, 11).

Mortimer (2000, 19-20) has suggested that either a green or pond to the south of the excavated area may have formed the focus around which the toft network was planned (Figure 6.10), but another possibility is that 'Middle Saxon' Cottenham possessed a church. The medieval parish church is located at the northern end of the High Street, but an earlier religious focus in the Lordship Lane area is hinted at by the presence of the 'Church Hill' name

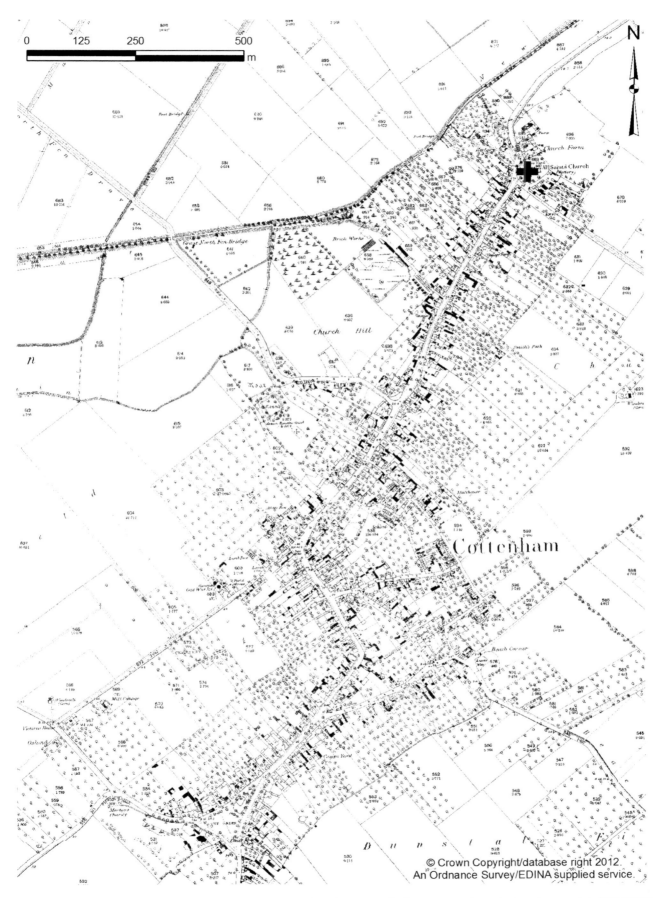

FIGURE 6.6 OS FIRST EDITION OF COTTENHAM SHOWING THE CROOKED HIGH STREET WITH ALL SAINTS CHURCH (CROSS) AT ITS NORTHERN END. EXCAVATIONS IN THE SOUTHERN CORE OF COTTENHAM SUGGEST THE VILLAGE PLAN WAS DEVELOPED AFTER A 'LATE SAXON' RESTRUCTURING OF AN EARLIER SETTLEMENT FOCUS (SEE BELOW). THE BLACK SQUARE DENOTES THE AREA OF FIGURE 6.7.

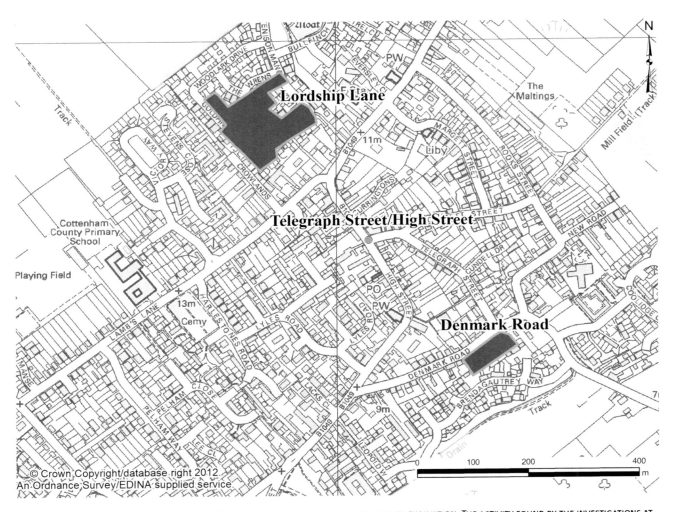

FIGURE 6.7: OS MODERN EDITION OF CENTRAL COTTENHAM, WITH AREAS OF ARCHAEOLOGICAL EXCAVATION. THE ACTIVITY FOUND BY THE INVESTIGATIONS AT TELEGRAPH STREET/HIGH STREET AND DENMARK WAS 'LATE SAXON', AND ONLY THE INTERVENTION AT LORDSHIP LANE LOCATED 'MIDDLE SAXON' EVIDENCE IN COTTENHAM FOR THE FIRST TIME.

recorded on the OS First Edition, referring either to a field or acknowledging the local name for this part of the village. Whilst not a dependable source, a local folk tale also tells of how villagers originally intended to build a church in the centre of the village, but had their attempts thwarted by the devil who continued to return building stones to the site of the current parish church (e.g. Ravensdale 1974, 123; Mortimer 2000, 20). The likelihood that this story preserves the garbled memory of an earlier church in the village centre is increased not only by the 'Church Hill' name, but also by the identification of human remains in the area during the nineteenth (Figure 6.11). Although no early structure has been excavated at Cottenham, if a 'Middle Saxon' church was present it could have formed the focus for the contemporary tenement arrangement at Lordship Lane.

The investigations undertaken at Lordship Lane, Cottenham, represent one of the most important contributions to early medieval settlement studies in Cambridgeshire. Following a period of bounded but relatively sparse occupation around the seventh century, the site underwent a marked transformation through the introduction of a new enclosure

network. This system, with one 'outhouse' structure per enclosure, almost certainly represents a series of tenement plots, arranged around an unexcavated focus to the south. Remarkably this 'toft' organisation at Cottenham, the form of which is more typically associated with later medieval villages, can be confidently attributed to the 'Middle Saxon' period. It is not possible to associate the arrangement as the start of the 'nucleated' village, as the excavator claimed, however (Mortimer 2000, 19). Indeed the enclosure system probably went out of use in the 'Late Saxon' period, as the settlement focus shifted away from the excavated area. It is around the tenth century that that the historic plan of Cottenham took shape, with the earlier principle of private land-use arrangements applied more extensively, and with more precision.

In a pattern that will be shown as a remarkably consistent feature of Cambridgeshire villages which possess 'Middle Saxon' settlement remains, the Domesday entry for Cottenham reveals that the manor was in the shared possession of the religious communities at Crowland and Ely by 1086. Although it is unreasonable to view ownership recorded in the eleventh century as evidence of monastic

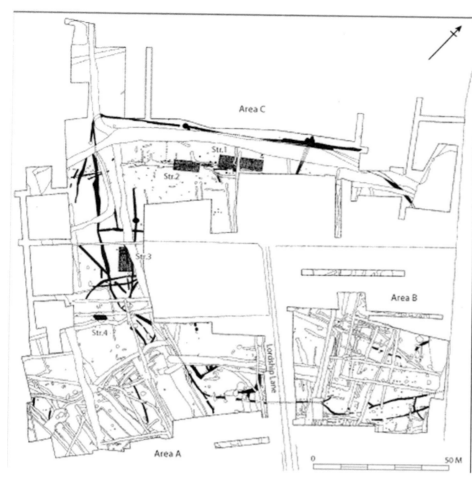

FIGURE 6.8: EXCAVATED FEATURES OF PHASE I, LORDSHIP LANE, COTTENHAM. THE LARGEST ENCLOSURE DEFINED THE EXTENTS OF MOST CONCENTRATED ACTIVITY, INCLUDING POST-BUILT STRUCTURES WHICH PROBABLY REPRESENT DOMESTIC HALLS (MORTIMER 2000, FIG. 7).

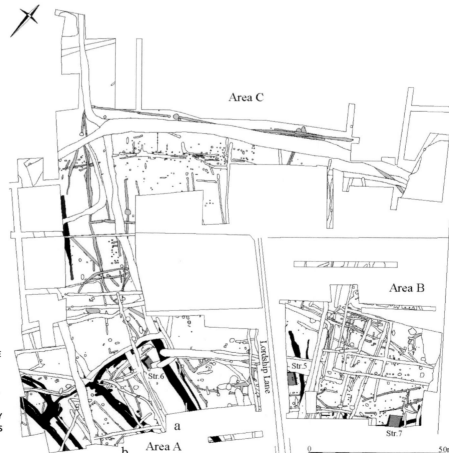

FIGURE 6.9: EXCAVATED FEATURES OF PHASE II, LORDSHIP LANE, COTTENHAM. DURING THE EIGHTH OR EARLY NINTH CENTURY, THE SETTLEMENT AT COTTENHAM UNDERWENT A MAJOR CHANGE WITH THE CONSTRUCTION OF A 'TOFT'-LIKE ARRANGEMENT, APPARENTLY DEFINING INDIVIDUAL PROPERTY BOUNDARIES (MORTIMER 2000, FIG. 9).

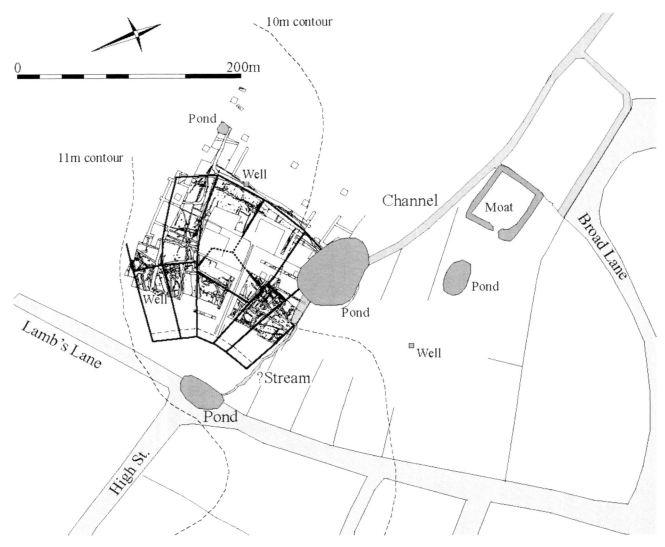

FIGURE 6.10: RICHARD MORTIMER'S RECONSTRUCTION OF THE PHASE II SETTLEMENT ARRANGEMENT AT LORDSHIP LANE, COTTENHAM. ALTHOUGH 'MIDDLE SAXON' SETTLEMENT WAS STRUCTURED AND SEMI-PERMANENT, IT IS CLEAR THAT IT WAS ONLY AFTER 'LATE SAXON' RE-ORDERING THAT THE HISTORIC VILLAGE PLAN WAS CREATED (MORTIMER 2000, FIG. 18).

influence in Cottenham's 'Middle Saxon' development, it is significant that in the history of Ely Abbey recorded in the *Liber Eliensis*, the manor is listed as an earlier holding. Compiled in the twelfth century from earlier material, the *Eliensis* states than an individual named *Uvi* or *Uva* granted land at Cottenham to the minster in the tenth century (Liber Eliensis Book II/84; Keynes 2003, 5-9). The grant recorded in the *Eliensis* may in fact be a forgery: an attempt to provide written integrity to a more ancient claim to Cottenham and its lands, and indeed, this was an approach adopted by many authors of early medieval charter declarations (Yorke 1995, 54–7). It therefore remains a distinct possibility that the monastic communities at Ely or Crowland were influential in the development of early Cottenham. The case for an ecclesiastical link in the establishment of semi-permanent and structured 'Middle Saxon' settlements in Cambridgeshire is also furthered by the evidence from Cottenham's neighbouring parish of Willingham.

The modern village of Willingham is situated in an extremely similar topographical position to Cottenham, and lies only 5km to the north-west. Even though Willingham is situated on a low ridge of greensand and Boulder Clay at 5m OD, even this moderate height was decisive in shaping the character of past human activity. Before the early medieval period, the location of Willingham on the fen-edge proved attractive to an Iron Age community who established a settlement to the east of the High Street. Similarly, in the Romano-British period the Peat Fen to the north of Willingham was used extensively for arable farming (Hall 1996a, 30-5). Until recently there was little archaeological or documentary material to suggest that Willingham was a pre-Conquest centre of any significance, although in his history of the parish church of Saint Mary and All Saints, the Reverend Watkins noted that the manor of Willingham was granted to to Ely Abbey by the same enigmatic *Uvi* that gifted Cottenham in the middle of the tenth century (Watkins 1896).

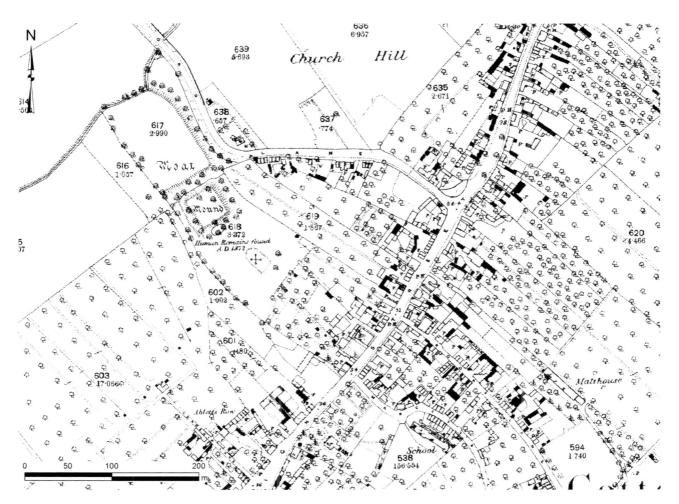

FIGURE 6.11: ORDNANCE SURVEY FIRST EDITION OF CENTRAL COTTENHAM. THE EXCAVATED SITE IS LOCATED IMMEDIATELY SOUTH OF CROWLANDS MOAT (CENTRE) WHICH IS IN THE 'CHURCH HILL' AREA OF THE VILLAGE. COMBINED WITH THE FIELD NAME, THE IDENTIFICATION OF HUMAN REMAINS IN THE AREA HINTS AT THE PRESENCE OF AN EARLIER RELIGIOUS FOCUS THAN THE CURRENT CHURCH LOCATED AT THE NORTHERN END OF THE HIGH STREET.

The only other indication that Willingham may have been a focus for early occupation is the small quantity of 'Late Saxon' masonry built into the fabric of the parish church (Pevsner 1954, 486-8). The church lies at the eastern end of Church Street, with tenements in the village also focused around the north-south orientated High Street (Figure 6.12) Far more compelling evidence for pre-Conquest settlement in Willingham has been derived from a series of archaeological excavations within the village core since the mid-1990s, which have identified evidence for settlement with occupation possibly beginning as early as the sixth century. Following archaeological evaluation that highlighted the presence of archaeological deposits, several plots of land were excavated to the east of the High Street by CAU in 1996 (CHER: CB17885). Excavation in advance of the 'infilling' of a previously undeveloped area, slightly removed from the historic core, is strikingly similar to the conditions of the investigations undertaken at Cottenham. Indeed, the evidence recovered from Willingham is also comparable, suggesting that both sites followed a similar path of development through the early medieval period.

The 1996 excavations in Willingham were somewhat piecemeal, being dictated by the proposed routes of service trenches, but the evaluations were nevertheless sufficient enough to locate a series of eight post-built structures, probably halls. The absence of beam-slot construction identified in the trenches led the excavators to suggest a possible 'Early Saxon' date for the structures (CHER: CB17885, 7), yet a similar lack of *Grubenhäuser* and the recovery of Ipswich Ware from stratified contexts instead demonstrates that this phase of occupation is datable to the eighth or early ninth centuries. In the succeeding phases, dated to the tenth and eleventh centuries by finds of St Neots Ware, activity was most concentrated in the northernmost excavated areas, although the focus of occupation is likely to have been located further north still. Occupation was characterised by a series of linear ditches orientated in an approximate north-south direction likely representing the boundaries of tenements fronting onto Church Street (CHER: CB17885, 9).

A more comprehensive understanding of Willingham's early medieval development was, however, provided by a CAU excavation in 2008, 10m west of the earlier evaluation trenches (Figure 6.13) (CHER: CB18148). Early medieval occupation on the site was represented by a post-built structure, enclosed by a ditch which appeared to define the area of domestic activity. This phase was dated

121

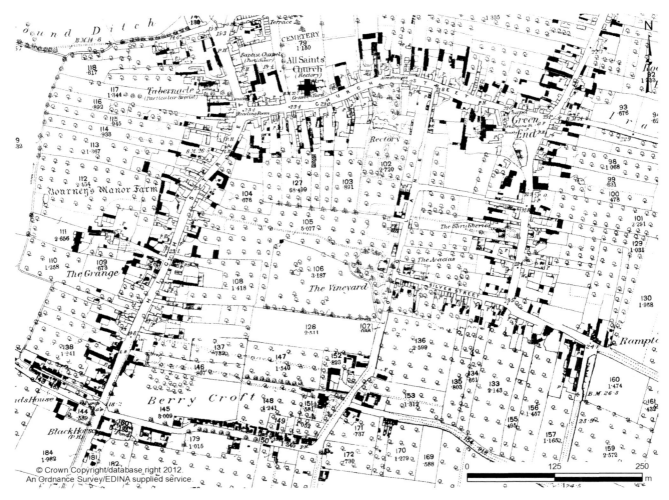

FIGURE 6.12: OS FIRST EDITION OF WILLINGHAM. THE HISTORIC VILLAGE PLAN WAS FOCUSSED AROUND TWO MAIN ROUTEWAYS; CHURCH STREET RUNNING WEST TO EAST, AND HIGH STREET ORIENTATED NORTH TO SOUTH. THE PARISH CHURCH OF ALL SAINTS (CROSS) IS SITUATED NEAR THE AXIS OF THE TWO.

to the eighth century by the recovery of Ipswich Ware and North French Blackware pottery (Blackmore 1988; CHER: CB18148, 10). A further north-south ditch in the eastern half of the site contained no dating material but was similarly dated to the 'Middle Saxon' period, based on stratigraphic relationships and the comparable form to the more westerly feature. Intriguingly, the enclosure on the western part of the site parallels the alignment of an earlier Romano-British boundary ditch. The recovery of a well-preserved sword and spear, broadly datable to the 'Middle Saxon' period from the bottom fill of the ditch may also represent a closing deposit after the feature had been 'ritually cleaned' before abandonment (CHER: CB18148, 16-8).

The second phase of the site, dated by pottery to the 'Late Saxon' period, was characterised by the replacement of the post-built building and the construction of a fenceline which again mirrored the alignment of the 'Middle Saxon' and Romano-British enclosure ditches. This period also saw the development of recognisable features of the medieval village for the first time, as two parallel ditches were also constructed in the western edge of the site. The features, which probably represent a new tenement arrangement, reflect closely the orientation of the historic

street plan (CHER: CB18148, 18). It is likely that around this time the focus of settlement relocated a short distance north to the area of the church, the 'Late Saxon' fabric of which supports the idea that it was founded at this date. Although Willingham does not feature the remarkable 'Middle Saxon' toft arrangement identified at Cottenham, the excavated evidence does suggest structured and semi-permanent settlement from around the eighth century. Also similar to Cottenham, this centre underwent a short shift and restructuring in the 'Late Saxon' period which probably resulted in the development of the recognisable historic village. Ely Abbey's ownership of Willingham from at least the tenth century is again intriguing, and along with Cottenham, suggests that the upland landscape of Cambridgeshire's fen-edge may have been targeted for exploited by 'Middle Saxon' religious houses.

The case-studies of Cottenham and Willingham demonstrate how the fen-edge of the Boulder Clay Plateau represented a particular focus for settlement during the 'Middle Saxon' period. Away from this area of interface, settlement in the *pays* appears to have been dictated by the proximity to water. The settlement excavated on the outskirts of Godmanchester, for instance, was located alongside the River Great Ouse and further south,

122

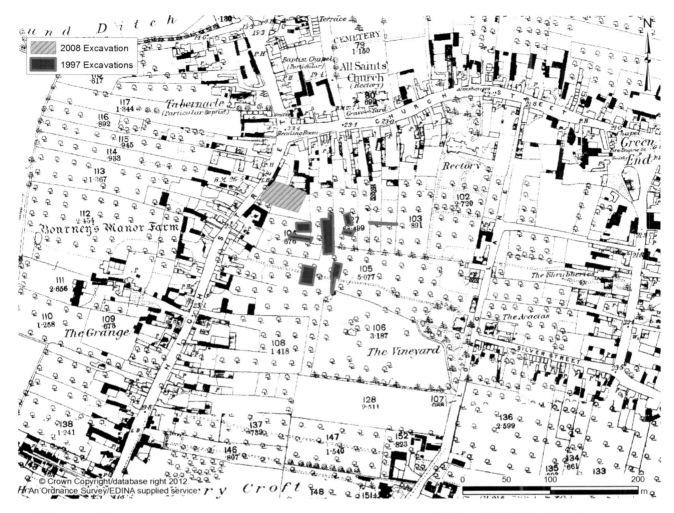

FIGURE 6.13: OS FIRST EDITION OF WILLINGHAM WITH THE AREAS INVESTIGATED BY EXCAVATION IN 1997 AND 2008. THE 'LATE SAXON' RELOCATION OF SETTLEMENT TO THE NORTH AND WEST FROM THE EXISTING 'MIDDLE SAXON' FOCUS IS LIKELY REFLECTIVE OF A 'TWO-STAGE' PROCESS OF EARLY MEDIEVAL SETTLEMENT DEVELOPMENT.

Oosthuizen has demonstrated extensive settlement and exploitation of the Bourn Valley from the eighth century (Gibson and Murray 2003; Oosthuizen 2006). Elsewhere on the River Great Ouse though, combined archaeological research from limited fieldwalking and excavation has located no sites in the St. Neots Valley (Spoerry 2000, 150-8). Elsewhere, in the Boulder Clay Plateau, the River Cam certainly did form a focus for 'Middle Saxon' communities and excavation in and around the county town of Cambridge has demonstrated the existence of a well-populated agricultural landscape. Archaeological interventions before the 1990s in Cambridge, failed to identify evidence even relating to the historically-documented 'Late Saxon' centre, although this may have been a consequence of the way in which 'dark-earth' formation processes reduce the archaeological visibility of early medieval settlement features (Cessford 2007, 219).

A handful of more recent investigations in Cambridge, however, have recovered early medieval occupation deposits suggesting that this part of the Cam Valley featured a concentration of 'Middle Saxon' settlements. Indeed, the Cambridge area was clearly a zone of dense

'Early Saxon' activity, with cemeteries identified at Girton College and Parker's Field (Meaney 1964; Hollingworth and O'Reilly 2012). Excavation in the town appears to confirm the assertions of Haslam (1984) who, on the basis of documentary evidence and the later topography of the town, suggested an early medieval settlement focus in the Castle Hill area. Haslam forwarded that the defended Roman town around Cambridge Castle was reoccupied during the eighth century, with an extra-mural market centre located to the north, preserved in the name Ashwyke (Haslam 1984b, 13-18; Taylor 1999, 43-5) The regular recovery of Ipswich Ware from this area supports this hypothesis, but more significant 'Middle Saxon' activity has been located closer to the River Cam. A keyhole excavation at Chesterton Lane Corner revealed evidence for an execution cemetery dated between the seventh to ninth centuries, with a *floruit* of use most likely occurring in the eighth century (Cessford and Dickens 2005; Cessford 2007). The cemetery was situated outside of the Roman town but at a nodal point in the landscape, parallel to the Roman road leading north from the crossing over the River Cam (Cessford 2007, 223). Although the Chesterton Lane Corner excavations identified no occupation deposits, the presence of the execution cemetery certainly supports the probability of settlement activity around this part of the Cam during the 'Middle Saxon' period.

For the 'Middle Saxon' elite, judicial executions were a crucial way of asserting authority, and the presence of an execution cemetery in Cambridge therefore hints that a high-status focus may have been located in the vicinity (Reynolds 2009a; 2009b). In the broader regional context, however, the finds of Ipswich Ware and Series R sceattas hint that Cambridge may have lain in the hinterland of Ipswich and could even have served as a secondary settlement for a 'productive site' that has been detected close by. The site, the exact location of which has been kept confidential to ensure that it is not targeted by night-hawkers, was identified through the recovery of numerous eighth-century sceattas (Blackburn and Sorenson 1984, 223-7; Scull 2002). The juxtaposition of the two sites conforms to the pattern recognised in Norfolk (Chapter VII), with 'productive sites' situated in close proximity to places that developed as important centres from the 'Late Saxon' period (Pestell 2003; Hutcheson 2006; Cessford 2007).

The character of 'Middle Saxon' settlement in and around Cambridge, however, cannot be determined with great clarity, but the activity detected around Castle Hill suggests that it formed one of numerous contemporary foci located to the west and north of the River Cam. Excavations in various locations across the modern town have revealed occupation remains, usually only datable by organic-tempered pottery to a broad 'Early-Middle Saxon' period. For instance, investigation at the Criminology Institute 250m west of the River Cam identified a single post-built hall (CHER: CB15349; Dodwell *et al.* 2004), and 3km south of the historic core of the town, excavation at Addenbrooke's Hospital found the remains of several post-built structures and *Grubenhäuser* (CHER: CB17800). The cumulative evidence for 'Early-Middle Saxon' settlement demonstrates the presence of a populated agricultural landscape, although it must be recognised that excavated sites can only be generally dated and may not be contemporary. Evidence for judicial executions in the Castle Hill area, however, illustrates that an elite element was present amongst the polyfocal settlement around the Cam. To date, though, the excavated early medieval settlements in and around Cambridge have been of more prosaic character, suggesting that the fertile river valley attracted a range of site-types by the 'Middle Saxon' period.

The archaeological evidence presented here demonstrates that settlement in the Boulder Clay Plateau of Cambridgeshire during the 'Middle Saxon' period was clearly influenced by the topographical variation within the *pays*. In particular, occupation was concentrated in and around the river valleys, which formed an important fertile zone within an otherwise quickly-draining landscape. Numerous 'Middle Saxon' sites were also developed around the fen-edge, where the Boulder Clay and greensand

of the *pays* meets the Peat Fen. The limited environmental evidence from sites such as Cottenham and Willingham suggest that wetland resources were a significant element of a mixed agricultural economy, with communities able to exploit a variety of conditions in their immediate vicinity. The excavated material from Cottenham and Willingham demonstrates that 'Middle Saxon' fen-edge settlement was not seasonal or transient as may have been anticipated, and which likely characterised occupation in such zones before the seventh century. Rather, from at least the eighth century if not a century earlier, more permanent centres were established along the fenland fringe which eventually emerged as later medieval villages.

At Cottenham in particular, 'Middle Saxon' settlement was not only more permanent but also clearly structured. The development of a toft arrangement, featuring individual property plots and buildings, represents a remarkable departure from the transient and boundless settlements of the 'Early Saxon' period. In turn, this approach to spatial organisation reflects a fundamental shift in the perception of land and property tenure, as the previous understanding of folk ownership was beginning to be replaced by private land holding, the extents of which began to be more regularly and permanently defined by the construction of boundaries. This process is far less discernible at Willingham, but it is nevertheless significant that the orientation of 'Middle Saxon' enclosures was mirrored by 'Late Saxon' fences and boundaries. It is intriguing and potentially significant that monastic houses held land at Cottenham and Willingham from at least the tenth century, and indeed it is possible that the newly semi-permanent and structured settlements of the 'Middle Saxon' period were influenced by the unique character of ecclesiastical lordship. Indeed, the possibility that the agency of Cambridgeshire's 'Middle Saxon' minsters communities was crucial in shaping settlement character may be supported by the evidence from the Cambridgeshire Heights, particularly the excavated evidence from the modern village of Fordham.

The Cambridgeshire Heights

The chalk escarpment that forms the Cambridgeshire Heights has been an open and largely treeless landscape since prehistoric times. By the time of Domesday, most townships in the *pays* were operating a system of 'sheep-corn' husbandry, whereby the agricultural economy was equally orientated to both sheep rearing and grain cultivation. The 'Late Saxon' farming regime of the Cambridgeshire Heights was therefore markedly different from that of the communities living on the Boulder Clay Plateau. Archaeological excavation in the village of Fordham, however, demonstrates that the fenland fringe at least was exploited in a similar fashion in both *pays* during the 'Middle Saxon' period. Located on the banks of the River Snail, the current village of Fordham is located only 1km south of the Peat Fen. Whilst not on the immediate interface between contrasting geologies such as Cottenham and Willingham, excavations within Fordham suggest that

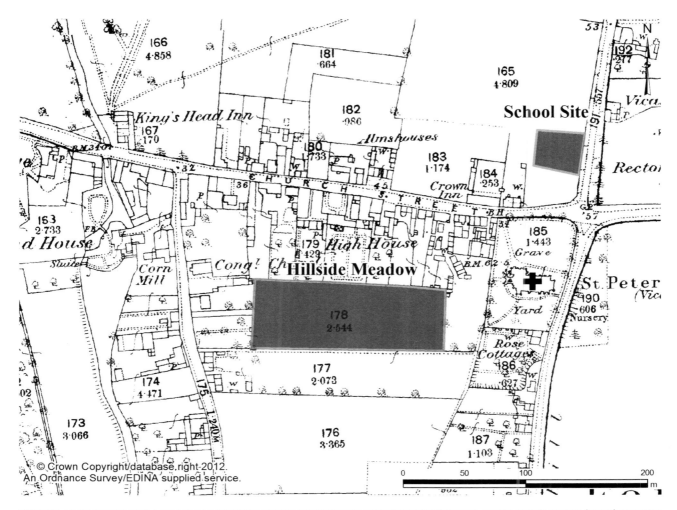

FIGURE 6.14: OS FIRST EDITION OF FORDHAM WITH THE LOCATIONS OF EXCAVATIONS CITED IN THE TEXT (SHADED), AND ST. PETER'S CHURCH (CROSS). NOTE THE SIMILARITY OF THE STREET PLAN TO THAT OF WILLINGHAM (ABOVE), WITH TENEMENTS ARRANGED AROUND AN WEST-EAST ORIENTATED CHURCH STREET AND A FURTHER NORTH-SOUTH ALIGNED ROUTEWAY. INTRIGUINGLY THE 'MIDDLE SAXON' EVIDENCE AT BOTH SITES HAS BEEN FOUND WITHIN THE ENCLOSURE FORMED BY THIS STREET-PLAN

its location close to the Peat Fen was an important factor in its earliest development. Indeed, during the 'Middle Saxon' period, a location such as Fordham's would have been ideal to take advantage of the episodic rise and fall in the local water table (Hall and Coles 1994, 125). The potential for 'Middle Saxon' activity in this part of the Cambridgeshire Heights was first revealed by the recovery of Ipswich Ware in the neighbouring parish of Snailwell, identified following fieldwalking as part of the Fenland Project. Significantly, the 'Middle Saxon' and subsequent settlement all lay close to the source of the river on which the medieval vill was later centred, reflecting the importance of water within a chalk landscape which is otherwise largely quickly-draining (Hall and Coles 1994, 129).

The most significant early medieval centre in the area recognisable through documentary evidence is Fordham's neighbouring village of Soham, located 4km to the north-west, and famous as the site of a 'Middle Saxon' minster . The *Liber Eliensis* documents the founding of a monastic community at Soham in 650, and although no archaeological evidence for settlement has so far been

recovered, a series of furnished burials found in the area indicate that it was likely an important area in the 'Early Saxon' period (Meaney 1964, 69; Blair 2005, 237). Soham was one of at least six minsters documented in the Cambridgeshire region before c.870, as the foundation of religious houses was a key means of colonising and consolidating land. Soham's establishment is a case in point, as it appears that south-eastern Cambridgeshire was situated on the border between the kingdoms of East Anglia and Mercia (Oosthuizen 2001, 54; Brown and Foard 2004, 89).

There is evidence that Fordham too occupied a frontier position in the early medieval period, as even today the parish church is under the jurisdiction of the archdeaconry of Sudbury and the Diocese of Norwich, contrasted to the rest of Cambridgeshire which lies within the Diocese of Ely (Oosthuizen 2001, 54; CHER: 17773). Whilst there is little documentary material to suggest that Fordham was a particularly significant centre in the early medieval period, archaeological excavation in the village has uncovered substantial evidence relating to 'Middle Saxon' occupation. The most extensive archaeological research within Fordham comprised the excavation of one hectare of land at Hillside Meadow by CAU in 1998 (Patrick and Rátkai 2011; CHER: CB14613). Following an initial site evaluation which revealed the presence of early medieval settlement deposits, the site was subject to comprehensive open area excavation (Figure 6.14). Investigation revealed four distinct phases of activity spanning the sixth century to the post-medieval period (Patrick and Rátkai 2011, 102-3).

The first activity identified on the site (Phase I) was characterised by a series of five enclosures, all aligned on a north-south axis, but of variable size and composition. Within the enclosure network were found four *Grubenhäuser*, three of which were located towards the western boundary of the site, and a series of pits (Figure 6.15). The recovery of organic-tempered wares combined with an absence of Ipswich Ware led Phase I to be attributed a rather vague date of *c*.500-725 (Patrick and Rátkai 2011, 103; CHER: CB14613, 3). The second phase of occupation was dated by Ipswich Ware to between *c*.725-850, although within this bracket two distinct periods of activity were discernible by stratigraphic relationships: Phase II (early) and Phase II (late). During Phase II (early) a number of the earlier enclosure ditches were reinstated, although the Phase I *Grubenhäuser* and pits apparently went out of use. The Fordham site underwent a more significant change in Phase II (late), however, as the previous enclosure arrangement was replaced by an entirely new series of boundary ditches. The features, orientated in a more uniform north-south and west-east manner, created a new and more regular enclosure network. Within the interior of one of the enclosures was dug a large pit and an elongated oval feature, and a further enclosure possessed a series of post-holes, perhaps indicative of hall structures (Patrick and Rátkai 2011, 103-4; CHER: CB14613, 4).

During Phase III of the site sequence, dated between the mid ninth and mid twelfth centuries on the basis of ceramic finds, some of the enclosures remained in use, but overall occupation on the Hillside Meadow site was not as concentrated (CHER: CB14613, 4). The most intense activity was located in the north-east corner of the excavated area, suggesting that the focus of settlement had shifted. A further evaluation trench excavated at the site of a school to the north of Church Street recovered evidence for 'Late Saxon' settlement but found no material dating to earlier phases (Figure 6.14) (CHER: CB14610). Investigation at the school site identified two parallel ditches, on an east west alignment and a series of post-holes in a similar orientation. These features were interpreted by the excavators as boundaries relating to property tenements of the tenth or eleventh centuries fronting onto Isleham Road (CHER: CB14610, 3). It therefore appears that at some point after the mid ninth century, settlement in Fordham shifted from the Hillside Meadow area towards the north-east, in the location occupied by the medieval parish church. Significantly, however, a number of the earlier Phase II (late) enclosures remained in use into the 'Late Saxon' period.

Displaying a comparable alignment to the historic street plan, one of the 'Middle Saxon' ditches was even reused as a property boundary, which historic maps show continued to be used into the nineteenth century (Figure 6.16). It remains difficult though, to determine exactly the relationship between the 'Middle Saxon' enclosure network excavated at Hillside Meadow, and the organisation of the later medieval village. There can be little doubt that it was changes dated to the 'Late Saxon' period that saw the development of Fordham's historic street and property network, and in a similar process to that noted at Cottenham and Willingham, the earlier settlement at Hillside Meadow was instead reverted to a backyard or paddock. Indeed, the 'Middle Saxon' archaeology of Fordham is also comparable to the excavated sites from the Boulder Clay Plateau, particularly the enclosures identified at Cottenham. At both sites, a radically new approach to settlement organisation was introduced into a pre-existing centre at some point during the 'Middle Saxon' period. In the case of Fordham, this development was likely dated to the late eighth or early ninth century, following occupation that may have begun as early as the early seventh century. Again it seems that these changes are likely due to deep-rooted transformations in the perception of property and ownership across society.

Attempting to discern the potential agents behind the 'Middle Saxon' restructuring of Fordham remains problematic, especially given the relative dearth of documentary sources relating to pre-Viking Cambridgeshire (Darby 1952, 310). Perhaps significantly though, Fordham is first recorded in 1086 as part of the royally-held demesne estate of the king's manor at Soham. The later association of the two centres is interesting, and given their close proximity, situated only 5km apart, it is possible that Fordham was located within the monastic estate of Soham before the eleventh century. The close geographical relationship of Fordham to the minster at Soham is similar to the situation recognisable in northern Wiltshire, where extensive 'Middle Saxon' settlement remains at Bremilham have been identified only 2.5km south-west of the historically-attested minster at Malmesbury (Chapter V; Hinchliffe 1986).

The settlement at Bremilham has been interpreted as a semi-monastic cell, acting as a 'grange' within the Malmesbury estate, and it seems probable that the 'Middle Saxon' site at Fordham fulfilled a similar function for the minster community at Soham. Not only are the Cambridgeshire sites comparably situated to those in Wiltshire, but it is also possible that Fordham's incorporation within the demesne of Soham recorded by Domesday actually preserves a far more antiquated association. There is little archaeological indication that 'Middle Saxon' Fordham was specialised towards a particular agricultural output, but instead environmental and macrofaunal evidence suggests that the site operated a mixed agrarian economy typical of the period (Patrick and Ratkai 2011, 80-5). It therefore appears that Fordham served as a centre for the production of agricultural surplus as part of the *inland* of Soham minster, an essential role for the functioning of any

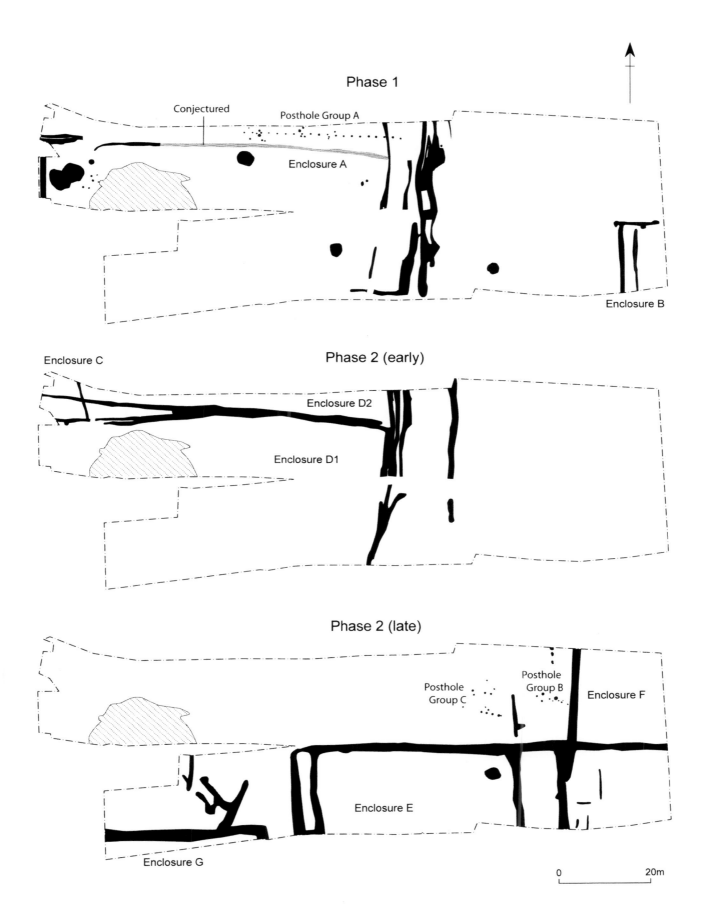

FIGURE 6.15: THE SIXTH TO NINTH CENTURY PHASES AT FORDHAM, CAMBRIDGESHIRE. A PRE-EXISTING SETTLEMENT UNDERWENT A DRASTIC REORDERING, PROBABLY IN THE EIGHTH CENTURY, WHEN A NEWLY REGULAR AND APPARENTLY PLANNED SERIES OF ENCLOSURES WAS ESTABLISHED (PATRICK AND RATKAI 2011, FIG 3.2).

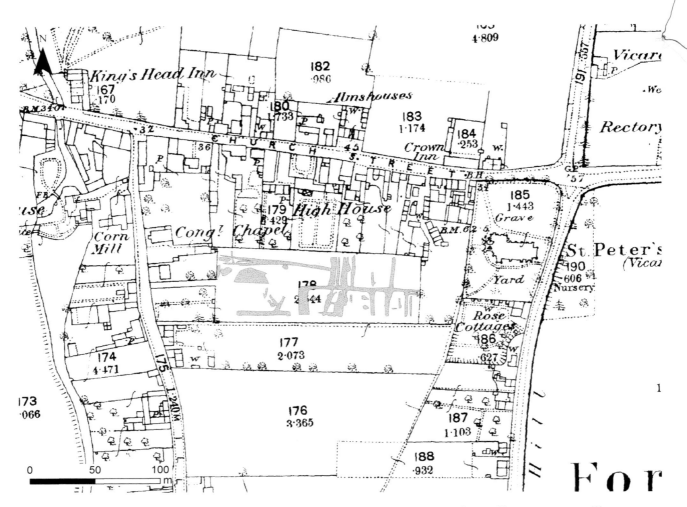

FIGURE 6.16: OS FIRST EDITION OF FORDHAM, DISPLAYING THE ENCLOSURE NETWORK REVEALED BY THE HILLSIDE MEADOW EXCAVATION. WHILST THE HISTORIC STREET-PLAN UNDOUBTEDLY EMERGED AFTER A 'LATE SAXON' RESTRUCTURING, THE EARLIER ENCLOSURES ARE OF A STRIKINGLY SIMILAR ALIGNMENT TO THE HISTORIC TENEMENT PATTERN, AND AT LEAST ONE BOUNDARY DITCHES OF THE HILLSIDE MEADOW SITE WAS REUSED TO ARTICULATE A LATER PROPERTY ALIGNMENT (AFTER PATRICK AND RATKAI 2011, FIG 3.25).

estate irrespective of how sophisticated and specialised its composition (Faith 1997, 15-18).

Although the Domesday entry for Fordham lacks the 'geld-free' details traditionally associated with *inland* sites, the archaeological evidence contributes to the pattern emerging from Cambridgeshire, and elsewhere in central and southern England, of settlements which possess apparently planned arrangements by the 'Middle Saxon' period that were likely associated with monastic establishments (Faith 1997, 36). In addition to the Cambridgeshire sites of Cottenham, and Fordham, can be added places such as Yarnton in Oxfordshire, where changes to the organisation and farming regime of the settlement may have been associated with its integration into the monastic estate of Eynsham (Chapter IV). In Cambridgeshire, the new approach to settlement organisation, coupled with farming economies that, whilst lacking the specialisation of sites such as Yarnton, appear to have been increasingly orientated towards the production of agricultural surplus, represent significant changes to the rural landscape. The monastic link with these transformations is also hinted at in the evidence from the Peat Fen and its Islands, where

excavation close to the minster at Ely has identified the most convincing evidence of a 'Middle Saxon' *inland* anywhere in England.

The Peat Fen and its Islands

More than any other part of Cambridgeshire, our understanding of early medieval settlement in the Peat Fens and its Islands has been substantially furthered by the fieldwalking undertaken as part of the Fenland Project. The programme fieldwalked at least parts of all Peat Fen parishes, providing an insight into pre-Conquest settlement patterns unparalleled elsewhere in the county. Systematic walking of fields supports the likelihood that there was a zone of 'Middle Saxon' settlements around the fen-edge of Cambridgeshire, complementing the excavated evidence from centres such as Willingham and Fordham. For instance, at Waterbeach two sites were identified on the gravel terraces of the River Cam, represented by burnt pebbles, domestic animal bone and organic-tempered pottery (Hall 1996b, 124). 'Early-Middle Saxon' domestic activity in the Waterbeach area had earlier been revealed by Thomas Charles Lethbridge, who excavated a

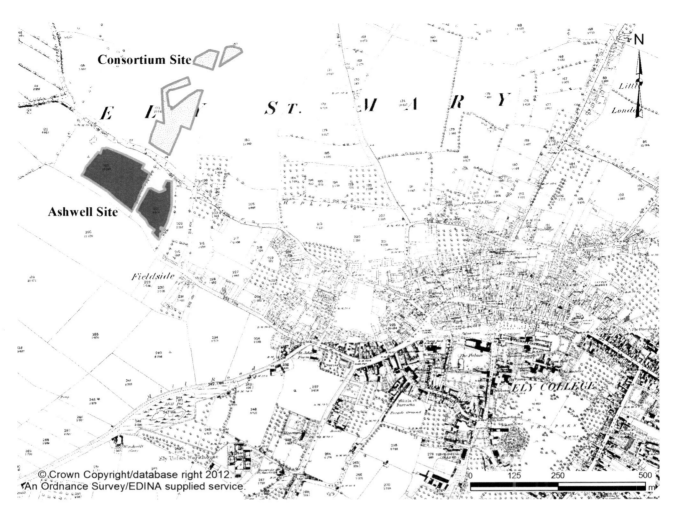

FIGURE 6.17: OS FIRST EDITION OF ELY, SHOWING THE EXCAVATED SITES AT WEST FEN ROAD, 1KM NORTH-WEST OF THE EXISTING CATHEDRAL AND TOWN CENTRE. GIVEN THE PROXIMITY OF THE 'MIDDLE SAXON' SETTLEMENT AT WEST FEN ROAD TO THE MINSTER AT ELY, IT SEEMS VERY LIKELY THAT IT FORMED PART OF THE 'PRODUCTIVE CORE' OF THE MONASTIC ESTATE (AFTER MORTIMER ET AL. 2005, FIG 1.1).

Grubenhäus at Car Dyke (Lethbridge 1927). In addition to the settlement evidence, the southern fen-edge was also clearly a focus for furnished burial, with cemeteries identified at Soham, Little Downham and Snailwell, amongst others (Hall 1987, 35-9).

In addition to sites located on the periphery of the *pays*, fieldwalking in the Peat Fen also demonstrates that the fen-islands provided important locations for 'Middle Saxon' settlement (Hall and Coles 1994, 128-31). 'Early Saxon' and 'Middle Saxon' pottery concentrations were noted particularly frequently on the low islands in the Welland Valley, and Ipswich Ware ceramics were also found at the deserted settlement on the upland of Sawtry Judith (Brown and Taylor 1980, 117; Hall and Coles 1994, 128). A significant observation made by the Fenland Project investigators though, is that far more early medieval activity is believed to exist under modern settlement centres on the fen-islands of the *pays* (Hall and Coles 1994, 128). The continued occupation of such sites throughout the historic period therefore obscures attempts by archaeologists to characterise the form and pattern of 'Middle Saxon' settlements. It is also notable

that whereas locations in other counties fieldwalked by the Fenland Project have been subject to targeted excavation (Crowson *et al.* 2005), until recently there had been little intrusive investigation into the 'Middle Saxon' artefact concentration on the fen-islands of Cambridgeshire. Since the introduction of statutory heritage protection in the early 1990s, however, several excavations have been undertaken on the largest of the fen-islands: the Isle of Ely.

Throughout the medieval period, Ely emerged as the centre of one of the most industrious and powerful minsters in the country. The *Liber Eliensis* suggests that the Abbey was founded as a double house by Æthelthryth in the middle of the seventh century, apparently located 1.5km away from the enigmatic centre of *Cratendune* (Garmonsway 1972, 34-5). Within the modern townscape of Ely, it is not certain whether the pre-Conquest house was situated on the site of the existing Abbey, and St. Mary's church and the hospital of St John the Baptist have both been suggested as possible alternatives (Keynes 2003, 32). Whilst the early history of Ely is recorded by Bede and the *Eliensis*, until 1990 there was little archaeological evidence for the Abbey or any associated settlement.

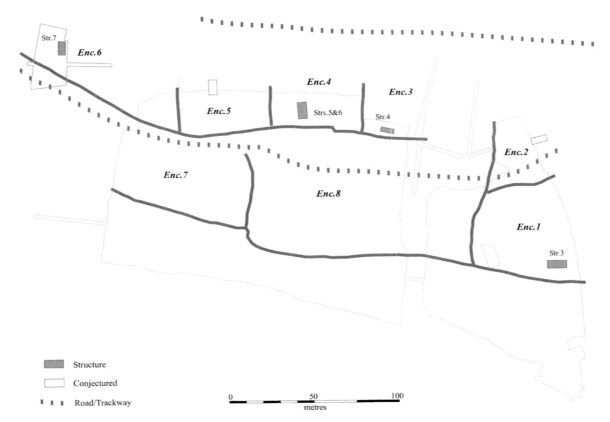

FIGURE 6.18: RECONSTRUCTION OF THE EARLY EIGHTH TO MID NINTH-CENTURY SETTLEMENT FEATURES EXCAVATED AT THE ASHWELL SITE OF THE WEST FEN ROAD SETTLEMENT, ELY. THE NETWORK OF ENCLOSURES AND STRUCTURES WERE ARRANGED AROUND A SPINAL TRACKWAY THAT RAN THROUGH THE SITE (MORTIMER ET AL. 2005).

Over the past two decades, however, a series of archaeological excavations has yielded evidence for 'Middle Saxon' activity within the modern town. Few structural features relating to the pre-Conquest settlement have been located to date, but Ipswich Ware has been recovered from limited excavations at St. Mary's Lodge (CHER: CB17818), Chapel Street (CHER: CB15532) and Chief's Street (CHER: CB15534). An evaluation trench south of the Lady Chapel also identified a large pit, within which was found the largest quantity of Ipswich Ware from an inland location outside of Suffolk or Norfolk (CHER: CB15021) (Mortimer et al. 2005, 2). These investigations strongly suggest that the current site of Ely Abbey and its immediate environs was a focus for 'Middle Saxon' activity, and probably represents the general location of the earliest minster. A more significant insight into the early development of Ely, however, was gained following excavations at West Fen Road, 1km to the north-west of the present cathedral. Open area excavations at the Ashwell Site in 1999 first identified a detailed sequence of 'Middle Saxon' and later settlement deposits to the south of West Fen Road (Mortimer et al. 2005). More recently published investigation at the Consortium Site, has revealed parts of the same complex, demonstrating that settlement also extended to the north of West Fen Road (Figure 6.17) (Mudd and Webster 2011). The combined evidence from these excavations has identified a site, the character and location of which strongly suggests was related to the religious community at Ely.

The excavation at the Ashwell Site was by far the most extensive of the two investigations and provides the main insight into the West Fen Road settlement. The recovery of Ipswich Ware and a single sceatta dated to c.730-40, combined with a lack of organic-tempered pottery finds across the Ashwell Site, suggests the West Fen Road settlement was established in the eighth century. Unlike other rural settlements in Cambridgeshire, such as Cottenham which demonstrates a restructuring of existing early medieval occupation, the site at West Fen Road appears to have been planned from its very inception. Eighth century activity was partly influenced by Romano-British earthworks, however, as the southern part of the settlement was bounded by a fourth-century enclosure ditch. Apart from this delineation, 'Middle Saxon' occupation at West Fen Road was characterised by a new settlement arrangement, with a series of shallow, ditched paddocks and more substantial enclosures ordered around a central trackway. A number of the enclosures, which were probably enhanced by hedges or fences, possessed post-built structures probably representing a combination of domestic and agricultural buildings. In addition to a total of at least six occupied enclosures and internal structures, two large empty enclosures to the south were identified, and interpreted as paddocks for cattle herding (Figure 6.18). This arrangement was subsequently developed after the middle of the ninth century, with the addition of further trackways, enclosures and structures, although the 'Middle Saxon' features continued to articulate the character of the medieval settlement, until its eventual abandonment during the fifteenth century (Mortimer *et al*. 2005, 25-32).

The environmental evidence from the 'Middle Saxon' phases at the Ashwell Site, represented by a large macrofaunal assemblage and charred plant remains, indicates that the site was operating a mixed farming economy, but one which was also geared to large-scale food production. Excavations have revealed little structural or artefactual material to suggest that West Fen Road was a high-status centre, but the regular and ordered approach to occupation does suggest a degree of planning from the outset (Mortimer *et al*. 2005, 33). Ordered occupation around a central track or road has been noted on other early medieval settlements, such as Catholme, Staffordshire, although contrary to West Fen Road it appears that tenements on the Trent Valley site developed in a more piecemeal fashion around the routeway (Losco-Bradley and Kinsley 2002). Such ordered approaches to settlement planning in the later medieval period are commonly related to the influence of lordly power: the deserted medieval settlements of Okehampton Park, Devon, for example are regularly spaced throughout the landscape and linked by a central trackway, which Oliver Creighton (2009) suggests is the product of a single lordly foundation.

The settlement arrangement identified at the Ashwell Site has been supplemented by further excavation to the north of West Fen Road, at the Consortium Site (Figure 6.19) (Mudd and Webster 2011). Although also excavated in 1999, the details of the 1.5ha open area site were not published until more recently. Similar to the Ashwell Site, Ipswich Ware pottery suggests that 'Middle Saxon' settlement was confined to the *c*.725-850 period, but within this two main phases of activity were identified; Phase I in which the basic site layout was established and Phase II when minor modifications were made. A large boundary ditch in the western part of the site formed a series of apparent tenement plots, defined by east-west and north-south ditches (Mudd and Webster 2011, 31). This arrangement gives the general impression that the enclosure network was orientated around a north-west track to the east of the excavated area. It would appear that this track may have connected the excavated areas of the Ashwell Site, located only 50m to the south and. Indeed the routeway excavated at the Ashwell Site does appear to bend to the north, further supporting this suggestion

Perhaps the most significant aspect of the entirety of the excavated West Fen Road complex is that more than any other 'Middle Saxon' centre in Cambridgeshire, the geographical proximity of the site to the early minster at Ely suggests that the planned approach to settlement was developed under the auspices of a minster community. As the excavators have already suggested, West Fen Road was probably not the site of the documented early minster, but more likely represents a settlement specifically geared to provide surplus for the neighbouring church group (Mortimer *et al*. 2005, 33-6). Located only 1km to the north-west of the 'Middle Saxon' activity recognised in

Ely town centre, it is likely that the settlement at West Fen Road was part of the early monastic estate from its first development in the eighth century. Indeed, West Fen Road adds weight to an increasing body of evidence suggesting that such core agricultural zones or 'proto-demesne' were a fundamental part of early monastic estates in central and southern England (Blair 2005, 256; Faith 1995, 36).

Together with the 'Middle Saxon' site at Fordham, which was likely developed as part of the agricultural core of the minster at Soham, the structured approach to the eighth century-settlement at West Fen Road is especially important to this book. These sites, together with the property arrangement recognised at Cottenham, adds to the growing body of evidence which demonstrates the likely influence of ecclesiastical communities in the development of an increasingly sophisticated 'Middle Saxon' settlement hierarchy (Wright 2010). John Blair has taken the association of planned settlements and monastic communities further, suggesting that sites under ecclesiastical ownership were gridded using a standard measures based on the techniques of Roman *agrimensores* (Chapter VII; Blair 2013). Before the Viking period, Blair argues, such an approach to settlement planning was restricted to monastic sites, and only in the centuries after *c*.850 did such gridding become more widespread to all settlement types.

Whilst it is not within the remit of this research to assess the potential standardisation of 'Middle Saxon' settlements in Cambridgeshire with Roman survey measures, it is certainly significant that monastic sites demonstrate a planned approach to occupation. The West Fen Road site is no exception, and the regular spacing of enclosures and structures certainly indicates a more considered approach to settlement planning than encountered on some other 'Middle Saxon' sites (e.g. Pine 2001). It is notable too that the investigators at West Fen Road noted that, whilst the faunal assemblage and plant remains from the site did not indicate a farming regime orientated to a particular product, the quantity of the excavated evidence did suggest that a mixed surplus was being created (Mortimer *et al*. 2005). Such findings conform to the generally-accepted view of the functioning of 'Middle Saxon' estates, whereby a series of dependent settlements involved with specialised resource procurement, were supplemented by a mixed surplus-producing agricultural core located close to the estate centre (e.g. Aston 1985).

The excavated settlement at West Fen Road thus represents a vital contribution to our understanding of 'Middle Saxon' occupation in the Peat Fen and its Islands, and indeed provides a broader insight into contemporary settlement development across Cambridgeshire. The fen-islands of the *pays* clearly formed important foci for 'Middle Saxon' activity, representing key dry areas upon which semi-permanent settlements were developed. The 'fen-islands' themselves consist of fertile and easily cultivable soils, which are otherwise rare within the Peat Fen, but the development of settlement centres also allowed

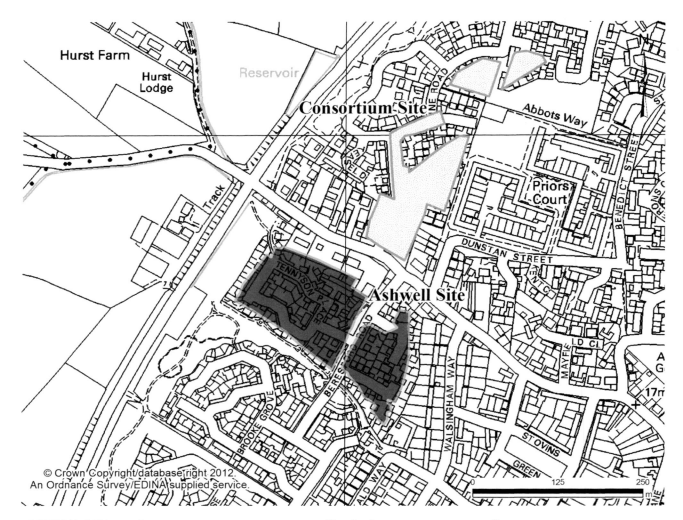

FIGURE 6.19: OS MODERN EDITION SHOWING THE LOCATION OF THE TWO WEST FEN ROAD EXCAVATIONS IN DETAIL. THE INVESTIGATIONS PROVIDE AN INSIGHT INTO THE FORM AND FUNCTION OF A MONASTIC INLAND UNPARALLELED IN ENGLAND.

communities to take advantage of other resources within the *pays*. The animal bone assemblage from West Fen Road demonstrates that fishing and wildfowl were clearly important aspects of 'Middle Saxon' agricultural regimes in the Peat Fen, but the landscape of the *pays* could also have been utilised for seasonal pasturing of animals (Mortimer *et al.* 2005; Rippon 2001, 152; Murray 2010). In addition to these practical considerations, there is also evidence that colonisation of islands in the Peat Fen would have been symbolically valuable throughout the medieval period, especially to monastic communities (e.g. Rippon 2004a, 129; see below).

The site at West Fen Road has revealed the most detailed archaeological evidence for a monastic *inland* anywhere in England, demonstrating the form and function that settlements within agriculture cores likely featured. The economy of the West Fen Road settlement was diverse, as might be expected of a 'proto-demesne', but vitally it seems that the site was specifically geared towards producing surpluses. In the well-recognised model of 'Middle Saxon' agricultural estates, farming yields produced by the West Fen Road community would have been rendered to the estate centre at Ely, from which it would have been either

utilised or the surplus sold for profit (Fleming 2011, 18). A comparable economy has already been noted at Fordham, where a mixed economic surplus was probably being rendered to the minster community at Soham. Also similar to Fordham, West Fen Road demonstrates a significant degree of settlement planning, with properties and enclosures arranged in a regular and ordered fashion, and were perhaps even laid out using standard measures. The delineation of private property boundaries appears to have been an integral part of the new arrangements detectable on such 'Middle Saxon' settlements, and again reflects a shift in the perception of private space and property ownership.

What the approach to the farming regime and settlement arrangement evident at West Fen Road demonstrates possibly more than anything is the sophistication and skill of early medieval communities to take advantage of resources, even in potentially difficult environments. This chapter has shown that in the Peat Fen, as elsewhere in Cambridgeshire, the rural landscape underwent drastic changes throughout the 'Middle Saxon' period. The majority of the evidence for such developments in Cambridgeshire has been derived from excavations within currently-occupied villages. Before the significance of the

Interventions in CORS	CORS interventions identifying archaeological deposits	CORS with 'Middle Saxon' artefactual material only	CORS with 'Middle Saxon' artefactual material and settlement structures from CORS
44	38	7	10

Table 6.1: Of the archaeological interventions undertaken within 'CORS' in Cambridgeshire, almost half have located potential evidence for occupation datable to the 'Middle Saxon' period.

'Middle Saxon' settlement archaeology of Cambridgeshire is discussed in more detail, it is first necessary to assess the consistency with which seventh to ninth century activity is found through such 'CORS' excavation. This evaluation will reveal the potential relationship, if any, of 'Middle Saxon' settlements with later historic villages, providing a gauge of how widespread the two-stage process of village formation, as identified at sites like Cottenham and Fordham, occurred across the county of Cambridgeshire.

'CORS': ASSESSING 'MIDDLE SAXON' POTENTIAL

As the above evidence demonstrates, a number of currently-occupied rural settlements in Cambridgeshire have been subject to archaeological excavation which has resulted in the identification of 'Middle Saxon' settlement evidence. Whilst the data from such places has a clear research value, of equal importance is assessing the frequency with which 'Middle Saxon' settlement material is found in 'CORS'. The AIP records that, of the archaeological interventions carried out in Cambridgeshire between 1990 and 2009, forty-four were undertaken in areas classified by this book as still-occupied rural settlements. Thirty-eight of these investigations located archaeological deposits of some type, seven of which detected 'Middle Saxon' artefacts only, and a further ten identified structural features relating to 'Middle Saxon' habitation. Archaeological work in Cambridgeshire's currently-occupied villages has therefore encountered 'Middle Saxon' material in seventeen out of the thirty-eight villages, in which stratified deposits were recorded, a detection rate of over forty-four percent. It must be remembered that the evidence derived from the AIP can only be realistically used as an approximate guide, and is not a completely comprehensive analysis (see Chapter II). Detection of 'Middle Saxon' settlement deposits in almost half of the 'CORS' excavated in Cambridgeshire is, nevertheless, extremely informative and suggests a significant relationship between existing villages and the later medieval landscape.

This chapter has thus far highlighted an apparent association between early minster communities in Cambridgeshire and the transformation of the landscape dated to the 'Middle Saxon' period. The following summary of the 'Middle Saxon' settlement archaeology of the county investigates the potential reasons for this association, but it will also show how difficult it is to associate specific sites or landscapes with ecclesiastical agency, given the inherently secular character of early minster foundations and their intimate familial links with 'Middle Saxon' royal houses. Rather, it will be demonstrated that the willingness to invest so heavily in the rural landscape was not the preserve of minsters or their clerics, but just one aspect of the more widespread changes across 'Middle Saxon' society in Cambridgeshire that resulted in new expressions within the material record.

SETTLEMENT IN 'MIDDLE SAXON' CAMBRIDGESHIRE

The settlement and landscape archaeology from the four *pays* of Cambridgeshire represents an important contribution to this research, and again demonstrates that significant changes occurred in the countryside during the 'Middle Saxon' period. By far the most poorly represented Cambridgeshire *pays* is the Siltlands in the far northern part of the county, where only slight 'Middle Saxon' activity has been detected, and no settlement sites have been excavated. The dearth of 'Middle Saxon' evidence is unsurprising given the moderate size of the Cambridgeshire Siltlands, and research elsewhere around the Wash demonstrates that the roddons of the intertidal silt landscapes were generally more densely settled than areas of peat. Indeed, the low rise of the Tydd St. Giles area which has yielded the only evidence for 'Middle Saxon' settlement from the Cambridgeshire Siltlands to date, hints that here too slight topographical variations were decisive in shaping early medieval activity. Conforming to the county-wide pattern of 'Middle Saxon' sites on fen-islands associated with religious houses by the 'Late Saxon' period, the manor of Tydd St. Giles is recorded as part of the liberty of Ely by 1086 (Darby 1952, 310).

It is not legitimate to associate the development of 'Middle Saxon' settlements on fen-islands with minster communities, based solely on their entries at Domesday, however. Indeed, by the eleventh century the entirety of the Siltlands and Peat Fen was incorporated into the two hundreds of Ely, following the generous endowments bestowed on the Abbey following its re-foundation in the tenth century (Keynes 2003, 29-32). It remains possible that the tenth-century grants of Cottenham and Willingham recorded in the *Liber Eliensis* were part of this same process (Liber Eliensis Book II/84; Keynes 2003, 5-9), but it is equally likely that such entries reflect an attempt to provide written integrity for more ancient claims, a possibility given extra credence by the semi-legendary details of the donation, including the shadowy benefactor *Uva*. Significant too, is the settlement character of sites such as 'Middle Saxon' Fordham and West Fen Road, the location and geographical proximity of which suggests they were probably *inland* centres for the minsters at Soham and Ely respectively. As anticipated of a 'proto-demesne', the economy of both sites was varied, yet was clearly orientated towards producing a surplus from a mixed farming regime. Further explanation for the lack of specialisation displayed by the *inland* settlements is likely the environmental conditions in which the sites were located. The often extensive low islands of the fenlands and its periphery would have represented valuable cultivable soils, especially when the extent of fenland coverage across northern Cambridgeshire is considered (Murray 2010).

Another characteristic of the *inlands* at Fordham and West Fen Road was the planned approach to their settlement. At Fordham, a new settlement arrangement of regular enclosures was introduced into a pre-existing centre, but at West Fen Road paddocks and tenements were developed on a site that was last occupied in the Romano-British period. Unlike Fordham and West Fen Road, Cottenham does not possess a close geographical relationship to a documented minster, and thus it is intriguing that the 'Middle Saxon' settlement presents a similarly structured approach to occupation. The excavated evidence at Cottenham again indicates a mixed farming economy, but there is little indication that the community were involved in the intensive production of surplus goods that characterised the centres at Fordham and West Fen Road. The establishment of the 'toft' network at Cottenham around the eighth century, apparently defining individual property plots, is nevertheless significant and implies that here also the community were influenced by changing perceptions of ownership and land tenure.

Although 'Middle Saxon' Cottenham was not located close to a known early minster, the influence of ecclesiastical agency in its development cannot be entirely dismissed. In addition to Ely's claim to land along the fen-edge from at least the tenth century, it is possible that the approach to settlement planning detectable at Cottenham was the preserve of monastic communities in the pre-Viking period. It has been noted that, whilst it cannot be proven that elite secular sites were monumental or more permanent before the tenth century, it appears that stable settlements were a key component of ecclesiastical establishments throughout the 'Middle Saxon' period (Blair 1996, 120-1). In Ireland, Charles Doherty has also asserted that minsters represent the earliest centres of permanently situated consumption, arguing that the eighth century Church was the 'only organisation that could produce a surplus, particularly of grain' (Doherty 1985, 55). The capacity to create such yields may have been due to the presence of monastic brethren with a semi-dependent status, whose ability to exploit the land more directly emancipated them from the process of tribute accumulation which so typified secular landownership up to *c.*850 (Blair 2005, 255; Fleming 2011, 22).

It is not only the permanence of settlement that may have been unique to monastic communities in the pre-Viking period, but it is even possible that sites under ecclesiastical ownership were subject to gridded planning using a standardised measure based on the techniques utilised by Roman *agrimensores* (Blair forthcoming). Indeed, the use of the Roman 'short-perch' has already been associated with the planning of eighth century Kentish churches, property boundaries at the likely ecclesiastically-planted trading centre at *Hamwih*, and the enclosure arrangements of numerous rural sites associated with early minsters. Whilst it is not within the remit of this research to assess the potential standardisation of 'Middle Saxon' settlements in Cambridgeshire with such measures, the excavation of planned arrangements on sites that may have been held by minsters is certainly significant. The introduction of bounded space into the landscapes of the wetlands and the fen-edge that had previously remained largely open and unenclosed in the 'Early Saxon' period may furthermore have been of symbolic value to the early Church.

It is likely that the colonisation of Cambridgeshire's fen-islands in particular would have represented a conspicuous statement of power, illustrating the rapidly increasing authority and economic viability of the 'Middle Saxon' minster communities which established them. Whilst it is unlikely that the early medieval Peat Fen was viewed as the entirely 'trackless waste' often depicted in hagiographies such as *The Life of Guthlac* (Roffe 2005), the 'wilderness' character of the *pays* outlined by such narratives likely represents an inflation of an environment that was nevertheless perceived as liminal. In Cambridgeshire, the evidence for 'Middle Saxon' colonisation of the Peat Fen and fen-edge in particular may have been seen as a manifestation of good over evil by ecclesiastics and others in society, and the development of settlements on the fen-islands could even have been viewed as a symbolic extension of the 'holy city' into marginal places (Blair 2005, 247-62).

A monastic-orientated outlook cannot adopted as a sole explanation for the 'Middle Saxon' colonisation and structured settlement of the Cambridgeshire wetlands, however, when the wider context of contemporary social change is considered. One of the clearest observations to be made is that although the use of standard measures may have been the preserve of church communities in the pre-Viking period, bounded space began to emerge on a range of rural settlements in England from as early as the sixth century (Reynolds 2003, 130). The varied approach to farming regimes, particularly notable on the fen-islands and along the fen-edge of Cambridgeshire, was also unlikely to have been restricted to monastic estates, as 'Middle Saxon' communities across the settlement hierarchy would have attempted to take advantage of such diverse resources. Where early minsters certainly profited though, was the scale of their endowments and the coherence of their estate organisation (Blair 2005, 254). Sustaining non-producing groups would probably have driven religious houses to intensify production across their lands, such as in Northamptonshire, where the 'Middle Saxon' minster at *Medeshamstede* is recorded as drawing renders from Lincolnshire properties up to forty kilometres away (Biddick 1989, 10-12).

It must be remembered though, that our understanding of such arrangements is due to the well-documented character of monastic institutions, and it is equally possible that secular estates employed similarly complex networks of dependencies. Scholars have probably over-emphasised the distinction between 'secular' and 'religious' centres and their estates, with archaeologists especially guilty of attempting to label individual sites as the product of specific agency (e.g. Loveluck 1998). As the work of Tim Pestell has shown, the archaeological record is not an adequate medium to make such rigid suppositions (Pestell 2003; 2004). It is even questionable whether such distinctions would even have been evident on the ground in 'Middle Saxon' Cambridgeshire, given the close involvement of royal authority in the development of religious houses as reflected in the familial nature of their personnel (Pestell 2004, 58).

In summary then, whilst there appears to be a compelling association between the new 'Middle Saxon' settlement forms of Cambridgeshire and early minsters, the transformations of the countryside is more usefully seen as the result of more widespread changes across society which was not peculiar to religious institutions. The identification of an execution site close to the crossing of the Cam in Cambridge is significant in this regard, as there is increasing evidence that such expressions of judicial authority were a crucial new manifestation of secular power in the 'Middle Saxon' period (Reynolds 2009a; 2009b). Rather than the product of specific establishments, it is thus clear that the transformation of Cambridgeshire's 'Middle Saxon' rural settlement was the result of more fundamental changes in the social, economic and political environment of central and eastern England. The picture emerging from archaeological evidence suggests that from the second quarter of the eighth century, an 'economic boom' took place in eastern England, reflected by increased agricultural production, the development of a more complex trade and redistribution network, and the more widespread use of coinage (Metcalf 1984; Blinkhorn 1999; Chapter VII).

In the countryside of Cambridgeshire, the increase in production on many rural settlements coincided with new approaches to settlement organisation, as semi-permanent and private property arrangements began to be defined for the first time. Whilst these changes were a clear departure from the 'Early Saxon' settlement forms which had preceded them, where such sites have been excavated within currently-occupied rural settlements, it is clear that historic village forms only emerged following a process of restructuring in the 'Late Saxon' and following periods. The sites at Cottenham, Willingham and Fordham, where still-occupied village excavations which have produced such significant settlement remains, it is clear that the 'Middle Saxon' phases are of different character to the village pattern detectable on later maps. Yet, investigation of the AIP for Cambridgeshire clearly shows a relationship between 'Middle Saxon' occupation and existing villages, with almost half of currently-occupied rural settlement

investigations locating evidence for pre-ninth century occupation.

What the excavations at Cottenham, Willingham, and Fordham demonstrate, however, is that the medieval village forms at each site only developed following a process of 'Late Saxon' restructuring. In each case, the earlier settlement foci were abandoned and emerged as 'backfields' to the new tenement arrangement as the historic village form began to take shape. There is only a slight possibility that settlements such as Fordham and Cottenham operated the type of 'proto common' field regimes detected by Oosthuizen in the Borne Valley, but such sites do not lie in the 'central province' in which common fields later emerged. Indeed, by projecting the 'Middle Saxon' centres explored by this book against Roberts and Wrathmell's (2000) 'central province, it is clear that there is little relationship between these early settlements and later 'nucleated' villages (Figure 6.20). It appears therefore, that it was only following later changes, probably from around the tenth century that recognisable historic villages gained their character. Thus, whereas it cannot be doubted that 'Middle Saxon' developments were a key influence for determining the location of later medieval sites, it was only after subsequent changes both in settlement and social environment that the historic landscape of Cambridgeshire was more permanently established.

CONCLUSION

Comparable to the previous counties researched by this book, this chapter has shown how the landscape of Cambridgeshire underwent significant changes during the 'Middle Saxon' period. In Cambridgeshire, our understanding of the early medieval settlement sequence has been particularly forwarded by excavation in currently-occupied villages. The contribution of such research is particularly welcome given the dearth of fieldwalking undertaking in the county, outside of the wetlands of the Siltlands and Peat Fen. Excavation within occupied villages in Cambridgeshire has demonstrated the development of semi-permanent and highly regular 'Middle Saxon' settlements, which may have even been planned according to a standardised grid or measure. The emergence of such an approach to occupation reflects fundamental transformations in the perception of land and property ownership, which itself is indicative of deep-rooted changes in society. Although Cambridgeshire is well-trodden ground for scholars searching for the origins of later medieval settlement character, this chapter has shown that the drastic 'Middle Saxon' restructuring of centres such as Fordham and Cottenham did not determine later centres of 'nucleation'. Rather, it was only following restructuring during the tenth century and later periods that such villages gained their medieval form, although 'Middle Saxon' occupation was undoubtedly a crucial influence in determining the site of such centres. It is unquestionable that the 'Middle Saxon' period saw the introduction of 'village-type' elements, such as the

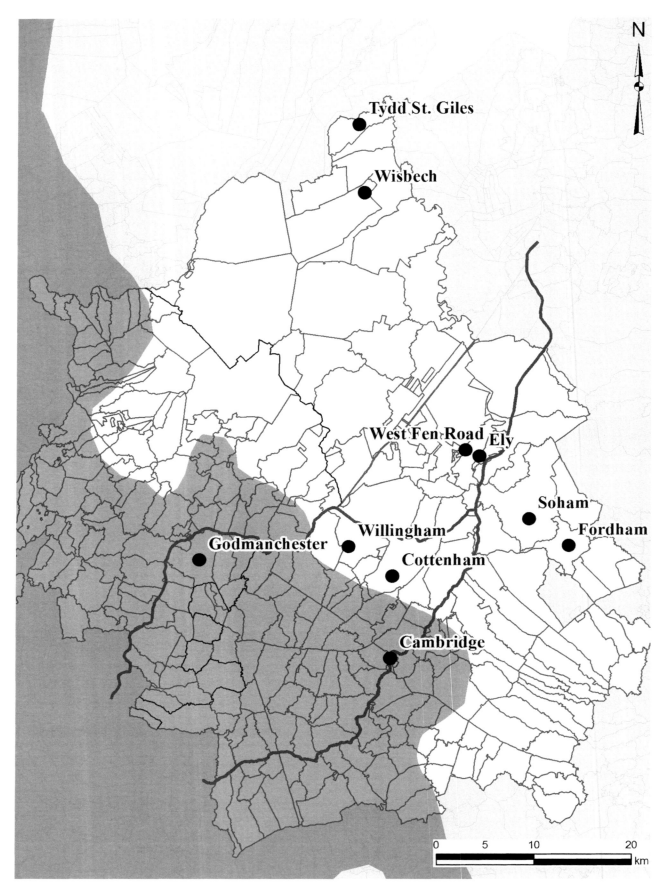

FIGURE 6.20: ROBERTS AND WRATHMELL'S (2002) 'CENTRAL PROVINCE (SHADED) AND 'MIDDLE SAXON' SETTLEMENTS MENTIONED IN THE TEXT. THE LACK OF JUXTAPOSITION BETWEEN THE 'CENTRAL PROVINCE' OF 'NUCLEATED' SETTLEMENTS AND COMMON FIELDS, AND 'MIDDLE SAXON' SITES, ESPECIALLY PLANNED SETTLEMENTS SUCH AS COTTENHAM, FORDHAM AND WEST FEN ROAD SUGGESTS THAT IT WAS LATER RESTRUCTURING THAT WAS CRUCIAL IN DETERMINING HISTORIC VILLAGE CHARACTER.

'toft' arrangement excavated at Cottenham but until the tenth century settlements will still prone to be reformed and reordered. Study of the 'Middle Saxon' settlement archaeology of Cambridgeshire is therefore of greatest value within its immediate chronological context, with the transformation of habitation and land use providing an insight into a changing society that was articulating power in the countryside by significant new means.

Chapter VII
Norfolk

For the final county-based chapter of this book, the emphasis of research shifts to Norfolk in the region of England known as East Anglia. Norfolk is in many ways a unique county, both in terms of its geographical conditions but also with regard to its history and archaeology. Bounded between the north and east by the North Sea, and to the west by the Fens, even today Norfolk is often regarded as a peculiar and marginal place. During the early medieval period, however, the North Sea provided a vital artery of trade and communication and, together with the fertile agricultural landscape of the region, contributed to the rise of the kingdom of the East Angles. The kingdom, which comprised modern-day Norfolk, the northern part of Suffolk, and possibly part of the fen basin, probably developed as a coherent political entity by the second half of the sixth century. Certainly by the early seventh century, the dynasty of the Wuffing kings of south-eastern Suffolk had assumed power and exerted their authority over the region, and it has been argued that the kingdom of the East Angles remained nationally prominent until the eventual creation of a unified England in the tenth century (Bassett 1989, 26; Scull 1992, 2-6).

In spite of the obvious significance of the region during the early medieval period, any attempt to research the history of Norfolk is hindered by the remarkably poor survival of relevant documentary material. Yet, the dearth of written records for Norfolk serves only to emphasise the significance of the archaeological evidence in providing an insight into the changing social and physical landscape of the early medieval period. Fortunately, Norfolk possesses an excellent archaeological record which surpasses that of any other county studied by this volume, both in terms of the quantity and quality of available data. In addition to the excavated evidence from currently-occupied villages, insights into broader 'Middle Saxon' settlement trends may be gleaned from the extensive fieldwalking projects undertaken in the county. In particular, Norfolk's continuous early medieval ceramic sequence has proven vital for the identification and phasing of 'Middle Saxon' sites (e.g. Blinkhorn 1999). Added to this body of material can be Norfolk's exceptional dataset of metalwork finds, largely the result of a consistently healthy relationship between detectorists and county authorities. Due to the value of this cumulative archaeological evidence, Norfolk and the wider region has often been the subject of early medieval settlement research, despite not being located in the traditional academic hot-bed of the English midlands. The work of Tom Williamson in particular, has sought to use East Anglia as a case-study for early medieval settlement research, the results from which he has used to model the *longue durée* of landscape change on a national scale (Williamson 2003; 2008).

The continued academic interest in the archaeology of the East Anglian region is represented by numerous other works, but perhaps most notably by the research of Tim Pestell and Richard Hoggett (Pestell 2003; 2004; Hoggett 2007; 2010a). Both researchers have focussed upon the influence of monastic activity in the region, with Hoggett attempting to trace the East Anglian conversion, and Pestell focussing on the prolonged importance of 'Middle Saxon' sites in shaping the location and character of later medieval religious establishments. What is notable about these pieces of research, however, is the regional focus which they adopt, which in many ways represents a logical approach when East Anglia's cohesion as an independent polity from the sixth century onwards is considered. These previous efforts have largely attempted to characterise the social and political makeup of what may possibly represent a peculiar early medieval social institution, however, and a similar endeavour here would not meet the main aims of this book. Rather, a more detailed approach which investigates Norfolk alone is more appropriate and is thus pursed in this chapter.

Researching the 'Middle Saxon' settlement and landscape of Norfolk provides an East Anglian case-study which may be used to compare and contrast the contemporary conditions already explored by the other county-based studies of this research. Most significantly, this approach will demonstrate whether the seventh to ninth centuries were also a period of fundamental change in the countryside of East Anglia, as was clearly the case in other parts of central and eastern England. Whilst the historical and archaeological evidence relating to other parts of the East Anglian region will not be ignored entirely, and in many instances provides useful contextual material, the primary focus of this chapter will remain on the northern part of the region. This chapter will begin with a brief introduction to Norfolk, followed by an account of the topographical *pays* of the county. A discussion of the landscape-orientated projects undertaken in Norfolk will then be succeeded by a detailed analysis of the evidence from currently-occupied rural settlements in the county, divided by *pays*. Analysis of material based on topographical zones is especially pertinent to study of the East Anglian countryside, as it has been previously asserted that physical conditions were fundamental in shaping the form of early medieval and later settlement across the region (e.g. Williamson 2003).

A *pays*-based approach will therefore allow such concepts to be assessed, both on a local level between the topographic zones of Norfolk itself, but also on a regional scale against the other counties investigated by this research. Rather than using evidence for 'Middle Saxon' settlement solely to understand later landscape character, however, this research is concerned with how such material can shed light on contemporary social conditions. This chapter will demonstrate that, although the landscape of Norfolk followed a divergent path of development to much of England from the 'Late Saxon' period, between the seventh and ninth centuries, the settlement character of the county underwent comparable changes to other places investigated by this research. These changes, it will be shown, were principally the result of fundamental transformations across society, as rapidly stratifying social institutions and lordly power was manifest in new ways, with rural communities becoming increasingly stable, specialised and hierarchical.

INTRODUCING NORFOLK

The county of Norfolk situated within the lowland region of East Anglia, today remains overwhelmingly rural with Norwich, Kings Lynn and Great Yarmouth the only substantial towns. The first written recording of the place-name 'Norfolk' is in Thurstan's will, dating to the eleventh century, but the shire is also referenced as *Norðfolc* and *Nordfolc* in the Anglo-Saxon Chronicle and Domesday Book respectively (Whitelock 1930, 82; Ekwall 1960, 353). The origins of a distinct northern-East Anglian territory are probably more ancient, though, as it appears that from the Iron Age the valleys of the rivers Gipping and Lark developed as a cultural watershed dividing the region. This apparent boundary, detectable through the distribution of coins and chariot fittings, and seems to have defined the extent of the Trinovantes to the south, from the looser political groupings of the Iceni to the north. This zone of cultural interface appears to have persisted throughout the medieval period, but it is hard to determine with certainty when the Norfolk-Suffolk border shifted to the River Stour, the course of which forms the county-boundary recorded on early mapping (Gurney 1994, 34; Rippon 2007, 25-35). Norfolk's limits in other areas are far easier to detect, with the North Sea surrounding the county from the east to the north-west, and the natural barrier of the fens forming the western extent of the territory. Norfolk has not been subject to significant boundary changes during recent history, and for the purposes of this research the historic extents of the county will be utilised, as this also represents the area covered by the Norfolk Historic Environment Record (NHER). For the purposes of this chapter, the landscape of Norfolk has been divided into seven distinct topographical *pays* (Figure 7.1).

THE *PAYS* OF NORFOLK

Marshland

Forming the western boundary of the county is an area commonly referred to as 'the fens'. An extremely low-lying and flat landscape, the fens is a former estuary of the rivers Ouse, Nene and Witham and extends into the neighbouring counties of Lincolnshire and Cambridgeshire. Although often viewed as a coherent whole, the fens actually comprise two distinct landscapes, the divergent character of which has been vital in shaping past human activity. These silts, known locally as 'Marshland', lie over a sequence of peat and clay deposits that had previously accumulated in the mouth of the estuary. The area between Downham Market and the Wash is characterised by deep silts deposited through marine incursions during the late prehistoric, Romano-British, and early medieval periods. This area of alluvial soils was colonised during the Romano-British period, but crucially for this study, also in the 'Middle Saxon' period after abandonment around the fifth century (Corbett and Dent 1994, 18; Crowson *et al.* 2005; Williamson 2006, 20). Vital to settlement development in the Marshland was the presence of roddons: raised banks of silt and sand which mark the line of earlier watercourses, providing essential drier places on which settlements could be sited. During the 'Late Saxon' period, several earlier settlements on the smaller roddons in Marshland appear to have been abandoned as the land was reclaimed (Silvester 1998, 158). The Domesday Book entries relating to Marshland townships demonstrates sophisticated exploitation of the *pays'* unique resources, detailing the presence of fisheries and salt works in addition to a mixture of arable and pastoral farming (Darby 1952, 151). Indeed, access to such resources led to the development of centres such as West Walton and Walpole St Peter into large and regionally important later medieval villages.

Peat Fen

To the south of the silt fen of Marshland is the Peat Fen, only a small portion of which lies within Norfolk. During prehistoric periods when sea levels were lower, the islands and fringes of the Peat Fen were successfully exploited. For much of the medieval period the *pays* was an un-reclaimed wetland subject to regular flooding, and large-scale permanent reclamation was only successful from the post-medieval period. This history has resulted in a landscape largely devoid of villages, with only secondary settlements such as Ten Mile Bank interrupting the stark landscape of straight roads and dykes (Williamson 1993, 14). It is not anticipated that any archaeological evidence relating to 'Middle Saxon' settlement will be identified in the Peat Fen, although this does not mean that the area was completely devoid of human activity during the period. The Peat Fen may have been used for fishing for instance, although the complete inundated nature of the landscape throughout the early medieval period is unlikely to have left any significant archaeological signature.

The Good Sands

The landscape of north-west Norfolk is characterised by gently rolling uplands, termed the 'Good Sands' by Arthur Young, as the acidic soils can be neutralised by digging pits into the underlying chalk and spreading it across farmland (Young 1809; Williamson 1993). The Good Sands appellation helps distinguish the area from the low-fertility sands of the Breckland to the south, where the

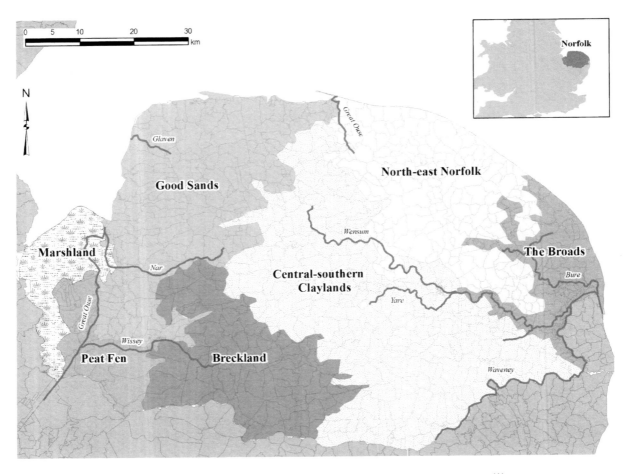

FIGURE 7.1: THE PAYS AND MAJOR RIVERS OF NORFOLK. SOURCE: HISTORIC PARISHES OF ENGLAND AND WALES ONLINE.

acidic soil has proved more restrictive to arable farming. Versatile brown earth and loamy soils on top of a subsoil of reddish-clay loam form the soil profile of the *pays*, which for the most part is a quickly-draining landscape. The location of historic villages has therefore largely been determined by the proximity of rivers and access to the water-retentive clays of river valleys. Most of the rivers cluster on the fringes of the *pays* where changes in geology are most frequent, although some minor watercourses on the upland also attracted settlement by the medieval period (Williamson 1993, 12-3). The importance of this part of west Norfolk during the 'Middle Saxon' period is evidenced by the identification of several potential 'productive sites' through the recovery of metalworking finds (Rogerson 2003, 110-5). Although the identity and role of 'productive sites' remains contested, the regular recovery of 'Middle Saxon' coinage in particular suggests that the Good Sands possessed a thriving economy before the development of centres such as King's Lynn (Richards 1999; Ulmschneider and Pestell 2003, 7-10; Hutcheson 2006, 74-80).

Breckland

The Breckland region of south-west Norfolk is formed by a low plateau, gently undulating between 25m and 100m OD, and features a geological profile of Aeolian Sands and a thin layer of clay, lying directly on porous chalk (Darby

1952, 150; Corbett and Dent 1994, 18). The resultant soils are highly acidic and infertile, creating poor arable farming conditions that are exacerbated by the tendency for water to drain quickly. The name 'Breckland', although probably only coined as late as the nineteenth century, refers to far older regional practice. The method of exploiting temporary areas of cultivation, known as outfields or 'brecks', usually over several years before allowing them to revert back to heathland, may have originated in the medieval period, but it is difficult to assign a definite provenance to the practice (Alison 1957, 28-30). Medieval settlement in the region typically comprised coalesced settlements, mostly focussed on the river valleys of the Wissey and Little Ouse, but villages also developed on the fringes of the region where geological variations provide more varied soil profiles (Williamson 1993, 11). Domesday Book records a low population and relatively few plough teams in Breckland, in addition to relatively little woodland. Rather, agricultural economies in 1086 appear to have been orientated to pastoral farming, with the stunted grass of the heathland more suited to sheep husbandry in particular (Darby 1952, 150).

The Central-southern Claylands

The Central-southern Claylands is an extensive area of Boulder Clay, situated largely between 75m and 150m OD, but with peaks occasionally rising to 200m OD in the north-west of the *pays*. The southern part of the region generally features more muted topography, which rarely rises over 125m OD. The clay geology results in heavy soils, best described as thick loams, which have historically proved hard to cultivate. By the end of the early medieval period, the region possessed an average population for the county and a similarly typical number of ploughteams, suggesting that mixed farming economies were being utilised by most townships. The eastern part of the *pays* was a particular concentration for medieval settlement, with the wide and deep river valleys in this area supporting the procurement of watermeadows. Pastoral farming, particularly of sheep was concentrated at the interface with Broadland. The uplands were originally densely wooded, and maintained relatively heavy wood cover by 1086 (Darby 1952, 148-9). Nearly the entirety of the area investigated by the Launditch Hundred Project falls within the Central-southern Claylands, providing a valuable insight into the changing character of the early medieval landscape, a picture which can be supplemented by a number of excavated currently-occupied rural settlement excavations in the *pays* (Wade-Martins 1980a).

North-east Norfolk

The north-eastern part of Norfolk possesses a varied geology, ranging between acidic sandy areas resulting in heathland similar to Breckland, to districts of deep, fertile and extremely easy-to-cultivate loams. Modern farming methods have lessened the impact of some of the less-fertile soils in the region, and in many cases the sandy heathlands have disappeared completely. Topographically, the North-east Norfolk *pays* is muted, and the landscape rarely rises above 80m OD (Darby 1952, 149). The medieval settlement pattern was for the most part dispersed, with loosely agglomerated villages and some common-edge settlements. Isolated churches, something of a characteristic Norfolk image, are especially prevalent in the area (Williamson 1993, 13). Domesday entries relating to the *pays* indicate an average population largely involved in arable-orientated farming, with relatively little meadowland or pastoral agriculture (Darby 1952, 150). Alan Davison has fieldwalked potions of several parishes around the Mannington area, but generally North-East Norfolk has not been subject to as much archaeological investigation as the western part of the county (Davison 1995).

Broadland

Located in the south-eastern part of Norfolk is an extensive area of drained marshland known as 'Broadland'. Before the medieval period, the area now occupied by Broadland was a massive estuary drained by the rivers Ant, Bure, Yare, Wensum and Waveney. Lying on the northern part of the estuary, the area of Flegg was an island throughout the Romano-British and 'Early Saxon' periods. This landscape gradually silted up and an extensive spit of land built up across the mouth of the estuary, upon which the town of Yarmouth was developed (Williamson 1993, 13).

The soils of the Flegg region are extremely fertile loams and the area was densely settled by the end of the early medieval period. The population density in this area was higher than any other part of Norfolk by 1086, all the more impressive considering that large parts of the landscape remained marshy at this time. A high proportion of sheep suggests that they were being fed on the marshes, possibly in order to prevent foot rot and liver fluke, a technique noted in other wetland areas of medieval England (e.g. Rippon 2001, 152). Desirable resources from the region included extensive woodland which fringed the Broads proper, but the landscape was also exploited for salt from at least the 'Late Saxon' period and throughout the later Middle Ages (Darby 1952, 149).

EARLY MEDIEVAL NORFOLK

Introduction

Both Norfolk, and East Anglia more generally, possess a rich tradition of archaeological research which has yielded extensive evidence for early medieval communities, crucially aided by an uninterrupted ceramic sequence. More than any other research, excavation of the princely burial site at Sutton Hoo in 1939 ensured an interest in the kingdom of the East Angles, even though the identification of the individual interred in Mound 1 as Rædwald is far from certain (cf. Bruce-Mitford 1974; Parker-Pearson *et al.* 1993; Carver 1998). From the post-War period there was a dramatic rise in archaeological discoveries of all periods, largely owing to the proactive approach of local authorities during redevelopment of centres such as Norwich. Combined with this pre-legislation concern for the historic environment, the publication of the East Anglian Archaeology monograph series and journal from 1975 ensured that the results of research were made widely available (Hoggett 2010a, 4-5). Further key contributions have been made by fieldwalking surveys and metal-detected finds, ensuring that the range of archaeological evidence from the county goes some way to negate the poor documentary record for early medieval Norfolk. For the 'Early Saxon' period, it is the material from cemeteries in particular that have preoccupied scholarly discourse.

'Early Saxon' Norfolk

The archaeological record for 'Early Saxon' Norfolk is dominated by artefactual material from funerary contexts, as numerous extensive cemeteries across the county have been subject to excavation. The most celebrated of these cemeteries is undoubtedly Spong Hill, located only 2.5km south of the 'Middle Saxon' centre of North Elmham (see below). Positioned in a typical 'Early Saxon' cemetery location within a river valley, excavations at Spong Hill identified one of the most extensive mixed-rite cemeteries in England (Hill and Penn 1981). Based on the few contemporary settlements that have been excavated in Norfolk, it seems that burial and occupation sites were situated in close proximity, whilst remaining distinct entities in the landscape throughout the fifth and sixth centuries

(Hills 1979, 310; Lucy *et al.* 2009). Richard Hoggett (2010a, 119-161; 2010b, 209-10) has viewed the changing geographical positioning of cemeteries and settlements throughout the early medieval period in East Anglia as the product of evolving religious beliefs. Although the restructuring of the landscape in 'Middle Saxon' England appears to have brought integration between habitation sites and burial grounds, associating these changes with the Christian conversion is questionable, especially given the eighth century and later production dates for diagnostic 'Middle Saxon' Ipswich Ware (see below; Blinkhorn 1999). Added to the character of 'Middle Saxon' ceramics, the difficulty of tracing the conversion process in East Anglia is compounded by the extremely poor survival of documentary evidence relating to the region.

Early Medieval Norfolk: The Documentary Evidence

Much to the frustration of early medieval scholars, East Anglia possesses an extremely sparse documentary record relating to the period and, with the exception of a few fragmentary accounts, written sources are almost non-existent until the eleventh century. The contrast between the evidence available in pre and post-Conquest periods is made all the more stark by the great detail in which East Anglia is covered in the 'Little Domesday'. Norfolk is one of the most fully described shires in the survey, detailing a sophisticated and hierarchical society that had previously been almost undetectable in terms of written evidence (Darby 1952; Roffe 2000, 224-35). In the pre-Conquest period, the dearth of East Anglian documentary sources is contrasted by the comparatively large quantities of material relating to the other English kingdoms (Yorke 1997, 58). The fragility of the records that are available is illustrated by the survival of the episcopal lists of the East Anglian see at *Dommoc* and *Elmham* only as they were integrated into a late eighth-century compilation of Mercian documents (Pestell 2004, 18). Yet, far from an illiterate or un-industrious kingdom, it would appear that the lack of sources detailing conditions amongst the East Angles is a result of the material not surviving, rather than never having been produced.

The poor survival of East Anglian records has traditionally been attributed to Viking raids on monastic establishments, as the region continued to be subject to Scandinavian attack, even after the West Saxon re-conquest of the eastern Danelaw. That the destruction or loss of documentary sources is not solely the result of Scandinavian activity, however, is demonstrated by the equally poor coverage of East Anglia in the post-Viking period. Rather, it is likely that the lack of adequate archival stewardship is an equally contributory factor in the lack of 'Middle Saxon' texts relating to Norfolk (Pestell 2004, 73-5). Compounding the loss of independent royal status is the dislocation and division of the East Anglian episcopal sees in the eleventh century, which surely would have impacted upon maintenance of their archives. As early post-Conquest historians appear to rely on the same sources available to us now, reveals that a significant proportion of documentary material is likely to have been lost by the time that the bishopric was permanently established at Norwich in 1095 (Yorke 1997, 58 Campbell 2000, 9; Hoggett 2010a, 23).

Historically-derived perspectives of the early medieval social and political environment of Norfolk are therefore hugely reliant on numismatic sources, in addition to Bede's *HE*, although closer inspection of the Northumbrian monk's likely sources raise further areas of uncertainty. Bede's account of the East Anglian kingdom is highly fragmented, with the details scattered sporadically both geographically and temporally. It is obvious that the Northumbrian cleric derived very little of his account from East Anglian sources, and much of the narrative is clearly transferred from Northumbrian, and to a lesser extent West Saxon and East Saxon traditions (Kirby 1966, 360-4). In spite of these issues, we are reliant upon the *HE*, together with a handful of other sources, to provide us with a historical insight into society in early medieval Norfolk. What can be deduced from Bede's history and other sources is that by at least the seventh century, leaders calling themselves the Wuffing kings had risen to regional prominence. Genealogical lists include *Wuffa* as an early leader, but this is likely to represent a phonological variant of Wulfingas or 'the offspring of the wolf', perhaps denoting a name with totemic origins (Williamson 1993, 75). The first historical East Anglian king that we can depict with any real certainty is Rædwald, who ruled in the first quarter of the seventh century. In spite of coming into contact with Christianity at Æthelberht's court in Kent, Rædwald famously housed altars to both pagan and Christian gods in the same temple (*HE* II, 15).

The arrival of the new ideology is not likely to have impacted the settlement landscape significantly until the reign of Sigeberht and Ecgric during the 630s. It is during this period that the first missionary activity is documented in East Anglia, bringing with them a new ideology and new expressions of material culture, including new forms of settlement. The Burgundian missionary Felix was established as the first bishop of the East Angles in the early 630s, but he is unlikely to have been a lone pioneer. Indeed, the rapidly growing momentum of the conversion process, and its impact upon the landscape of East Anglia is also demonstrated by the founding of a monastery at Iken by Botolph in 653 (*ASC* 653; Hoggett 2010a, 32). Establishment of Felix's bishopric at *Dommoc* was decisive, however, as it continued as the only East Anglian see until *c.*673. Although the location of *Dommoc* remains debated, the two most likely sites of the centre are both located in Suffolk (for discussion see Whitelock 1972, 4; Rigold 1961, 55; 1974, 100; Hoggett 2010a, 36-40).

More pertinent to this study was the division of the East Anglian see by Archbishop Theodore *c.*673, with evidence from the Council of *Clovesho* identifying the new centre as *Elmham* (Haddan and Stubbs 1964, 547). The location of the see has also been disputed, with the debate mostly focussing around two possible locations; North Elmham in

Norfolk and South Elmham in Suffolk. The case for both sites has been described numerous times, most recently by Hoggett (2010a, 40-44), and thus the full details of the arguments will not be rehearsed here. It appears that North Elmham in Norfolk is by far the most likely candidate for *Elmham*, however, based primarily on the results of excavations at both sites (Wade-Martins 1980b; Heywood 1982). Both East Anglian dioceses were impacted by Viking incursions, but the lasting power of the Norfolk see is demonstrated by its sole restoration upon the West Saxon re-conquest in the tenth century (Whitelock 1972, 15-20).

Whilst historical documents therefore give us some insight into the activities of royal and clerical authorities in the 'Middle Saxon' period, the picture remains fragmentary at best. In addition to providing only a minimal coverage of elite activity, written sources provide little information of more widespread social, economic and political changes between the seventh and ninth centuries. By examining the settlement archaeology of Norfolk, this chapter will demonstrate how material evidence is able to provide a unique insight into the effectively proto-historic communities of 'Middle Saxon' Norfolk. Significantly, it will be shown how similar transformations to the landscape were occurring in Norfolk as elsewhere in England during the 'Middle Saxon' period, suggesting that an increasingly stratified society was expressing itself in new ways, partly as a result of the rapidly changing character of lordship. In a departure from other areas of England though, it will be shown that 'Late Saxon' Norfolk featured an alternative pattern of development which significantly impacts the range of data available to modern archaeologists.

The other county-based chapters of this book have demonstrated that from around the tenth century, settlements underwent a restructuring which often resulted in the creation of recognisable historic villages. In Norfolk, however, occupation in many places apparently continued to shift into the post-Conquest period, with settlements being established around commons and heathlands, greens and fens, from which the resultant villages often took their names. In many areas the migration to these areas was so comprehensive that the parish church was left standing in complete isolation (Fox 1980, 96-9; Williamson and Bellamy 1987, 84). Vital for this research, however, these later developments ensure that significant quantities of early medieval settlement evidence is located in undeveloped portions of Norfolk's landscape, allowing archaeological investigation through pervasive methods such as metal-detecting, and in particular fieldwalking.

THE EVIDENCE FROM THE LANDSCAPE

Introduction

In terms of researching changes to landscape and settlement patterns through the early medieval period, Norfolk possesses among the best conditions anywhere in England. One of the most notable features of rural Norfolk is the high percentage of the landscape that remains under arable farming. Although modern ploughing can potentially damage archaeological deposits, the same action provides ideal conditions for fieldwalking (Chester-Kadwell 2009, 52). The potential for fieldwalking to enhance our understanding of changing settlements patterns has been recognised in Norfolk since the 1960s, and a number of extensive projects have recovered crucial evidence relating to early medieval occupation (e.g. Wade-Martins 1980a; 1980b; Rogerson 1995). The identification of 'Middle Saxon' settlement sites, both via fieldwalking and through more intrusive archaeological investigation is substantially improved in Norfolk by the prevalence of a durable and diagnostic pottery type: Ipswich Ware.

Ipswich Ware was first comprehensively categorised and described in the 1950s, and has since emerged as the archetypal indicator for 'Middle Saxon' settlement in East Anglia (Hurst and West 1957). The ceramic is rarely recovered in prolific quantities, but survives well in all soil types, is resistant to taphonomic processes, and occurs with sufficient frequency to allow conclusions to be drawn regarding settlement frequency and arable exploitation (Rogerson 1995, 101). Ipswich Ware also represents the re-emergence of industrial-scale production of ceramics in East Anglia for the first time since the end of the Roman period, and was wheel-thrown, kiln-fired and crucially for this research, widely-distributed in the northern part of the region. As such, Ipswich Ware marked a significant departure from the handmade, bonfire-fired and restricted distribution of most other 'Middle Saxon' ceramics from East Anglia. First identified after excavation of kiln sites in Ipswich during the 1920s and 1930s, the eponymous *wic* remains the sole recognised centre of production. The ware therefore provides a useful indicator of Ipswich's zone of influence, and indeed probably the influence of the East Anglian elite, throughout its period of production. Although the material is found as far afield as Yorkshire, Kent and the Upper Thames Valley, in the southern part of East Anglia, distribution of Ipswich Ware suggests that the overlordship of the kingdom may have extended along the Rivers Gipping and Lark, and the Orwell Estuary, rather than along the Stour where the historic county boundaries of Essex and Suffolk met (Figure 7.2) (Rippon 2007, 25-7). Outside of East Anglia, Ipswich Ware has often been linked to elite centres, but in Norfolk and Suffolk it appears that the material was used in a much more prosaic fashion, representing an excellent indicator of 'Middle Saxon' settlements of all types (Hurst and West 1956, 30-2; Blinkhorn 1996, 6).

Primarily on the basis of artefact association, the production of Ipswich Ware was initially dated to between *c.*650-850, although Hurst (1959) subsequently refined the first date of production to *c.*625-650 (Hurst and West 1956, 32-8). The chronological phasing of Ipswich Ware has since been significantly revised, however, following an English Heritage-funded initiative headed by Paul Blinkhorn (1999). Succeeding a critique of previous artefact-orientated dating, and comprehensive analysis of

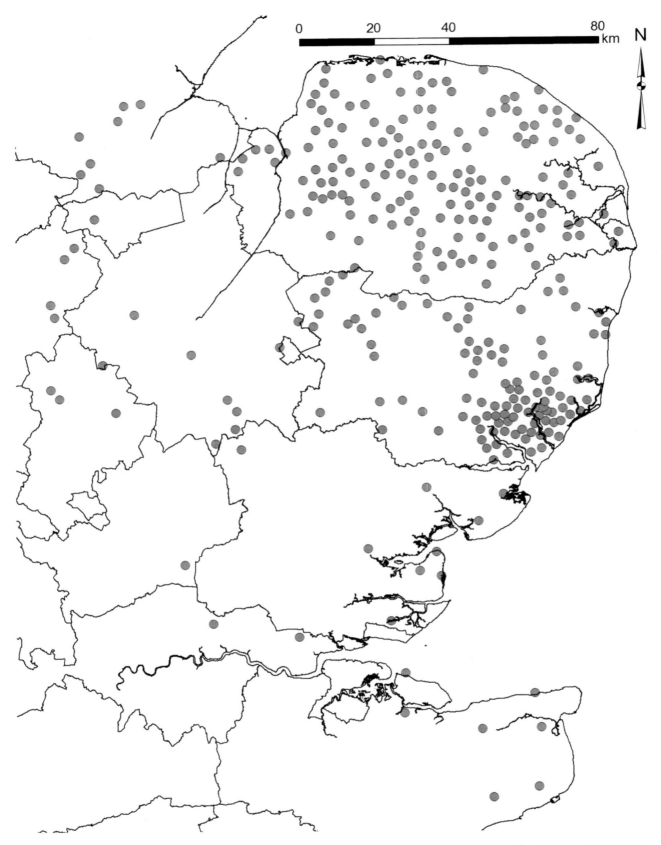

FIGURE 7.2: DISTRIBUTION OF IPSWICH WARE FINDS SHOWS THAT THE SOUTHERN BOUNDARY OF THE KINGDOM OF THE EAST ANGLES IS LIKELY TO HAVE SHIFTED (AFTER BLINKHORN 2009). TEST-PITTING AT GAYWOOD IN NORTH-WEST NORFOLK IS THE LARGEST CONCENTRATION OF THE CERAMIC OUTSIDE OF THE EPONYMOUS WIC (SEE BELOW).

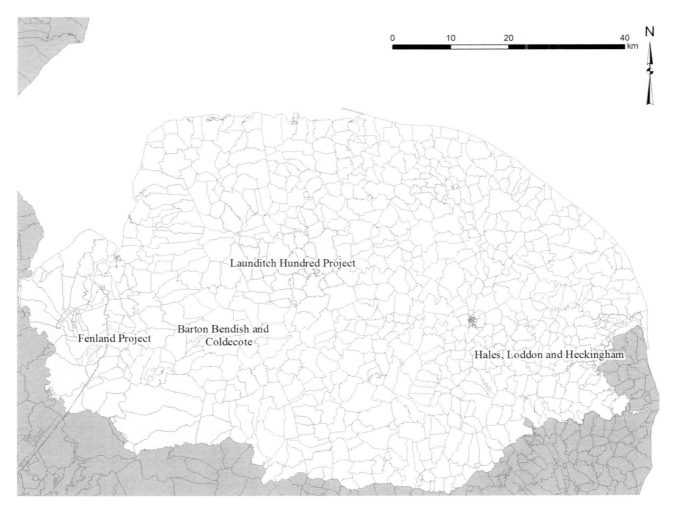

FIGURE 7.3: MAP OF FIELDWALKED PARISHES IN NORFOLK. ALTHOUGH SURVEYS RARELY COVER AN ENTIRE, OR EVEN THE MAJORITY OF A PARISH, IT HAS BEEN ESTIMATED THAT TEN PERCENT OF NORFOLK'S LANDSCAPE HAS BEEN FIELDWALKED. SOURCE FOR MAPPING: HISTORIC PARISHES OF ENGLAND AND WALES ONLINE.

ceramic composition and the context of Ipswich Ware's recovery, Blinkhorn suggests that pottery production did not begin until *c.*700-725. The alternative dating attributed to Ipswich Ware is far from certain, although an eighth century start-date is not contradicted by the lack of the material in the final phase of accompanied burials in East Anglia (Pestell 2004, 28). Somewhat hopefully, Hoggett has maintained the original early seventh century date for the initial production of Ipswich Ware, based on its recovery from the last phases of settlement occupation at West Stow, Suffolk (Hoggett 2007, 10-11; 2010a, 5-6).

It is very possible that occupation at West Stow persisted into the eighth century, however, and Hoggett is perhaps over-eager to view Ipswich Ware as a seventh-century product, so that it can be used as a marker for settlement during the earliest years of the East Anglian conversion (e.g. Hoggett 2010a, 6). Of the evidence that contradicts such an early interpretation, perhaps the most significant is the likelihood that Ipswich did not develop as a proto-urban centre until the later seventh century, following the emergence of *Lundenwic* in the middle of the same century (Wade 1993, 144-48). The *c.*625-650 interpretation for Ipswich Ware's first use therefore implies the production

of the material possibly before the actual development of the *wic*. Indeed, archaeologists risk falling into circular arguments, as the first production of Ipswich Ware has been used to date the earliest development of the *emporium* and vice-versa. The overwhelming proportion of evidence from East Anglia, however, suggests that Ipswich Ware was first produced in the earliest years of the eighth century, probably going out of widespread usage in the middle of the ninth century (Blinkhorn 1999, 4-8). The prevalence of durable and datable ceramics, together with a significant quantity of ploughed fields, has resulted in the successful identification of 'Middle Saxon' sites in Norfolk through systematic fieldwalking survey.

Fieldwalking Projects in Norfolk

The landscape of Norfolk has been subject to two large-scale fieldwalking projects, the Launditch Hundred Project and the Fenland Project, both of which have covered several parishes. In addition, a number of smaller-scale surveys, often the result of industrious local groups or enthusiasts, supplement our picture of landscape change throughout the early medieval period. Figure 7.3 illustrates the fieldwalked parishes of Norfolk, although

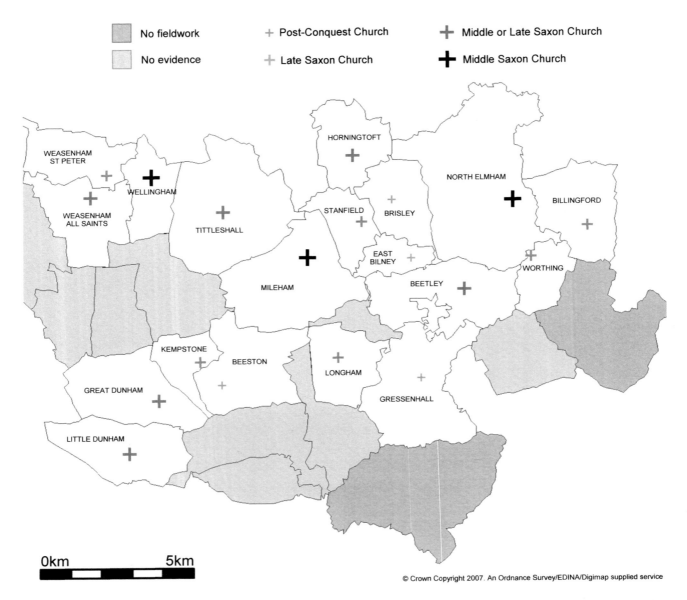

No fieldwork   + Post-Conquest Church   + Middle or Late Saxon Church

No evidence   + Late Saxon Church   ✚ Middle Saxon Church

0km   5km

© Crown Copyright 2007. An Ordnance Survey/EDINA/Digimap supplied service

FIGURE 7.4: THE NINETEEN PARISHES SURVEYED BY THE LAUNDITCH HUNDRED PROJECT AND THE POSTULATED DATE OF CHURCH FOUNDATIONS, BASED ON CERAMIC SCATTERS IN THEIR ENVIRONS (AFTER HOGGETT 2007, FIG 32).

it should be noted that projects have rarely investigated the entirety, or even the majority of the area in parishes. Rather, most surveys have been somewhat biased towards research of the landscape surrounding historic churches and settlements. Despite this caveat it has been estimated that approximately ten percent of the total land area of the county has been fieldwalked, and even limited projects provide potentially significant information for researchers (Chester-Kadwell 2009, 57).

The first significant fieldwalking project in Norfolk to locate extensive evidence for early medieval settlement was the Launditch Hundred Survey (Wade-Martins 1980a). Fieldwalking by Peter Wade-Martins between 1967 and 1970 in the central Norfolk hundred of Launditch focussed on the landscape surrounding currently-occupied villages and churches, thus providing comparative evidence for

settlement change from the nineteen parishes surveyed (Figure 7.4) (Wade-Martins 1980a, 3-7).

Of the Launditch parishes 'walked', a total of eight yielded evidence for 'Middle Saxon' activity (Wade-Martins 1980a, 19-21). In two parishes, at Mileham and Wellingham, fieldwalking around the parish church located distinct concentrations of Ipswich Ware. It is likely that the churches at Mileham and Wellingham were founded during the 'Middle Saxon' period, only for the settlement focus to migrate before the ninth century, thus accounting for the lack of 'Late Saxon' pottery in the immediate vicinity of the church. At both sites, settlement shifted only a short distance, with the identification of Thetford Ware scatters within the existing village demonstrating that the historic settlement pattern had become crystallised by the 'Late Saxon' period (Figure 7.5) (Wade-Martins

1980a, 34-8). Fieldwalking at Mileham and Wellingham therefore reveals a two-stage progression of historic village development, a process consistently recognised in other counties studied by this volume.

The two-stage process of village development was also potentially identified in the parishes of Longham, Weasenham All Saints, Horningtoft and Tittleshall, although the foundation date of the churches at these sites is less certain (Figure 7.5) (Wade-Martins 1980a, 19-23). The churches at Longham and Tittleshall appear to have been founded in the 'Late Saxon' period, as their immediate environs were surrounded solely by scatters of Thetford Ware. At both sites, settlement apparently expanded in the 'Late Saxon' period from an existing 'Middle Saxon core. The provenance of the churches at Weasenham All Saints and Horningtoft is less secure, however, surrounded by a combination of Ipswich and Thetford Wares. Irrespective of the date of church foundation, the evidence from Weasenham and Horningtoft also suggests a ninth century or later growth from an extant 'Middle Saxon' focus (Wade-Martins 1980a, 24-8). Whilst not repeating an identical pattern of settlement change, all of the above sites demonstrate an apparent expansion or shift of occupation from existing foci, which Ipswich Ware dates to the eighth or early ninth centuries.

Added to this corpus in the Launditch Hundred can be North Elmham, where excavation located settlement likely related to the historically-attested 'Middle Saxon' bishopric (see below). By the eleventh century, the growth of North Elmham witnesses the expansion of the cathedral cemetery over the earlier occupation site. The extant parish church was founded in the late eleventh century immediately south of the 'Middle Saxon' settlement, although activity apparently continued to shift south as the current village is somewhat removed from this area (Wade-Martins 1980b, 628-32). That survey by Launditch Hundred Project did not detect the North Elmham site illustrates that fieldwalking cannot be used as an absolute indicator for early medieval activity. Indeed, the single sherds of Ipswich Ware recovered by Wade-Martins in the parishes of Great and Little Dunham perhaps indicates further foci in Launditch Hundred, although these fragments may equally be the result of arable farming (Wade-Martins 1980a, 84-5). It is therefore clear that in order to provide the clearest possible picture of the early medieval settlement sequence in Norfolk, fieldwalking data needs to be supplemented by other types of archaeological evidence whenever available.

The other substantial programme of fieldwalking undertaken in Norfolk was that associated with the Fenland Project. Founded in 1981 with the aim of systematically surveying as much of the fen basin as possible during the six years allotted to the scheme, the Fenland Project focussed on three areas of Norfolk: Marshland, the Nar Valley and the Wissey Embayment (Figure 7.6) (Silvester 1988; 1991). Fieldwalking in the Nar Valley and Wissey Embayment identified little evidence for 'Middle Saxon' activity, with the notable exception of Wormegay. Located on an island in the Nar Valley, Wormegay actually represents the only village centre surveyed by the Fenland Project in Norfolk (Silvester 1988, 172-3). An extensive pottery scatter comprising both Ipswich Ware and Thetford Ware was recovered from the southern part of the raised silt that forms Wormegay Island, immediately adjacent to the parish church. The likely exceptional status of the 'Middle Saxon' Wormegay site is evidenced by the retrieval of concentrations of contemporary metalwork, including styli and coinage (Rogerson 2003, 118-21). At some point in the 'Late Saxon' period though, occupation relocated to the western part of the island where a castle was also established (Silvester 1988, 143-6).

The distance of settlement relocation at Wormegay is much more substantial than any of those illustrated by the Launditch Hundred Project, with the later centre situated some 750m west of the 'Middle Saxon' focus (Figure 7.7). The cause behind this more extensive shift is possibly due to the topographical situation of Wormegay, an island upon which the western portion represents the driest area for occupation. That Wormegay was a focus for early medieval settlement at all, though, was likely its status as the only substantial island in the Nar Valley (Silvester 1988, 143-6). Indeed, the positioning of Middle Saxon sites upon low islands is a characteristic of the neighbouring Marshland district, from which more extensive evidence for settlement was identified by the Fenland Project, where fieldwalking identified a total of seven concentrations of Ipswich Ware located on roddons.

The geographical pattern of these 'Middle Saxon' concentrations in Marshland is particularly significant, as they are spaced at regular intervals of 1.5-2km apart (Figure 7.8) (Silvester 1988, 158). It has been suggested that this distribution indicates a degree of deliberate planning, perhaps under the authority of the surrounding upland communities (Silvester 1988, 158; Hall and Coles 1994, 126). Alternatively, Robert Silvester (1988, 156) has indicated that the pattern may have developed more organically, with origins as temporary occupation sites for the seasonal pasturing of stock on the saltmarshes that were later settled permanently. Of the seven settlements recognised, the site at Hay Green in the parish of Terrington St Clement appears exceptional, with significant quantities of pottery recovered over an area extending approximately 1.5km (Silvester 1988, 37). Targeted excavation undertaken on the basis of the fieldwalked finds located a series of 'Middle Saxon' structural features, mostly comprising north-south orientated ditches along the edge of the roddon. As suspected by the fieldwalking results, the site appears to have been abandoned at the end of the 'Middle Saxon' period with no sign of 'Late Saxon' habitation (Crowson et al. 2005, 170-1).

During the same project, excavation at West Walton also confirmed the presence of 'Middle Saxon' settlement under an artefact concentration. Earlier fieldwalking had detected a scatter of 'Middle Saxon' and later ceramics, located 300m west of the parish church. A surprising

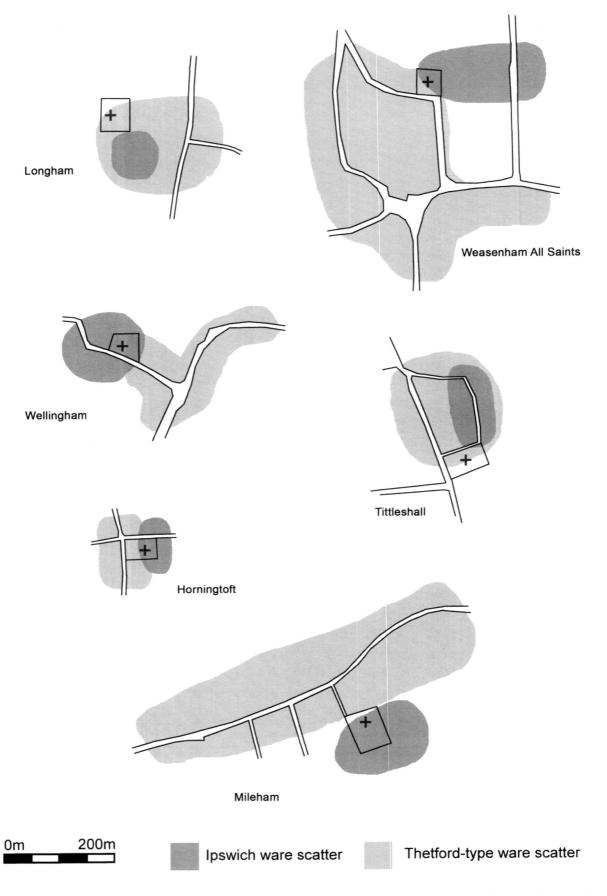

Longham

Weasenham All Saints

Wellingham

Tittleshall

Horningtoft

Mileham

0m   200m

    Ipswich ware scatter   Thetford-type ware scatter

FIGURE 7.5: DISTRIBUTION OF 'MIDDLE SAXON' AND 'LATE SAXON' POTTERY SCATTERS AROUND CHURCHES AND VILLAGES IN LAUNDITCH HUNDRED. SUCH SURVEY SUGGESTS VARIATION IN EARLY MEDIEVAL SETTLEMENT DEVELOPMENT, A THEME PARALLELED BY OTHER ARCHAEOLOGICAL EVIDENCE (AFTER WADE-MARTINS 1980A).

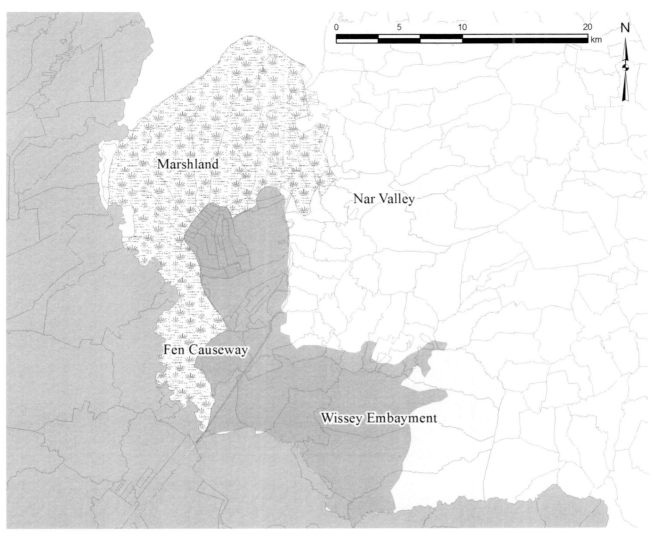

FIGURE 7.6: PARISHES SURVEYED BY THE FENLAND PROJECT. THE EXTENT OF PEAT FEN IS SHADED, AND THE SILT FEN IS INDICATED WITH A 'MARSH' SYMBOL. FIELDWALKING IN MARSHLAND IDENTIFIED SEVERAL 'MIDDLE SAXON' SITES, BUT THE OTHER REGIONS WERE APPARENTLY NOT AS INTENSIVELY OCCUPIED IN THE PERIOD.

element of the excavation was the identification of crop remains and crop-processing residues, which suggests that arable activity was practiced at the site around the eighth century (Penn *et al*. 2005; Crowson et al 2005, 189). The location of the settlement close to the church is not dissimilar to the pattern noticed in some of the parishes researched by the Launditch Hundred Project, and the likelihood that West Walton was a 'Middle Saxon' estate centre is evidenced by its entry in Domesday, recorded as owning two extensive manors, one of which was held by the Abbey at Ely (Silvester 1988, 92). Among the most populous vills in Norfolk, the estate of West Walton is likely to have included parts of the historic parishes of Walpole and Walsoken, and at least suggests its role as a former 'central place' (Crowson *et al*. 2005, 190).

Whilst fieldwalking and targeted excavation has noted numerous 'Middle Saxon' settlements in Marshland, scholars have disagreed over the interpretation of their geographical distribution. Following the original conclusions of the Fenland Project investigators, David

Roffe (2005, 286) has deemed it unlikely that sites such as Hay Green or West Walton were themselves estate centres (Silvester 1988, 158; Hall and Coles 1994, 126), but rather posits that they were more likely the product of colonisation from upland communities located around the fen-edge. Kenneth Penn, however, has asserted that the evidence points to more self-contained groups, permanently inhabiting the landscape with a self- sufficient, and probably non-specialised agricultural economy (Penn 2005, 299). Perhaps the most likely candidate for an estate centre is West Walton, with the 'Middle Saxon' focus located close to the parish church which may have originated in the same period (Hoggett 2007, 131). Indeed, West Walton is the only site in Marshland that has been labelled as 'productive', on the basis of recovered metalwork, although again the character and function of such places is not entirely clear (see below) (e.g. Pestell 2003; Rogerson 2003).

The nature of the current evidence from Marshland does not therefore allow confirmation of either of the

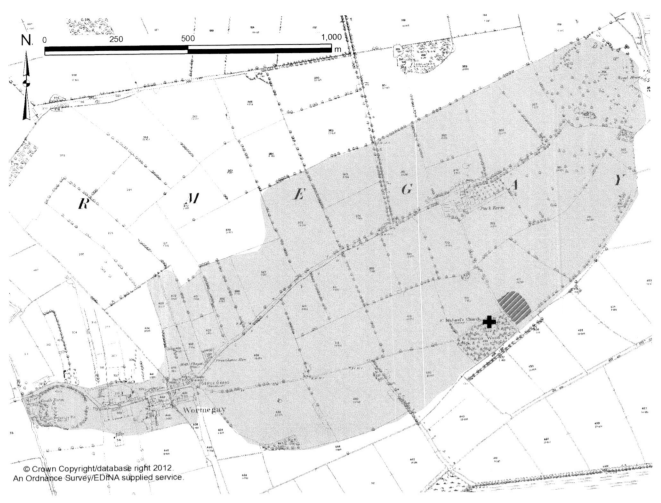

FIGURE 7.7: OS FIRST EDITION OF WORMEGAY SHOWING THE AREA ABOVE THE 3M CONTOUR (SHADED), THE CONCENTRATION OF 'MIDDLE SAXON' IPSWICH WARE (HACHURED), AND THE PARISH CHURCH OF ST MICHAEL (CROSS). THE FOCUS OF OCCUPATION RELOCATED FROM THE 'MIDDLE SAXON' CHURCH AND SETTLEMENT TO THE AREA OF THE EXISTING VILLAGE AND CASTLE, FURTHER EAST, IN THE 'LATE SAXON' PERIOD.

two models forwarded to date, with the key interpretive problem related to the difficulty of distinguishing estate centres from more typical rural sites through archaeological evidence. What can be said with greater conviction is that the data from fieldwalking and excavation demonstrates an increased exploitation of the wetland environment of the Marshland from the eighth century, following a period of almost total abandonment during the initial centuries of the early medieval period (Silvester 1988, 156-8; Rippon 2001, 145). The only exception to this pattern is the 'Early Saxon' focus located on the silted ridge of the Aylmer Hall canal in Tilney. Excavation here revealed little evidence for the drainage systems that characterise the 'Middle Saxon' sites, and the 'Early Saxon' ceramics recovered instead suggests the existence of a small and seasonally-occupied settlement (Silvester 1988, 156; Leah and Crowson 1993, 46; Murphy 1993).

The regular spacing of 'Middle Saxon' occupation sites in Marshland strongly suggests at least some degree of planning though, either organised by the inhabitants of the Marshland settlements themselves, or through the agency of those located on the upland margins. It is intriguing to

consider, although not possible to demonstrate, whether the Marshland settlements possessed their own territories, perhaps in the form of a proto-parish arrangement. Whether such an approach to settlement planning was the result of elite lordship or industrious peasant communities is similarly difficult to establish with confidence, but it is highly probable that the changing character of 'Middle Saxon' society was decisive in the increased exploitation and colonisation of Marshland. Indeed, the model of development identified in Marshland appears to have been common to coastal wetlands throughout the southern part of England during the early medieval period; small-scale and seasonal exploitation in the 'Early Saxon' period, followed by more permanent colonisation in the 'Middle Saxon' period, was eventually succeeded by complete reclamation in 'Late Saxon' times (Rippon 2000a; 2001; 2004b). In Norfolk, lasting reclamation of the Marshland was probably achieved around the tenth century, with the construction of the sea wall, and the development of farms operating in freshwater conditions (Silvester 1988, 37-8).

In addition to the extensive fieldwalking surveys of the Launditch and Fenland projects, a number of smaller

FIGURE 7.8: DISTRIBUTION OF 'MIDDLE SAXON' SITES IDENTIFIED BY THE FENLAND PROJECT, WITH THE EXCEPTIONAL SITES OF HAY GREEN AND WEST WALTON LABELLED. THE EQUAL SPACING OF THE SITES, ALMOST ONE TO A PARISH, SUGGESTS A DEGREE OF SETTLEMENT PLANNING PERHAPS WITHIN ADMINISTRATIVE UNITS. SOURCE FOR MAPPING: HISTORIC PARISHES OF ENGLAND AND WALES ONLINE.

projects elsewhere in Norfolk have also yielded significant results for 'Middle Saxon' landscape research. The dedication of the late Alan Davison is particularly notable, whose numerous fieldwalking projects form the majority of the smaller-scale surveys undertaken in the county. Amongst Davison's surveys was the fieldwalking of the three adjacent parishes of Hales, Loddon and Heckingham in south-east Norfolk, within the Central-southern Clayland *pays* (Figure 7.3) (Davison 1990). The project benefited from previous study in the area, which had combined fieldwalking evidence with hedgerow dating (Addington and Cushion 1981). The 'Three Parish Survey' demonstrated a dispersed and ephemeral 'Early Saxon' settlement pattern, apparently followed by a marked shift in character around the eighth century which conformed to the then well-established 'Middle Saxon shuffle' model (Arnold and Wardle 1981). The densely-settled core of Loddon village meant that it could not be surveyed, but walking in the rest of the parish showed a tendency for 'Middle Saxon' occupation to shift to the lower ground of the River Chet and its tributaries. A similar shift occurred

in Heckingham, but here survey also illustrated a 'Middle Saxon' focus adjacent to the parish church. In Hales, however, walking adjacent to the parish church did not detect any 'Middle Saxon' material (Davison 1990, 11-16).

Located in the Breckland of south-west Norfolk, fieldwalking in the parish of Barton Bendish has been complemented with excavation of the current village centre (Rogerson and Davison 1997; Pritchard 1997). The same project also undertook a concentrated fieldwalking survey of a single field in the adjacent Caldecote parish (Silvester 1997). Fieldwalking across Barton Bendish parish noted a pattern of 'drastically dwindled' 'Early Saxon' occupation, comparable to that noted in the Three Parish Survey, although the more comprehensive coverage of the survey in Barton is more likely to indicate actual absence of settlement. Significantly, the main 'Middle Saxon' focus detected in Barton Bendish parish was located in a field only 100m west of St. Mary's church. The investigators, however, did not deem the scatter of thirteen Ipswich Ware sherds as intense enough to be classed as a 'site', and instead interpreted the concentration as the result of intense manuring (Rogerson and Davison 1997, 21). This analysis notably contrasts with Davison's (1990, 11-12) model of site definition which posits that even three or four sherds of ceramic could represent a former occupation site. It is possible that a further 'Middle Saxon' focus was located to the north-west of St. Mary's Church, although village expansion means that this area currently lies under housing (Rogerson and Davison 1997, 22-5). In the neighbouring parish of Caldecote, fieldwalking appeared to demonstrate the occurrence of short-range settlement shift in the 'Late Saxon period from an earlier focus, with the now-deserted settlement and church probably becoming established around the tenth century (Silvester 1997, 79-85).

Fieldwalking has also been productive in dating the likely foundation of churches in other parts of Norfolk. At Illington, a parish in the southern part of Breckland, survey identified a small concentration of 'Middle Saxon' pottery located 500m of the church, but the medieval building was also surrounded by dense concentrations of 'Late Saxon' Thetford Ware (Davison *et al.* 1993, 3-4). In the adjacent parish of Little Hockham, recovery of both 'Middle Saxon' and 'Late Saxon' sherds around the church hint at an eighth-century foundation, the associated settlement of which later relocated. Fewer sherds but a similar pattern of development was also detected in the neighbouring parish of Great Hockham, which together with Little Hockham, probably formed part of an early medieval estate (Davison 1987). A more convincing 'Middle Saxon' site, although not located close to a parish church was recognised at the Hargham Estate, in an area of rich loamy soils in southern-central Norfolk (Davison and Cushion 1999). A discrete scatter of over one-hundred Ipswich Ware sherds was found, along with imported 'Middle Saxon' ceramic types, a rare occurrence on rural sites of this period. The concentration of material, which most likely dated from the eighth century, was situated on an area of light, freely-draining soils close to the line of a Roman road. Settlement in the area remained mobile until the medieval period, when the present common-edge village took shape (Davison and Cushion 1999, 271-3).

Also located on loamy soils, survey at Park Farm in the north-western parish of Snettisham, detected a density of Ipswich Ware sherds approximately 350m from the parish church. The church of St. Mary's is now isolated, suggesting shift in the very late medieval or early post-medieval period (Leah and Flitcroft 1993, 477). Further north, fieldwalking at Witton recovered a substantial number of 'Middle Saxon' artefacts. Rather confusingly, subsequent excavation only identified features dating from the tenth century onwards (Lawson 1983, 70-1). The archaeological evidence produced by such small-scale fieldwalking projects in Norfolk is testament to the groups and individuals involved in the often painstaking method of recovery. Whilst the data recovered to date certainly indicates varying methods of settlement development, even on a local scale, it is significant that 'Middle Saxon' activity is regularly found in close proximity to later

medieval parish churches. Indeed, this association has been recognised by researchers for some time, many of whom have targeted churchyards for further investigation as a consequence.

The research potential of the isolated churches located in many parts of the Norfolk landscape has been recognised for some time, often surrounded by arable farmland and ideal for archaeological investigation. In addition to the methodical recovery of evidence through fieldwalking projects, the NHER also contains information of chance finds or occasional discoveries found in churchyards and their environs. In Norfolk and Suffolk combined, twenty-eight churchyards have yielded 'Middle Saxon' artefacts, and a further seventy have produced 'Late Saxon' material, mostly pottery. 'Middle Saxon' sherds alone have been identified at twelve sites, with the lack of later material suggesting foundation followed by settlement shift before the tenth century (Hoggett 2010a, 145-7). The information from churchyards across the region therefore supports the work of individuals such as Richard Morris, who asserted that a moderate number of churches were founded during the 'Middle Saxon' period, which was followed by a far greater number of centres being established from the late ninth century (Morris 1989; 2010). Quantifying instances of churchyard finds remains difficult however, relying as we do on chance discoveries and, just as importantly, reporting by members of the public. Norfolk does though benefit from a good relationship between county authorities and metal-detectorists, whose work contributes further to the landscape-scale evidence from the county.

Metal-detected Evidence

The hobby of metal-detecting, which first gained popularity in the 1970s, is often looked upon with scorn by archaeologists who view the practice as damaging to potentially significant archaeological deposits. In East Anglia, however, a tradition of good relations between detectorists and regional archaeologists has led to far greater recording of metalwork finds and as a consequence, a better understanding of the early medieval landscape. A wealth of information is now recorded in the HERs of both East Anglian counties, reflected by the review of recent annual reports on the results of the Portable Antiquity Scheme (PAS) which shows somewhat remarkably that Norfolk accounts for a third of the artefacts recorded nationally through the initiative (Hutcheson 2006, 79). The most unique and valuable addition to 'Middle Saxon' settlement research made by metal-detecting has been the identification of probable settlements, commonly referred to as 'productive sites'.

The term 'productive sites' originally named by numismatists has, in recent years, been seen as unhelpful and not suitable as a description for what appear to have been centres of greatly varying character (cf. Richards 1999; Ulmschneider and Pestell 2003; Pestell 2004, 31-6; Davies 2010). It is increasingly clear that 'productive sites' do not necessarily share common attributes, besides the

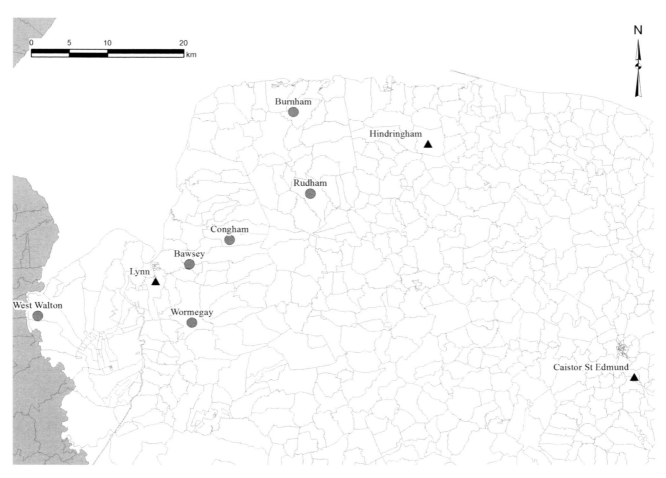

FIGURE 7.9: LOCATION OF 'PRODUCTIVE SITES' IDENTIFIED BY ROGERSON (CIRCLES) AND FURTHER POSSIBLE EXAMPLES AS SUGGESTED BY PESTELL (TRIANGLES) (ROGERSON 2003; PESTELL 2003). THE POSSIBLE SITES HAVE BEEN FAR LESS RICH IN METALWORK BUT INTERESTINGLY STILL DISPLAY A CONCENTRATION IN WEST NORFOLK. SOURCE FOR MAPPING: HISTORIC PARISHES OF ENGLAND AND WALES ONLINE.

manner in which they were discovered though recovery of metalwork (Hoggett 2010a, 77). In East Anglia, Tim Pestell has undertaken particularly concerted research upon the corpus of potentially diverse 'productive sites', attempting to highlight their potential ecclesiastical associations (Pestell 2003; 2004). Pestell notes the coincidence of post-Conquest monastic foundations with sites known to have had an importance in the early medieval period. Norman ecclesiastical centres appear to have sometimes been structured by sites of the tenth or eleventh century, but the evidence for reuse of important 'Middle Saxon' foci is less convincing (Pestell 2004, 194-9). Furthermore, Pestell has noted the problems with attempting to associate evidence from 'productive sites' to sites of religious and secular character, suggesting that archaeologists should not attempt to make clear or rigid distinctions between the two. Indeed, the intimate involvement of secular power with religious houses is reflected in the familial nature of 'Middle Saxon' foundations (Pestell 2004, 31-60).

As a consequence, archaeologists should attempt to better understand the character of individual 'productive sites' of Norfolk and they way in which they integrated into the social and settlement hierarchy, whilst avoiding arbitrary labels such as 'religious' or 'secular' as scholars have

tended to apply in the past (e.g. Hoggett 2007; 2010a). Andrew Rogerson (2003, 110-2) has outlined a total of six 'productive sites' in Norfolk: West Walton situated in Marshland, and Bawsey, Burnham, Congham, Rudham and Wormegay, all located in the Good Sands (Figure 7.9). On the basis of recovered coinage, three further locations in Norfolk have been noted as likely 'productive sites': Hindringham and Lynn, again situated in the Good Sands of west Norfolk, and Caistor St Edmund in the Central-southern Claylands (Pestell 2003, 129-31).

In terms of the metalwork recovered, the site at Bawsey, located on a peninsula of the River Gaywood, is the most prolific of Norfolk's 'productive sites'. Unsystematic fieldwalking survey and metal-detecting on the site since the 1980s has focussed on an apparent ditched enclosure, visible on aerial photographs (Figure 7.10) (NHER 25962). The density of finds recovered from Bawsey makes it the most likely of the 'productive sites' in the county to have been occupied on a permanent basis, rather than seasonally. Indeed, Andrew Rogerson has pushed the interpretation still further, suggesting that Bawsey is a leading contender as the estate centre from which the apparent systematic settling of Marshland was conducted (see above) (Rogerson 2003, 113-120). Unfortunately, the

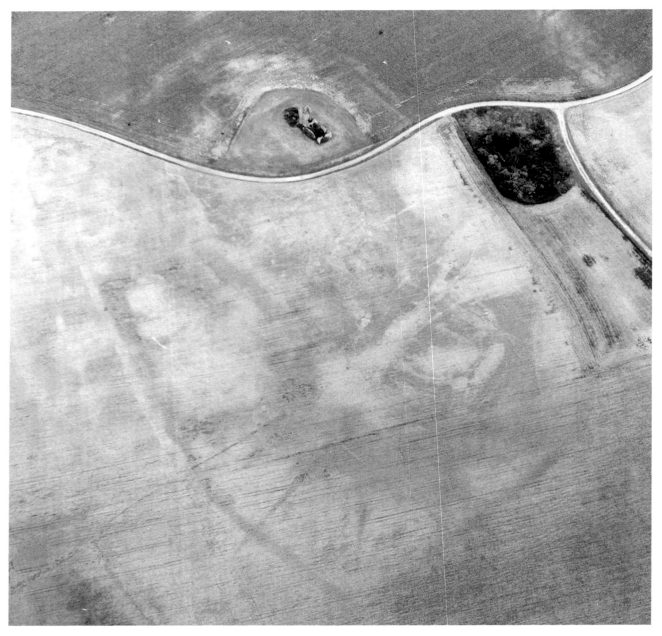

FIGURE 7.10: AERIAL PHOTOGRAPH OF THE 'PRODUCTIVE SITE' AT BAWSEY

results from evaluation trenches excavated by the 'Time Team' at Bawsey remain unpublished, but Ipswich Ware was recovered from the fill of the enclosure ditch. The potential that Bawsey formed one of several significant settlements in this part of the Good Sands is supported by test pitting at Gaywood, now a suburb of King's Lynn, where significant quantities of Ipswich Ware hint at a possible redistribution centre of regional significance (see below).

At Burnham, 'Middle Saxon' occupation has been located alongside the Goose Beck, a tributary of the River Burn (NHER 28127). The site was initially detected through fieldwalking in 1983 but, similar to Bawsey, no systematic survey has been undertaken at Burnham. Restricted

excavation by Norfolk Archaeology Unit has, however, extended the known area of occupation, suggesting a secondary focus perhaps meant solely for habitation (NHER 28127; Rogerson 2003, 114-5). Excavation has also been undertaken at Congham, situated next to a branch of the Icknield Way (NHER 25765). Fieldwalking had indicated that the site may extend over a 10ha area, perhaps on the site of an earlier Roman villa. Targeted excavation identified the post holes of a single 'Middle Saxon' building, typical of settlement sites dating to the period (NHER 25765; Rogerson 2003, 115-6).

Elsewhere, the distribution of finds from Wormegay suggests that 'Middle Saxon' settlement on the island may have been zoned here too, with occupation and metalwork finds forming separate and quite discrete concentrations. At West Walton, the only 'productive site' in the Marshland *pays* identified to date, a similar situation is apparent, with the 'productive' area apparently distinct from the area of domestic activity (Silvester 1988, 37; Rogerson 2003, 119; Crowson *et al.* 2005, 189). Outside of the areas investigated by the Fenland Project, the 'productive site' at Rudham apparently features a double focus of activity, located across the parish boundary of East and West Rudham on a tributary of the River Wensum. Artefact recovery has been far more prolific in West Rudham, with the greatest concentration occurring adjacent to the graveyard of the parish church (NHER 30883; Rogerson 2003, 116-8).

The industrious work of metal-detectorists in Norfolk has thus produced a potentially useful alternative dataset for research, identifying six 'productive sites' and a handful of possibly comparable centres. In spite of the recognition of such sites, however, their analysis in Norfolk suffers from a lack of further investigation, and the often unsystematic way in which the existing material has been recovered. No 'productive site' in Norfolk has been subject to more than trial trenching, and indeed no truly extensive open area excavation has been undertaken on any settlement site in the county since the investigation of North Elmham in 1971, perhaps with the exception of Sedgeford (see below; Wade-Martins 1980b; Rogerson 2003, 120). It is tempting to use the 'productive site' at Brandon, Suffolk, as a comparator to the Norfolk examples, as here more comprehensively excavation identified a three-celled timber church and two cemeteries, but also evidence for river-borne trade, a mixed agricultural regime and light industry (Carr *et al.* 1988).

Recent research of 'productive sites', however, cautions against such simplistic associations (e.g. Ulmschneider and Pestell 2003), and the six foci in Norfolk may represent centres of greatly different character; distinct both from each other, and from more thoroughly investigated sites that were found through metal-detecting, such as Brandon. Hoggett (2010a, 77-8) has urged that 'productive sites' be seen as ecclesiastical, yet even the gold plaque depicting Saint John the Evangelist, found at Brandon, cannot be viewed as evidence of monasticism when it is considered that secular individuals are equally likely to have carried such religious accoutrements (Pestell 2004, 36). Elsewhere, A.R.J. Hutcheson's (2006) assertion that Norfolk's six 'productive sites' were primarily points of tax collection, forming a network of dispersed economic centres in the north-west of the county before the development of King's Lynn, is difficult to corroborate. The location of 'productive sites' situated close to the coast, or major waterways or routeways certainly advocates a trade and commerce-centred outlook though, an analysis which is supported by the large numbers of coins which characterise activity (Hutcheson 2006, 82-4). The unsystematic recording of metal-detecting, however, makes it difficult to be certain how 'typical' so-called 'productive sites' really are. Many 'productive sites' have been recognised for several decades, and the assemblage of metalwork from them is

at least partly a product of their continued investigation by metal-detectorists, due to their status as known fruitful areas.

The activity of metal-detectorists may therefore be creating something of a self-fulfilling prophecy, as concerted investigation of 'productive sites' perpetuates their apparently unique character. It therefore remains uncertain to what extent the recovery of large quantities of coinage in particular is indicative of specialism or a bias of research, and archaeologists must be wary of adopting models such as Hutcheson's uncritically. The research of five west Norfolk sites undertaken by Gareth Davies, utilising an integrated survey methodology consisting of overlaid plotting of metal-detected finds, geophysics, fieldwalking and trial-trench excavation, is particularly relevant in this regard (Davies 2010). The differing find-loss signatures, Davies asserts, is indicative of the contrasting economic fortunes of the settlements at Burnham, Congham, Rudham, Sedgeford and Wormegay. Davies' work underlines the increasing settlement hierarchy that developed during the 'Middle Saxon' period, and emphasises the problems with using a blanket term such as 'productive sites' (Davies 2010, 117). It is probably through more excavation that the understanding of sites labelled as 'productive' will most effectively be furthered, and the current evidence lends itself only to the most general of conclusions. As Rogerson has indicated, without more thorough research of 'Middle Saxon' East Anglia we can 'go little further in understanding the economic, political and social dynamics which were at play' (Rogerson 2003, 121). Indeed, the most effective way of achieving a more comprehensive understanding of 'Middle Saxon' settlement in Norfolk is by combining the evidence from landscape-scale research with the evidence from archaeological excavations.

THE EVIDENCE FROM EXCAVATIONS

Introduction

The rich material record for 'Middle Saxon' settlement derived from landscape-scale investigation in Norfolk is somewhat contrasted by the relatively sparse evidence from archaeological excavations. The site at North Elmham remains the only 'Middle Saxon' settlement in the county subject to large-scale investigation, and although the long-term research of the Sedgeford Historical and Archaeological Project has yielded impressive results (Cabot *et al.* 2004), the majority of excavations have been piecemeal or restricted in extent. Fortunately for this work, a good deal of research has been undertaken within currently-occupied rural settlements, the archaeological evidence from which provides a valuable insight into potential 'Middle Saxon' antecedents of many existing villages. 'Middle Saxon' settlements found in currently-occupied rural settlements are also significant in what they reveal about contemporary society, as their character is indicative of fundamental landscape restructuring dating to around the eighth century. In spite of the dearth in supporting documentary material, the cumulative

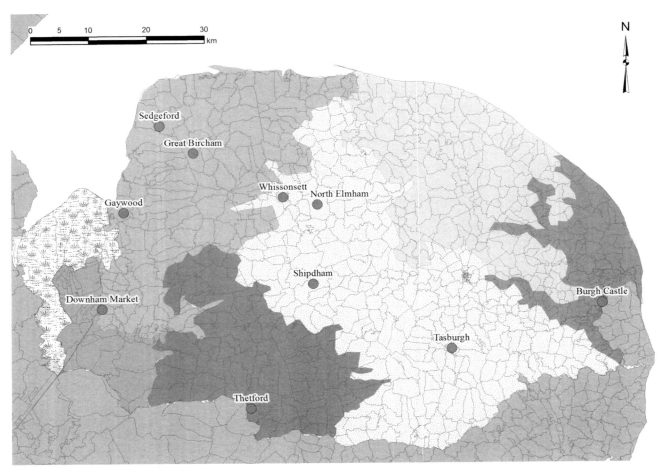

FIGURE 7.11: LOCATION OF EXCAVATED SITES MENTIONED IN THE TEXT AND THE PAYS OF NORFOLK. 'MIDDLE SAXON' SETTLEMENT EVIDENCE IS PARTICULARLY WELL REPRESENTED IN THE GOOD SANDS AND CENTRAL-SOUTHERN CLAYLANDS PAYS. SOURCE FOR MAPPING: HISTORIC PARISHES OF ENGLAND AND WALES ONLINE

archaeological evidence from excavation, fieldwalking and metal-detection, makes it clear that northern East Anglia was subject to similar social changes to the other counties studied by this research during the 'Middle Saxon' period. Settlement development from the tenth century, however, appears to have been markedly different in some parts of Norfolk than elsewhere in central and eastern England, resulting in the unique material record now available for study. With an emphasis on investigation within currently-occupied villages, which represents a unique new dataset for study, this chapter will now assesses the excavated evidence for 'Middle Saxon' settlement in Norfolk, with discussion divided by the county's geographical *pays* (Figure 7.11).

The Good Sands

As the above analysis of fieldwalked and metal-detected evidence has demonstrated, the Good Sands *pays* represents one of the richest areas for 'Middle Saxon' settlement archaeology in Norfolk. Indeed, the relatively fertile landscape, combined with an extensive coastline, and several navigable rivers made the Good Sands an attractive region for occupation throughout the early medieval period. Supplementing the material from fieldwalking, but especially metal-detecting, which led to the identification

of several 'productive sites', the Good Sands also has a significant corpus of 'Middle Saxon' settlement evidence derived from excavation. Other than North Elmham, the most extensively-excavated seventh to ninth-century settlement investigated in Norfolk is Sedgeford, located in the northern part of the *pays* on the River Reedham, roughly 5km east from the coast. In addition to evidence for settlement, excavation at Sedgeford since the 1950s has also identified a cemetery complex containing over two hundred west-east orientated burials. More comprehensive excavations of 'Middle Saxon' occupation and burial have been ongoing at Sedgeford since 1996, made possible thanks to a slight westward shift of the 'Late Saxon' focus (Cabot *et al.* 2004; NHER 1605 and NHER 1609).

Initial results from the 'Boneyard' area, located 200m south-east of the present parish church recognised three groups of 'Middle Saxon' linear features and three similarly-dated rubbish pits, one of which contained a high quality Ipswich Ware pitcher within which were found two burnt deposits (Figure 7.12). Further excavation 50m north, alongside the river, revealed further ditches, pits and gullies all dating to the 'Middle Saxon' period. Structural evidence was found in the form of a pit, filled with layers of rammed chalk, which probably represents part of a building foundation (Faulkner 1997). Excavation of the

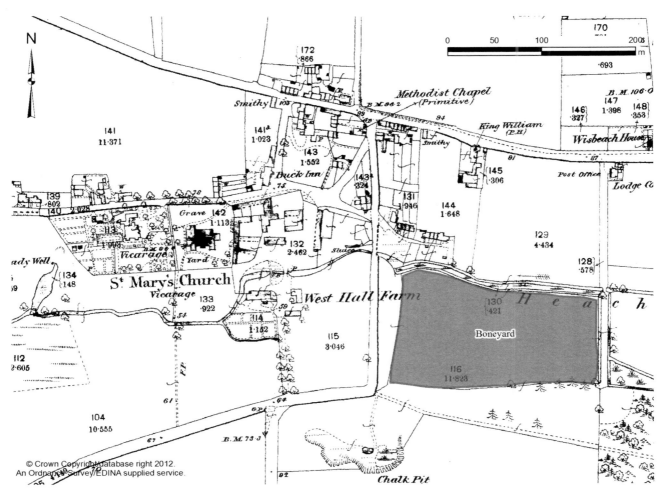

FIGURE 7.12: OS FIRST EDITION OF SEDGEFORD ILLUSTRATING THE AREA KNOWN AS THE BONEYARD. EXCAVATION HERE HAS LOCATED A 'MIDDLE SAXON' SETTLEMENT AND CEMETERY FOCUS. THE SITE APPEARS TO HAVE BEEN ABANDONED IN THE 'LATE SAXON' PERIOD, AND FOCUS SHIFTED NORTH OF THE RIVER TO THE AREA OF THE PRESENT VILLAGE.

accompanying burials in the Boneyard has not located an attendant church, however, leading Hoggett to suggest that the burial ground itself formed the first 'Christian focus' at Sedgeford (Hoggett 2010a, 136). The lack of evidence for a church within the 'Middle Saxon' cemetery at Sedgeford indicates that burial did not become the preserve of churches until perhaps the ninth century, when activity was relocated north of the river to the area now occupied by the present village.

The evidence from Sedgeford therefore conforms to the trend derived from evidence elsewhere in England, which suggests that burial did not become the preserve of the Church until at least the ninth century (Blair 2005 241-5). The extensive excavation programme undertaken at Sedgeford therefore conforms to a pattern already recognised in Norfolk through landscape-orientated projects: a 'Middle Saxon' settlement focus succeeded by relocation over a short distance, probably around the tenth century, to form the medieval village-plan of Sedgeford. The increased willingness to transform the landscape in the 'Late Saxon' period is represented by the construction of a dam, which created a *vivarium* and mill pond (Cabot *et al.* 2004, 319). The management of such specialised

technology has been viewed as a key element of the construction of early medieval lordship (e.g. Saunders 1990), and at Sedgeford the development of the dam and mill hints at the increased power of lordship which typifies the social environment of 'Late Saxon' England (Reynolds 1999, 62-3).

Whilst intensified from around the tenth century, manifestation of such power through investment in landscape and settlement was not an innovation just of the 'Late Saxon' period in the Good Sands of Norfolk, as demonstrated by excavation at Downham Market. Whilst the excavated site at Downham Market was located on the freely-draining sands of the Good Sands, the evidence from the site revealed exploitation of the Peat Fen, located only 0.5km to the west (NHER 30228). 'Middle Saxon' settlement evidence was first identified through evaluation trenches dug by the Norfolk Archaeological Unit (NAU) in 1999 and 2000, which led to the excavation of five more extensive trenches. 'Middle Saxon' activity consisted of a series of ditches apparently forming large enclosures (NHER 30228). The macrofaunal evidence suggests that the enclosures may have been used for penning of livestock, rather than for drainage as was the likely purpose

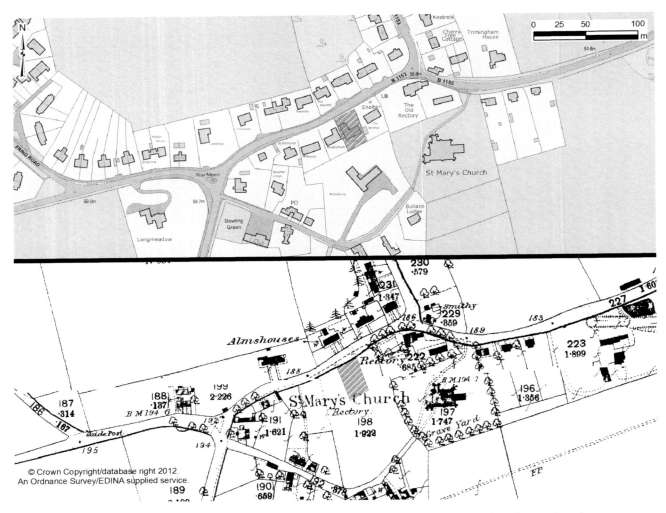

FIGURE 7.13: MODERN AND FIRST EDITION OS MAPS SHOWING THE EXCAVATED AREA AT GREAT BIRCHAM (SHADED). THE 'MIDDLE SAXON' EVIDENCE WAS FOUND DURING IN-FILLING OF AN ENCLOSURE FORMED BY THE HISTORIC STREET PATTERN, FRAMED TO THE SOUTH-EAST BY ST. MARY'S CHURCH.

of the ditch networks of the Marshland settlements (e.g. Silvester 1998).

The Downham Market site, located at the interface between Peat Fen and the Good Sands, probably demonstrates the seasonal movement of livestock, with animals moved onto the wetlands during the drier summer months. Initial occupation possibly developed into more permanent settlement, however, as evidence for non-wild food plants were also recovered (NHER 30228). The evidence for more sustained habitation is fragmentary though, and it is difficult to positively associate the 'Middle Saxon' focus with a later relocation to the present site of Downham Market, located 0.5km to the east. Nevertheless, the site of 'Middle Saxon' Downham Market does demonstrate exploitation of the marginal landscape of the Peat Fen, probably by industrious communities who grazed their animals on the uplands during the winter. It is likely that several early medieval estates were exploiting the wetland in such a manner from around the eighth century, for the first time since the Romano-British period.

The close relationship between 'Middle Saxon' settlements and later village centres, whilst not evidenced

at Downham Market, is demonstrated by investigation at Great Bircham situated in the centre of the Good Sands *pays* (Figure 7.11). Development of houses immediately west of the parish church of St. Mary during the mid-1970s was undertaken with an archaeological watching brief, and the subsequent excavation of a single evaluation trench (Figure 7.13) (NHER 6062). The most impressive discovery of these interventions was undeniably a 'Late Saxon' pottery kiln, but occupation on the site had started in the 'Middle Saxon' period. A series of ditches, dated by Ipswich Ware to the eighth century, were found in addition to domestic refuse and building material (NHER 6062). The restricted nature of research at Great Bircham makes it difficult to assess comprehensively the development of the early medieval settlement sequence, but occupation appears to have been more intense from around the tenth century. It is possible that excavation only encountered the edge of 'Middle Saxon' activity, with a subsequent shift towards the area of the church around the tenth century, leading to the discovery of more dense habitation and specialised industry in the form of pottery kilns on the site. It is possible that Great Bircham was important centre amongst a polyfocal settlement pattern, as occasional 'Middle Saxon' finds have been discovered adjacent to the

FIGURE 7.14: OS FIRST EDITION SHOWING THE RUINED CHURCH OF ST ANDREW'S IN BIRCHAM (CROSS), THE IPSWICH WARE FROM WHICH SUGGESTS THE PRESENCE OF A POLYFOCAL 'MIDDLE SAXON' SETTLEMENT PATTERN IN GREAT BIRCHAM.

ruined St Andrew's church, located 800m to the east of the excavated site (Figure 7.14).

The density of 'Middle Saxon' sites in the northern part of the Good Sands *pays* as evidenced by 'productive sites, and the excavated material from Sedgeford is corroborated by investigations undertaken by the HEFA project at Gaywood. Now a suburb of King's Lynn, Gaywood was a separate village until the middle of the twentieth century, situated on a river bearing the same name. During the summer of 2010, the HEFA project investigated five test-pits in the suburb, three of which yielded a total of over five-hundred sherds of Ipswich Ware. The quantity of sherds was found on the western side of Wootton Road, where probable 'Middle Saxon' structural remains were also identified within the three test-pits (HEFA Website-Gaywood). Added to the corpus of artefacts identified by the HEFA scheme can be the one-hundred plus Ipswich Ware sherds found by a resident in the back garden of 139 Wootton Road during 2009 (Figure 7.15) (NHER 52930).

The quantity of Ipswich Ware found at Gaywood is truly remarkable even for East Anglia, and especially given

the restricted area of investigation, representing the largest collection of sherds recovered from a single site in Norfolk. To place the assemblage in context, Alan Davison considered that when fieldwalking, as few as four sherds may indicate a 'Middle Saxon' settlement (Davison 1990 11-12). Situated on a navigable river near to the coast, the extent of ceramics recovered from Gaywood indicates a specialist function for the centre, probably as a trading place from which goods were redistributed to the northern part of the East Anglian kingdom. Indeed, the intensity of seaborne trade around the Wash from at least the eighth century is reflected more generally by the heavy concentrations of Ipswich Ware from the coast of north-west Norfolk, the density of which is only paralleled by Ipswich itself. Far less likely, although still possible, is that Gaywood represents another place of Ipswich Ware production; the first identified outside of the eponymous *wic*. No evidence for kilns has yet been discovered, however, and on the current evidence it seems more probable that the high quantities of pottery found in the test pits is the product of Gaywood's nodal location within north-west Norfolk's 'Middle Saxon' communication network.

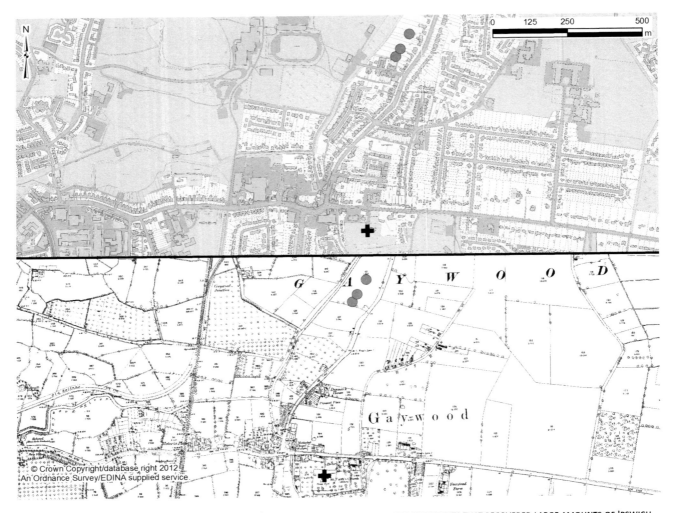

FIGURE 7.15: OS MODERN AND FIRST EDITION MAPS OF GAYWOOD, SHOWING THE LOCATIONS OF TEST-PITS THAT RECOVERED LARGE AMOUNTS OF IPSWICH WARE (CIRCLED) AND THE SITE OF THE MEDIEVAL PARISH CHURCH (CROSS). TWO FURTHER TEST PITS (SQUARED) TO THE EAST OF WOOTTON ROAD RECOVERED NO MATERIAL, INDICATING THAT SETTLEMENT WAS CONCENTRATED TO THE WEST. THE SITE CANNOT BE CLASSIFIED AS A 'CORS', HOWEVER, LOCATED OVER 500M NORTH OF THE PARISH CHURCH (AFTER HEFA WEBSITE-GAYWOOD.

Overall, the Good Sands is amongst the best-represented of Norfolk's *pays* in terms of excavated evidence for 'Middle Saxon' settlement, having been subject to a decent quantity of research-based and development-led investigation. Excavated material, in addition to that derived from fieldwalking and metal-detecting makes it plain that north-west Norfolk was an area of intense settlement around the eighth century. Although the Wash and its river network was central to the development of centres in the northern part of the *pays*, in the south the excavated 'Middle Saxon' site at Downham Market demonstrates that the Peat Fen also began to be exploited, probably on a seasonal basis. The relatively densely populated landscape of the Good Sands is contrasted by Breckland, from which only Thetford has yielded substantial excavated evidence for 'Middle Saxon' occupation.

Breckland

The freely-draining and infertile sandy soils of the Breckland provided challenging environments for settlement and agriculture throughout the later historic period, and also appears to have restricted the extent of 'Middle Saxon' activity in the region. Excavated material relating to 'Middle Saxon' settlement is sparse in Breckland, although some evidence for occupation has been found in the Thetford area. Thetford emerged as an important town located on the Little Ouse River in the tenth century, although the fact that it was chosen as an overwintering site by Scandinavian forces in 870 hints at an earlier significance of the area (*ASC* 870). Evidence for 'Middle Saxon' settlement from the centre of Thetford has not been forthcoming though. For instance, investigation at Mill Lane, at the centre of the defended 'Late Saxon' town revealed Iron Age, Romano-British, Late Saxon and medieval occupation but no material dating to the 'Middle Saxon' period (Wallis 2003). The 'Late Saxon' settlement of Thetford was largely situated in the northern part of the modern town, but excavation suggests that a 'Middle Saxon' focus lay to the south of the river (Figure 7.16).

Archaeological evidence for 'Middle Saxon' settlement at Thetford was first discovered during excavation of a low earthwork enclosure at Red Castle in 1957. The feature,

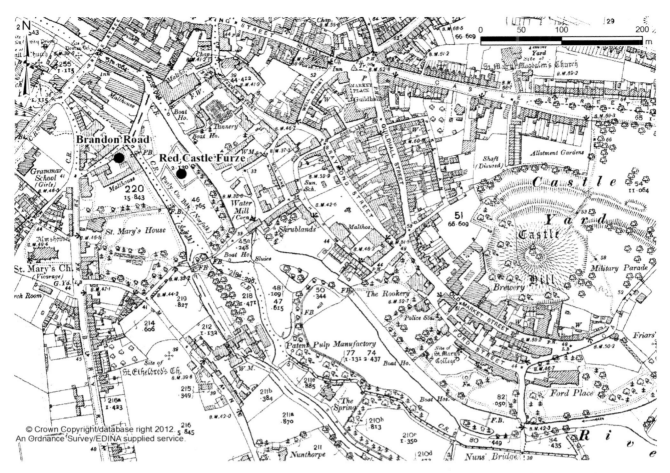

FIGURE 7.16: OS FIRST EDITION REVISION OF THETFORD. INVESTIGATION AT RED CASTLE FURZE AND BRANDON ROAD LOCATED 'MIDDLE SAXON' SETTLEMENT DEPOSITS. THE 'LATE SAXON' TOWN, HOWEVER, DEVELOPED ON THE NORTHERN SIDE OF THE RIVER.

which had previously gone unrecognised, was subject to a series of archaeological evaluation trenches which revealed the remains of a church and cemetery. Although the majority of this activity appeared to be 'Late Saxon' and later, many of the grave fills contained 'Middle Saxon' Ipswich Ware and similarly-dated occupation debris and postholes were also recovered (Knocker 1967). Further indication that the south bank of the river represented the focus of 'Middle Saxon' Thetford was found during construction of the bypass in 1988-90 (NHER 24849). 'Middle Saxon' finds were recovered from much of the area disturbed by groundworks along the Brandon Road, and although targeted excavation was restricted to only thirteen evaluation trenches, a series of pits, ditches and a probable hall structure were all identified. The settlement features were dated to the eighth or early ninth centuries by ceramics, on a site that also possessed evidence for prehistoric, Romano-British and 'Early Saxon' activity (NHER 24849).

The cumulative evidence from Thetford therefore suggests that 'Middle Saxon' settlement was centred on the south bank of the Little Ouse River, and not in the area of the 'Late Saxon' town (Figure 7.16). The excavators of the Red Castle site tentatively suggested that the church within the earthwork enclosure was of 'Middle Saxon' origin,

although there is no secure dating evidence to corroborate such a hypothesis (Knocker 1967). Indeed, there is currently little archaeological evidence from Thetford to suggest a 'Middle Saxon' centre of exceptional status, and the recovered material instead seems typical of more average rural settlements of the period. It is possible that the presence of 'Middle Saxon' settlement, located 200m to the south-west of 'Late Saxon centre at Thetford, may simply be the result of a coincidental juxtaposition, yet the existence of a well-populated settlement landscape is likely to have been important in the decision of the Scandinavian army to overwinter in the area in 870. The 'Late Saxon' town may have developed as the result of short-range relocation from an existing settlement on the south bank of the river towards the area of the Iron Age *oppidum*, which most scholars also believe was reused by Viking forces as their overwintering base (e.g. Everson and Jecock 1999). Whilst Thetford is therefore a place of 'Middle Saxon' and later interest in the Breckland *pays*, settlement remains dating from the seventh to ninth centuries are better represented in Norfolk's Central-southern Claylands.

Central-southern Claylands

The boulder clay of the Central-southern Claylands, prone to water logging and difficult to cultivate, still provided

FIGURE 7.17: AERIAL PHOTOGRAPH OF NORTH ELMHAM, SHOWING THE EXCAVATED AREA AROUND THE PARK LODGE (TOP), 'LATE SAXON' CATHEDRAL RUINS (CENTRE) AND MEDIEVAL PARISH CHURCH (TOP LEFT). THE EXISTING CHURCH IS PROBABLY THE SITE OF BISHOP DE LOSINGA'S (1091-1119) FOUNDATION, AND THE RUINS LIKELY THE REMAINS OF A NORMAN CHAPEL BUILT ON THE SITE OF THE EARLIER CATHEDRAL (HEYWOOD 1982, 1-5). SOURCE FOR PHOTO: NHER.

more attractive conditions for early medieval settlement than areas such as Breckland. Indeed, the high potential for 'Middle Saxon' settlement is highlighted by fieldwalking surveys such as the Launditch Hundred Project, potential that is also reflected in the record of excavated material from the *pays*. Located on the upper extents of the River Wensum, the site of North Elmham is arguably the most celebrated of Norfolk's 'Middle Saxon' settlements. This part of the Central-southern Claylands has a well-established pattern of 'Early Saxon' activity, with the mixed rite cemetery of Spong Hill located only 2.5km south of North Elmham village (Hills and Penn 1981). The Spong Hill cemetery probably served a number of settlements in the surrounding area, one of which was situated on the periphery of the burial ground (Rickett 1995). North Elmham itself has also been a focus for academic research, due to its possible status as the historically-documented see of *Elmham* from the final quarter of the seventh century.

Until the 1950s it was thought that the ruined church at North Elmham represented the remains of an early medieval cathedral, later altered around the fourteenth century. Excavations led by Stuart Rigold, however, identified a series of 'Late Saxon' occupation phases beneath the standing remains, which have since been reinterpreted as a private early Norman chapel (Figure 7.17) (Rigold 1962). Together with the lack of Ipswich Ware detected by the Launditch Hundred Project, it was only further excavation from 1967 at North Elmham Park, 50m south-west of the ruined church, which first detected 'Middle Saxon' settlement in the parish (Figure 7.18). The excavations by Peter Wade-Martins, who also led the Launditch Hundred Project, identified 'Middle Saxon' occupation comprising long, straight boundary ditches, structures with foundation trenches and deep, timber-lined wells (Wade-Martins 1980b). Settlement comprised three phases, gradually intensifying over time, with the focus apparently shifting to the site of the ruined church in the eleventh century (Wade-Martins 1980b, 110-24). Excavation of 'Middle Saxon' settlement remains at North Elmham Park represents the strongest and perhaps decisive indicator that the site in Norfolk can be associated with East Anglian see of *Elmham*, especially when compared with the relatively weak case for South Elmham, Suffolk.

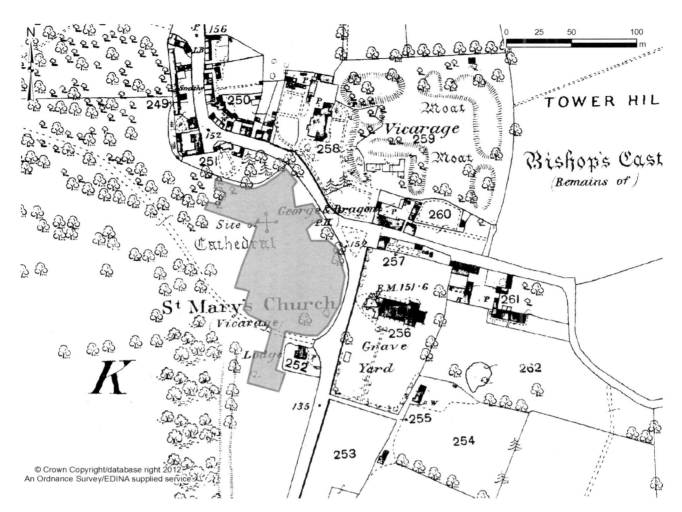

FIGURE 7.18: OS FIRST EDITION SHOWING THE EXCAVATED AREA AT NORTH ELMHAM PARK (SHADED), SITUATED 50M SOUTH-WEST OF THE EARTHWORKS OF THE NORMAN CATHEDRAL. THE PHASES EXCAVATED AT NORTH ELMHAM STRONGLY SUGGEST THAT THIS IS THE SITE OF THE HISTORICALLY-ATTESTED SEE OF ELMHAM, RATHER THAN SOUTH ELMHAM, SUFFOLK, AS SOME HAVE ARGUED.

Elmham is first recorded in the signatories of the Council of Clovesho dated to 803, but there is no specific written evidence to suggest where the site of the see was situated. Crucially, however, the document describes *Elmham* as an *Ecclesia*, which may indicate, as Hoggett (2010a, 40) has argued, that the site did not have a recognisable Roman inheritance (Haddan and Stubbs 1964, 547; Campbell 1979). Whilst extensive excavations in and around the ruined church at North Elmham have detected no evidence for Romano-British activity (Rigold 1962; Wade-Martins 1980b), the site of South Elmham is situated within a square enclosure of probable Roman date (Smedley and Owles 1970, 5-6; Hoggett 2010a, 41-2). This philology, combined with the excavated 'Middle Saxon' settlement from North Elmham, and the lack of comparable evidence from South Elmham, makes it highly likely that the Central-southern Claylands of Norfolk possessed an episcopal see from the seventh century.

One aspect of the North Elmham Park excavations that the investigators found surprising was the moderate quantities of 'Middle Saxon' ceramics recovered, totalling one-hundred and fourteen sherds of Ipswich Ware (Wade-Martins 1980b, 124). On the basis of this evidence, Wade-Martins even suggested that one of the 'Middle Saxon' phases may have been aceramic (Wade-Martins 1980b, 120). For a high-status site such as North Elmham this appears improbable and the dearth of Ipswich Ware may instead be the result of the sampling methodology used; the excavations did not sieve material systematically and, given the clayey nature of the local soil, pottery may have gone unidentified in large soil clods (Rogerson 2010 pers. comm.). A shortage of portable material culture is not an unprecedented phenomenon of elite early medieval sites, however, such as Yeavering, Northumbria, where the site appeared to have been 'cleaned' on abandonment (Hope-Taylor 1977). The moderate amount of 'Middle Saxon' pottery from North Elmham Park therefore cautions against using quantities of material to characterise settlement sites in Norfolk, in the same way that Pestell (2004, 31-64) has shown how artefact type cannot be used to determine the status of 'Middle Saxon' settlements.

Elsewhere in the Central-southern Claylands, the enigmatic site of Tasburgh has yielded evidence for 'Middle Saxon' settlement through archaeological excavation. Located on

FIGURE 7.19: AERIAL PHOTOGRAPH OF TASBURGH, SHOWING THE LARGE ENCLOSURE (CENTRE) PRESERVED BY FIELD BOUNDARIES BUT ALSO VISIBLE AS CROPMARKS (RIGHT CENTRE). THE PARISH CHURCH IS VISIBLE IN THE CENTRE-LEFT OF THE IMAGE. THE EXACT ORIGIN OF THE ENCLOSURE IS NOT KNOWN BUT IT CERTAINLY APPEARS TO HAVE BEEN PARTIALLY OCCUPIED DURING THE 'MIDDLE SAXON' PERIOD. SOURCE FOR PHOTO: NHER.

the Norwich to Ipswich section of the Roman road from *Venta Icenorum* (Caistor St. Edmund) to *Camulodunum* (Colchester), Tasburgh features an extraordinary enclosure situated on a spur of land overlooking the confluence of the River Tas, and two of its minor tributaries (Figure 7.19). The broadly oval monument is formed by a single bank and ditch, within which the parish church and part of the modern village have encroached into the southern third (Rogerson and Lawson 1991, 31-5). The Tasburgh enclosure has previously been identified as the Roman station of *Ad Taum*, although from as early as the 1930s this has been subject to question (Figure 7.20) (NHER 2258). Rather, the form of the earthwork bears closer resemblance to an Iron Age hillfort, although investigation has yet to recover evidence to support such a hypothesis. 'Middle Saxon' evidence at Tasburgh has been found in the form of over one- hundred and thirty sherds of Ipswich Ware, recovered through excavation in the vicinity of the parish church. Similarly large quantities of Thetford Ware and the foundations of a 'Late Saxon' timber structure indicate that occupation continued to focus on the church site into the 'Late Saxon' period, during which settlement apparently shifted to the south-east where the current core of Tasburgh is now situated (Figure 7.20) (NHER 2258; Rogerson and Lawson 1991, 57).

At Whissonsett in central Norfolk, excavation has similarly demonstrated 'Middle Saxon' occupation followed by a 'Late Saxon' shift in focus. Located near the interface between the Boulder Clay and Good Sands, excavation in the central Norfolk village revealed 'Middle Saxon' settlement 60m north of the parish church (Figure 7.21) (NHER 40453). 'Middle Saxon' evidence comprised the footing of two post-hole structures, probably halls, and nineteen inhumation burials. This activity was bounded to the south by a west-east orientated double-ditched enclosure, which subsequent keyhole excavation demonstrated turned to the north, a feature that crucially conforms to the later village plan (Figure 7.22). In the 'Late Saxon' period the cemetery apparently went out of use, and a series of settlement enclosures extended across the site. It is likely that during this period the centre of occupation was located to the area of the parish church to the south, a possibility that is supported by the identification of a 'Late Saxon' cross in the churchyard (NHER 40453). Whissonsett therefore demonstrates a familiar pattern of 'Middle Saxon' structured settlement, succeeded by a 'Late Saxon' reordering, which probably resulted in the formation of the historic village pattern.

A similar settlement sequence to that identified at Whissonsett was detected through excavation at Shipdham, also located in the western part of the *pays*. Investigation at Church Close, situated 150m south of All Saints' church, revealed a long-lived occupation site (Figure 7.23) (NHER 42664). 'Early Saxon' activity was evidenced by the

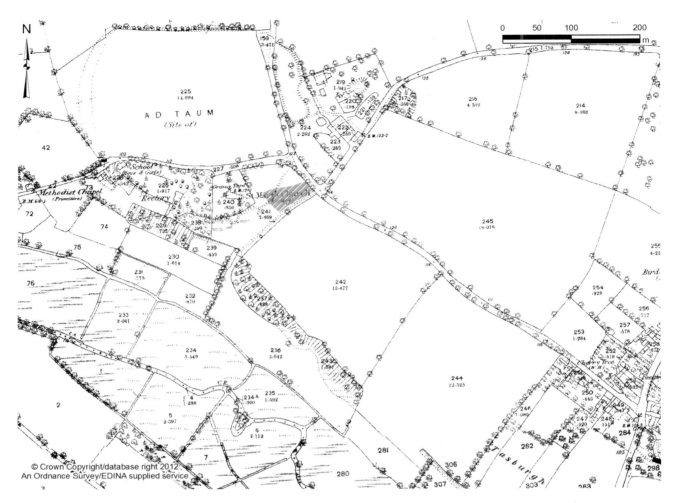

FIGURE 7.20: OS FIRST EDITION OF TASBURGH. THE RECOVERY OF 'MIDDLE SAXON' SHERDS THROUGH EXCAVATION (SHADED AND BOXED) IN CLOSE VICINITY TO THE CHURCH LIKELY INDICATES THAT IT WAS INSERTED INTO THE SOUTHERN PART OF THE ENCLOSURE AT THIS TIME. SETTLEMENT AROUND THE CHURCH SUBSEQUENTLY SHIFTED TO THE SOUTH-EAST (BOTTOM-RIGHT), PROBABLY DURING THE 'LATE SAXON' PERIOD.

recovery of a sixth-century gusset plate and twenty sherds of organic-tempered pottery, although no structural features were recorded. During the eighth century, however, several ditches, two post-built structures, and pits were developed across the site. The 'Middle Saxon' ditch arrangement at Shipdham is similar to that excavated at North Elmham, suggesting that occupation was structured perhaps into individual tenements (NHER 42664). Ipswich Ware and imported continental pottery provided the 'Middle Saxon' provenance for the settlement, supported by the recovery of four sceattas (AD 710-765) and two cut dirhams (AD 754-775 and 813-825). In spite of Shipdham's land-locked location, such coinage indicates its position within a trade network able to import material from distant foreign locations. 'Late Saxon' settlement in the village appears to have been centred northwards towards the present parish church, as two ditch systems excavated at Shipdham Place produced tenth and eleventh century pottery, on a site which later developed as a moated manor (NHER 42664).

Broadland

Together with North-west Norfolk, Broadland is amongst the most poorly represented *pays* in the county in terms

of early medieval settlement archaeology. Whereas this research has found little 'Middle Saxon' occupation evidence in North-west Norfolk, in Broadland investigation of Burgh Castle has located early medieval activity within the walls of the Roman fort. Burgh Castle was previously positioned on the southern side of the Great Estuary, at the tidal interface of the rivers Bure, Yare and Waveney. Constructed as part of the defences known as the 'Saxon Shore', the site has traditionally been associated with the monastic site of *Cnobheresburg*, given to the Irish monk Fursa by Siegberht in the 630s (*HE* III, 19; e.g. Johnson 1987). The association of Burgh Castle with *Cnobheresburg* is far from straightforward, however, but archaeological evidence has certainly demonstrated that the fort formed a 'Middle Saxon' focus (Hoggett 2010a, 56). Excavations by Charles Green in the north-eastern corner of the fort produced over two-hundred and fifty sherds of Ipswich Ware, although few were recovered from stratified contexts. The density of recovered ceramics suggests the presence of settlement, and although a 'Middle Saxon' cemetery has been excavated, no associated occupation site has yet been found. It is possible that structural features at Burgh Castle have suffered from post-depositional destruction, being ploughed from at least the sixteenth century, and it should

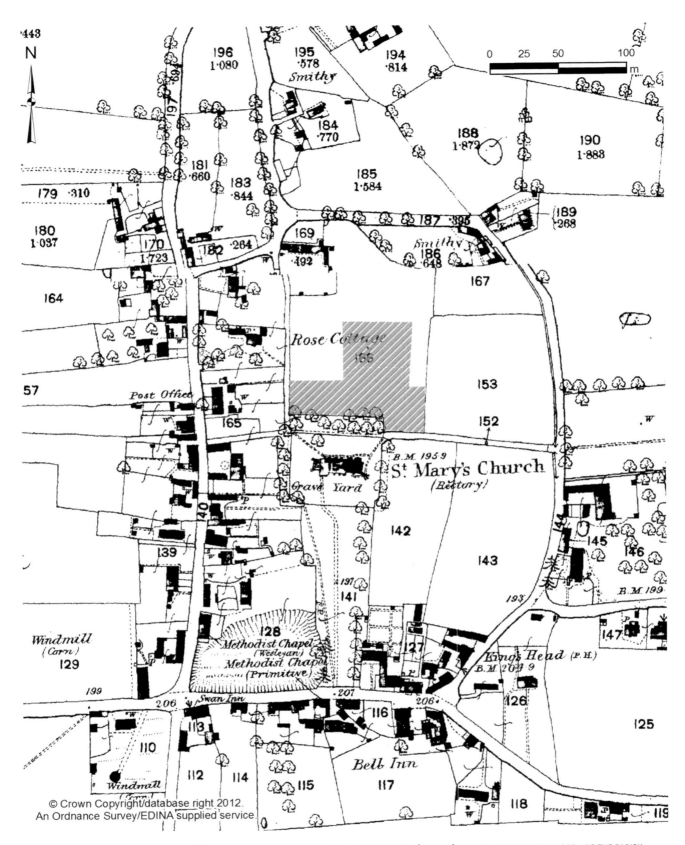

FIGURE 7.21: OS First Edition of Whissonsett, illustrating the area of excavation (shaded), located immediately north of the parish churchyard. 'Middle Saxon' activity detected in the northern part of the excavation was followed by a shift of focus southwards towards the area of the church during the 'Late Saxon' period.

also be considered that even if antiquarian investigation is taken into account, only a quarter of the fort interior has been excavated (Johnson 1987, 45-50; Hoggett 2010, 56-9).

'CORS': ASSESSING 'MIDDLE SAXON' POTENTIAL

As the above discussion demonstrates, numerous currently-occupied rural settlements in Norfolk have been subject to archaeological excavation which has resulted in the identification of 'Middle Saxon' settlement remains. Whilst the evidence from such sites has clear significance for research, of equal importance is assessing the frequency with which 'Middle Saxon' material in general is found in currently-occupied villages. The AIP records that, of the archaeological interventions carried out in Norfolk between 1990 and 2009, forty two were undertaken in areas classified by this research as 'currently occupied'. Thirty three of these investigations located archaeological deposits of some kind, six of which detected 'Middle Saxon' artefacts only, and a further ten identified structural features relating to 'Middle Saxon' occupation. Archaeological work in Norfolk's still-occupied rural settlements has therefore encountered 'Middle Saxon' material in sixteen out of the thirty three villages, in which stratified deposits were recorded, a detection rate of over forty-eight percent. It must be remembered that the evidence derived from the AIP can only be realistically used as an approximate guide, and is not a completely comprehensive analysis (see Chapter II). Detection of 'Middle Saxon' settlement deposits in almost half of the currently-occupied rural settlements excavated in Norfolk is, nevertheless, extremely informative and suggests a significant relationship between existing villages and the later medieval landscape.

The regular discovery of 'Middle Saxon' settlement evidence from Norfolk's extant villages is especially surprising when the continued settlement mobility of the 'Late Saxon' and subsequent periods is considered. One factor that likely skews the results of the AIP somewhat though is the dislocation between parish churches and current village centres in the county. As this research classifies currently-occupied rural settlement on the basis of any area lying within 100m of settlement extents recorded on OS First Edition maps, *and* any area which falls within a 500m radius of the parish church (Chapter II), several villages in Norfolk actually have dual 'currently occupied' foci, often quite geographically separate from each other. The phenomenon of isolated churches in Norfolk therefore creates in some parishes double the extent of an area classified as a 'currently-occupied' rural settlement by this book when compared to other counties. Indeed, it is notable that several of the interventions which have recovered 'Middle Saxon' evidence are actually represented by investigations located adjacent, or in close proximity to, the parish church which now lies in a discrete location to the villages it serves.

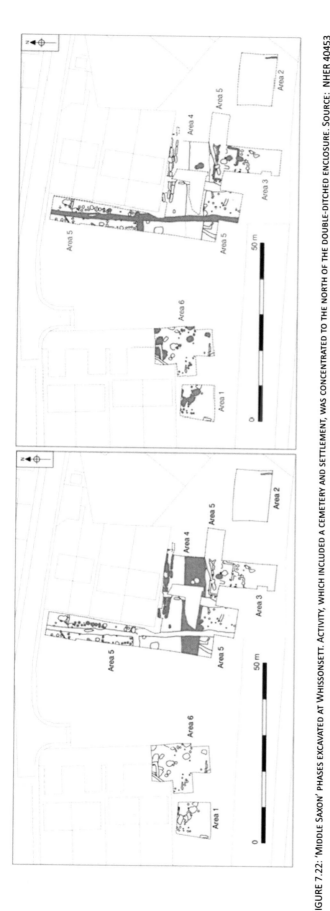

FIGURE 7.22: 'MIDDLE SAXON' PHASES EXCAVATED AT WHISSONSETT. ACTIVITY, WHICH INCLUDED A CEMETERY AND SETTLEMENT, WAS CONCENTRATED TO THE NORTH OF THE DOUBLE-DITCHED ENCLOSURE. SOURCE: NHER 40453

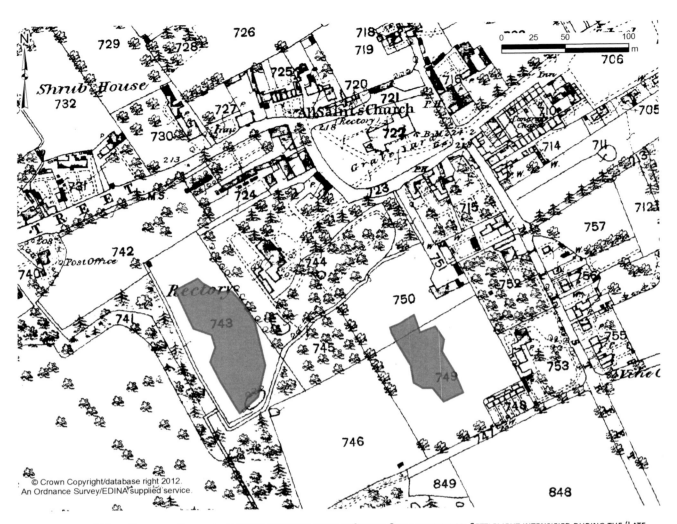

FIGURE 7.23: OS FIRST EDITION OF SHIPDHAM. THE TWO EXCAVATED AREAS AT CHURCH CLOSE ARE SHADED. SETTLEMENT INTENSIFIED DURING THE 'LATE SAXON' PERIOD BUT WAS CONCENTRATED IN THE NORTHERN PART OF THE EXCAVATIONS, SUGGESTING THAT THE PRESENT VILLAGE FORM WAS DEVELOPED DURING THIS TIME.

Interventions in 'CORS'	'CORS' interventions identifying archaeological deposits	'CORS' with 'Middle Saxon' artefactual material only	'CORS' with 'Middle Saxon' artefactual material and settlement structures from 'CORS'
42	33	6	10

Table 7.1: Of the archaeological interventions undertaken within 'CORS' in Norfolk, almost half have located potential evidence for occupation datable to the 'Middle Saxon' period.

The identification of 'Middle Saxon' occupation adjacent to churches does suggest however, a trend towards church foundation around the eighth century in some parishes, followed by subsequent settlement shift. Whilst Norfolk therefore demonstrates mobility for a more prolonged period, and indeed over greater distances than any other county studied by this research, this chapter has shown clear instances of currently-occupied village in the county with apparent 'Middle Saxon' antecedents. Excavation in close proximity to the parish church has located settlement evidence dated to the eighth or early ninth centuries in villages such as Shipdham, Whissonsett and Great Bircham. The character of investigation at these sites, comprising

excavation close to the parish church but not adjacent to it, makes it difficult to assess whether churches were a component of settlement at this time. More promising in this regard is the evidence from fieldwalking projects such as the Launditch Hundred Project, which appears to show some 'Middle Saxon' church foundations, followed by a far more comprehensive second wave of establishments in the 'Late Saxon' period.

The AIP for Norfolk thus at first appears to show a close correlation between still-occupied villages and 'Middle Saxon' settlement, but on closer inspection, a far more complex picture is revealed. Evidence for currently-occupied rural settlement investigation in Norfolk is partly distorted by the regular occurrence of parish churches located in distinct locations to their dependent villages, thus increasing the area classed as 'currently occupied' in some parishes. Excavations have revealed 'Middle Saxon' remains next to churches and within *truly* currently occupied rural settlements in Norfolk, indicating that developments which occurred around the eighth century were significant for the development of both church and village in at least some parishes. Churches should not be viewed as an essential component of 'Middle Saxon' communities in Norfolk, however, as evidenced at Sedgeford where extensive excavation of settlement and cemetery has revealed no church-type structure. Fieldwalking is the most effective method of assessing the period in which churches were established, and in many cases can also shed light on the relationship of 'Middle Saxon' settlements with later medieval villages if any exists. Perhaps the most clear deduction from fieldwalking results, similar to the picture emerging from currently-occupied rural settlement excavation, is one of a variable path of early medieval settlement development in Norfolk, reflective of industrious and capable communities shaping their own environment.

SETTLEMENT AND SOCIETY IN 'MIDDLE SAXON' NORFOLK

More than any other county researched by this book, archaeological investigation in Norfolk provides a vital contribution to our understanding of 'Middle Saxon' settlement and society. The lack of documentary material for East Anglia has meant that archaeological research in the region has adopted a leading role in providing insights into changing social conditions as reflected in the physical remains of settlements and landscapes. To this end, researchers are fortunate that Norfolk possesses one of the richest archaeological records anywhere in England. The range and quantity of evidence available is largely the result of a proud research tradition, but 'Middle Saxon' settlement research also benefits from tenth century and later developments peculiar to the county. A tendency for settlements in Norfolk to remain mobile well into the medieval period means that many abandoned 'Middle Saxon' centres now lie in agricultural land. Fieldwalking and metal-detecting is able to define the location and extent of such sites, and more detail can be gained from excavation of deposits that have not been damaged or truncated by later settlement.

It is the evidence derived from landscape-scale research, from fieldwalking and metal-detecting, that is perhaps the most unique of Norfolk's archaeological datasets. It has been estimated that approximately ten percent of the total land area of the county has been fieldwalked, surely representing the best coverage of any county in England. Metal-detecting too has been extensive, and has proved beneficial, and whilst this approach remains more effective in identifying funerary remains (e.g. Chester-Kadwell 2009), it has also been central in providing evidence for metal-rich settlement sites. Added to such landscape-orientated investigation, the results from excavations help to characterise the form and development of settlement sites in Norfolk more closely. Although the county possesses a dearth of extensive excavations, with the notable exceptions of North Elmham and Sedgeford, development within currently-occupied rural settlements has led to a number of investigations that have located early medieval settlement.

Combining these various strands of evidence together, it is possible to gain a significant insight into the 'Middle Saxon' settlement landscape of Norfolk. This evidence demonstrates that, although the kingdom of the East Angles represents one of the most poorly understood early medieval English polities in terms of historical narrative, developments in the northern part of the region between the seventh to ninth centuries were comparable to conditions in the other areas of central and eastern England studied by this book. Of the material presented above, a series of key deductions can be made which suggest that the 'Middle Saxon' period was a time of fundamental social change, and this was manifest in transformation of settlements and exploitation of the land. Perhaps one of the most notable expressions of this new environment is the increased adaptation and use of different Norfolk's topographical *pays*, particularly wetlands. The poor record of 'Middle Saxon' activity in the Broadland *pays* is somewhat anticipated, as industrial peat extraction in the fringes from the medieval period onwards is likely to have had a detrimental impact on archaeological deposits. The exception to this situation is Burgh Castle, the standing Roman remains of which may have formed a focus for the development of a 'Middle Saxon' elite centre (Johnson 1983).

Despite the relative lack of archaeological evidence from the Broadland, the pattern of parishes in the region suggests that the landscape may have been utilised in the 'Middle Saxon' period. Parishes such as Chedgrave and Stockton, situated at some distance from the Broads proper, still have detached portions in the marsh. These historic arrangements illustrate the value of wetland environments, and in this instance particularly the access to woodlands and salt-pans, for the agricultural regimes of early medieval communities (Rackham 1986, 381). At the time of the Domesday survey, Broadland is recorded as possessing one of the highest densities of 'free peasants' anywhere in the county, probably the result of economic expansion through conversion of wastes to arable by industrious farming groups (Darby 1952, 149). The other 'poorly manorialised' region of Norfolk in 1086 was the silt fen of Marshland, the early medieval development of which is far better represented in the archaeological record.

Combining fieldwalking with targeted excavation, the research of the Fenland Project in particular has transformed our understanding of 'Middle Saxon' Marshland, and it is now clear that from around the eighth century the silt fen was subject to limited but permanent settlement. Hay

Green has produced the greatest density of ceramics of any 'Middle Saxon' settlement identified in Marshland but, as demonstrated by North Elmham, artefact densities cannot be used as a reliable indicator of status. Indeed, subsequent excavation of pottery concentrations at Hay Green revealed what appeared to be an average 'Middle Saxon' settlement operating a mixed farming economy (Silvester 1988, 37). West Walton too has been noted as a site of likely exceptional 'Middle Saxon' status, on the basis of its metalwork yield (Rogerson 2003, 110), and later administrative history, but again the evidence does not allow for more concrete interpretation (Silvester 1988, 92).

On balance, it appears probable that Hay Green and West Walton were centres of at least regional importance from around the eighth century, yet more impressive is the apparent planned approach to the colonisation of Marshland around this time. Whether directed by established upland communities or industrious self-contained groups, the settlement of Marshland gives an appearance of being planned, or at least regulated, with sites evenly spread across the *pays*, possibly adhering to defined territorial units. It is easy to see such distributions as the work of an individual lord, but scholars are advised caution when interpreting 'dots on maps' as single premeditated events. Whilst Ipswich Ware provides the Marshland settlements as broadly 'Middle Saxon', their establishment may not have been entirely contemporary and could have emerged more organically than it would first appear. The capability of peasant groups in orchestrating such an approach to landscape organisation should also not be underestimated, as rural communities appear equally able to instigate changes to their living conditions throughout the medieval period (e.g. Dyer 1985).

It is tempting nevertheless to interpret the Marshland sites as the work of elite, perhaps monastic groups, as it has already been shown that settlement of wetland islands and its fringes, such as in Cambridgeshire, was possibly undertaken under the guidance of 'Middle Saxon' minster communities (Chapter VI). Similarly, in the wetlands of Somerset, Stephen Rippon has shown that the lordly influence of Glastonbury Abbey was probably central in effecting early medieval settlement change, even if the clerics themselves were not involved directly in the process (Rippon 2008, 104). The population capacity to exploit the silt Marshland may have been provided by monastic brethren with a semi-dependant status, who were free from the process of tribute accumulation which characterised secular landownership up to *c.* 800 (Blair 2005, 255; Fleming 2011, 22). Interpreting the 'Middle Saxon' Marshland settlements as the result of ecclesiastical agency is at best speculative, however, and it is not clear that the sites were even founded by lordly rather than peasant groups. What the archaeological evidence demonstrates without doubt though is a fundamental change to the use of Marshlands during the 'Middle Saxon' period, as permanent settlements were established in the silt fen for the first time.

The increased ability and willingness to exploit the Marshland is indicative of increasingly sophisticated economic and social structures which emerged from the seventh century in England. Such changes are also likely behind the emergence of more diverse settlement types in Norfolk, like the 'productive sites' identified in the north-west of the county. Although the term 'productive sites' potentially encompasses settlements of various character and function, the recovery of coinage in large quantities is undoubtedly significant. The prolific numbers of eighth-century coins found at sites such as Bawsey and Wormegay represent high monetary values and their density either reflcets control of resources within a proto-monetary society or centralised production. In the expanding commercial environment of the late seventh and early eighth centuries, development of coinage seems to have been a priority for royal authority as part of the control and centralisation of trade (Pestell 2004, 33). Indeed, that trade was a key element of Norfolk's 'productive sites' is shown by their distribution on navigable rivers or close to the coast.

More than any other *pays* the Good Sands reflects the growth of a more complex rural settlement network in Norfolk, marked by the development of numerous specialist centres. The expansion and intensification of trade networks was certainly not the preserve of Norfolk's six 'productive sites, however, as rural settlements across the county show evidence of outside influence. The land-locked centre at Shipdham, for instance, yielded coins from the Byzantine Empire and although 'productive sites' are perhaps the most clear signifiers of a stratifying settlement hierarchy, even more typical rural communities are likely to have been influenced by widespread 'Middle Saxon' economic and social change. Whilst the spread of coinage is perhaps the most obvious portable artefact expressing new forms of royal power, from the late seventh century the church developed as a key new medium for elite investment. Archaeological investigation in Norfolk has yet to identify convincing structural evidence for a 'Middle Saxon' church, probably the result of the limited excavations undertaken in the county to date. Even at the extensively investigated site of North Elmham, the probable site of the East Anglian see of *Elmham*, no church was revealed, demonstrating the difficulty of detecting such structures.

That religious buildings began to be situated within 'Middle Saxon' settlements in East Anglia is demonstrated by the excavated three-celled structure from Brandon in Suffolk, which almost certainly represents a church (Carr *et al.* 1988). In Norfolk, the most convincing evidence for 'Middle Saxon' church foundations is actually derived from fieldwalking; Ipswich Ware concentrations surrounding parish churches indicates eighth or ninth-century origins for centres that have since been rebuilt. In some places, only Ipswich Ware is found in church environs, suggesting church foundation within a 'Middle Saxon' settlement that subsequently shifted focus before the end of the ninth century. In many such instances, such as at Mileham and Wellingham, it is notable that relocation is minimal, with 'Late Saxon' scatters found almost contiguous to 'Middle Saxon' concentrations (Wade-Martins 1980a). This research has shown that this process of settlement drift is a consistent phenomenon detectable across central and eastern England, although similar to the rest of the counties researched by this volume, detecting actual 'Middle Saxon' church structures 'Middle Saxon' has proven problematic. Whilst the relative lack of written material makes it uncertain who established such centres, it is likely that pre-Viking churches were almost totally royally-founded, monastic institutions (Blair 2005, 84-8). In other parishes, Ipswich Ware and 'Late Saxon' wares have been found in combination, suggesting that the settlement is likely to have remained adjacent to the eighth century church for a more prolonged period, before relocating.

Establishment of church buildings was therefore an important process within some, but by no means all, 'Middle Saxon' settlements in Norfolk. At Sedgeford, for example, extensive excavation of a large cemetery and settlement complex has yet to identify a church and it is probably only around the eleventh century that the centre possessed a dedicated structure for religious worship. Indeed, fieldwalking and excavated evidence suggests that church foundation rapidly increased in the centuries after c.850, as at Whissonsett where a shift in the 'Late Saxon' settlement focus was apparently accompanied by church establishment. Significantly, though, the 'Middle Saxon' ditch at Whissonsett conformed to the later street-plan, demonstrating the lasting significance at some sites of developments dated to the period. Whilst Norfolk's early medieval settlement sequence therefore presents a picture of overwhelming variation, on a regional and even local scale, this chapter has shown the way in which 'Middle Saxon' occupation consistently demonstrates fundamental changes to the character of existing 'Early Saxon' habitation forms. Excavation has shown the introduction of boundaries on 'Middle Saxon' sites, perhaps indicative of tenement plots, such as revealed at North Elmham.

In Norfolk, as elsewhere in England, such changes show that the perceptions of property were developing, with the concept of private space being manifest in settlement arrangements for the first time (e.g. Reynolds 2003). This change is perhaps most clearly seen in place-names, as the *gens*-orientated designations such as Happing, -OE '*Hæps* people' (Sandred 1996, 84) which probably originated in the sixth century, were replaced by a landscape dotted with location-specific elements during the 'Middle Saxon' period. Whilst personal elements are by no means eliminated from later place-names, it is probably from the 'Middle Saxon' period that the settlements themselves, usually in the form of 'tun' and 'ham', are more consistently referred to (Gelling 2011, 993-7). Elsewhere in England, this book has shown that the introduction of more permanent sites and lasting boundary features may represent the first stage in the development of later, more lasting settlements, but in Norfolk communities appear to have been willing to relocate until well into the medieval period.

Elucidating the precise reasons behind the continued mobility of rural settlements is not within the remit of this research, but it appears that differing circumstances from the 'Late Saxon' period were likely key, as this chapter has demonstrated the comparable conditions of Norfolk's 'Middle Saxon' social and settlement landscape with other areas of England. Ongoing at the time of writing, research by John Blair is noting the consistency with which gridded elements were introduced to early medieval settlements in central England after the Viking period, an approach which was apparently much less common in regions such as Norfolk (Blair 2013). Gridded plans, Blair argues, utilising two standard measurements based on the approaches used by Roman *agrimensores* but utilising indigenous units, are likely to have been the preserve of monastic communities before c.850 but became a more widespread approach to organising all settlement types after this date. Taking the model a step further, Blair suggests that standard grids formed the basis of many settlement plans within the 'central province' of central England where 'nucleated' medieval villages are more typically encountered. Whilst an interesting and potentially revolutionary thesis, the reasons why gridded plans were not adopted in places like East Anglia remains unclear. Whatever the causes of Norfolk's divergent path, this book benefits from the rich material record that it has produced, providing a crucial understanding of the changing character of 'Middle Saxon' settlement and landscape, and a unique insight into contemporary society.

CONCLUSION

The modern landscape of Norfolk is in many ways unique, and is undoubtedly largely a product of its development during the historic period. The presence of features such as isolated churches and common-edge settlement types, however, are largely a product of changes that occurred in 'Late Saxon' and subsequent periods. Continued mobility of settlement well into the late medieval period led to 'Middle Saxon' and 'Late Saxon' churches situated in location often far-removed from their associated settlements. The causes behind Norfolk's alternative path of development have not been explored in detail, and the key conclusion of this chapter has instead been the apparently comparable conditions in the county during the 'Middle Saxon' period. Similar to the other four counties studied by this research, the landscape of Norfolk underwent fundamental transformations during the 'Middle Saxon' period, with increased exploitation of marginal land, the foundation of churches, development of structured and semi-permanent occupation, and increasingly hierarchical and specialised settlements. Again, it appears that these features are the result of key changes in society, including new perceptions of property and space, and the developing character of lordship. Indeed, the almost complete dearth of documentary material for early medieval East Anglia should not prevent us seeing new powers at work in the

'Middle Saxon' landscape of Norfolk. It is notable that for the 'Late Saxon' period, the emergence of features such planned settlements are roundly accepted as products of elite authority, supported by scant documentary references, such as that found in *Geþyncðo*. Similar to the other thematic studies of this volume, this chapter demonstrates that such forces were likely at work earlier than is generally appreciated, even in areas where there is little written material to corroborate the archaeological material.

Chapter VIII
Discussion

This book began with the central aim of assessing the way in which 'Middle Saxon' settlement archaeology can contribute to our understanding of society between the seventh and ninth centuries. Within this aim, this also research sought to critically re-examine the character and chronology of early medieval settlement change, and more specifically, looked to challenge the popular scholarly outlook that it was the later ninth to eleventh centuries that witnessed the first key transformation of rural communities which affected the lived experience of inhabitants. In addition, this volume looked to assess whether there is regional variation in the archaeological evidence to 'Middle Saxon' settlement and land use, and whether these discrepancies represent actual differences in the character of the countryside between the seventh and ninth centuries, or indicate instead alternative traditions of research. In order to fulfil these aims and objectives, this study explored the archaeological evidence for 'Middle Saxon' settlements across five counties in central and eastern England. The contribution of archaeological investigation into currently-occupied rural settlements has been especially significant, representing a unique dataset of great research value.

By combining such data and other unpublished 'grey-literature', together with the more widely disseminated published material, and placing it within the context of the historic landscape, this research has produced a series of important insights of 'Middle Saxon' communities. This section will bring together the data from the five case studies, and emphasise both the common themes, but also the disparities in the evidence offered. The preceding chapters have presented five counties characterised by great topographical diversity, but it is also clear that the differing regions possess divergent traditions of early medieval settlement research. Where the evidence has allowed, a consistent approach to investigation has been made in each county, but flexibility has been required where there exists clear inconsistencies in available data. Attempting to gauge the influence of topography on 'Middle Saxon' communities, for instance, resulted in a *pays*-based investigation for most chapters, yet in Oxfordshire the lack of archaeological evidence outside of the Thames Valley required a different approach. Fortunately the material evidence from Oxfordshire's central *pays* was sufficient to allow an alternative analysis, which examined the developing settlement hierarchies of the 'Middle Saxon' period through the likely status of sites.

It is the role of this chapter to scrutinise this often inconsistent evidence, in order to provide a greater understanding of 'Middle Saxon' settlement and landscape character, but also to generate an insight into the changing conditions in society between the seventh and ninth centuries. This book has presented evidence that directly challenges the prevailing scholarly understanding of early medieval landscape change, illustrated, for example, by Lewis *et al.* (1997, 198), who argue that 'for the first five centuries after the collapse of the Roman province, until the ninth century or later, rural settlement generally consisted of small dispersed settlements, mostly scattered on lighter and more fertile soils...abandoned some time after 850, and replaced by villages'. Contrary to this popular perception, research has emphasised the case for 'Middle Saxon' landscape transformation, and it has been suggested that this wholesale restructuring of settlement character and function was part of deep-rooted social change that significantly impacted rural communities and the lived experience of the inhabitants.

This chapter will explore the evidence for 'Middle Saxon' settlement change through a series of central themes: the developing permanence and internal organisation of settlements, the expanding geographical locations of rural occupation, the developing economies of rural communities, and finally the relationship between 'Middle Saxon' settlement and the later landscape. Before the fundamental outcomes of the book are investigated in greater detail, however, it is first necessary to place the archaeological evidence within its wider context. This research has continually asserted that transformation of 'Middle Saxon' rural settlement was part of a broader phenomenon of social, economic and political change that occurred between the seventh and ninth centuries. But what is the evidence for these developments, and how do we gauge their likely relationship with contemporary rural settlement? Drawing on archaeological and other material from across 'Middle Saxon' England, the following section will demonstrate that the modifications undergoing rural communities in the five counties was part of more comprehensive transformation affecting society.

SETTLEMENT AND SOCIAL CHANGE IN 'MIDDLE SAXON' ENGLAND

Introduction

To provide a greater understanding of 'Middle Saxon' England requires the drawing together of often disparate stands of evidence, but through this process it becomes clear that the seventh to ninth centuries was a dynamic period of great change in society (Rippon 2010, 45). Beginning with the broadest of scales, the seventh century is marked by greater stabilisation of political entities, as kin-based groups began to be replaced by the more extensive overlordship exercised by increasingly powerful individuals. The earliest evidence for 'kingship', outlined within written documents from the end of the sixth century, indicates an institution already well-established, no matter how precarious the position of individual rulers may have been (Bassett 1989, 3). By the seventh century, however, there can be little questioning that individuals calling themselves 'kings' possessed more deep-rooted and wide ranging authority. Archaeologically-speaking, detecting such power on the ground has often proved challenging, and indeed whole volumes have been dedicated to the subject and its inherent difficulties (e.g. Dickinson and Griffiths ed. 1999).

The 'princely burials' dated to the first quarter of the seventh century, such as Taplow and Sutton Hoo, have quite reasonably been associated with royal authority (e.g. Carver 2005) and represent our most likely material evidence for particular early 'kings'. The evidence from settlement is often regarded as less compelling, however (cf. Stoodley 1999). Indeed, it has been suggested that archaeology can little distinguish kings from their aristocrats, or the nobility in general from the rest of society, especially when considering the evidence for occupation (Bassett 1989, 5). Part of the difficulty is the way in which the archaeological material has been treated, as attempts are made to associate the specific kings, places or events recorded in written sources with physical remains. Material culture, especially of the early medieval period, can rarely be associated with such specifics, and researchers instead benefit from attempting to perceive the broader chronological narrative provided by the archaeological record.

The Changing Face of Elite Settlement

Despite despondency in some quarters about the potential that settlement archaeology has to explore social hierarchies, clearly early elite occupation sites have been identified at a number of locations across England, the most famous and best-excavated example being Yeavering, Northumberland (Hope-Taylor 1977). The 'palace' complex at Yeavering demonstrates the pinnacle of the development of the great hall, featuring a meticulously-planned group of central buildings. Carefully aligned, and featuring spatial arrangements actively controlled by enclosures, the buildings at Yeavering were also rebuilt on the same plot, unlike most halls of the period (Hope Taylor 1977; Blair 2005, 54-7; Ulmschneider 2011, 159). Settlement complexes bearing some resemblance to Yeavering have also been partially investigated at Cowdery's Down in Hampshire, and Bremilham in Wiltshire, and identified elsewhere through aerial photography at places such as Hatton Rock, Warwickshire and Atcham, Shropshire (Hirst and Rahtz 1973; Millett and James 1983; Hinchliffe 1986; Pretty 1999).

Perhaps surprisingly, the limited dating evidence derived from this corpus of undeniably high-status settlements suggests that they were all abandoned by the middle of the seventh century (Hope-Taylor 1977; Hinchliffe 1986, 250-253). The disappearance of ostentatious 'palatial' complexes such as Yeavering and Bremilham thus rather unfortunately coincides with the chronological starting-point of this study, which itself has sought to argue for steadily increasing investment in landscape and settlement beginning as early as c.600. Whilst a handful of possible 'Middle Saxon' palace sites have been suggested on the basis of archaeological and historical evidence (Bruce-Mitford 1974, 75; Williams et al. 1985), identifying the high-status centres of the 'Middle Saxon' period is obscured by the close association between sites of secular and ecclesiastical character.

The impact of the Augustinian Church upon all aspects of English life cannot be exaggerated, and is explored in remarkable depth and scale in John Blair's *Church in Anglo-Saxon Society* (Blair 2005). From the middle of the seventh century, the Church became the primary medium for elite investment, as communities of religious people were established by royal authorities throughout England. Scholars have preferred to adopt the term 'minster' to refer to all types of church centre dating to the 'Middle Saxon' period, as deployment of this modernised version of an Old English term usefully avoids making judgments about the character of places, especially when their identify remains uncertain or debated (Blair 2005, 2-5). From as early as the 1970s, however, archaeologists have recognised the difficulty of detecting minsters on the ground (e.g. Rahtz 1973), and despite the vast increase in archaeological recording in the past forty years, the issue continues to draw significant debate. Discussion in recent years had tended to be drawn to three sites, at Brandon in Suffolk, Flixborough in Lincolnshire, and Northampton (Gittos 2011, 827-8).

Listing a collection of attributes which are consistent of minsters, Blair has argued that the excavated remains at Northampton, amongst other places, actually represent a religious community, and not a royal palace as originally interpreted by the excavators (Williams et al. 1985; Blair 2005, 204-11). Based on the excavated sequence from Flixborough, Christopher Loveluck has also suggested that secular sites may be distinguished through their comparatively high consumption of wild animals, likely obtained through hunting (Loveluck 2007, 148-59). As explored in Chapter VII, Tim Pestell is amongst a number of scholars who have directly challenged outlooks such as Blair's and Loveluck's, illustrating that even the most 'religious-type' material culture may have been used on high-status sites of any type (Pestell 2004, 40-50). A further concern is the apparent ubiquity of minsters, as Church activity has been used to interpret sites of apparently varying character, occupied between the seventh and ninth centuries (Gittos 2011, 828).

A lack of detailed comparison between sites of specifically ecclesiastical and secular nature may represent another problem, but more critically, it is possible that scholars are searching for a distinction on the ground that never actually existed in 'Middle Saxon' England. One aspect of interpretation that has gone largely unrecognised is the likely anachronistic connotations that researchers currently back-project onto early medieval society. This research therefore adopts a more cautious approach, but one which perhaps provides a more accurate projection of the perceived reality, by classing sites simply as of 'elite' character. Written sources can of course be insightful in identifying the likely activities of a specific place (e.g. Campbell 1979), but the archaeological evidence from 'Middle Saxon' England rarely allows us to be so explicit. Whilst the vast discrepancies in wealth between 'Early Saxon' centres such as Mucking and Yeavering remain undetectable in 'Middle Saxon' society, it is nevertheless obvious that the period did witness great expansion in types of site, with the development of a gradually more sophisticated settlement hierarchy, linked to rapidly changing economy.

Developing Hierarchies: Settlement and Economy

As this research has shown, the 'Middle Saxon' period in central and eastern England was characterised by a marked increase in settlement type, developed partly as a consequence of rapidly changing economic conditions. Archaeologically, the most prominent new settlement form are the *emporia* that developed along the south and east coasts from the latter part of the seventh century, principally at *Hamwih* (Southampton), *Lundenwic* (London), *Gippeswic* (Ipswich) and *Eoforwic* (York). The *emporia* were certainly amongst the foremost of the nexus of centres engaged in continental trade around the English Channel and the North Sea, utilising an unprecedented quantity of coinage that would not be exceeded for another five centuries (Blackburn 2003, 31). These centres also stand out in other ways, primarily with regard to their great size compared to other sites of the period, but also in their evidence for planned layouts (Pestell 2011, 569). Excavations at *Hamwic*, the most comprehensively-investigated of the *emporia*, identified evidence for occupation extending almost fifty hectares, arranged around a gridded pattern of metalled roads probably established around 700 (Birbeck *et al.* 2005, 86-9). In London, more limited excavations hint at a similarly-sized centre, with roads also indicating a likely structured method of settlement layout (Malcolm *et al.* 2003, 145).

The seemingly planned approach to arrangement of such centres has lead to the widespread view that they were established by a central authority, and there can be little doubt of elite influence of some description in their operation (Birbeck *et al.* 2005, 196; Leary 2004, 142). *Emporia* can no longer be reasonably viewed, however, as singular channels of elite exchange for the kingdom in which they were situated (cf. Hodges 1982, 197). Rather, places such as *Hamwih* and *Gippeswic* represent the most prominent examples of an emerging group of diverse 'Middle Saxon' sites that illustrate fundamental development of a sophisticated settlement hierarchy. Current scholars have found Richard Hodges' (1982, 50-2) traditional classification of exchange centres somewhat restrictive, and have attempted instead to contextualise *emporia* within their hinterlands. Where *emporia* were once viewed as a stimulus for settlement development in their surrounding countryside, the evidence presented by this research complements the revisionist view of John Moreland (2000), who suggests that 'Middle Saxon' agricultural changes facilitated the foundation of large, non-producing populations. Indeed, research on animal bone assemblages in particular has supported the likelihood that growing rural productivity sustained the inhabitants of large *emporia* (e.g. Crabtree 1994).

Together with the *emporia*, the proliferation of minster communities required similar provision from their hinterlands, creating 'central places' important for economic development, and perhaps eventually precipitating the growth of small towns (Blair 2005, 245-60). The whole of rural society should not be seen as producing renders directly for such centres, however, and if anything, medieval landscape research has consistently illustrated the complexity of rural organisation (e.g. Jones 1979). Whilst the growth of non-farming populations undeniably placed new pressures on rural populations, further evidence that *emporia* did not act as lone centres in a regional trade network is demonstrated by the development of so-called 'productive sites'. In Chapter VII, the evidence from Norfolk, illustrated the emergence of places that have yielded significant quantities of metalwork, which although continue to be defined as a singular corpus, probably represent centres of various status and function.

The evidence from 'productive sites' such as Bawsey and Wormegay undoubtedly hints at increasing settlement specialisation, and it is likely that some possessed specific functions, such as points for tax collection (Hutcheson 2006; Loveluck and Tys 2006). Indeed, documentary sources supporting the existence of toll collection, and the evidence from the continent suggests that such renders were highly lucrative for elite authorities (Kelly 1992, 18; Pestell 2011, 573). Few productive sites have been comprehensively studied, however, and this pattern of piecemeal investigation makes generalisation hazardous (cf. Hutcheson 2006). Amongst the rare unifying characteristics of 'productive' sites, is their consistent positioning close to the coast or navigable rivers. Such locations are indicative of the trade and communication that was integral to their function, but whether this in turn is representative of a new economic and social environment remains debated (Davies 2010, 50-1). James Campbell (2000b), for instance, has argued that trade was at least as extensive in the 'Early Saxon' period as it was in the subsequent centuries.

In a related point, Chris Wickham (2005, 344-51) has noted the prolific use of eighth-century coinage across East Anglia was not associated with state development, yet from the more complex social milieu of contemporary Mercia has emerged little evidence for either coinage or 'productive sites'. Such observations are part of a much wider debate amongst scholars over the function of coinage in eighth and ninth-century England, with the key point of divergence being whether more widespread coin use represents a highly monetised and market-based economy, or whether instead it was rooted in socially-embedded transactions which had little, if any, economic importance. The sheer quantity of sceattas known from 'Middle Saxon' England does suggest a link between coinage and trade, but further research is required to extrapolate this relationship in greater detail (Astill 2011, 504-5). The step-change in landscape investment from the seventh century also alludes to a changing economic environment, though, not simply in terms of establishment of 'special purpose' centres such as 'productive sites' and *emporia*, but the developments that occurred throughout the settlement hierarchy. Furthermore, the increase in site-types and locations occasionally provides an insight into contemporary political conditions, with the minsters and settlements established around the fen of eastern England reflecting the struggles between increasingly powerful polities (Pestell 2011, 574; Chapter VI). Whilst this discussion has so far continued to emphasise the evidence from 'Middle Saxon' settlement centres that indicates changes to social and economic conditions, an analysis of other types of landscape investment similarly hints at new powers at work in the countryside.

Industry and Infrastructure in 'Middle Saxon' England

The increasing types of settlement that emerged in 'Middle Saxon' England represent just one aspect of the central theme of growing landscape investment that characterised the period. Whereas consumption of wealth through burial dropped off markedly during the second half of the seventh century, other mediums became the focus of investment, and for the elite and emerging aristocracy, wealth was largely obtained from possession of estates. In addition to developing more sophisticated settlement networks on such properties, individuals also began to foster industry and infrastructure (Rippon 2010, 47). At Ebbsfleet in Kent, for instance, a tidal-powered horizontal mill was dendrochronological dated to the 690s, and at Tamworth a similar construction may have originated as early as the eighth century (Rahtz and Meeson 1992; Buss 2002). A number of industrial metal-working producing centres have also been identified in southern England, such as the excavated site at Ramsbury in Wiltshire (Haslam 1980; Chapter V), and at Worget in Dorset where a probable mill structure dated to *c.*664-709 was filled with slag and furnace residues, suggesting that processing was being undertaken at the site or close by. Also in Dorset, archaeomagnetic dating of probable corn drying ovens at Gillingham resulted in a date centring on the eighth century (Heaton 1992), and a similar type of site has also been detected at Hereford (Shoesmith 1982).

The prosaic but essential raw material of salt also seems to have been more consistently procured during the 'Middle Saxon' period. In addition to the considerable coastal salt production recorded by Domesday, documentary and archaeological evidence from sites such as Droitwich, Warwickshire, show the brine springs were increasingly

exploited throughout the 'Middle Saxon' period (Keen 1988; Maddicott 2005). Significantly, written sources for Droitwich demonstrate that both secular and ecclesiastical authorities profited from Droitwich's salt industry, illustrating once again the matching interests of the entire social elite (Hurst 1997). A further notable theme of the evidence for industrial production in 'Middle Saxon' England is that many processing sites were positioned in land-locked locations. Whilst water transport was clearly vital, evidenced both by the geographical positioning of 'productive sites', and the consistent attempts by Mercia to control the Thames Valley, goods must also have been distributed overland (e.g. Blair ed. 2007). Indeed, the presence of such a transport network complements other evidence for infrastructural development, which demonstrates the material and manpower resources available to major landowners between the seventh and ninth centuries (Rippon 2010, 49). Whilst little is known about the upkeep of roads themselves, existence of some form of integrated overland transport network is supported by the clear importance that kings and bishops placed on bridge maintenance.

The detailed written records regarding the bridge at Rochester, Kent, for instance illustrate that neighbouring estates were held responsible for the upkeep of specific lengths of the causeway (Brookes 1994). Bridge construction and maintenance was one of the three 'common burdens', together with fortress building and army service, identified by historians as exercised by early medieval English kings, and first recorded in a charter of Æthelbald dated to 749 (S 92; John 1958). Associating such obligation with the fortress network of the Burghal Hidage has proved a particular focus of academic interest, but from at least the eighth century, a series of strongholds were developed in Mercia. The earliest documentary reference relating to the construction of defensive enclosures is recorded in the Synod of Gumley, also dating to 749, and by the end of the century, Offa is recorded as requesting obligations of fortress and bridge investment from the people of Kent (S 92; Williams 2005, 103). Archaeologically-speaking, the evidence for eighth and early ninth-century-defences within Mercia has been less forthcoming, with perhaps the most convincing evidence coming from Hereford, where the estate centre featuring grain driers (above) was likely developed as a defensible place (Shoesmith 1982, 74).

Assessing the material data from possible 'Middle Saxon' *burhs* in Mercia, Steven Bassett has posited likely eighth-century defensive works at Tamworth in Staffordshire, Winchcombe in Gloucestershire, Worcester, and Hereford (Bassett 2007; 2008). With the exception of Hereford, though, such an interpretation has yet to be sustained by dating evidence from the defensive circuit. The lack of contemporary activity from within the defences, however, should not be taken as testifying against a 'Middle Saxon' origin, as illustrated by recent work at Wallingford, Oxfordshire, which shows that the fortifications may not have attracted immediate intramural (Christie and

Creighton 2010). More convincing evidence for 'Middle Saxon' defences, indicative of extensive overlordship, is derived from frontier works, such as the great linear earthwork known as Wansdyke. Running between the Bristol Channel and Hampshire, Wansdyke has recently been re-dated to the seventh or eighth centuries, hinting that it may have originated as a boundary between Wessex and Mercia (Reynolds and Langlands 2006).

Wansdyke is thus likely to have been developed in a similar period to the more celebrated Offa's Dyke, traditionally viewed as marking the western edge of the Mercian Kingdom. Comparable to the bridge at Rochester, the alternative construction techniques evident in the built fabric of Offa's Dyke suggests the involvement of numerous teams in its building, likely derived from the vast corpus of estates under Mercian lordship (Hill and Worthington 2002). The evidence from archaeology and other sources therefore suggests that the 'Middle Saxon' period was characterised by marked development of industry and infrastructure, but largely due to the lack of diagnostic ceramics compared to eastern England, the south-west and western coast have in the past often been seen as an exception to this prevailing trend (e.g. Moreland 2000; Griffiths 2003). As Rippon (2010) has shown, however, the differing types of material culture outside of the intensively-researched regions of central and eastern England has skewed the existing scholarly outlook, and it appears that landscape change was equally significant in areas such as south-west England as it was within the more comprehensively investigated 'central province'.

Increasingly powerful kings, together with ecclesiastical authorities, from the seventh century sought to exploit the countryside and its resources through new and ever-more sophisticated means, as developing overlordship ensured that the social elite had unprecedented manpower and resources at their disposal. This capital was invested heavily into the landscape, through construction of centres for industrial processing, but also through the development of an integrated transport network, able to link important nodal places. Not all innovation, whether in infrastructure or of any other kind, should be viewed as 'top-down', however. Scholars should not be misled into thinking that the lack of documentary evidence relating to all but the upper echelons of society determines that rural communities were not themselves powerful. Rather, scholars should be aware of the changes that a rapidly stratifying society are likely to have instigated, and consider in particular the way in which a growing number of powerful landowners are likely to have affected settlement form, function and location.

Summary

The above assessment of numerous aspects of social, economic and political conditions in 'Middle Saxon' England demonstrates that the seventh to ninth centuries was a period of significant transformation. It must be acknowledged, however, that the broad-brush approach of contextualisation adopted here runs the risk of purporting a picture of everywhere that does not describe anywhere. In order to counter this, a series of specific sites, landscapes and other evidence have been cited in order to provide specific examples that support the general themes. Using this approach, it has been shown that, from the seventh century, elite investment into the rural landscape was inherently linked to the Church, as the new ideology became the primary focus for consumption of wealth. The wider settlement picture of the period also suggests that society was undergoing important changes, as the variety of site-types expanded rapidly. The most prominent new 'Middle Saxon' settlement form were the large coastal *emporia*, yet they represent just one aspect of a rapidly growing settlement hierarchy which also featured greater specialisation of many centres.

Expansion and specialisation themselves hint at the development of more sophisticated economic arrangements, a likelihood which is supported by the more widespread use of coinage across much of central and eastern England. The exploitation of differing economic conditions made greater wealth available to elite authorities, who invested more heavily into industry and infrastructure. This book has demonstrated that greater investment also occurred in the 'Middle Saxon' rural landscape, as the character of settlement in particular underwent radical transformation. The archaeological evidence for these developments in rural settlement will now be explored through a series of central themes, which together complement the evidence already present for the 'Middle Saxon' period as a time of significant and lasting change.

SETTLEMENT CHANGE IN 'MIDDLE SAXON' ENGLAND

Permanence and Structure: 'Middle Saxon' Settlement Organisation

One of the most prominent findings of this research has been that a significant quantity of the 'Middle Saxon' settlements discussed are of definitively different character to the Mucking-type sites that many scholars argue persisted into the period. Amongst the most common distinctive aspects of the settlement evidence offered by this volume has been the frequency with which sites appear to have been at least semi-permanent in character. 'Middle Saxon' buildings on rural sites were far more frequently rebuilt in the same location, with occupation sometimes persisting for several centuries. This research has also demonstrated a relationship between more permanent 'Middle Saxon' sites and existing villages, and although in most instances it was only following subsequent restructuring that historic centres developed, pre-ninth century phases were often crucial in establishing the pattern of subsequent settlement. In addition, it is clear that the type of structures present on settlements changed over time, with *Grubenhäuser* far more common on sites predating the seventh century, but rarely in use during the second half of the 'Middle Saxon' period (Tipper 2004, 3-10).

177

It has been demonstrated too, that 'Middle Saxon' settlements were subject to a greater degree of internal organisation than their earlier counterparts. The study of settlement layout, and especially the recognition of enclosures and boundaries from the seventh century, has been advanced significantly over recent decades (Hamerow 2011a, 122). In each of the five counties studied by this book, archaeological evidence has illustrated the introduction semi-permanent and increasingly structured 'Middle Saxon' settlement forms into the rural landscape. The likely minster sites at Oundle and Brixworth in Northamptonshire both possessed substantial ditched enclosures around their communities, with the excavated feature at the former site perhaps enhanced by the documented 'great thorn hedge', which is recorded as surrounding Wilfrid's minster (*VSW* c. 67, 146). Enclosure was clearly fundamental to the monastic ideal, and a *vallum* or *septum monasterii* has also been located at other possible minster centres such as Abingdon, Bampton, and Prescote, in Oxfordshire (Chapter IV; Blair 2005, 196).

Caution is advised, however, before associating large enclosing boundaries only with religious communities during the 'Middle Saxon' period. The keyhole-shaped enclosure ditch at Higham Ferrers, for instance, was identified by the excavators as a likely stock-pen, operated under the direct supervision of the adjacent *villa regalis* at Irthlingborough (Hardy *et al.* 2007, 30-5). As a royal estate centre, Irthlingborough is likely to have possessed at least one church, again raising the issue of the way settlement status is identified in the archaeological. Andrew Reynolds has argued that, from as early as the late sixth century, boundaries began to be introduced into many types of rural settlement in England (Reynolds 2003, 98-9) Corroborating this picture, internal ditched enclosures appear as a regular feature of apparently various classes of 'Middle Saxon' settlement investigated by this research. Perhaps the most impressive enclosure arrangements are those excavated within the village centres of Cottenham and Fordham, in Cambridgeshire, the regularity of which suggests that a standard survey measure may have been used to plan them, but in each of the counties 'Middle Saxon' occupation sites featuring ditched boundaries have been identified. Although in many cases the excavated ditches were probably relatively insubstantial, it is likely that the features were augmented by less-traceable banks, fences or hedges. Significantly, evidence for repeated re-cutting of many features suggests maintenance over relatively long periods, with enclosures delineating at least semi-permanent settlement arrangements (Hamerow 2011a, 122).

The development of semi-permanent ditched features has previously been associated with a shift in agricultural economies, as rural communities previously involved in subsistence farming, began to adopt more intensive stock-rearing practices around the early seventh century (Blinkhorn 1999, 16). Practical considerations would definitely have played a part in the development of more regular ditched boundaries, and the use of enclosures to control livestock is a common feature of early medieval sites in England, such as Yeavering (Northumberland), and Warmington (Northamptonshire) (Hope-Taylor 1977; Chapter III). Such rationales do not, however, rule out the possibility that ideological motivations were also responsible for the changing internal organisation of 'Middle Saxon' centres. In the same way that the regular tenement plots of the 'Late Saxon' period are commonly related to a rapidly changing social environment, Reynolds has asserted that earlier planned layouts reflect new forms of 'Middle Saxon' lordship (Reynolds 2003, 131-3).

The degree to which 'Middle Saxon' lords could exert control over peasant communities has, though, been rightly questioned by Helena Hamerow, and the ability of non-elite groups to plan their settlement space should not be undermined (Hamerow 2011, 125). Utilising documentary sources dating from the twelfth century onward, Christopher Dyer has shown that peasant groups were equally capable of changing their occupation arrangements as their lords, and it seems plausible that their 'Middle Saxon' counterparts possessed similar agency (Dyer 1985). It is almost certain that the gradual increase of ditched features detectable on rural sites from the 'Middle Saxon' period onward does suggest changing social conditions, however, and it is likely that increasingly powerful elites were at least partly responsible for their development. Central to the transformation of settlement space were changing perceptions of land and property tenure, shifting from earlier communal attitudes. The development of private land ownership is also supported by early West Saxon legal codes, many of which contain a strong emphasis on rules and regulations regarding property. Such legal prescriptions likely describe experiences of social regulation that existed by the sixth century, but ones which are only rarely visible on exceptional settlement sites such as Cowdery's Down, Hampshire (Reynolds 2003, 101-3).

The semi-permanent and structured settlements of the 'Middle Saxon' period presented by this book are therefore of plainly different character to the dispersed and shifting sites that many scholars suggest were typical of the period. Interpretation of the early medieval landscape is partly restricted by the unsuitability of the traditional tripartite chronology, as archaeological sites often stretch across the arbitrarily-defined periods, and researchers need to be careful not to assign particular features to certain phases too strictly. However, the 'Middle Saxon' occupation evidence, within the study area and further afield, demonstrates that the view of largely unchanged rural settlement forms persisting until the mid-ninth century is no longer tenable. Whilst unplanned settlements such as Mucking were likely occupied into the traditionally defined 'Middle Saxon' period (Rippon 2007, 172), from as early as the seventh century, organisation of communities in the countryside underwent significant transformation. The lack of social differentiation apparent on fifth and sixth-century settlements, which is reflective of the power that 'resided in persons rather than places' (Loseby 2000, 345) therefore began in the 'Middle Saxon' period to be replaced by new views of property and privacy.

Increasingly powerful, if largely undocumented, aristocrats are likely to have been at least partly responsible for the introduction of new settlement arrangements, but similarly the capacity of peasant communities to effect change themselves cannot be dismissed. We should be wary not to view the early medieval landscape of the five counties on a singular evolutionary path of development from unplanned 'Early Saxon' forms, to the regularly arranged villages of the 'Late Saxon' period, however. For example, at West Heslerton, North Yorkshire, the earliest phases of the early medieval site appears to have featured boundaries, and the excavators also suggest that occupation was structured and zoned from its inception in the fifth century (Powlesland 1990; 1997). Clearly then, archaeological models must allow for a certain degree of leeway, but there can be little doubt that the 'Middle Saxon' period in central and eastern England was characterised by increasingly complex and sophisticated settlement forms. It has been demonstrated that increasing permanence and order apparent on rural settlements, and the new perceptions of space and ownership that undoubtedly accompanied them, were a product of the changing social environment of 'Middle Saxon' England; conditions that also influenced the location of habitation sites in the period.

Pushing the Margins: The Location of 'Middle Saxon' Settlements

The developing topographical positioning of early medieval settlements has for a long time been a source of scholarly discussion. Based on a growing body of excavated and fieldwalking data, a view emerged from the early 1980s that occupation sites underwent a significant shift in the 'Middle Saxon' period (Arnold and Wardle 1981). 'Early Saxon' settlements were seen to be disproportionately linked with well-drained but interfile soils, and it was suggested that their abandonment was associated with a shift to heavier soils, due to wholesale reorganisation of land-use and territorial arrangements around the eighth century (Arnold and Wardle 1981, 145-9). The data upon which this so-called 'Mid-Saxon shuffle' model was based has been comprehensively critiqued, and in particular the idea of wholesale settlement abandonment around the eighth century has been seriously questioned (Hamerow 1991, 1-17). The restricted scale of archaeological excavations, especially in comparison to some sites on the other side of the North Sea, continues to cause problems for interpretation, especially when it is considered that many rural settlements may have retained at least a degree of mobility into the 'Late Saxon' period (Hamerow 2011, 121).

Despite these difficulties, this book has illustrated a changing picture of settlement location during the 'Middle Saxon' period, although there is little to support the fundamental dislocation of sites suggested by the previous 'Mid Saxon shuffle' hypothesis. Indeed, many of the settlements that featured structured 'Middle Saxon' layouts, discussed above, appear to have been introduced into pre-existing foci occupied in the sixth and seventh centuries, such as at Cottenham and Ely, Cambridgeshire, and Avebury, Wiltshire. Although the 'Middle Saxon' period does not seem to have been characterised by widespread upheaval of rural settlement patterns, this research has illustrated communities inhabiting a more diverse range of landscapes. This conclusion builds on similar sequences of development that have been detected by previous archaeological research, such as at Whittlewood in Northamptonshire, where existing centres appear to have been targeted for development (Jones and Page 2006, 156). In areas where diagnostic ceramics are available, fieldwalking projects have especially contributed to our understanding of the increasing environments settled by 'Middle Saxon' communities. In the Marshland of Norfolk, for example, seven sites located on roddons were probably newly founded in the seventh or eighth century, as people sought to exploit resources in marginal landscapes in more systematic fashion (Silvester 1988, 158). Stephen Rippon has demonstrated that colonisation of coastal wetlands was widespread in southern England in the 'Middle Saxon' period, before permanent reclamation of such environments was pursued from around the tenth century (Rippon 2000a; 2001; 2004b).

The processes by which the Marshland settlements were established remains a source of contention, with some arguing that seasonal sites were subsequently developed as more permanent centres (e.g. Silvester 1988, 156). The regular spacing of the 'Middle Saxon' settlements, however, may indicate that a greater degree of planning was involved (Chapter VII; Hall and Coles 1994, 126), with sites perhaps located within an otherwise undetectable administrative framework. Whilst the 'marginal' character of fen areas may previously have been overstated (e.g. Roffe 2005; Rippon 2001, 152), there can be little doubt that establishment of settlements on the Marshland roddons represented an expansion from more densely-settled areas. At Wormegay in the Nar Valley of Norfolk, the presence of a 'Middle Saxon' settlement also hints at growth from more well-settled locations (Silvester 1988, 172-3), development of new centres in the 'Middle Saxon' period was not restricted to wetland landscapes. The chalk downlands of central-southern England appear to have been more densely settled from the seventh century, with sites particularly focussing on the spring-line between Upper and Middle Chalk (Holbrook and Thomas 1996; Williams and Newman 1998). At Wantage, Oxfordshire and Market Lavington, Wiltshire, slight 'Early Saxon' activity is detectable, but it was not until the 'Middle Saxon' period that settlement seems to have become more permanent. The evidence from such places represents a more convincing case for seasonal sites that were later targeted for more lasting settlement, a process that was likely intensified in the 'Late Saxon' period (Gardiner 2011, 212).

The evidence presented by this research therefore does not support the tenets of the 'Middle Saxon Shuffle' model, but nevertheless suggests that significant changes in location of occupation sites did occur in the 'Middle Saxon' period. It now appears that some previous investigators placed too great an emphasis on settlement relocation (e.g. Arnold and Wardle 1981; Newman 1989; Moreland 2000), given the tendency for 'Early Saxon' sites to shift across the landscape (Hamerow 1991). Investigation since the 1980s has demonstrated that 'Early Saxon' occupation was not restricted to freely-draining locations, as previously believed (e.g. Powlesland 1990), and indeed, a number of the 'Middle Saxon' settlements presented in this book clearly had earlier foundations, such as at Daventry, Northamptonshire and Collingbourne Ducis, Wiltshire. The misconception of a widespread step-change in the location of sites is also likely to have been influenced by the changing character of 'Middle Saxon' settlements. The introduction of semi-permanent settlement arrangements across the study area from the seventh century, together with the adoption of more durable ceramics especially in the east of England, results in greater visibility of 'Middle Saxon' sites than earlier sequences.

It is thus likely that in many cases 'Middle Saxon' habitation identified in ostensibly new locations actually possess earlier origins that have gone undetected. The settlement at Yarnton, Oxfordshire, provides a useful case in point; if investigation was restricted to fieldwalking, the assemblage of organic-tempered ceramics and Ipswich Ware could have been taken as indicative of purely 'Middle Saxon' occupation, albeit intensive in character. The excavations in the landscape around Yarnton and its neighbouring villages, however, demonstrated both 'Early Saxon' and 'Middle Saxon' occupation, with the latter sequence characterised by more intensive and permanent settlement (Hey 2004, 42-8). Whilst many 'Middle Saxon' sites may therefore have possessed earlier antecedents, there is evidence for settlement *expansion* into new locations around the eighth century. The clearest example comes from the Marshland of Norfolk, where fieldwalking and subsequent trenching identified a series of apparently *de novo* sites probably founded around the eighth century (Silvester 1988, 156-8; Crowson *et al.* 2005, 170-1). Following almost total abandonment in the earliest post-Roman centuries, the roddons of Marshland were targeted for the establishment of more permanent sites, surrounded by networks of drainage ditches (Silvester 1988, 156; Leah and Crowson 1993, 46; Murphy 1993).

The widespread colonisation of coastal wetlands in the 'Middle Saxon' period makes it likely that the degree of settlement expansion may be somewhat unrepresented by the chosen study area of this research, with Norfolk the only county featuring a coastline. Outside of East Anglia though, expansion of settlement may also have occurred onto the chalk uplands of Oxfordshire and Wiltshire, where small, seasonal 'Early Saxon' sites were later developed and occupied more permanently. It is notable that 'Middle Saxon' settlements at Wantage and Market

Lavington both later developed as medieval villages, following short-range drift and restructuring in the 'Late Saxon' period. With the exception of Wormegay, the lack of village-centre investigation undertaken by the Fenland Project in the Norfolk wetlands makes it uncertain whether similar processes occurred here. The seven Marshland sites detected by fieldwalking, however, were all abandoned by the 'Late Saxon' period, perhaps representing a shift away from pastorally-orientated farming regimes (Crowson *et al.* 2005, 170-1). Indeed, the expansion of 'Middle Saxon' settlements into more diverse regions is itself indicative of the changing character of the agricultural economy, a feature that also emerged as a major finding of this research.

New Pressures: The Changing Economies of 'Middle Saxon' Communities

A range of evidence from the five counties suggests that the physical restructuring of the 'Middle Saxon' countryside, evident in developing settlement plans and new site locations, was part of a more comprehensive process of landscape exploitation (Rippon 2010, 57). In Oxfordshire, replacement of the unstructured 'Early Saxon' landscape of dispersed settlement in the landscape around Yarnton and Cassington coincided with agricultural intensification, with increased arable production and the introduction of new crops. The development of semi-permanent and structured habitation in the 'Middle Saxon' period at Yarnton was also associated with the first systematic management of the Thames floodplain, as the first gravel terrace was developed for meadow (Hey 2004, 45). In the Thames Valley generally, there is evidence for increased alluviation around the eighth and ninth centuries, suggesting that communities along the river were involved in similar reclamation activities (Robinson 1992, 204-7). In Northamptonshire too, the palaeoeconomic evidence from Raunds and West Cotton indicates increased alluviation of the Nene Valley floodplain (Campbell 1994, 78-82). Meadowland frequently occurs in early medieval charters, and indeed in the laws of *Ine* (Whitelock 1955, 368), but it has been argued that in 'Early Saxon' times it was a relatively rare feature of the landscape. Tom Williamson, for example, has posited that only during the 'Middle Saxon' period, perhaps in order to support growing populations and larger numbers of draft oxen, were meadows more consistently developed (Williamson 2003, 164).

The shift towards more intensive agricultural production, if not specialisation, is also detectable at a number of sites in Cambridgeshire. At West Fen Road, Ely, the community were apparently involved in producing a mixed farming surplus, most likely for the neighbouring monastic community (Mortimer *et al.* 2005; Mudd and Webster 2011). At Fordham, also in Cambridgeshire, the somewhat limited palaeoeconomic data is also indicative of intensification around the 'Middle Saxon' period, although the site retained an economy geared towards producing a mixed agricultural surplus. The location of sites on the fen-islands and along the fen-edge clearly allowed exploitation of varied resources by the inhabitants, although the emphasis of production was likely to have shifted dramatically between seasons. The presence of rectilinear enclosures at both sites reflects the need to keep livestock near the settlements within a landscape that was too wet for winter grazing, but which in the drier months provided a valuable resource for sheep grazing in particular (Rippon 2001, 152; Hamerow 2011, 123).

Whilst palaeoenvironmetal evidence is limited on many excavated sites, targeted pollen sequences support the likelihood that the 'Middle Saxon' period was characterised by agricultural intensification. A closely-dated pollen sequence at Scole, on the Norfolk-Suffolk border, indicates that around the eighth century, the landscape mostly consisted of arable cultivation. At Diss and Old Buckenham the cultivation of hemp was similarly dated to the 'Middle Saxon' period, suggesting that agricultural regimes in southern Norfolk underwent both diversification and intensification at this time (Peglar 1993). Evidence such as this from the study area contributes to a growing picture of widespread agricultural intensification that took place across southern England in the 'Middle Saxon' period, recently highlighted by Stephen Rippon (2008; 2010). The changing approaches of exploitation, Rippon asserts, was part of a more fundamental increase of landscape investment, which included utilisation of greater manpower and resources (Rippon 2010, 63-4). It is possible that such changes apparent around the eighth century were part of a more protracted process which began c.600, as the English became more interested in the formal articulation of the landscape recognisable in a range of phenomena, such as planning of cemeteries in orderly rows and aligning buildings on apparently 'ritual' axes (Blair 2005, 52). These changes, which intensified and diversified in the 'Middle Saxon' period not only influenced the contemporary landscape, but were to have a lasting impact upon the countryside of central and eastern England.

The Lasting Influence: 'Middle Saxon' and Later Landscapes

It has repeatedly been stressed that explanation of historic village and field character was not amongst the primary aims of this book, yet the frequency with which 'Middle Saxon' settlement remains have been detected within currently-occupied rural settlements cannot be ignored, and some assessment of the relationship between pre-ninth century and later occupation is clearly appropriate. This research assumed a more critical definition of the term 'currently-occupied' than previous studies, which allowed quantitative assessment of 'Middle Saxon' occupation deposits identified through evaluation trenches or more extensive excavation. The AIP assessment of 'CORS' investigation within the five counties has yielded significant results, summarised in the table below (Table 8.1).

The AIP assessment produced varied results across the five counties, with Wiltshire possessing a markedly limited number of currently-occupied interventions. The few investigations that have been carried out in Wiltshire, however, detected 'Middle Saxon' deposits half of the time, a frequency only bettered by the results from Northamptonshire. Cambridgeshire and Norfolk present similarly high rates of 'Middle Saxon' settlement detection, and of the five counties studied, identification of less than forty percent only occurred in Oxfordshire. Indeed, if the results from Oxfordshire were to be removed from the assessment, 'Middle Saxon' settlement discovery within currently-occupied villages in the remaining four counties averages almost fifty percent. The reasons why Oxfordshire stands out as an anomaly are not entirely clear, but it should be emphasised that the 'Middle Saxon' remains that have been found in the county are substantial, especially when compared to somewhere like Wiltshire where the excavated archaeological evidence is far more fragmentary. Also noteworthy is the relatively high percentage of detection relating to Norfolk, a result which is skewed by the high proportion of churches in locations distinct from their associated settlement centres (see Chapter VII).

As has been emphasised previously, the AIP analysis was designed only to provide an approximate guide, and does not represent a comprehensive assessment of all currently-occupied rural settlement investigations undertaken within the study area. The results from this somewhat general examination are nevertheless considerable, suggesting a significant relationship between 'Middle Saxon' and later settlements. A consistent pattern that has been recognised over the preceding five chapters is that 'Middle Saxon' occupation, falling within the 'currently-occupied' curtilage defined by this research, is most commonly situated in areas slightly removed from the historic village core. It could be argued that this simply reflects the well-settled character of the 'Middle Saxon' countryside, and that the presence of earlier activity within villages is therefore simply a result of geographical juxtaposition. Indeed, just such an argument has recently been made by Paul Everson and David Stocker, amongst their contributions to the final volume of the 'Wharram: A Study of Settlement in the Yorkshire Wolds' series (Everson and Stocker 2012, 164-173).

Contrary to the view of the editor, Stuart Wrathmell, and other contributors to the volume, Everson and Stocker assert that the evidence for 'Middle Saxon' settlement in and around the deserted village of Wharram Percy, North Yorkshire, bears no relationship to the later medieval site (e.g. Wrathmell 2012, 178-10). Central to their argument, the pair suggest that *Grubenhäuser* were likely used as temporary sites, and that the network of overlapping enclosures that characterise the excavated 'Butterwick-type' complexes are similarly indicative of seasonal sheep-farming activity (Everson and Stocker 2012, 164-6). Equally critical, in Everson and Stocker's view, is the lack of post-built structures excavated at Wharram,

COUNTY	'CORS' interventions identifying archaeological deposits	'CORS' with 'Middle Saxon' artefactual material only	'CORS' with 'Middle Saxon' artefactual material and settlement structures	Regularity of 'Middle Saxon' detection (%)
Northamptonshire	23	5	8	56.5
Oxfordshire	49	8	6	28.6
Wiltshire	12	3	3	50.0
Cambridgeshire	38	7	10	44.7
Norfolk	33	6	10	48.5
			AVERAGE (%)	35.7

Table 8.1: Cumulative totals of the AIP 'CORS' assessment, demonstrating that where archaeological deposits have been detected within existing villages in the study area, 'Middle Saxon' activity has been located on over a third of sites, on average.

suggesting the lack of residential halls substantiates the premise that permanent habitation did not occur during the 'Middle Saxon' phases. Wrathmell (2012, 178) though, has challenged this position, emphasising the difficulty of detecting post-built structures, and the significant investment required to construct new enclosures year-on-year, as the pair imply.

Part of the reason behind such divergence in opinion is the way in which 'villages' are defined and perceived by researchers, with Everson and Stocker aligned with the more popular opinion which continues to underline the rather straightforward observation that 'Middle Saxon' occupation and later villages are of clearly different character (e.g. Lewis et al. 1997, 198-9). Similarly though, there can be little disputing that the 'Middle Saxon' settlement evidence presented by this work differ markedly from the dispersed and transient occupation more typical of the earliest medieval centuries. The establishment of enclosures, for instance, introduced a means of controlling and restricting movement, and indeed a way of creating and reproducing social relationships that earlier communities probably had not experienced. It could be argued that the toft-like arrangements of 'Middle Saxon' settlements represent an indisputably 'village-like' feature, and although there is a dearth of excavated evidence for church foundations dated to this period, the fieldwalking data from Norfolk in particular may hint that religious foci were being established within at least some rural communities at this time (e.g. Wade-Martins 1980a). As Richard Jones has demonstrated though, attempts to fulfil arbitrary and most likely anachronistic 'tick-lists' of village characteristics has to-date not proved a fruitful avenue of research (e.g. Jones 2010). Rather, this book has served to emphasise the way in which the changing character of early medieval settlements was understood and perceived by the inhabitants, experiences that would again have been again changed in the 'Late Saxon' period as the modification of existing foci led to the crystallisation of historic village forms.

First advocated by Tony Brown and Glen Foard in 1998, the evidence both from currently occupied rural settlement excavations, and other forms of archaeological investigation presented by this volume, support a two-stage process of village formation in some places (Brown and Foard 1998). Unlike Wharram Percy, where a lack of post-built structures allowed an interpretation of seasonal occupation to be forwarded, this research has illustrated indisputably semi-permanent 'Middle Saxon' settlements adjacent to historic village centres. Post-built structures, most likely representing residential halls have been located regularly, including at Daventry and Warmington in Northamptonshire, Wantage in Oxfordshire, Avebury in Wiltshire, Cottenham and Fordham in Cambridgeshire, and Whissonsett in Norfolk. Although relatively rare, occasionally ditched features established in the 'Middle Saxon' period were subsequently used to articulate the later village plan. For instance, linear ditches have been reused during 'Late Saxon' restructuring at centres like Daventry, Fordham and Whissonsett. Slightly more ambiguously, although certainly significant, in many cases the orientation of 'Middle Saxon' settlement structures can be seen to paralleled the historic village plan, also alluding to some form of reuse, or at least respect for antecedent landscape features.

In the past, such 'Middle Saxon' phases in and around historic villages have been assigned terms such as 'initial nucleation' or 'proto-nucleation' (Brown and Foard 1998; Jones and Page 2006; Rippon 2008). This study adopts a more conservative interpretation, however, as it has been shown that 'Middle Saxon' remains in currently occupied rural villages occur in both areas of traditionally 'nucleated' and 'dispersed' medieval settlement character (Chapter VI). It has not proved possible to specifically relate 'Middle Saxon' activity with the process of village 'nucleation', and instead it appears that changes after the mid-ninth century were decisive in determining later medieval village form, and in this regard, it is interesting to note the varying degree with which settlement shifted in order to create the historic settlement. At Yarnton, for instance, the 'Middle Saxon' settlement focus was probably located some 300m west of the manor and church, likely established when the centre of occupation shifted around the tenth century (Hey 2004, 42-3), yet at places such as Fordham, the earlier remains are all but contiguous with the medieval village tenements. This close geographical relationship raises the possibility that at some sites 'Middle Saxon' deposits remain undetected beneath existing buildings and gardens, and that perhaps the two-stage process of settlement change has been overemphasised, but whilst it is possible that 'Middle Saxon' settlement material does underlie existing villages in some instances, the cumulative evidence does suggest that settlements underwent a process of relocation and restructuring beginning around the tenth century.

The preceding five chapters have consistently identified semi-permanent 'Middle Saxon' sites adjacent to villages becoming deserted before or during the 'Late Saxon' period. Not only is the shift in focus usually manifest in the excavated sequence, but development of new arrangements around the tenth century is demonstrated by the frequency of 'Late Saxon' fabric in parish churches at locations as far afield as Avebury, Whissonsett and Willingham. In Norfolk, the tendency for settlements to remain mobile continued into the post-Conquest period, with some centres only becoming fixed in the landscape as late as the thirteenth century. In the remainder of the study area, however, it is likely that 'Late Saxon' reorganisation was associated with the laying out of common fields, as seen at Raunds, Northamptonshire, and in the Bourn Valley of Cambridgeshire (Parry 2006, 275; Oosthuizen 2006). The inhabitants of 'Late Saxon' settlements certainly adopted a more rigorous approach to spatial arrangements than their forebears, and this concern was also likely transmitted to the agricultural landscape as intermixed holdings gradually became more consistently established (Williamson 2003, 127).

Whilst contributing only slightly to the 'nucleation' debate that continues to dominate academic discourse, this research has nevertheless provided an insight into the changing character of early medieval occupation, and the way in which such phenomena was likely experienced by rural communities. Although the close physical relationship of seventh to ninth-century settlements and later villages has been established, one significant uncertainty that remains is what the 'Middle Saxon' sites identified within currently occupied rural settlements were actually called. For example, was the 'Middle Saxon' site excavated in the backyards of modern Fordham known by the name first recorded in the tenth century? A particular issue surrounding shifting settlement types is that we do not know the degree to which a site could relocate whilst retaining the same name (see discussion in Hooke 1997). Compounding the problem, in many instances, the entries in Domesday often represents the earliest recorded naming of settlements which potentially possess far more ancient origins (e.g. Gelling 1978; Fox 2008).

Some of the sites discussed by this research, however, are recorded in earlier documents, such as the fen-edge settlements of Cambridgeshire which had been assigned their names by at least the tenth century (*Liber Eliensis* II/84). Indeed, the majority of place-names in southern England are commonly assigned 'Middle Saxon' origins by the majority of specialists, with subsequent Scandinavian influences largely impacting the north and east of the country (Gelling 2011, 993; Wrathmell 2012, 179). It is likely that the increasingly fixed place of habitation, together with the changing social conditions, led to a shift from *'folc'* names denoting allegiance to an individual, to the development of location-specific names in the 'Middle Saxon' period. The OE *-ingas* and *-ingāham* names which likely dated to the fifth and sixth centuries were thus superseded by a more common practice of naming newly stable settlements after their topographical characteristics (Gelling 2011, 993-7). In places such as the Marshland of Norfolk, farmers infiltrating previously unsettled areas began to name their settlements after the distinct geographical environments in which they were located.

The issue of place-names has been emphasised here as it underlines the likelihood that it was during the 'Middle Saxon' period that the *identity* of settlements was first widely established in the landscape. Settlements in wholly new locations clearly continued to be founded throughout the 'Late Saxon' and subsequent periods (e.g. Chapman 2010), but in other places, existing occupation centres were restructured from the tenth century. In Norfolk, however, whilst restructuring may have occurred around the 'Late Saxon' period, its influence was clearly not nearly as decisive as in other areas. In northern East Anglia, rural communities had a greater tendency to continue reorganising and relocating themselves well into the medieval period proper, even after the establishment of churches which in other areas of England created lasting foci for settlement. Even in Norfolk though, it is likely that most settlements had been assigned their names and indeed, obtained their identities by the mid-ninth century. In the majority of central and eastern England, however, it was only after subsequent restructuring did the physical and perceived position of such centres become permanently fixed in the landscape. This 'Late Saxon' and subsequent transformation completed a two-stage process of settlement development, which further research in currently-occupied villages and elsewhere will no doubt substantiate (e.g. Rippon 2008, 260-3).

Summary

The key observations of this volume have thus been divided into four broad themes, each of which points to significant 'Middle Saxon' landscape and settlement change. It has been shown that from around the seventh century, communities in the countryside of the five counties began to establish new forms of habitation, often characterised by semi-permanent ditched enclosures. The formalisation of space was not completely unknown in the preceding centuries, but the 'Middle Saxon' period witnessed an unprecedented adoption of boundaries and internal enclosures, used both for practical purposes but also to shape and reinforce experiences of social regulation. Settlements also began to expand into landscapes that had previously been unoccupied or utilised only seasonally. For the first time, groups living in settlements year-round were established in locations such as the wetlands of eastern England, and the upland chalk landscapes of central and southern England, hinting at new powers behind exploitation of the countryside.

Across the study area, we have also seen the intensification of agricultural regimes dated to the 'Middle Saxon' period. Evidence for specialisation in some areas, is combined with an overarching picture of increasing production notable in the rural landscape of central and eastern England. Although somewhat limited in extent, the palaeoenvironmetal material again suggests a growing investment in the countryside, and a greater concern for its management and utilisation. Finally, the lasting impact of 'Middle Saxon' landscape transformation has also been illustrated, as in many places the restructuring of settlements began a two-stage process of village formation. Moreover, it was from the seventh century that the identity of rural communities began to be shaped, attaching names to the places where they lived, rather than to real or imagined individuals which had previously been more commonplace. Whilst settlements of this period were undoubtedly more permanent than those of the fifth or sixth centuries, and possessed elements such as tenement arrangements and possibly church centres, rural groups were subject to further change in the 'Late Saxon' and subsequent periods, as new forms of order were once again manifest in the landscape.

Indeed, it is around the tenth century onwards that archaeologists have more readily attributed the developments in the archaeological record to broader social conditions. The introduction of more regulated village plans, together with other elements such as manorial centres and churches, are quite rightly recognised as the product of the changing character of lordship, with the identification of 'thegnly' sites such as West Cotton in Northamptonshire, and Goltho in Lincolnshire, likely representing a fair reflection of the historical reality (Beresford 1987; Chapman 2010). Insights into 'Late Saxon' society provided by archaeology, with a thegnly class able to exercise power over space and resources, can further be supplemented by documentary sources, such as the details listed in *Geþyncðo* (Gardiner 2011, 199). The close association that scholars attach to lordship and landscape from the tenth century, however, is not usually transferred to earlier centuries. Part of the problem is that researchers have often failed to see the scale and significance of landscape change predating the mid-ninth century (e.g. Lewis *et al.* 1997). Contrary to the prevailing academic view, this research has demonstrated without doubt that the countryside of central and eastern England underwent widespread and fundamental transformation in the 'Middle Saxon' period. These 'Middle Saxon' developments, akin to the later period, were also inherently linked to wider changes taking place across society, which archaeology is able to explore through the dynamic relationship between human action and material culture. Together with the archaeological and other evidence presented here, the evidence from rural settlement presents

central and eastern England during the 'Middle Saxon' period in a new light, inhabited by increasingly complex, sophisticated and hierarchical communities, investing in settlement and landscape in new and more lasting ways.

CONCLUSION: 'MDDLE SAXON' SETTLEMENT AND SOCIETY

The above discussion has reemphasised the central observations made by this book, in addition to providing a wider context by outlining the depth and extent of change that occurred between the seventh and ninth centuries in central and eastern England. The picture emerging from archaeology and other sources strongly indicates transformation of social, economic and political composition from the seventh century. On a national scale, the formation of relatively stable political entities is all but indistinguishable from the process of conversion, given that the writings introduced by the early Church provide our first glimpse of English 'kingship'. As minsters became the primary medium for elite investment, distinguishing between the possible character of elite activity has proved extremely difficult, and it is likely that 'secular' and 'ecclesiastical' definitions have been applied too strictly. Whilst the influence of minsters communities cannot be underestimated, scholars are yet to agree on how, or even if, they can be defined. An intriguing possibility currently being explored by John Blair, is that clerics in the pre-Viking period were the only elite authorities to structure their settlement space around on gridded patterns based on the techniques of Roman *agrimensores* (Blair, pers. comm.). The results of this research will undoubtedly be significant, but it is unlikely to convince all archaeologists and historians that any particular material culture was peculiar to the pre-ninth century Church (e.g. Pestell 2004, 40-50; Gittos 2011, 828).

If there remains debate regarding the character of high-status centres themselves, there can be little doubt as to the wider influence of the elite upon the English landscape. From the late seventh century, a plethora of new settlement types emerge in the archaeological record, but elite authority is most easily detected by the extensively planned layouts of the coastal *emporia*. Indeed, both with regard to settlement planning, and their sheer scale, the *emporia* are exceptional in a 'Middle Saxon' context, but they can no longer be reasonably viewed as singular channels of elite trade and exchange. Rather, the foundation of *emporia* was just one facet of more fundamental changes that occurred across the settlement hierarchy, as various new types of site were developed from the late seventh century. The term 'productive' site likely masks places of varying form and function, but some sites at least possessed specialist functions, perhaps as seasonal markets or points of tax collection. The significant quantity of sceattas in particular, recovered from 'productive' places and elsewhere, is indicative of a step-change in trade dating to the eighth century, which in turn suggests deep-rooted economic growth.

Although the relationship between increased coin use and the economy has yet to be investigated in great detail, enhancing the perception of economic transformation is the increased investment in industry and infrastructure associated with 'Middle Saxon'-period England. Whilst elite authorities clearly sought to exploit the countryside in more intensive and sophisticated means, it is important to remember that the wealth of kings and bishops remained primarily based upon agricultural production. It is in this respect that the two narratives of this chapter, and indeed this book, converge. The demonstrated transformation of the rural landscape of the five counties must be viewed as part of more deep-rooted social, economic and political change. These developments did not impact rural communities alone, but various aspects of the lives of 'Middle Saxon' people, as change, innovation and expansion impacted even the most seemingly prosaic settlement sites.

In addition to the newly semi-permanent and structured arrangements on rural sites, indicative both of practical considerations and new perceptions of space and ownership, communities were also either encouraged, or took it upon themselves, to develop settlements in previously uninhabited or seasonally-occupied locations. The positioning of sites in such locations allowed the occupants to exploit a more diverse range of resources, a practice which was part of more comprehensive agricultural diversification and exploitation. Such changes to the rural landscape provide great insight into 'Middle Saxon' social conditions in their own right, but it is also obvious that they had a more enduring influence upon the countryside. It was during the 'Middle Saxon' period that settlements, and indeed the people that inhabited them, began to change their identity. By the mid-ninth century, many communities had gained both their name, and their place in the landscape. Only following subsequent changes, likely dated to the tenth century and later, did settlements become more firmly fixed, and it was the developments in this period that shaped the character of medieval villages, and indeed continues to shape the rural landscape of central and eastern England even today.

Chapter IX
Conclusion

This book has explored the experiences of rural communities who lived between the seventh and ninth centuries in central and eastern England. Adopting an archaeologically-orientated approach, but one which also utilised alternative sources where relevant, this research has provided significant new insight into 'Middle Saxon' society. With regard to the material data, the archaeological evidence from currently-occupied rural settlements has proved a particularly unique and informative source. The value of the evidence from still-occupied villages has been crucially contextualising, though, with alternative archaeological and other datasets, which together helped develop a more comprehensive and meaningful understanding settlement and society. Further research into these conditions is no doubt desirable, and in this regard, currently-occupied rural settlement study will surely prove amongst the most fruitful avenues of scholarship. Whilst many of the key conclusions of this research have been the product of currently-occupied rural settlement, this book has equally highlighted the potential of this dataset which could be realised through more study.

Through the approaches adopted by this volume, it has been seen that, contrary to the opinion of many early medieval landscape scholars, communities in the countryside of the five county study area underwent significant change in the 'Middle Saxon' period. These changes included the introduction of new property arrangements, expansion of occupation into previously unsettled or sparsely populated areas, and the development of new types of settlement centre, many of which were specialised towards a particular product or service. Settlements also began to be settled more permanently, as new perceptions of space and ownership began to be etched onto the landscape through ditched enclosures, their reinstatement and reuse, sometimes over many decades, demonstrating that their spatial, social and legal significance was passed onto subsequent generations. These changes were part of a process of increased interest in the articulation of the landscape, which began as early

as *c*.600, but which intensified and diversified from the middle of the seventh century.

The transformation of settlement, which would have had a marked impact on the lived experience of people living in rural areas did not occur in isolation, however, but was part of broader, deep-rooted changes that were occurring across society. The 'Middle Saxon' period has been illustrated as a time which witnessed fundamental modification to political, social and economic systems in southern England, as early medieval society became increasingly sophisticated and stratified. Major landowners, particularly kings and clerics, began to display their power by new means; advancing industry and infrastructure such as bridges, and defence and road networks, and developing specialised settlement centres like *emporia*. Much of this authority was expressed through the material culture of the Augustinian Church, which from the mid-seventh century became the primary focus of elite consumption.

Crucially though, the increasing wealth available to the socially powerful continued to be primarily derived from agricultural production, and it is perhaps because of this that archaeologists are able to detect such significant investment in the rural landscape during the 'Middle Saxon' period. Whilst the changing character of lordship surely lies behind the transformations, we must be wary not to wholly undermine the potential of rural communities to themselves modify their lived environment. Indeed, assigning particular agency to detectable phenomena has proved challenging, and the changes to rural communities are best seen as the result of broader social transformation. That developments in society were manifest in the physical environment of settlement, not only provides us with an insight into the lived experience of 'Middle Saxon' people, but also allows us to trace the way in which such communities precipitated changes that would shape the landscape of central and eastern England into the present day.

References

PRIMARY SOURCES

Anglo-Saxon Chronicle, ed/trans. C. Plummer, 1892-9, *Two of the Saxon Chronicles Parallel (II Volumes)*, Oxford: Clarendon Press

Bede, 'Historia Ecclesiastica Gentis Anglorum' (Ecclesiastical History of the English People), ed/trans. B. Colgrage and R.A.B. Mynors, 1969, Oxford: Clarendon Press

Gildas, 'De Excidio Britonum' (The Ruin of Britain), ed/trans. M. Winterbottom, 1978: *Gildas: The Ruin of Britain and Other Works*, Chichester: Phillimore, 87-142

OTHER SOURCES

Addington, S. and Cushion, B. 1981: 'Landscape and Settlements in south Norfolk', *Norfolk Archaeology* 38, 97-139

Addyman, P.V. 1964: 'A Dark-Age Settlement at Maxey, Northamptonshire', *Medieval Archaeology* 8, 20-73

Addyman, P.V. 1972: 'Anglo-Saxon Houses at Chalton, Hampshire: Second Interim Report', *Medieval Archaeology* 16, 13-31

Alcock, L. 1995: *Cadbury Castle: The Early Medieval Archaeology*, Cardiff: University of Wales Press

Allen, G.W.G. 1938: 'Marks Seen from the Air in the Crops near Dorchester', *Oxoniensia* 3, 169-171

Allen, T., Hayden, C., and Lamdin-Whymark, H. 2008: *From Bronze Age Enclosure to Anglo-Saxon Settlement: Archaeological Excavations at Taplow Hillfort, Buckinghamshire* (Thames Valley Landscape Monograph), Oxford: Oxford University School of Archaeology

Allisson, K.J. 1957: 'The Sheep-Corn Husbandry of Norfolk in the Sixteenth and Seventeenth Centuries', *Agricultural History Review* 5, 12-30

Allison, K.J., Beresford, M.W. and Hurst, J.G. 1966: *The Deserted Villages of Northamptonshire*, Department of Local History, Occasional Papers 18, Leicester: Leicester University Press

Alternberg, K. 2003: *Experiencing Landscapes*, Stockholm: Almqvist and Wiksell

Anderton, M. 1999: 'Beyond the Emporia', in Anderton, M. (ed.) *Anglo-Saxon Trading Centres: Beyond the Emporia*, Glasgow: Cruithne Press, 1-3

Arnold, C.J. 1984: *Roman Britain to Anglo-Saxon England*, London: Croom Helm

Arnold, C.J. 1997: *An Archaeology of the Early Saxon Kingdoms*, London: Routledge

Arnold, C.J. and Wardle, P. 1981: 'Early Medieval Settlement Patterns in England', *Medieval Archaeology* 25, 145-149

Asser, *The Life of King Alfred* (W. Stevenson (ed.)) 1959, Oxford: Clarendon Press

Arthur, B.V. and Jope, E.M. 1962-3: 'Early Saxon Pottery Kilns at Purwell Farm, Cassington, Oxfordshire', *Medieval Archaeology* 6-7, 1-14

Astill, G. 1985: 'Archaeology, Economics and Early Medieval Europe', *Oxford Journal of Archaeology* 4 (ii), 215-231

Astill, G. 2011: 'Overview: Trade, Exchange and Urbanisation', in H. Hamerow, D.A. Hinton, and S. Crawford (eds.) *The Oxford Handbook of Anglo-Saxon Archaeology*, Oxford: Oxford University Press, 503-514

Aston, M. 1985: *Interpreting the Landscape: Landscape Archaeology and Local History*, London/New York: Routledge

Aston, M. and Gerrard, C. 1999: 'Unique, Traditional and Charming: The Shapwick Project, Somerset', *Antiquaries Journal* 79, 1-58

Attenborough, F. L. 1922: *The Laws of the Earliest English Kings,* Cambridge: Cambridge University Press

Audouy, M. and Chapman, A. 2009: *Raunds: The Origin and Growth of a Midland Village, AD 450-1500: Excavations in North Raunds, Northamptonshire 1977-87*, Oxford: Oxbow

Austin, D. 1985: 'Dartmoor and the Upland Village of the South-West of England' in D, Hooke. (ed.) *Medieval Villages: A Review of Current Work,* Oxford: Oxford University Committee for Archaeology, 71-80

Austin, D. 1990: 'The Proper Study of Medieval Archaeology', in Austin, D. and Alcock, L. (eds.) *From the Baltic to the Black Sea: Studies in Medieval Archaeology*, London: Routledge, 9-42

Bailey, R.N. 1996: *England's Earliest Sculptors*, Toronto: Pontifical Institute of Mediaeval Studies

Baldwin-Brown, G. 1915: *The Arts in Early England*, London: Murray

Baker, R.S. 1880: 'On the Discovery of Anglo-Saxon Remains at Desborough, Northamptonshire', *Archaeologia* 45, 466-471

Barndon, R. 2006: 'Myth and Metallurgy: Some Cross-cultural Reflections on the Social Identity of Smiths', in Andrén, A., Jennbert K., and Raudvere, C. (eds.) *Old Norse Religion in Long-term Perspectives*, Lund: Nordic Academic Press, 99-103

Bassett, S. 1989: 'In Search of the Origins of Anglo-Saxon Kingdoms', in S. Bassett (ed.) *The Origins of Anglo-Saxon Kingdoms*, Leicester: Leicester University Press, 3-27

Bassett, S. 2007: 'Divide and Rule? The Military Infrastructure of Eighth and Ninth-Century Mercia', *Early Medieval Europe* 15, 53-85

Bassett, S. 2008: 'The Middle and Late Anglo-Saxon Defences of Western Mercian Towns', *Anglo-Saxon Studies in Archaeology and History* 15, 180-239

Bateman, C. Enright, D. and Oakley, N. 2003: 'Prehistoric and Anglo-Saxon Settlements to the Rear of Sherbourne House, Lechlade: Excavations in 1997', *Transactions of the Bristol and Gloucestershire Archaeological Society* 121, 23–96

Beresford, G. 1987: *Goltho: The Development of an Early Medieval Manor c. 850-1150*, London: RCHME

Beresford, M. and Hurst, J, 1990: *Wharram Percy Deserted Medieval Village*, London: English Heritage

Beresford, M. and Joseph, K. 1969: *New Towns of the Middle Ages (Second Edition)*, London: Lutterworth Press

Bersu, G. 1938: 'The Excavation at Woodbury, Wiltshire in 1938', *Proceedings of the Prehistoric Society* 4, 308-313

Biddle, M. 1975: 'The Evolution of Towns: Planned Towns Before 1066', in M.W. Barley (ed.) *The Plans and Topography of Medieval Towns in England and Wales*, York: CBA Research Report 14, 19-31

Biddle, M. 1989: 'A City in Transition: 400-800', in M.D. Lobel (ed.) *The City of London from Prehistoric Times to c. 1520*, Historic Town Atlas 3, Oxford: Clarendon Press, 20-29

Biddick, K. 1989: *The Other Economy: Pastoral Husbandry on a Medieval Estate*, Berkeley: University of California Press

Birbeck, V., with Smith, R.J.C., Andrews, P., and Stoodley, N. 2005: *The Origins of Mid Saxon Southampton: Excavation at the Friends Provident St. Mary's Stadium 1998-2000*, Salisbury: Trust for Wessex Archaeology

Blackburn. M. 2003 'Productive Sites and the Pattern of Coin Loss in England, 600-1180', in T. Pestell and K. Ulmschneider (eds.) *Markets in Early Medieval Europe: Trading and 'Productive Sites', 650-850*, Macclesfield: Windgather Press, 20-36

Blackburn, M. And Sorenson, D. 1984: 'Sceattas from an Unpublished Site Near Cambridge', in D. Hill and D.M. Metcalf (eds.) *Sceattas in England and on the Continent*, Oxford: British Archaeological Report 128, 223-227

Blackmore, L. 1988: 'The Anglo-Saxon Pottery', in R.L. Whytehead and R. Cowie (eds.) Two Middle Saxon Occupation Sites: Excavations at Jubilee Hall and 21-22 Maiden Lane, *Transactions of the London and Middlesex Archaeological Society* 39, 81-110

Blair, J. 1985: 'Secular Minster Churches in Domesday Book', in P. Sawyer (ed.), *Domesday Book: A Reappraisal*, London: Edward Arnold, 104-142

Blair, J. 1987: 'St Frideswide Reconsidered', *Oxoniensia* 52, 71-128

Blair, J. 1989: 'Frithuwold's Kingdom and the Origins of Surrey', in S. Bassett (ed.) *The Origins of Anglo-Saxon Kingdoms*, 97-107

Blair, J. 1998: 'Bampton: An Anglo-Saxon Minster', *Current Archaeology* 160, 124-130

Blair, J. 1994: *Anglo-Saxon Oxfordshire*, Oxford: Oxfordshire Books

Blair, J. 1996: 'Palaces or Minsters: Northampton and Cheddar Reconsidered', *Anglo-Saxon England* 25, 97-121

Blair, J. 2000: 'Late Anglo-Saxon Oxfordshire, 700-1100', *Oxoniensia* 65, 1-6

Blair, J. 2002: 'Anglo-Saxon Bicester: The Minster and the Town', *Oxoniensia* 67, 133-140

Blair, J. 2005: *The Church in Anglo-Saxon Society*, Oxford: Oxford University Press

Blair, J. (ed.) 2007: *Waterways and Canal-building in Medieval England*, Oxford: Oxford University Press

Blair, J. 2010a: 'The Anglo-Saxon Minsters', in K. Tiller and G. Darkes (eds.) *An Historical Atlas of Oxfordshire*, Chipping Norton: Oxfordshire Record Society, 26-27

Blair, J. 2010b: 'Bampton: A Minster Town', in K. Tiller and G. Darkes (eds.) *An Historical Atlas of Oxfordshire*, Chipping Norton: Oxfordshire Record Society, 30-31

Blair, J. 2013: 'Grid-planning in Anglo-Saxon Settlements: The short perch and four perch module, *Studies in Anglo-Saxon Archaeology and History* 18, 18-61.

Blinkhorn, P. 1999: 'Of Cabbages and Kings: Production, Trade and Consumption in Middle-Saxon England, in Anderton, M. (ed.) *Anglo-Saxon Trading Centres: Beyond the Emporia*, Glasgow: Cruithne Press, 4-23

Blinkhorn, P. 2002: 'The Anglo-Saxon Pottery', in S. Foreman, J. Hillier and D. Petts (eds.) *Gathering the People. Settling the Land: The Archaeology of a Middle Thames Landscape*, Oxford: Oxford Archaeology Thames Valley Landscapes Monograph 14, 35

Blinkhorn, P. 2004: 'Early and Middle Saxon Pottery', in G. Hey, *Yarnton, Saxon and Medieval Settlement and Landscape*, Thames Valley Landscapes Monograph 20, Oxford: Oxford Archaeology, 267-273

Boddington, 1996: *Raunds Area Project (Report 1) Raunds Furnells: The Anglo-Saxon Church and Churchyard*, London: RCHME

Bonney, D. 1979: 'Early Boundaries and Estates in Southern England', in P. Sawyer (ed.) *English Medieval Settlement*, London: Edward Arnold, 41-51

Booth, P. 2010: 'Roman Oxfordshire', in K. Tiller and G. Darkes (eds.) *An Historical Atlas of Oxfordshire*, Chipping Norton: Oxfordshire Record Society, 16-17

Bourdillon, J. 1994: 'The Animal Provisioning of Saxon Southampton', in J. Rackham (ed.) *Environment and Economy in Anglo-Saxon England (Proceedings of a Conference held at The Museum of London 9th-10th April 1990*, CBA Research Report 89, York: Current British Archaeology 120-125

Boyle, A. 2001: 'Excavations in Christ Church Cathedral Graveyard', *Oxoniensia* 66, 337-368

Bradley, R. 1978: 'Rescue Excavations in Dorchester-on-Thames', *Oxoniensia* 43, 17-39

Bradley, R. 1984: *The Social Foundations of Prehistoric Britain: Themes and Variations in the Archaeology of Power*, London: Longman

Brodribb, A.C.C., Hands, A.R. and Walker, D.R. 2005: *The Roman Villa at Shakenoak Farm, Oxfordshire, Excavations 1960-76*, British Archaeological Reports 395, Oxford: Archaeopress

Brooks, N. 1974: 'Anglo-Saxon Charters: The Work of the Last Twenty Years', *Anglo-Saxon England* 3, 211-231

Brooks, N. 1984: The *Early History of the Church at Canterbury*, Leicester: Leicester University Press

Brooks, N. 1989: 'The Formation of the Mercian Kingdom', in S. Bassett (ed.) *The Origins of Anglo-Saxon Kingdoms,* Leicester: Leicester University Press, 159-170

Brooks, N. 1994: 'Rochester Bridge, AD 43–1381', in N. Yates and J.M. Gibson (eds.) *Traffic and Politics: The Construction and Management of Rochester Bridge AD 43–1993*, Woodbridge: Boydell, 1-40

Brooks, N. 2000: 'Canterbury, Rome and the Construction of the English Identity', in J.M.H. (ed.) *Early Medieval Rome and the Christian West: Essays in Honour of Donald A. Bullough*, Leiden: Brill, 221-247

Brooks, N. And Kelly, S.E. forthcoming: *Charters of Christ Church Canterbury*

Brown, A.E. 1991: *Early Daventry*, Leicester: University of Leicester

Brow, A.E. and Taylor, C.C. 1980: 'Cambridgeshire Earthwork Surveys (4)', *Proceedings of the Cambridgeshire Antiquarian Society* 70, 113-125

Brown, T. and Taylor, C.C. 1978: 'Settlement and Land Use in Northamptonshire: a Comparison Between the Iron Age and the Middle Ages', in B. Cunliffe and T. Rowley (eds.) *Lowland Iron Age Communities in Europe*, BAR International Supplementary 48, Oxford: British Archaeological Reports, 77-89

Brown, T. and Foard, G. 1998: 'The Saxon Landscape: A Regional Perspective', in P. Everson and T. Williamson (eds.) *The Archaeology of Landscape: Studies Presented to Christopher Taylor*, Manchester: Manchester University Press, 67-94

Brown, T. and Foard, G. 2004: 'The Anglo-Saxon Period', in M. Tingle (ed.) *The Archaeology of Northamptonshire*, Northampton: Northamptonshire Archaeological Society, 78-101

Brown, O.F. and Roberts, G.J. 1973: *Passenham: The History of a Forest Village*, Chichester: Phillimore

Bruce-Mitford, R. 1974: *Aspects of Anglo-Saxon Archaeology: Sutton Hoo and Other Discoveries*, London: Gollancz

Brugmann, B. 2011: 'Migration and Endogenous Change', in H. Hamerow, D.A. Hinton, and S. Crawford (eds.) *The Oxford Handbook of Anglo-Saxon Archaeology*, Oxford: Oxford University Press, 30-45

Brück, J. 2005: 'Experiencing the Past? The Development of a Phenomenological Archaeology in British Prehistory', *Archaeological Dialogues* 12 (i), 45-72

Buss, B. 2002: 'Ebbsfleet Saxon Mill', *Current Archaeology* 183, 93

Butterworth, C. and Seager Smith, R. 1997: 'Excavations at the Hermitage, Old Town, Swindon', *Wiltshire Archaeological and Natural History Magazine* 90, 55-76

Cabot, S., Davies, G., and Hoggett, R., 2004: 'Sedgeford: Excavations of a Rural Settlement in Norfolk', in J. Hines, A. Lane and M. Redknap (eds.) *Land, Sea and Home*, Leeds: Maney, 313-324

Cadman, G.E. and Audouy, M. 1990: 'Recent Excavations on Saxon and Medieval Quarries in Raunds, Northamptonshire, in D. Parsons (ed.) *Stone Quarrying and Building in England AD43-1525*, Chichester: Phillimore, 187-206

Campbell, G. 1994: 'The Preliminary Archaeobotanical Results from Anglo-Saxon West Cotton and Raunds', in J. Rackham (ed.) *Environment and Economy in Anglo-Saxon England*, Council for British Archaeology Report 89, York: Council for British Archaeology, 65-82

Campbell, J. 1979: 'Bede's Words for Places', in P.H. Sawyer (ed.) *Places, Names and Graves: Early Medieval Settlement*, Leeds: The University of Leeds, 34-64

Campbell, J. 1986: 'Some Twelfth Century Views of the Anglo-Saxon Past', in J. Campbell (ed.) *Essays in Anglo-Saxon History*, London: Hambledon Press, 209-228

Campbell, J. 2000a: 'The East Anglian Sees Before the Conquest', in J. Campbell (ed.) *The Anglo-Saxon State*, London: Hambledon, 107-128

Campbell, J. 2000b: 'The Sale of Land and the Economics of Power in Early England: Problems and Possibilities', in J. Campbell (ed.) *The Anglo-Saxon State*, London: Hambledon and London

Carver, M.O.H. 1990: 'Pre-Viking Traffic in the North Sea, in S. McGrail (eds.) *Maritime Celts, Frisians and Saxons*, CBA Research Report 71, London: Council for British Archaeology, 117-25

Carver, M.O.H. 1998: *Sutton Hoo: Burial Ground of Kings?*, London: The British Museum Press

Carver, M.O.H. 2005: *Sutton Hoo: A Seventh Century Princely Burial Ground and its Context*, London: British Museum Press

Carr, R.D., Tester, A. and Murphy, P. 1988: 'The Middle-Saxon Settlement at Staunch Meadow, Brandon', *Antiquity* 62, 371-377

Cessford, C. 2007: 'Middle Anglo-Saxon Justice: The Chesterton Lane Corner Execution Cemetery and Related Sequence, Cambridge (with A. Dickens, N. Dodwell and A. Reynolds), *The Archaeological Journal* 164, 197-226

Cessford, C. and Dickens, A. 2005: 'Cambridge Castle Hill: Excavations of Saxon, Medieval and Post-Medieval Deposits, Saxon Execution Site and a Medieval Coinhoard', *Proceedings of the Cambridge Antiquarian Society* 94, 73-101

Chadwick, H.M. 1940: 'Who Was He?', *Antiquity* 14, 76-87

Chambers, R.A. 1976: 'Eynsham, Oxfordshire 1975', *Oxoniensia* 41, 355-356

Chambers, R.A. 1987: 'The Late- and Sub-Roman Cemetery at Queenford Farm, Dorchester-on-Thames, Oxon', *Oxoniensia* 52, 35-70

Chambers, R.A. 2007: *Excavation at Barrow Hills, Radley, Oxfordshire, 1983-5*, Oxford: Oxford Archaeology

Chapman, J. 2010: *West Cotton, Raunds: A study of the Medieval Settlement Dynamics AD 450-1450: Excavation of a Deserted Medieval Hamlet in Northamptonshire 1985-89*, Oxford: Oxbow

Chapman, J. and Hamerow, H. 1997: 'Introduction: On the Move Again- Migrations and Invasions in Archaeological Explanation', in J. Chapman and H. Hamerow (eds.) *Migrations and Invasions in Archaeological Explanation*, Oxford: British Archaeological Reports, 1-10

Chester-Kadwell, M. 2009: *Early Saxon Communities in the Landscape of Norfolk*, British Archaeological Report 481, Oxford: Archaeopress

Childe, V.G. 1925: *The Dawn of European Civilisation*, London: Kegan Paul

Christie, N. 2004: 'Landscapes of Change in Late Antiquity and the Early Middle Ages: Themes Directions and Problems', in N. Christie (ed.) *Landscapes of Change: The Evolution of the Countryside in Late Antiquity and the Early Middle Ages*, Aldershot: Ashgate, 1-38

Christie, N. and Creighton, O. with Edgeworth, M. and Fradley, M. 2010: "Have You Found Anything Interesting?' Exploring Early Medieval and Medieval Urbanism at Wallingford: Sources, Routes and Questions', *Oxoniensia*, 35-48

Clark, G. 1966: 'The Invasion Hypothesis in British Archaeology', *Antiquity* 40, 172-189

Clarke, A., Fulford, M.G., Rains, M. And Tootell, K. 2007: 'Silchester Roman Town Insula IX: The Development of an Urban Property *c*. AD 40-50-*c*. AD 250' *Internet Archaeology* 21 (ISSN 1363-5387)

Clarke, J. 1993: *The Book of Brackley: The First Thousand Years*, Northampton: Northampton Records Office

Clarke, H.B. and Simms, A. 1985: 'Towards a Comparative History of Urban Origins', in H.B. Clarke and A. Simms (eds.) *The Comparative History of Urban Origins in Non-Roman Europe*, Oxford: British Archaeological Reports, 669-714

Clarke, R.R. 1955: 'The Fossditch: A Linear Earthwork in south-west Norfolk', *Norfolk Archaeology* 31, 178-196

Clayton, N.B. 1973: 'New Wintles Farm, Oxfordshire', *Oxoniensia* 38, 382-4

Collard, M. and Havard, T. 2011: 'The Prehistoric and Medieval Defences of Malmesbury: Archaeological Investigations at Holloway, 2005-2006', *Wiltshire Archaeological and Natural History Magazine* 104, 79-94

Cool, H.E.M. 2000: 'The Parts Left Over: Material Culture into the Fifth Century', in T. Wilmott and P.Wilson (eds.) *The Late Roman Transition in the North*, British Archaeological Reports 299 Oxford: Archaeopress, 47-65

Corbett, W. and Dent, D. 1994: 'The Soil Landscapes', in P. Wade-Martins (eds.) *An Historical Atlas of Norfolk* (2ⁿᵈ edition), Norwich: Norwich Museums Service, 18-19

Costen, M. 1994: 'Settlement in Wessex in the Tenth Century: The Charter Evidence', in A.M. Aston and C. Lewis (eds.), *The Medieval Landscape of Wessex*, Oxford: Oxbow, 97-107

Crabtree, R. 1994: 'Animal Exploitation in East Anglian Villages', in J. Rackham (ed.) *Environment and Economy in Anglo-Saxon England*, Current British Archaeology Research Report 89, York: Council for British Archaeology, 40-54

Crawford, O.G.S 1928: *Air Survey and Archaeology*, London: HMSO

Crawford, S. 2008: 'The Early Medieval Period', Unpublished Report for the Solent Thames Research Framework Regional Assessment

Creighton, O. H. 2009: *Designs Upon the Land*, Woodbridge: Boydell Press

Crick, J. 2007: *Charters of St Albans*, Anglo-Saxon Charters 12, Oxford: Oxford University Press (The British Academy)

Crick, J. 2009: 'Nobility', in P. Stafford (ed.) *A Companion to the Early Middle Ages: Britain and Ireland c.500-c.1100*, Chichester: Wiley-Blackwell, 414-431

Crowley, D.A. 1987: 'Tisbury', in *Victoria County History: A History of the County of Wiltshire, Volume 13*, 195-248

Crowson, A., Lane, T., Penn, K. and Trimble, D. 2005: 'The Excavations', in A. Crowson, T. Lane, K. Penn and D. Trimble (eds.) *Anglo-Saxon Settlement on the Siltland of Eastern England*, Lincolnshire Archaeology and Heritage Reports No 7, Sleaford: Heritage Trust of Lincolnshire, 12-205

Cubitt, C. 1995: Anglo-*Saxon Church Councils c.650-c.850*, London/New York: Leicester University Press

Darby, H.C. 1952: *The Domesday Geography of Eastern England*, Cambridge: Cambridge University Press

Darby, H.C. and Finn, R.W: 1967: *The Domesday Geography of South-west England*, Cambridge: Cambridge University Press

Dark, K. 2004: 'The Late Antique Landscape of Britain, AD300-700', in N. Christie (ed.) *Landscapes of Change: The Evolution of the Countryside in Late Antiquity and the Early Middle Ages*, Aldershot: Ashgate, 279-300

Darkes, G. 2010: 'Topography', in K. Tiller and G. Darkes (eds.) *An Historical Atlas of Oxfordshire*, Chipping Norton: Oxfordshire Record Society, 6-7

Davison, A. 1987: 'Little Hockham', *Norfolk Archaeology* 40, 84-93

Davison, A. 1990: *The Evolution of Settlement in Three Parishes in South East Norfolk*, East Anglian Archaeology 49, Norwich: Norfolk Archaeology Unit and Norfolk Museums Service

Davison, A. 1995: 'The Field Archaeology of the Mannington and Wolterton Estates', *Norfolk Archaeology* 42, 160-84

Davison, A. 2003: 'The Archaeology of the Parish of West Acre: Part 1: Field Evidence', *Norfolk Archaeology* 44 (ii), 202-221

Davison, A. and Cushion, B. 1999: 'The Archaeology of the Hargham Estate', *Norfolk Archaeology* 43, 257-274

Davison, A., Green, A., and Milligan, B. 1993: *Illington: A Study of a Breckland Parish and its Anglo-Saxon Cemetery*, East Anglian Archaeology Report 63, Gressenhall: Field Archaeology Division, Norfolk Museums Service

Davies, G. 2010: 'Early Medieval 'Rural Centres' and West Norfolk: A Growing Picture of Diversity, Complexity and Changing Lifestyles', *Medieval Archaeology* 54, 89-122

Davies, J.A. 1996: 'Where Eagles Dare: The Iron Age of Norfolk', *Proceedings of the Prehistoric Society* 62, 63-92

Davies, R. 2003: 'The Medieval State: the Tyranny of a Concept?', *Journal of Historical Sociology* 16 (ii), 280-300

Davies, W. 1973: 'Middle Anglia and the Middle Angles', *Midland History* 2, 18-20

Dawson, G.J. 1961-2: 'Excavations at Purwell Farm, Cassington', *Oxoniensia* 26-27, 1-6

Dickinson, T.M. 1973: 'Excavations at Standlake Down in 1954: The Anglo-Saxon Graves', *Oxoniensia* 38, 329-257

Dickinson, T.M. 1976: *The Anglo-Saxon Burial Sites of the Upper Thames Region, and their bearing on the History of Wessex,* c. *AD 400-700*, Unpublished DPhil Thesis, The University of Oxford

Dickinson, T. M. 1983: 'Anglo-Saxon Archaeology: Twenty Five Years On', in D. A. Hinton (ed.) *25 Years of Medieval Archaeology,* Sheffield: University of Sheffield, 33-47

Dickinson, T. 1991: 'Material Culture as Social Expression: The Case of Saxon Saucer Brooches with Running Spiral Decoration', *Studien zur Sachsenforschung* 7, 39-70

Dickinson, T. and Griffiths, D. (eds.) 1999: *The Making of Kingdoms: Anglo-Saxon Studies in Archaeology and History 10*, Oxford: Oxford University School of Archaeology

Dixon, P. 1982: 'How Saxon is the Saxon House?', in P. Drury (ed.) *Structural Reconstruction*, Oxford: British Archaeological Reports, 275-287

Dobinson, C. and Denison, S. 1995: *Metal Detecting and Archaeology in England*, London: RCHME and Council for British Archaeology

Dodd, A. 2003: *Oxford before the University: The Late Saxon and Norman Archaeology of the Thames Crossing, the Defences and the Town*, Landscapes Monograph 17, Oxford: Oxford Archaeology Thames Valley

Dodd, A. 2010: 'Early Anglo-Saxon Settlement', in K. Tiller and G. Darkes (eds.) *An Historical Atlas of Oxfordshire*, Chipping Norton: Oxfordshire Record Society, 18-19

Dodwell, N., Lucy, S. and Tipper, J. 2004: 'Anglo-Saxons on the Cambridge Backs: The Criminology Site Settlement and King's Garden Hostel Cemetery', *Proceedings of the Cambridge Antiquarian Society* 93, 95-123

Doherty, C. 1985: 'The Monastic Town in Early Medieval Ireland', in H.B. Clarke and A. Simms (eds.) *The Comparative History of Urban Origins in Non-Roman Europe: Ireland, Wales, Denmark, Germany, Poland and Russia from the Ninth to the Thirteenth Century*, Oxford: British Archaeological Reports, BAR International Series 255, 45-75

Doucet, A. 1994: 'Agriculture in the 20th Century', in P. Wade-Martins (ed.) *An Historical Atlas of Norfolk*, Hunstanton: Norfolk Museums Service, 176-177

Draper, S. 2006: *Landscape, Settlement and Society in Roman and Early Medieval Wiltshire*, BAR Series 419, Oxford: Archaeopress

Draper, S. 2008: 'The Significance of *OE* Burh in Anglo-Saxon England', *Anglo-Saxon Studies in Archaeology and History* 15, 240-253

Draper, S. 2011: 'Language and the Anglo-Saxon Landscape: Towards an Archaeological Interpretation of Place-names in Wiltshire', in N.J. Higham and M.J. Ryan (eds.) *Place-Names, Language and the Anglo-Saxon Landscape*, Woodbridge: Boydell & Brewer, 85-104

Drury, P.J. and Rodwell, W. 1978: *Excavations at Little Waltham 1970-1*, CBA Research Report, London: Council for British Archaeology

Dunning, G.C. 1932: 'Bronze Age Settlements and a Saxon Hut near Bourton-on-the-Water, Gloucestershire', *Antiquaries Journal* 12, 279-292

Dunning, G. C. and Hawkes, S.C. 1961: 'Soldiers and Settlers in Britain, Fourth or Fifth Century', *Medieval Archaeology* 5, 1-70

Durham, B. 1977: 'Archaeological Investigations in St Aldate's, Oxford', *Oxoniensia* 42, 83-203

Dyer, C. 1985: 'Power and Conflict in the Medieval Village', in D. Hooke (ed.) *Medieval Villages*, Oxford: Oxford University Committee for Archaeological Monographs, 27-32

Dyer, C. 1999: The Medieval Settlement Research Group Whittlewood Project', *Annual Report, Medieval Settlement Research Group* 14, 16-17

Dyer, C. 2003: *Making a Living in the Middle Ages: The People of Britain 850-1520*, London: Penguin

Eagles, B. 1994: 'The Archaeological Evidence for Settlement in the Fifth to Seventh Centuries AD', in A.M. Aston and C. Lewis (eds.), *The Medieval Landscape of Wessex*, Oxford: Oxbow, 13-32

Eagles, B. 2001: 'Anglo-Saxon Presence and Culture in Wiltshire *c.*450-*c.*675', in P. Ellis (ed.) *Roman Wiltshire and After: Papers in Honour of Ken Annable*, Bristol: Wiltshire Archaeological and Natural History Society, 199-233

Eagles. B. 2004: 'Britons and Saxons on the Eastern Boundary of the Civitas Durotrigum', *Britannia* 35, 234-240

Earle, T. 1997: *How Chiefs Come to Power: The Political Economy in Prehistory*, Stanford: Stanford University Press

Edgar, W. 1923: *Borough Hill (Daventry) and its History*, London: Taylor and Francis

Ekwall, E. 1960: *The Concise Oxford Dictionary of English Place Names*, Oxford: Clarendon Press

Everitt, A. 1979: 'Country, County and Town: Patterns of Regional Evolution in England', *Transactions of the Royal Historical Society*, Fifth Series, 29, 79-108

Everson, P. 1977: 'Excavations in the Vicarage Garden at Brixworth', *Journal of the British Archaeological Association* 130, 55-122

Everson, P. And Jecock, M. 1999: 'Castle Hill and the Early Medieval Development of Thetford in Norfolk', in P. Pattison, D. Field and S. Ainsworth (eds.) *Patterns of the Past: Essays in Landscape Archaeology for Christopher Taylor*, Oxford: Oxbow, 97-106

Faulkner, N. 1997: 'Sedgeford Historical and Archaeological Research Project. 1996: First Interim Report', *Norfolk Archaeology* 42, 532-535

Faull, M. 1977: 'British Survival in Anglo-Saxon Northumbria', in L. Laing (ed.) *Studies in Celtic Survival*, British Archaeological Report 37, Oxford: Archaeopress 1-55

Faith, R. 1997: *The English Peasantry and the Growth of Lordship*, Leicester: Leicester University Press

Foard, G. 1978: 'Systematic Fieldwalking and the Investigation of Saxon Settlement in Northamptonshire', *World Archaeology* 9, 357-374

Foard, G. 1984: *Raunds Area Project: Research Design*, unpublished

Foard, G. 1985: 'The Administrative Organisation of Northamptonshire in the Saxon Period', *Anglo-Saxon Studies in Archaeology and History* 4, 185-222

Foard, G., Hall, D. and Partida, T. 2009: *Rockingham Forest: An Atlas of the Medieval and Early-Modern Landscape*, Northampton: Northamptonshire Record Society

Foard, G. and Pearson, T. 1985: 'The Raunds Area Project: First Interim Report, *Northamptonshire Archaeology* 20, 3-21

Foot, S. 2000: *Veiled Women, I: The Disappearance of Nuns from Anglo-Saxon England*, Aldershot: Ashgate

Ford, S. 1995: 'The Excavation of a Saxon Settlement and a Mesolithic Flint Scatter at Northampton Road, Brixworth, Northamptonshire, 1994', *Northamptonshire Archaeology* 21, 3-22

Ford, S. and Hazell, A. 1989: 'Prehistoric, Roman and Anglo-Saxon Settlement Patterns at North Stoke, Oxfordshire', *Oxoniensia* 65, 7-24

Forster, R., Rodwell, K., Squires, R. and Turner, H. 1975: 'Wantage', in K. Rodwell (ed.) *Historic Towns in Oxfordshire: A Survey of the New County*, Oxford: Oxford Archaeological Unit, 3

Fowler, P.J. 1971: 'Hillforts A.D. 400-700', in D. Hill and M. Jesson (eds.) *The Iron Age and its Hillforts*, Southampton: Southampton University, 203-213

Fox, H. 1980: 'Approaches to the Adoption of the Midland System', in T. Rowley (ed.) *The Origins of Open Field Agriculture*, London: Croom Helm, 64-110

Fox, H. 2008: 'Butter Place-names and Transhumance, in O.J. Padel and D.N. Parsons (eds.) *A Commodity of Good Names: Essays in Honour of Margaret Gelling*, Donington: Shaun Tyas

Funnell, B. 1994a: 'Solid Geology', in P. Wade-Martins (ed.) *An Historical Atlas of Norfolk*, Hunstanton: Norfolk Museums Service, 12-13

Funnell, B. 1994b: 'Glaciers Change the Landscape', in P. Wade-Martins (ed.) *An Historical Atlas of Norfolk*, Hunstanton: Norfolk Museums Service, 14-15

Funnell, B. 1994c: 'Recent Geology, in P. Wade-Martins (ed.) *An Historical Atlas of Norfolk*, Hunstanton: Norfolk Museums Service, 16-17

Fleming, A. 1988: *The Dartmoor Reaves: Investigating Prehistoric Land Divisions*, London: Batsford

Fleming, A. 2007: 'Don't Bin Your Boots', *Landscapes* 8 (i), 85-99

Frodsham, P. and O'Brien, C. 2005: *Yeavering: People, Power, Place*

Foard, G. 1978: 'Systematic fieldwalking and the investigation of Saxon settlement in Northamptonshire', *World Archaeology* 9 (iii), 357-374

Fowler, P.J. 1976: 'Agriculture and rural settlement', In D. M. Wilson (ed.) *The Archaeology of Anglo-Saxon England*, London: Methuen, 23-48

Fowler, 2000: *Landscape Plotted and Pieced: Landscape History and Local Archaeology in Fyfield and Overton, Wiltshire*, London: Society of Antiquaries

Franklin, M.J. 1988: 'The Secular College as a Focus for Anglo-Norman Piety: St Augustine's, Daventry', in J. Blair (ed.) *Minster and Parish Churches: The Local Church in Transition 950-1200*, Oxford University Committee for Archaeology Monograph 17, Oxford: Oxbow

Frere, S.S. 1962: 'Excavations at Dorchester-on-Thames, 1962', *Archaeological Journal* 119, 114-149

Gardiner, M. 2011: 'Late Saxon Settlements', in H. Hamerow, D.A. Hinton, and S. Crawford (eds.) *The Oxford Handbook of Anglo-Saxon Archaeology*, Oxford: Oxford University Press, 198-217

Gates, T. 2005: 'Yeavering and Air Photography: discovery and interpretation', in P. Frodsham and C. O'Brien (eds.) *Yeavering: People, Power and Place*, Stroud: Tempus, 65-83

Geake, H. 2002: 'Persistent Problems in the Study of Conversion-Period Burials in England', in S. Lucy and A. Reynolds (eds.) *Burial in Early Medieval England and Wales*, London: Society for Medieval Archaeology

Gelling, M. 1974: *The Place-Names of Berkshire, Part II*, Cambridge: English Place-Name Society

Gelling, M. 1978: *Signposts to the Past*, London: Dent

Gelling, M. 2011: 'Place-Names and Archaeology', in H. Hamerow, D.A. Hinton, and S. Crawford (eds.) *The Oxford Handbook of Anglo-Saxon Archaeology*, Oxford: Oxford University Press, 986-1002

Gem, R. 2009: 'Architecture, Liturgy and *Romanitas* at All Saints' Church, Brixworth' (27th Brixworth Lecture, 2009), *The Brixworth Lectures (Second Series)* 8, Northampton: Friends of Brixworth Church

Gerrard, C. 1999: 'The Shapwick Project', in C. Webster (eds.) *A Century of Archaeology in Somerset: Papers to Mark 150 Years of the Somerset Archaeological and Natural History Society*, Taunton: Somerset County Council, 67-93

Gerrard, C. 2003: *Medieval Archaeology: Understanding Traditions and Contemporary Approaches*, Abingdon: Routledge

Gerrard, C. 2007: *The Shapwick Project, Somerset: A Rural Landscape Explored*, The Society for Medieval Archaeology Monograph 25, Leeds: Society for Medieval Archaeology

Gerrard, C. and Rippon, S. 2007: 'Artefacts, Sites and Landscapes: Archaeology and Medieval Studies', in A. Deyermond (ed.) *A Century of British Medieval Studies*, Oxford: Oxford University Press, 525-555

Giandrea, M.F. 2007: *Episcopal Culture in Late Anglo-Saxon England*, Woodbridge: Boydell and Brewer

Gibson, C. and Murray, J. 2003: 'An Anglo-Saxon Settlement at Godmanchester, Cambridgeshire', *Anglo-Saxon Studies in Archaeology and History* 12, 136-217

Gilbert, D. 2008: 'Excavations at St. Mary's Church, Black Bourton, Oxfordshire': Early, Middle, and Late Saxon Activity', *Oxoniensia* 73, 147-160

Gilmour, B. 1979: 'The Anglo-Saxon Church at St Paul-in-the-Bail', *Medieval Archaeology* 23, 214-218

Gingell, C. 1978: 'The Excavation of an Early Anglo-Saxon Cemetery at Collingbourne Ducis', *Wiltshire Archaeological and Natural History Magazine* 70/71, 61-98

Gingell, C. 1983: 'A Fieldwalking Survey in the Vale of Wardour' (with P. Harding), *Wiltshire Archaeological and Natural History Magazine* 77, 11-25

Gittos, H. 2011: 'Christian Sacred Places and Spaces', in H. Hamerow, D.A. Hinton, and S. Crawford (eds.) *The Oxford Handbook of Anglo-Saxon Archaeology*, Oxford: Oxford University Press, 824-843

Goodier, A. 1984: 'The Formation of Boundaries in Anglo-Saxon England: A Statistical Study', *Medieval Archaeology* 28, 1-21

Gover, J.E.B., Mawer, A. and Stenton, F.M. 1933: *The Place-Names of Northamptonshire*, Cambridge: Cambridge University Press

Gover, J.E.B., Mawer, A. and Stenton, F.M. 1939: *The Place-Names of Wiltshire*, Cambridge: Cambridge University Press

Gray, H.L. 1915: *English Field Systems*, Harvard: Harvard University Press

Gray, M. and Clayton, N. 1978: 'Excavations on the Site of Eynsham Abbey, 1971', *Oxoniensia* 43, 100-122

Graham-Campbell, J. 2000: *The Anglo-Saxon State*, London: Hambledon

Green, J.R. 1881: *The Making of England*, London: MacMillan and Co

Griffiths, D. 2003: 'Markets and "Productive" Sites: A View from Western Britain', in T. Pestell and K. Ulmschneider (eds.) *Markets in Early Medieval Europe: Trading and 'Productive Sites', 650-850*, Macclesfield: Windgather Press, 62-72

Gurney, D. 1994: 'The Roman Period', in P. Wade-Martins (ed.) *An Historical Atlas of Norfolk*, Hunstanton: Norfolk Museums Service, 34-35

Haddan, A.W. and Stubbs, W. 1964: *Councils and Ecclesiastical Documents Relating to Great Britain and Ireland*, Oxford: Clarendon Press

Hall, D. 1981: 'The Origins of Open-Field Agriculture: The Archaeological Fieldwork Evidence', in T. Rowley (ed.) *The Origins of Open-Field Agriculture*, London: Croom Helm, 22-38

Hall, D. 1982: *Medieval Fields*, Aylesbury: Shire

Hall, D. 1985: 'Late Saxon Topography and Early Medieval Estates', in Hooke, D. (ed.) *Medieval Villages*, Oxford: Oxford University Press, 61-69

Hall, D. 1987: *The Fenland Project, Number Two: Fenland Landscapes and Settlement between Peterborough and March*, Cambridge: Cambridge Archaeological Committee

Hall, D. 1988: 'The Late Saxon Countryside: Villages and Their Fields', in D. Hooke (ed.) *Anglo-Saxon Settlements*, Oxford: Blackwell, 99-122

Hall, D. 1995: *The Open Fields of Northamptonshire*, Northampton: Northamptonshire Record Society

Hall, D. 1996a: *The Fenland Project, Number Six: The South-western Cambridgeshire Fenlands*, Cambridge: Cambridgeshire Archaeological Committee

Hall, D. 1996b: *The Fenland Project, Number Ten: Cambridge Survey, Isle of Ely and Wisbech*, Cambridge: Cambridgeshire Archaeological Committee

Hall, D. and Coles, J. 1994: *Fenland Survey: An Essay in Landscape and Persistence*, Royal Commission on the Historical Monuments of England Archaeological Report 1, London: Royal Commission on the Historical Monuments of England

Hall, D. and Hutchings, J.B. 1972: 'The Distribution of Archaeological Sites Between the Nene and the Ouse Valleys', *Bedfordshire Archaeological Journal* 7, 2-16

Hall, D. and Martin, P. 1979: 'Brixworth, Northamptonshire- An Intensive Field Survey, *Journal of the British Archaeological Association* 132, 1-6

Hallam, H.E. 1988: 'England Before the Norman Conquest', in H.E. Hallam (ed.), *The Agrarian History of England and Wales, Volume II, 1042-1350*, Cambridge: Cambridge University Press 1-44

Hamerow, H. 1991: 'Settlement Mobility and the "Middle Saxon Shift": Rural Settlements and Settlement Patterns in Anglo-Saxon England', *Anglo-Saxon England* 20, 1-17

Hamerow, H. 1992: 'Settlement on the Gravels in the Anglo-Saxon Period', in M. Fulford and L. Nichols (eds.) *Developing Landscapes of Lowland Britain: The Archaeology of the British Gravels*, London: Society of Antiquaries, 39-46

Hamerow, H. 1993: *Excavations at Mucking, Volume 2: The Anglo-Saxon Settlement*, London: English Heritage

Hamerow, H. 1997: 'Migration Theory and the Anglo-Saxon "Identity Crisis"', in J. Chapman and H. Hamerow (eds.) *Migrations and Invasions in Archaeological Explanation*, Oxford: British Archaeological Reports, 33-43

Hamerow, H. 2000: 'Anglo-Saxon Oxfordshire, 400-700: The Tom Hassall Lecture for 1998', *Oxonniensia* 64, 23-38

Hamerow, H. 2002: *Early Medieval Settlements: The Archaeology of Rural Communities in North-West Europe 400-900*, Oxford: Oxford University Press

Hamerow, H. 2006: '"Special Deposits" in Anglo-Saxon Settlements', *Medieval Archaeology* 50, 1-30

Hamerow, H. 2010: 'The Development of Anglo-Saxon Rural Settlement Structure, *Landscape History* 31 (i), 6-22

Hamerow, H. 2011a: 'Overview: Rural Settlement', in H. Hamerow, D.A. Hinton, and S. Crawford (eds.) *The Oxford Handbook of Anglo-Saxon Archaeology*, Oxford: Oxford University Press, 119-127

Hamerow, H. 2011b: 'Anglo-Saxon Timber Buildings and their Social Context', in H. Hamerow, D.A. Hinton, and S. Crawford (eds.) *The Oxford Handbook of Anglo-Saxon Archaeology*, Oxford: Oxford University Press, 128-155

Hamerow, H., Hayden, C. and Hey, G. 2007: 'Anglo-Saxon and Earlier Settlement near Drayton Road, Sutton Courtenay, Berkshire', *Archaeological Journal* 164, 109-198

Hanson, L. and Wickham, C. (eds.) 2000: *The Long Eighth Century: Production, Distribution and Demmand*, Leiden: Brill

Harding, P.A. and Andrews, P. 2002: 'Anglo-Saxon and Medieval Settlement at Chapel Street, Bicester: Excavations 1999-2000', *Oxoniensia* 67, 179-198

Hardy, A. and Blair, J. 2003: 'Introduction', in A. Hardy, A. Dodd and G.D. Keevill (eds.) *Aelfric's Abbey: Excavations at Eynsham Abbey, Oxfordshire, 1989-92*, Oxford: Oxford Archaeology/Oxford University School of Archaeology

Hardy, A., Dodd, A. and Keevill, G.D. 2003: *Aelfric's Abbey: Excavations at Eynsham Abbey, Oxfordshire, 1989-92*, Oxford: Oxford Archaeology/Oxford University School of Archaeology

Hardy, A. and Lorimer, P. 2004: *Roots of an English Town: Exploring the Archaeology of Higham Ferrers*, Oxford: Oxford Archaeology

Hardy, H., Mair Charles, B. and Williams, R.J. 2007: *Death and Taxes: The Archaeology of a Middle Saxon Estate Centre at Higham Ferrers, Northamptonshire*, Oxford: Oxford Archaeology

Härke H. 1990: 'Warrior graves? The Background of the Anglo-Saxon Weapon Burial Rite, *Past and Present* 126 (i), 22–43

Harrison, S. 2002: 'Open Fields and Earlier Landscapes: Six Parishes in South-east Cambridgeshire', *Landscapes* 3 (i), 35-54

Harrison, S. 2003: 'The Icknield Way: Some Queries', *The Archaeological Journal* 160, 1-22

Harrold, B. 2003: *An Enigma of Ancient Suffolk*, Colchester: Red Bird Press

Hart, C. 1970: *The Hidation of Northamptonshire*, Leicester: Leicester University Press

Hart, J. Collard, M. and Holbrook, N. 2005: 'A New Roman Villa near Malmesbury', *Wiltshire Archaeological and Natural History Magazine* 98, 297–306

Haslam, J. 1976: *Wiltshire Towns: The Archaeological Potential*, Devises: Wiltshire Archaeological and Natural History Society

Haslam, J. 1980: 'A Middle Saxon Iron Smelting Site at Ramsbury, Wiltshire', *Medieval Archaeology* 24, 1-68

Haslam, J. 1984a: *Anglo-Saxon Towns in Southern England*, London: Phillimore

Haslam, J. 1984b: 'The Development and Topography of Saxon Cambridge', *Proceedings of the Cambridge Antiquarian Society* 72, 13-29

Haslam, J. 2003: 'Excavations at Cricklade, Wiltshire, 1975', *Internet Archaeology* 14

Haslam, J. 2005: 'King Alfred and the Vikings: Strategies and Tactics 876-886 AD', in S. Semple (ed.) *Anglo-Saxon Studies in Archaeology and History 13*, Oxford: Oxford University School of Archaeology, 121-153

Haslam, J. 2010: 'The Two Anglo-Saxon *Burhs* of Oxford', *Oxoniensia* 75, 15-34

Hassall, T.G. 1972: 'Excavation at the Saxon Church at Waterperry, Oxfordshire', *Oxoniensia* 37, 245

Hatcher, J. and Bailey, M. 2001: *Modelling the Middle Ages: The History and Theory of England's Economic Development*, Oxford: Oxford University Press

Hawkes, S.C. 1986: 'The Early Saxon Period', in G. Briggs J. Cook and T. Rowley (eds.) *The Archaeology of the Oxford Region*, Oxford: Oxford University Dept for External Studies

Heaton, M.J. 1992: Two Mid-Saxon Grain Driers and Later Medieval Features at Chantry Fields, Gillingham, Dorset', *Proceedings of the Dorset Natural History and Archaeological Society* 114, 96-126

Hearne, C. and Smith, R. 1991: 'A Late Iron Age and Black Burnished Ware Production Site at Worgret, near Wareham, Dorset (1986-7)', *Proceedings of the Dorset Natural History and Archaeological Society* 113, 54-105

Henig, M. and Booth, P. 2000: *Roman Oxfordshire*, Stroud: Tempus

Hesse, M. 1992: 'Fields, Tracks and Boundaries in the Creakes, north Norfolk', *Norfolk Archaeology* 41, 305-324

Hey, G. 2004: *Yarnton, Saxon and Medieval Settlement and Landscape*, Thames Valley Landscapes Monograph 20, Oxford: Oxford Archaeology

Heywood, S.R. 1982: 'The Ruined Church at North Elmham', *Journal of the British Archaeological Association* 135, 1-10

Higham, N. 1992: *Rome, Britain and the Anglo-Saxons*, London: Seaby

Higham, N. 2010: 'The Landscape Archaeology of Anglo-Saxon England', in N.J. Higham and M.J. Ryan (eds.) *The Landscape Archaeology of Anglo-Saxon England*, Woodbridge: Boydell and Brewer, 1-21

Hill, D. 1981: *An Atlas of Anglo-Saxon England*, Oxford: Blackwell

Hill, D., and Worthington, M. 2002: *Offa's Dyke*, Stroud: Tempus

Hills, C. 1979: 'The Archaeology of Anglo-Saxon England in the Pagan Period: A Review', *Anglo-Saxon England* 8, 297-329

Hills, C. 1999: 'Early Historic Britain', in J. Hunter and I. Ralston (ed.) *The Archaeology of Britain: An introduction from the Upper Palaeolithic to the Industrial Revolution*, London: Routledge, 176-193

Hills, C. 2003: *Origins of the English,* London: Duckworth

Hills, C. 2011: 'Overview: Anglo-Saxon Identity', in H. Hamerow, D.A. Hinton, and S. Crawford (eds.) *The Oxford Handbook of Anglo-Saxon Archaeology*, Oxford: Oxford University Press, 3-12

Hills, C. and Penn, K. 1981: *The Anglo-Saxon Cemetery at Spong Hill, North Elmham, Part II: Catalogue of Cremations*, East Anglian Archaeology Report 11, Gressenhall: Field Archaeology Division, Norfolk Museums Service

Hinchliffe, J. 1986: 'An Early Medieval Settlement at Cowage Farm, Foxley, near Malmesbury', *Archaeological Journal* 143, 240-259

Hindley, G. 2006: *The Anglo-Saxons*, London: Constable and Robinson

Hines, J. 1984: *The Scandinavian Character of Anglian England in the Pre-Viking Period*, Oxford: British Archaeological Reports

Hinton, D.A. 1990: *Archaeology, Economy and Society: England from the fifth to the fifteenth century*, London: Seaby

Hinton, D. A. 1992: 'Revised Dating of the Worgret Structure' *Proceedings of the Dorset Natural History and Archaeological Society* 114, 258-260

Hinton, D.A. 1994: 'The Archaeology of Eighth to Eleventh-Century Wessex', in A.M. Aston and C. Lewis (eds.), *The Medieval Landscape of Wessex*, Oxford: Oxbow, 33-46

Hinton, D.A. 1997: 'The 'Scole-Dickleburgh Field System' Examined', *Landscape History* 19, 5-12

Hirst, S. and Rahtz, P. 1973: 'Hatton Rock, 1970', *Transactions of the Birmingham and Warwickshire Archaeological Society* 85, 161-177

Hodge, C.A.H., Burton, R.G.O., Corbett, W.M., Evans, R. and Seale, R.S. 1984: *Soils and Their Uses in Eastern England*, Soil Survey of England and Wales Bulletin 13

Hodges, R. 1982: *Dark Age Economics: The Origins of Towns and Trade, AD 600-1000*, London: Duckworth

Hodges, R. 1989: *The Anglo-Saxon Achievement*, London: Duckworth

Hoggett, R.S. 2007: *Changing Beliefs: The Archaeology of the East Anglia Conversion*, Doctoral Thesis submitted to the University of East Anglia

Hoggett, R.S. 2010a: *The Archaeology of the East Anglian Conversion*, Woodbridge: The Boydell Press

Hoggett, R.S. 2010b: 'The Early Christian Landscape of East Anglia' in N.J. Higham and M.J. Ryan (eds.) *The Landscape Archaeology of Anglo-Saxon England*, Woodbridge: Boydell and Brewer, 193-210

Holbrook, N. And Thomas, A. 1996: 'The Roman and Early Anglo-Saxon Settlement at Wantage, Oxfordshire. Excavations at Mill Street', *Oxoniensia* 61, 109-180

Hollingworth, E.J. and O'Reilly, M.M. 2012: *The Anglo-Saxon Cemetery at Girton College, Cambridge*, Cambridge: Cambridge Library Collection

Hooke, D. 1985: *The Anglo-Saxon Landscape: The Kingdom of the Hwicce*, Manchester: Manchester University Press

Hooke, D. 1988: 'Early Forms of Open-Field Agriculture in England', *Geografiska Annaler* 70B, 123-131

Hooke, D. 1994: 'The Administrative and Settlement Framework of Early Medieval Wessex', in A.M. Aston and C. Lewis (eds.), *The Medieval Landscape of Wessex*, Oxford: Oxbow, 83-95

Hooke, D. 1996: 'Changing Settlement Patterns and Land Use in Midland and Southern England in the Early Medieval and Medieval Period', *Ruralia* I, 80-89

Hooke, D. 1997: 'The Anglo-Saxons in the Seventh and Eighth Centuries: Aspects of Location in Space', in J. Hines (ed.) *The Anglo-Saxons from the Migration Period to the Eighth Century*, Woodbridge: Boydell Press, 65-100

Hooke, D. 1998: *The Landscape of Anglo-Saxon England*, Leicester: Leicester University Press

Hope-Taylor, B. 1977: *Yeavering: An Anglo-British Centre of Early Northumbria*, London: Department of the Environment Archaeological Reports 7

Hoskins, W.G. 1955: *The Making of the English Landscape*, London: Hodder and Stoughton

Hull, G. And Preston, S. 2002: 'Excavation of Late Saxon, Medieval and Post-Medieval Deposits of Land at Proctor's Yard, Bicester', *Oxoniensia* 67, 199-286

Hurst, J.D. (ed.) 1997: *A Multi-Period Salt Production Site at Droitwich: Excavations at Upwich*, Current British Archaeology Research Report 107, York: Current British Archaeology

Hurst, J.G. 1976: 'The Pottery' in D. Wilson (ed.) *The Archaeology of Anglo-Saxon England*, London: Methuen, 283-347

Hurst, J. G. and West, S.E. 1956: 'Saxo-Norman Pottery in East Anglia, Part II', *Proceedings of the Cambridge Antiquarian Society* 50, 29-42

Hutcheson, A.R.J. 2006: 'The Origins of King's Lynn? Control of Wealth on the Wash Prior to the Norman Conquest, *Medieval Archaeology* 50, 71-104

Jackson, D.A. 1993/4a: 'The Iron Age Hillfort at Borough Hill, Daventry, Excavations in 1983', *Northamptonshire Archaeology* 25, 63-68

Jackson, D.A. 1993/4b: 'Archaeological Evaluation at Upton, Northampton', *Northamptonshire Archaeology* 25, 69-76

Jackson, D.S. 1993/4c: 'Iron Age and Anglo-Saxon Settlement Activity around Hunsbury Hillfort, Northampton', *Northamptonshire Archaeology* 25, 35-46

Jackson, D.A. 1995: 'Archaeology at Grendon Quarry, Northamptonshire. Part 2: Other Prehistoric, Iron Age and Later Sites excavated in 1974-75 and Further Observations between 1976-80', *Northamptonshire Archaeology* 26, 3-32

Jenkyns, J. 1999: 'Charter Bounds', in M. Lapidge, J. Blair, S. Keynes and D. Scragg (eds.) *The Blackwell Encyclopaedia of Anglo-Saxon England*, Oxford: Blackwell, 97-99

Jessup, M. 1975: *A History of Oxfordshire*, London: Phillimore

John, E. 1958: 'The Imposition of the Common Burdens on the Lands of the English Church', *Historical Research* 31, 117–129

Johnson, A. G. 1993/4: 'Excavations in Oundle, Northants: Work Carried Out at Stoke Doyle Road 1979, Black Pot Lane 1985 and St. Peter's Church 1991', *Northamptonshire Archaeology* 25, 99-117

Johnson, M. 2007: *Ideas of Landscape*, Oxford: Blackwell

Johnson, S. 1987: *Burgh Castle: Excavations by Charles Green 1958-61*, East Anglian Archaeology Report 20, Gressenhall: Norfolk Archaeological Unit

Jones, G. 1979: 'Multiple Estates and Early Settlement', in P.H. Sawyer (ed.), *English Medieval Settlement*, London: Edward Arnold, 9-34

Jones, L., Woodward, A. and Butuex, S. 2006: *Iron Age, Roman and Saxon Occupation at Grange Park: Excavations at Courteenhall, Northamptonshire, 1999*, Birmingham Archaeology Monograph Series 1 (BAR Series 245), Oxford: Archaeopress

Jones, M.U. 1980: 'Mucking and the Early Saxon Rural Settlement in Essex', in D. Buckley (ed.) *Archaeology in Essex to AD 1500*, London: CBA Report 34, 82-95

Jones, M.U. and Jones, W.T. 1974: 'An Early Saxon Landscape at Mucking, Essex', In T. Rowley (ed.) *Anglo-Saxon Settlement and Landscape. Papers presented to a Symposium, Oxford 1973*, British Archaeology Report 6, Oxford: Oxford University, Department for External Studies, 20-35

Jones, R. 2010: 'The Village and the Butterfly: Nucleation Out of Chaos and Complexity', *Landscapes* 11(i), 25-46

Jones, R. and Page, M. 2006: *Medieval Villages in an English Landscape: Beginnings and Ends*, Macclesfield: Windgather Press

Jones, R. and Pears, B. 2003: *Excavation and Geophysical Survey at St Mary's Church, Whittlebury, Northamptonshire in Advance of the Laying of Pipes and the Sinking of a Septic Tank Within the Churchyard: Interim Report*, University of Leicester Unpublished Report, The Whittlewood Project Archive (ADS Online)

Jorgensen, L. 2003: 'Manor and Market at Lake Tisso in the Sixth to Eleventh Centuries: The Danish 'Productive' Sites, in T. Pestell and K. Ulmschneider (eds.) *Markets in Early Medieval Europe: Trading and 'Productive Sites', 650-850*, Macclesfield: Windgather Press, 175-207

Keen, L. 1988: 'Coastal Salt Production in Norman England', *Anglo-Norman Studies* 11, 133-179

Keevill, G.D. 1992a: 'Life on the Edge: Archaeology and Alluvium at Redlands Farm, Stanwick, Northamptonshire', in S. Needham and M. Macklin (eds.) *Alluvial Archaeology in Britain: Proceedings of a Conference Sponsored by the RMC Group*, Oxford: Oxbow, 25-32

Keevill, G.D. 1992b: 'An Anglo-Saxon Site at Audlett Drive, Abingdon, Oxfordshire', *Oxoniensia* 57, 55-79

Keevill, G.D. 2003: 'Archaeological Investigations in 2002 at the Abbey Church of St. Peter and St. Paul, Dorchester on Thames, Oxfordshire', *Oxoniensia* 68, 313-362

Kelly, S.E. 1992: 'Trading Privileges from Eighth-Century England', *Early Medieval Europe* 1 (1), 3-28

Kelly, S.E. 1996: *Charters of Shaftesbury Abbey*, Anglo-Saxon Charters 5, Oxford: Oxford University Press (The British Academy)

Kelly, S. E. 2001: *Charters of Abingdon Abbey*, Anglo-Saxon Charters 7, Oxford: Oxford University Press (The British Academy)

Kelly, S.E. 2005: *Charters of Malmesbury Abbey*, Anglo-Saxon Charters 11, Oxford: Oxford University Press (The British Academy)

Kelly, S.E. 2009: *Charters of Peterborough Abbey*, Anglo-Saxon Charters 14, Oxford: Oxford University Press (The British Academy)

Kemble, J.M. 1849: *The Saxons in England*, London

Keynes, S. 2003: 'Ely Abbey 672-1109', in P. Meadows and N. Ramsay (eds.) *A History of Ely Cathedral*, Woodbridge: Boydell Press, 3-58

Kidd, A. 2004: 'Northamptonshire in the First Millennium BC', in M. Tingle (ed.) *The Archaeology of Northamptonshire*, Northampton: Northamptonshire Archaeological Society, 44-62

Kirby, D.P. 1966: 'Bede's Narrative Sources for the 'Historia Ecclesiastica'', *Bulletin of the John Rylands Library* 48, Manchester: The John Rylands University Library, 341-371

Kirk, J.R. and Leeds, E.T. 1954: 'Three Early Saxon Graves from Dorchester, Oxfordshire', *Oxoniensia* 17/18, 6376

Knapp, A.B. 1988: 'Ideology, Archaeology and Polity' *Man* 23 (i), 133-163

Knight, D. 1993: 'Late Bronze Age and Iron Age Pottery from Pennyland and Hartigans', in Williams, R.J. (ed.) *Pennyland and Hartigans: Two Iron Age and Saxon sites in Milton Keynes*, Buckinghamshire Archaeological Society Monograph 4, Buckingham: Buckinghamshire Archaeological Society

Knocker, G.M. 1967: 'Excavations at Red Castle, Thetford', *Norfolk Archaeology* 34, 119-186

Lake, J. 2007: 'The English *Pays*: Approaches to Understanding and Characterising Landscapes and Places', *Landscapes* 8 (ii), 28-39

Larwood, G.P. and Funnell, B.M. 1961: 'The Geology of Norfolk', in F. Briers (ed.) *Norwich and its Region*, Norwich: Norwich Local Committee of the British Association, 18-30

Lawson, A.J. 1983: *The Archaeology of Witton, near North Walsham*, East Anglian Archaeological Report 18, Gressenhall: Norfolk Archaeological Unit

Leah, M.D. and Crowson, A. 1993: 'Norfolk Archaeological Unit: The Fenland Management Project', *Fenland Research* 8, 43-50

Leah, M.D. and Flitcroft, M. 1993: 'Archaeological Surveys at Park Farm, Snettisham and Courtyard Farm, Ringstead', *Norfolk Archaeology* 41 (iv), 462-281

Leary, J. 2004: *Tatberht's Lundenwic: Archaeological Excavations in Middle Saxon London*, Pre-Construct Archaeology Monograph 2, London: Pre-Construct Archaeology

Leeds, E.T. 1913: *The Archaeology of the Anglo-Saxon Settlements*, Oxford: Clarendon Press

Leeds, E.T. 1923: 'A Saxon Village at Sutton Courtenay, Berkshire, *Archaeologia* 73, 47-192

Leeds, E.T. 1924: 'An Anglo-Saxon Cremation Burial of the Seventh Century at Asthall Barrow, Oxfordshire' *Antiquaries Journal* 4, 113-126

Leeds, E.T. 1927: A Saxon Village at Sutton Courtenay, Berkshire (Second Report)', *Archaeologia* 76, 59-80

Leeds, E.T. 1936: *Early Anglo-Saxon Art and Archaeology (Rhind Lectures 1935)*, Oxford, Clarendon Press

Leeds, E.T. 1947: A Saxon Village at Sutton Courtenay, Berkshire (Third Report)', *Archaeologia* 92, 79-93

Leeds, E.T. and Riley, M. 1942: 'Two Early Saxon Cemeteries at Cassington, Oxfordshire', *Oxoniensia* 7, 62-70

Leeds, E.T. and Short, H. 1953: *An Anglo-Saxon Cemetery at Petersfinger near Salisbury, Wiltshire*, Salisbury: Salisbury Museum

Lethbridge, T.C. 1927: 'An Anglo-Saxon hut on the Car Dyke at Waterbeach', *Antiquaries Journal* 8, 141-146

Lethbridge, T.C. and Tebutt, C.F. 1933: 'Huts of the Anglo-Saxon Period', *Proceedings of the Cambridge Antiquarian Society* 33, 133-151

Lewis, C. 1994: 'Patterns and Processes in the Medieval Settlement of Wiltshire', in A.M. Aston and C. Lewis (eds.), *The Medieval Landscape of Wessex*, Oxford: Oxbow, 171-193

Lewis, C. 2007: 'New Avenues for the Investigation of Currently Occupied Medieval Rural Settlement: Preliminary Observations from the Higher Education Field Academy', *Medieval Archaeology* 51, 134-162

Lewis, C. 2010: 'Exploring Black Holes: Recent Investigation in Currently Occupied Rural Settlements in Eastern England', in N.J. Higham and M.J. Ryan (eds.) *The Landscape Archaeology of Anglo-Saxon England*, Woodbridge: Boydell Press, 83-106

Lewis, C. 2011: 'Test Pit Excavation within Currently Occupied Rural Settlements- Results of the HEFA CORS Project 2010, *Medieval Settlement Research* 26, 48-59

Lewis, C., Mitchell-Fox, P. and Dyer, C. 1997: *Village, Hamlet and Field: Changing Medieval Settlements in Central England*, Manchester: Manchester University Press

Lewis, J.M. 1957: 'The Launditch: A Norfolk Linear Earthwork', *Norfolk Archaeology* 31, 419-426

Liber Eliensis, (Blake, E.O. 1962 (ed.)), London: Royal Historical Society

Longman, T. 2006: 'Iron Age and Later Defences at Malmesbury: Excavations 1998-2000', *Wiltshire Archaeological and Natural History Magazine* 99, 104-164

Loseby, S.T. 2000: 'Power and Towns in Late Roman Britain and Early Anglo-Saxon England', in G. Rippoll and J.M. Gurt (eds.) *Sedes Regiae (ann. 400-800)*, Barcelona: Reial Acadèmia de Bones Lletres, 319-370

Losco-Bradley, S. 1977: *The Archaeology of Anglo-Saxon England*, London: Methuen, 49-98

Losco-Bradley, S. and Kinsley, G. 2002: *Catholme: An Anglo-Saxon Settlement on the Trent Gravels in Staffordshire*, Nottingham: Nottingham Studies in Archaeology Monograph 3

Loveluck, C. 1998: 'A high-status Anglo-Saxon Settlement at Flixborough, Lincolnshire', *Antiquity* 72, 146-161

Loveluck, C. 2007: *Rural Settlement, Lifestyles and Social Change in the Later First Millennium AD: Anglo-Saxon Flixborough in its Wider Context*, Excavations at Flixborough 4, Oxford: Oxbow

Loveluck, C. and Tys, D. 2006: 'Coastal Societies, Exchange and Identity along the Channel and southern North Sea Shores of Europe', AD 600-1000', *Journal of Maritime Archaeology* 1, 140-169

Loyn, H. 2007: 'Anglo-Saxon England', in A. Deyermond (ed.) *A Century of British Medieval Studies*, Oxford: Oxford University Press, 7-26

Lucy, S., Tipper, J., and Dickens, A. 2009: *The Anglo-Saxon Settlement and Cemetery at Bloodmoor Hill, Carlton Colville, Suffolk*, East Anglia Archaeology Report 131, Cambridge: Cambridge Archaeological Unit

MacDougall, H.A. 1982: *Racial Myth in English History: Trojans, Teutons and Anglo-Saxons*, Montreal: Harvest House

MacKreth, D. 1996: *Orton Hall Farm: A Roman and Early Anglo-Saxon Farmstead*, Manchester: The University of Manchester

Maddicott, J.R. 1997: 'Plague in 7th Century England', *Past and Present* 156, 7-54

Maddicott, J.R. 2005: 'London and Droitwich, *c*.650-750: Trade, Industry and the Rise of Mercia', *Anglo-Saxon England* 34, 7-58

Malcolm, G., Bowsher, D., and Cowie, R. 2003: *Middle Saxon London: Excavations at the Royal Opera House 1989-99*, Museum of London Archaeology Service Monograph 15, London: Museum of London

Malim, T., Penn, K., Robinson, B., Wait, G., and Welsh, K. 1997: 'New Evidence on the Cambridgeshire Dykes and Worsted Street Roman Road' *Proceedings of the Cambridgeshire Antiquarian Society* 85, 27-122

Malone, C. 1989: *Avebury*, London: English Heritage

Margary, I.D. 1955: *Roman Roads in Britain*, London: Baker

Martin, E. 1999: 'Suffolk in the Iron Age', in J. Davies and T. Williamson (eds.) *The Iron Age in Northern East Anglia*, Norwich: Centre of East Anglian Studies

Martin, E. And Satchell, M. 2008: *Where Most Inclosures Be: History, Morphology and Management*, Ipswich: Suffolk Archaeological Service

Masefield, R. 2008: *Prehistoric and Later Settlement and Landscape from Chiltern Scarp to Aylesbury Vale: The Archaeology of the Aston Clinton Bypass, Buckinghamshire*, British Archaeological Report 473, Oxford: Archaeopress

May, J. 1977: 'Romano-British and Saxon Sites near Dorchester-on-Thames', *Oxoniensia* 42, 42-79

Mayes, A., Hardy, A. and Blair, J. 2000: 'The Excavation of Early Iron Age and Medieval Remains on Land to the West of Church View, Bampton, Oxfordshire', *Oxoniensia* 65, 267-290

McOmish, D., Field, D. and Brown, G. 2002: *The Field Archaeology of the Salisbury Plain Training Area*, Swindon: English Heritage

Meadows, I. 1996: 'Wollaston', *Current Archaeology* 150, 212-215

Meadows, I. 2009: 'The Roman and Early Saxon Periods', in I. Meadows, W.A. Boismier and A. Chapman (eds.) *Synthetic Survey of the Environmental, Archaeological and Hydrological Record for the River Nene from its Source to Peterborough*, Swindon: RCHME, 89-124

Meaney, A.L. 1964: *A Gazetteer of Early Anglo-Saxon Burial Sites*, London: Allen and Unwin

Meaney, A.L. 1997: 'Hundred Meeting-places in the Cambridge Region', in A.R. Rumble and A.D. Mills (eds.) *Names, Places and People: An Onomastic Miscellany in Memory of John McNeal Dodgson*, Stamford: Watkins, 195-240

197

Medlycott, M. and Germany, M. 1994: 'Archaeological Fieldwalking in Essex, 1985-1993: Interim Results', *Essex Archaeology and History* 25, 14-27

Mellor, M. 2003: 'Pottery from Excavations at All Saints Church 1973-4', in A. Dodd (ed.) *Oxford before the University: The Late Saxon and Norman Archaeology of the Thames Crossing, the Defences and the Town*, Landscapes Monograph 17, Oxford: Oxford Archaeology Thames Valley, 336-339

Metcalf, D. 1984: 'Monetary Circulation in Southern England in the First Half of the Eighth Century, in D. Hill and D. Metcalf (eds.) *Sceattas in England and on the Continent*, Oxford: British Archaeological Report 128, 27-69

Metcalf, M. 1988: 'The Coins', in P. Andrews (ed.) *The Coins and Pottery from Southampton*, Southampton Finds Volume One, Southampton: Southampton City Museums, 17-59

Miket, R. 1980: 'A Re-statement of Evidence from Bernician Burials' in P. Rahtz, T. Dickinson and L. Watts (eds.) *Anglo-Saxon Cemeteries*. Oxford: BAR, 289-305

Millett, M. 1990: *The Romanisation of Britain*, Cambridge: Cambridge University Press

Millett, M. and James, S. 1983: 'Excavations at Cowdery's Down, Basingstoke, Hampshire', *Archaeological Journal* 140, 151-279

Miles, D. 1986: *Archaeology at Barton Court Farm, Abingdon, Oxfordshire*, Oxford: Oxford Archaeology Unit

Miles, D., Palmer, S., Smith, A. and Jones, P. 2007: *Iron Age and Roman Settlement in the Upper Thames Valley: Excavations at Claydon Pike and other sites within the Cotswold Water Park*, Thames Valley Landscapes Monograph No. 26, Oxford: Oxford Archaeology

Moffat, J.M. 1805: *History of the Town of Malmesbury*, Tetbury: J.G. Goodwyn

MoLAS, 2004: *The Prittlewell Prince: The Discovery of a Rich Anglo-Saxon Burial in Essex*, London: The Museum of London Archaeology Service

Moore, J. 2004: 'St Ebbe's Church', *Oxoniensia* 69, 422

Moore, W.R.G. 1981: 'The Development of Archaeology in Northamptonshire', *Northamptonshire History News*

Moreland, J. 2000: 'Concepts of the Early Medieval Economy', in I.L. Hansen and C. Wickham (eds.) *The Long Eighth Century*, Liede: Boston, 1-34

Morris, J. 1973: *The Age of Arthur: A British History of the British Isles from 350 to 650*, London: Phillimore

Morris, R. 2010: *Churches in the Landscape*, London: Dent

Morris, R. 2010: 'Local Churches in the Anglo-Saxon Countryside', in H. Hamerow, D.A. Hinton, and S. Crawford (eds.) *The Oxford Handbook of Anglo-Saxon Archaeology*, Oxford: Oxford University Press, 172-197

Morrison, W.A. 2009: *A Synthesis of Antiquarian Observation and Archaeological Excavation at Dorchester-on-Thames, Oxfordshire*, Oxford: British Archaeological Reports Series 491

Mortimer, R. 2000: 'Village Development and Ceramic Sequence: The Middle to Late Saxon Village at Lordship Lane, Cottenham, Cambridgeshire, *Proceedings of the Cambridge Antiquarian Society* 89, 5-34

Mortimer, R., Roderick, R. And Lucy, S. 2005: *The Saxon and Medieval Settlement at West Fen Road, Ely: The Ashwell Site*, East Anglian Archaeology 110, Cambridge: Cambridge Archaeological Unit

Mudd, A. 2002: *Excavations at Melford Meadows, Brettenham, 1994: Romano-British and Early Saxon Occupations*, East Anglian Archaeology Report 99, Oxford: Oxford Archaeological Unit

Mudd, A. and Webster, M. 2011: *Iron Age and Middle Saxon Settlements at West Fen Road, Ely, Cambridgeshire: The Consortium Site*, BAR Archaeological Report 538, Oxford: Archaeopress

Murphy, P. 1993: 'Anglo-Saxon Arable Farming on the Silt-fens: Preliminary Results, Fenland Research 8, 75-9

Murphy, P. 1994: 'The Anglo-Saxon Landscape and Rural Economy: Some Results from Sites in East Anglia and Essex', in J. Rackham (ed.), *Environment and Economy in Anglo-Saxon England*, York: Council for British Archaeology, 23-39

Murphy, P. 2005: 'Coastal Change and Human Response', in T. Ashwin and A. Davison (eds.) *An Historical Atlas of Norfolk*, Chichester: Phillimore, 6-7

Murray, P. 2010:'The Landscape and Economy of the Anglo-Saxon Coast', , in N.J. Higham and M.J. Ryan (eds.) *The Landscape Archaeology of Anglo-Saxon England*, Woodbridge: Boydell Press, 211-221

Musty, J. and Stratton, J.E.D. 1964: 'A Saxon Cemetery at Winterbourne Gunner, near Salisbury', *Wiltshire Archaeological and Natural History Magazine* 59, 86-109

Myres, J.N.L. 1969: *Anglo-Saxon Pottery and the Settlement of England*, Oxford: Clarendon Press

Myres, J.N.L. and Green, B. 1973: *The Anglo-Saxon Cemeteries of Caistor-by-Norwich and Markshall, Norfolk*, London: Society of Antiquaries

Newman, J. 1992a: 'The Late Roman and Anglo-Saxon Settlement Pattern in the Sandlings of Suffolk', in M. Carver (ed.) *The Age of Sutton Hoo: The Seventh Century in North-western Europe*, Woodbridge: Boydell, 2-38

Newman, J. 1992b: 'Sutton Hoo-East Anglian or East Saxon King?', *Saxon- The Newsletter of the Sutton Hoo Society* 17, 4-5 (http://www.suttonhoo.org/Saxon/Saxon_pdf/Saxon17.pdf)

Northamptonshire Heritage, 1996: *Policy Report on Saxon and Medieval Ceramics in Northamptonshire*, Unpublished Northamptonshire County Council Planning and Transportation Report, NHER Reference: SNN105665

Oosthuizen, S. 1997: 'Medieval Settlement Relocation in West Cambridgeshire: Three Case Studies', *Landscape History* 19, 43-55

Oosthuizen, S. 1998a: 'Prehistoric Fields into Medieval Furlongs? Evidence from Caxton, south Cambridgeshire', *Proceedings of the Cambridgeshire Antiquarian Society* 86, 145-152

Oosthuizen, S. 1998b: 'The Origins of Cambridgeshire', *The Antiquaries Journal* 78, 85-109

Oosthuizen, S. 2001: 'Anglo-Saxon Minsters in South Cambridgeshire', *Proceedings of the Cambridge Antiquarian Society* 90, 49-67

Oosthuizen, S. 2006: *Landscapes Decoded: The Origins and Development of Cambridgeshire's Medieval Fields*, Explorations in Local and Regional History 1, Hatfield: University of Hertfordshire

Oosthuizen, S. 2007: 'Mercia and the Origins and Distribution of Common Fields', *The Agricultural History Review* 55 (ii), 153-180

Oosthuizen, S. 2010: 'Medieval Field Systems and Settlement Nucleation: Common or Seperate Origins', in N.J. Higham and M.J. Ryan (eds.) *The Landscape Archaeology of Anglo-Saxon England*, Woodbridge: Boydell Press, 107-132

Oosthuizen, S. 2011: 'Anglo-Saxon Fields', in H. Hamerow, D.A. Hinton, and S. Crawford (eds.) *The Oxford Handbook of Anglo-Saxon Archaeology*, Oxford: Oxford University Press, 377-401

Page, M. 2010: 'Domesday Landscape and Land Use', in K. Tiller and G. Darkes (eds.) *An Historical Atlas of Oxfordshire*, Chipping Norton: Oxfordshire Record Society, 34-35

Pantos, A. 2004: 'The Location and Form of Anglo-Saxon Assembly-places: Some 'Moot Points', in A. Pantos and S. Semple (eds.) *Assembly Places and Practices in Medieval Europe*, 155-180

Parker-Pearson, M., Van de Noort, R., and Woolf, A. 1993: 'Three Men and a Boat: Sutton Hoo and the East Anglian Kingdom', *Anglo-Saxon England* 22, 27-50

Parry, S. 2006: *The Raunds Area Survey: An Archaeological Study of the Landscape of Raunds, Northamptonshire, 1985-94*, Oxford: Oxbow Books

Parsons, D. 1977: 'Brixworth and its Monastery Church', in A. Dornier (ed.) *Mercian Studies*, Leicester: Leicester University Press, 173-189

Patrick, C. and Rátkai, S. 2011: 'Chapter 3: Hillside Meadow, Fordham', in R. Cuttler, H. Martin-Bacon, K. Nichol, C. Patrick, R. Perrin, S. Rátkai, M. Smith and J. Williams (eds.) *Five Sites in Cambridgeshire: Excavations at Woodhurst, Fordham, Soham, Buckden and St Neots, 1998–2002*, BAR 258, Oxford, 41–122

Pearce, S. 2003: 'Processes of Conversion in North-west Roman Gaul', in M. Carver (ed.) *The Cross Goes North: Processes of Conversion in Northern Europe AD 300-1300*, Woodbridge: Boydell, 61-78

Peglar, S.M. 1993: 'The Development of the Cultural Landscape Around Diss Mere, Norfolk, UK, During the Past 7000 Years', *Review of Palaeobotany and Palynology* 76, 1-47

Penn, K. 1993: 'Early Saxon Settlement', in P. Wade-Martins (ed.) *An Historical Atlas of Norfolk*, Hunstanton: Norfolk Museums Service, 36-37

Penn, K, 1998: *An Anglo-Saxon Cemetery at Oxborough, West Norfolk: Excavations in 1990*, East Anglian Archaeology Occasional Papers 5, Norfolk Museums and Field Archaeological Service

Penn, K. 2000: *Excavations on the Norwich Southern Bypass, 1989–91. Part II: The Anglo-Saxon Cemetery at Harford Farm, Caistor St Edmund, Norfolk*, East Anglian Archaeology 92, Gressenhall: Norfolk Archaeology and Museum Service

Penn, K. 2005a: 'Introduction', in A. Crowson, T. Lane, K. Penn and D. Trimble (eds.) *Anglo-Saxon Settlement on the Siltland of Eastern England*, Lincolnshire Archaeology and Heritage Reports No 7, Sleaford: Heritage Trust of Lincolnshire, 1-8

Penn, K. 2005b: 'Discussion and Conclusions', in A. Crowson, T. Lane, K. Penn and D. Trimble (eds.) *Anglo-Saxon Settlement on the Siltland of Eastern England*, Lincolnshire Archaeology and Heritage Reports No 7, Sleaford: Heritage Trust of Lincolnshire, 289-300

Percival, S. and Williamson, T. 2005: 'Early Fields and Medieval Furlongs: Excavations at Creake Road, Burnham Sutton, Norfolk', *Landscapes* 6 (i), 1-17

Pestell, T. 2003: 'The Afterlife of 'Productive' Sites in East Anglia', in T. Pestell and K. Ulmschneider (eds.) *Markets in Early Medieval Europe: Trading and Productive Sites, 650-850*, Macclesfield: Windgather Press, 122-137

Pestell, T. 2004: *Landscapes of Monastic Foundation: The Establishment of Religious Houses in East Anglia c. 650-1200*, Woodbridge: The Boydell Press

Pestell, T. 2011: 'Markets, Emporia, Wics and 'Productive' Sites', in H. Hamerow, D.A. Hinton and S. Crawford (eds.) *The Oxford Handbook of Anglo-Saxon Archaeology*, Oxford: Oxford University Press, 556-579

Pevsner, N. 1954: *The Buildings of England: Cambridgeshire*, London: Harmondsworth

Philips, C.W. 1939: *Britain in the Dark Ages (memoir with south-sheet)*, London: Ordnance Survey

Pine, J. 2001: 'The Excavation of a Saxon Settlement at Cadley Road, Collingbourne Ducis, Wiltshire', *Wiltshire Archaeological Magazine*, 88-117

Pine, J. And Ford, S. 2003: 'Excavation of Neolithic, Late Bronze Age, Early Iron Age and Early Saxon Features at St. Helen's Avenue, Benson, Oxfordshire', *Oxoniensia* 68, 131-178

Pitt, J. 2003: 'Minster Churches and Minster Territories in Wiltshire', *Anglo-Saxon Studies in Archaeology and History* 12, 58-71

Plumber, C. 1986:

Plunkett, S. 2005: *Suffolk in Anglo-Saxon Times,* Stroud: Tempus

Pollard, J. and Reynolds, A. 2002: *Avebury: The Biography of a Landscape*, Stroud: Tempus

Poore, D., Norton, A. and Dodd, A. 2009: 'Excavations at Oxford Castle: Oxford's Western Quarter from the Mid Saxon Period to the Late Eighteenth Century (Based on Daniel Poore's Tom Hassall Lecture for 2008), *Oxoniensia* 74, 1-18

Postgate, M.R. 1964: *The Open Fields of Cambridgeshire*, Unpublished PhD thesis, University of Cambridge

Powell, P. 2010: 'Geology', in K. Tiller and G. Darkes (eds.) *An Historical Atlas of Oxfordshire*, Chipping Norton: Oxfordshire Record Society, 8-9

Powlesland, D. 1990: 'West Heslerton: the Anglian settlement. Interim report on excavations in 1989', *Medieval Settlement Research Group Annual Report* 4, 46

Powlesland, D. 1997: 'Anglo-Saxon Settlements, Structures, Form and Layout', in J. Hines (ed.) *The Anglo-Saxons from the Migration Period to the Eighth Century*, Woodbridge: Boydell Press, 101-116

Pretty, K. 1999: 'Defending the Magonseate', in S. Bassett (ed.) *The Origins of Anglo-Saxon Kingdoms*, Leicester: Leicester University Press, 171-183

Pritchard, D. 1997: 'Excavations at Church Street, Barton Bendish', in A. Rogerson, A. Davison, D. Pritchard, and R. Silvester (eds.) *Barton Bendish and Caldecote: Fieldwork in south-west Norfolk,* East Anglia Archaeology Report 80, Gressenhall, Norfolk Museums Service, 43-77

Rackham, O. 1986: *The History of the Countryside*, London: Dent

Radford, C.A.R. 1954: 'Trial Excavations at Jarrow', *The Archaeological Journal* 111, 205-9

Radford, C.A.R. 1957: 'The Saxon House: A Review and some Parallels, *Medieval Archaeology* 1, 27-38

Rackham, O. 1986: 'The Ancient Woods of Norfolk', *Transactions of the Norfolk and Norwich Naturalists' Society* 27, 161-177

Rahtz, P. 1973: 'Monasteries as Settlements', *Scottish Archaeological Forum* 5,125-135

Rahtz, P. 1976: 'Buildings and Rural Settlement', in D. Wilson (eds.) *The Archaeology of Anglo-Saxon England*, London: Methuen, 49-98

Rahtz, P. And Meeson, R. 1992: *An Anglo-Saxon Watermill at Tamworth: Excavations in the Bolebridge Street Area of Tamworth, Staffordshire, in 1971 and 1978*, London: Council for British Archaeology

Ravensdale, J.R. 1974: *Liable to Floods: Village Landscape on the Edge of the Fens AD 450-1850*, Cambridge: Cambridge University Press

Renfrew and Bahn 2000: *Archaeology: Theories, Methods and Practice*, London: Thames and Hudson

Reynolds, A. 1995: 'Avebury, Yatesbury and the Archaeology of Communications', *Papers from the Institute of Archaeology* 6, 21-30

Reynolds, A. 1999: *Later Anglo-Saxon England: Life and Landscape,* Stroud: Tempus

Reynolds, A. 2003: 'Boundaries and Settlements in later Sixth to Seventh-Century England', *Anglo-Saxon Studies in History and Archaeology* 12, Oxford: Oxbow, 98-136

Reynolds, A. 2006: 'The Early Middle Ages', in N. Holbrook and J. Jurica (eds.) *25 Years of Gloucestershire Archaeology*, Cirencester: Cotswold Archaeology, 133-160

Reynolds, A. 2009a: *Anglo-Saxon Deviant Burial Customs*, Oxford: Oxford University Press

Reynolds, A. 2009b: *The Emergence of Anglo-Saxon Judicial Practice: The Message of the Gallows*, The Agnes Jane Robertson Memorial Lectures on Anglo-Saxon Studies 1, Aberdeen: The Centre for Anglo-Saxon Studies, University of Aberdeen

Reynolds, A. and Langlands, A. 2006: 'Social Identities on the Macro Scale: A Maximum View of Wansdyke', in W. Davies, G. Halsall, and A. Reynolds (eds.) *People and Space in the Middle Ages 300-1300*, Turnhout: Brepols, 13-44

Reynolds, S. 1985: 'What do We Mean by "Anglo-Saxon" and "Anglo-Saxons"?', *The Journal of British Studies* 24 (iv), 395-414

Rickett, R. 1995: *The Anglo-Saxon Cemetery at Spong Hill, North Elmham Part VII: The Iron Age, Roman and Early Saxon Settlement.* East Anglian Archaeology Report 73, Gressenhall: Norfolk Museums Service

Richards, J.D. 1999: 'What's so Special about 'Productive Sites'? Middle Saxon Settlements in Northumbria, in T. Dickinson and D. Griffiths (eds.) *The Making of Kingdoms,* Anglo-Saxon Studies in Archaeology and History 10, Oxford: Oxford University School of Archaeology, 71-99

Richards, J.D. and Naylor, J. 2009: 'The Real Value of Buried Treasure. VASLE: The Viking and Anglo-Saxon Landscape and Economy Project', in S. Thomas and P. G. Stone (eds.) *Metal Detecting and Archaeology*, Woodbridge: Boydell Press, 167-180

Rigold, S.E. 1961: 'The Supposed See of Dunwich', *Journal of the British Archaeological Association* 24, 5-59

Rigold, S.E. 1962: 'The Anglian Cathedral of North Elmham, Norfolk', *Medieval Archaeology* 6, 67-108

Rigold, S.E. 1974: 'Further Evidence about the Site of Dommoc', *Journal of the British Archaeological Association* 37, 97-102

Rigold, S.E. 1977: 'Litus Romanum – The Shore Forts as Mission Stations', in D. Johnson (ed.) *The Saxon Shore*, Council for British Archaeology Research Report 18, London: Council for British Archaeology, 70-75

Rippon, S. 1991: 'Early Planned Landscapes in Essex', *Essex Archaeology and History* 22, 46-60

Rippon, S. 2000a: *The Transformation of Coastal Wetlands*, London: British Academy

Rippon, S. 2000b: 'Landscapes in Transition: The Later Roman and Early Medieval Periods', in D. Hooke (ed.) *Landscape: The Richest Historical Record*, Amesbury: Society for Landscape Studies, 47-61

Rippon, S. 2001: 'Reclamation and Regional Economies of Medieval Marshland in Britain', in B. Raftery and J. Hickey (eds.) *Recent Developments in Wetland Research.* Dublin: University College Dublin, 139-158

Rippon, S. 2004a: 'Making the Most of a Bad Situation? Glastonbury Abbey, Meare and the Medieval Exploitation of Wetland Resources in the Somerset Levels', *Medieval Archaeology* 40, 91-130

Rippon, S. 2004b: *Historic Landscape Analysis: Deciphering the Countryside*, Practical Handbooks in Archaeology 16, York: Council for British Archaeology

Rippon, S. 2007: 'Focus or Frontier? The Significance of Estuaries in the Landscape of Southern Britain', *Landscapes* 8 (i), 23-38

Rippon, S. 2008: *Beyond the Medieval Village*, Oxford: Oxford University Press

Rippon, S. 2009: '"Uncommonly Rich and Fertile" or "Not Very Salubrious" The Perception and Value of Wetland Landscapes', *Landscapes* 10 (i), 39-60

Rippon, S. 2010: 'Landscape Change during the 'Long Eighth Century' in Southern England', in N.J. Higham and M.J. Ryan (eds.) *The Landscape Archaeology of Anglo-Saxon England*, Woodbridge: Boydell Press, 39-64

Roberts, B.K. 1990: 'Rural Settlement and Regional Contrasts: Questions of Continuity and Colonisation', *Rural History* 1 (i), 51-72

Roberts, B.K. and Wrathmell, S. 2000: *An Atlas of Rural Settlement in England*, London: English Heritage

Roberts, B.K. and Wrathmell, S. 2002: *Region and Place*, London: English Heritage

Roberts, B.K. and Wrathmell, S. 1998: 'Dispersed Settlement in England: A National View, in P. Everson and T. Williamson (eds.) *The Archaeology of Landscape: Studies Presented to Christopher Taylor*, Manchester: Manchester University Press, 95-116

Robinson, M. 1992: 'Environment, Archaeology and Alluvium on the River Gravels of the South Midlands', in S. Needham and M.G. Macklin (eds.) *Alluvial Archaeology in Britain*, Oxbow Monographs in Archaeology 27, Oxford: Oxbow, 197-208

Rodwell, W. 1978: 'Relict Landscapes in Essex', in H.C. Bowen and P.J. Fowler (eds.) *Early Land Allotment in the British Isles*, British Archaeological Reports 48, Oxford: BAR, 89-98

Roffe, D. 2000: *Domesday: The Inquest and the Book*, Oxford: Oxford University Press

Roffe, D. 2005: 'The Historical Context', in A. Crowson, T. Lane, K. Penn and D. Trimble (eds.) *Anglo-Saxon Settlement on the Siltland of Eastern England*, Lincolnshire Archaeology and Heritage Reports No 7, Sleaford: Heritage Trust of Lincolnshire, 264-288

Rogerson, A. 1995: *Fransham: An Archaeological and Historical Study of a Parish on the Norfolk Boulder Clay*, Doctoral Thesis submitted to the University of East Anglia

Rogerson, A. 2003: 'Six Middle Saxon Sites in West Norfolk', in T. Pestell and K. Ulmschneider (eds.) *Markets in Early Medieval Europe: Trading and Productive Sites, 650-850*, Macclesfield: Windgather Press, 110-121

Rogerson, A. and Davison, A. 1997: An Archaeological and Historical Survey of the Parish of Barton Bendish, Norfolk, in A. Rogerson, A. Davison, D. Pritchard and R. Silvester (eds.) *Barton Bendish and Caldecote: Fieldwork in south-west Norfolk,* East Anglia Archaeology Report 80, Gressenhall, Norfolk Museums Service, 1-42

Rogerson, A. and Lawson, A. 1991: 'The Earthwork Enclosure at Tasburgh', in J. Davies, T. Gregory, A. Lawson, A. Rickett and A. Rogerson (eds.) *The Iron Age Forts of Norfolk*, East Anglian Archaeology Report 54, Gressenhall: Norfolk Archaeology and Museums Service

Rowley, T. and Brown, L. 1981: 'Excavations at Beech House Hotel, Dorchester-on-Thames 1972', *Oxoniensia* 46, 1-55

RCHME, 1968: *An Inventory of the Historical Monuments in the County of Cambridge, Vol 1: West Cambridgeshire*, London: Royal Commission on the Historical Monuments of England

RCHME, 1975: *An Inventory of the Historical Monuments in the County of Northampton, Volume I: Archaeological Sites in North-East Northamptonshire*, London: Her Majesty's Stationery Office

RCHME, 1979: *An Inventory of the Historical Monuments in the County of Northampton, Volume II: Archaeological Sites in Central Northamptonshire*, London: Her Majesty's Stationery Office

RCHME, 1981: *An Inventory of the Historical Monuments in the County of Northampton, Volume III: Archaeological Sites in North-West Northamptonshire*, London: Her Majesty's Stationery Office

RCHME, 1982: *An Inventory of the Historical Monuments in the County of Northampton, Volume IV: Archaeological Sites in South-West Northamptonshire*, London: Her Majesty's Stationery Office

RCHME, 1993: *Guilsborough, Northamptonshire: An Archaeological Survey by the RCHME, January 1993*, Unpublished Field Survey Report, Swindon: English Heritage

Rumble, A. 2001: 'Edward the Elder and the Churches of Winchester and Wessex', in N.J. Higham and D.H. Hill (eds.) *Edward the Elder, 899-924*, London: Routledge, 230–47

Salisbury, H. 2002: 'Preface', in S. Losco-Bradley and G. Kinsley *Catholme: An Anglo-Saxon Settlement on the Trent Gravels in Staffordshire*, Nottingham: Nottingham Studies in Archaeology Monograph 3, xi-xii

Sandred, K.I. 1996: *The Place-Names of Norfolk*, Nottingham: English Place-Name Society

Saunders, T. 1990: 'The Feudal Construction of Space: Power and Domination in the Nucleated Village', in R. Sampson (ed.) *The Social Archaeology of Houses*, Edinburgh University Press, 180-196

Scarfe, N. 1976: 'The Place-name Icklingham: a Preliminary Re-Examination', *East Anglian Archaeology Report* 3, 127-134

Scull, C. 1991: 'Post-Roman Phase 1 at Yeavering: A Reconsideration', *Medieval Archaeology* 35, 51-63

Scull, C. 1992: 'Before Sutton Hoo: Structures of Power and Society in Early East Anglia', in M.O.H. Carver (ed.) *The Age of Sutton Hoo: The Seventh Century in North-West Europe*, Woodbridge: Boydell Press, 3-23

Scull, C. 1993: 'Archaeology, Early Anglo-Saxon Society and the Origins of Kingdoms', *Anglo-Saxon Studies in Archaeology and History* 6, 65-82

Scull, C. 2002: 'Ipswich: Development and Contacts of an Urban Precursor in the Seventh Century', in B. Hardh and L. Larsson (eds.), *Central Places in the Migration and Merovingian Periods. Papers from the 52nd Sachsensymposium, Lund, August 2001*, Stockholm: Almqvist and Wiksell International, 303-316

Seebohm, F. 1883: *The English Village Community*, London: Longmans

Shaw, M. 1991: 'Saxon and Earlier Settlement at Higham Ferrers, Northamptonshire', *Medieval Settlement Research Group Annual Report* 6, 15-21

Shaw, M. 1993: 'A Changing Settlement Pattern at Warmington, Northamptonshire', *Medieval Settlement Research Group Annual Report* 8, 41-47

Shaw, M. 1993/4: 'The Discovery of Saxon Sites below Fieldwalking Scatters: Settlement Evidence from Brixworth and Upton Northamptonshire', *Northamptonshire Archaeology* 25, 77-92

Shoesmith, R. 1982: *Hereford City Excavations, Volume 2: Excavations on and close to the Defences*, London: Council for British Archaeology

Silvester, R.J. 1988: *The Fenland Project, Number 3: Norfolk Survey, Marshland and Nar Valley*, East Anglian Archaeology Report Number 45, Gressenhall: Norfolk Archaeological Unit

Silvester, R.J. 1993: 'The Addition of More-or-Less Undifferentiated Dots to a Distribution Map: The Fenland Survey in Retrospect', in J. Gardiner (ed.) *Flatlands and Wetlands: Current Themes in East Anglian Archaeology*, East Anglian Archaeology 50, Norwich: Scole Archaeological Committee for East Anglia, 24-39

Silvester, R. J. 1997: 'Multi-Period Occupation at Caldecote, West Norfolk', in A. Rogerson, A. Davison, D. Pritchard and R. Silvester (eds.) *Barton Bendish and Caldecote: Fieldwork in South-west Norfolk,* East Anglia Archaeology Report 80, Gressenhall, Norfolk Museums Service, 77-90

Sims, R.E. 1978: 'Man and Vegetation in Norfolk, in Limbrey, S. and Evans, J.G. (eds.) *The Effect of Man on the Landscape: The Lowland Zone*, London: Council for British Archaeology Research Report, 57-62

Sims-Williams, P. 1987: 'The Settlement of England in Bede and the Chronicle', *Anglo-Saxon England* 12, 1-41

Sims-Williams, P. 1990: *Religion and Literature in Western England, 600-800*, Cambridge: Cambridge University Press

Smedley, N. and Owles, E. 1970: 'Excavations at Old Minster, South Elmham', *Proceedings of the Suffolk Institute of Archaeology and Natural History* 32 (i), 1-16

Smith, C. 1980: 'The Survival of Romano-British Toponymy', *Nomina* 4, 27-40

Soden, I. 1994/5: 'Saxon and Medieval Settlement Remains at St John's Square, Daventry, Northamptonshire, July 1994-February 1995', *Northamptonshire Archaeology* 27, 51-99

Speake, G. 1989: *A Saxon Bed Burial on Swallowcliffe Down. Excavations by F de M Vatcher*, London: English Heritage

Spoerry, P. 2000: 'Estate, Village, Town? Roman, Saxon and Medieval Settlement in the St Neots Area', in Dawson, M. (ed.) *Prehistoric, Roman and post-Roman landscapes of the Great Ouse Valley*, CBA Research Report 119, York: Council for British Archaeology, 145-160

Stafford, P. 2009a: 'Introduction, in P. Stafford (ed.) *A Companion to the Early Middle Ages: Britain and Ireland c.500-c.1100*, Chichester: Wiley-Blackwell, 3-8

Stafford, P. 2009b: 'Historiography', in P. Stafford (ed.) *A Companion to the Early Middle Ages: Britain and Ireland c.500-c.1100*, Chichester: Wiley-Blackwell, 9-22

Steane, J. 1974: *The Northamptonshire Landscape*, London: Hodder and Stoughton

Steedman, K. 1995: 'Excavation of a Site at Riby Crossroads, Lincolnshire', *The Archaeological Journal* 151, 212-306

Stenton, F.M. 1933: 'Medeshamstede and its Colonies', in J.G. Edwards (ed.) *Historical Essays in Honour of James Tait*, Manchester (Subscription), 313-326

Stenton, F.M. 1943: *Anglo-Saxon England*, Oxford: Oxford University Press

Stenton, F.M. 1953: *The Latin Charters of the Anglo-Saxon Period*, Oxford: Clarendon Press

Stenton, F.M. 1970: 'The East Anglian Kings of the Seventh Century', in D.M. Stenton (ed.) Preparatory *to Anglo-Saxon England: Being the Collected Papers of Frank Merry Stenton*, Oxford: Clarendon Press, 394-402

Stenton, F.M. 1971: *Anglo-Saxon England* (3rd Edition), Oxford: Oxford University Press

Stevens, C. 2004: 'Iron Age and Saxon Settlement at Jugglers Close, Banbury', *Oxoniensia* 69, 385-416

Stoddart, S. 2000: 'The Impact of Aerial Photography', in S. Stoddart (ed.) *Landscapes from Antiquity: Antiquity Papers 1*, Cambridge: Antiquity Publications, 75-78

Stone, S. 1859a: 'Account of Certain (supposed) British and Saxon Remains, Recently Discovered at Standlake, in the county of Oxford, *Proceedings of the Society of Antiquaries of London* 4, 92-100

Stoodley, N. 1999: 'Burial Rites, Gender and the Creation of Kingdoms: The Evidence from Seventh-Century Wessex', *The Making of Kingdoms*, Anglo-Saxon Studies in Archaeology and History 10, Oxford: Oxford University Committee for Archaeology, 99-107

Stone, S. 1859b: 'Anglo-Saxon Remains at Ducklington near Witney', *Proceedings of the Society of Antiquaries of London* (Second Series) 1, 100-1

Sumner, H. 1913: *The Ancient Earthworks of Cranborne Chase*, Gloucester: Alan Sutton

Tate, W.E. 1944: 'Cambridgeshire Field Systems', *Proceedings of the Cambridge Antiquarian Society* 40, 56-88

Taylor, C.C. 1973: *The Cambridgeshire Landscape: Cambridgeshire and the Southern Fens*, London: Hodder and Stoughton

Taylor, C.C. 1989: 'Whittlesford: The Study of a River Edge Village', in Aston, M., Austin, D. and Dyer, C. (eds.) *The Rural Settlements of Medieval England*, London: George Allen and Unwin, 207-230

Taylor, C.C. 1981: 'Archaeology and the Origins of Open Field Agriculture', in T. Rowley (ed.) *The Origins of Open Field Agriculture*, London: Croom Helm, 13-22

Taylor, C.C. 1983: *Village and Farmstead: A History of Rural Settlement in England*, London: George Philip

Taylor, C.C. 1999: *Cambridge: The Hidden History*, Stroud: Tempus

Taylor, C.C. 2002: 'Nucleated Settlement: A View from the Frontier, *Landscape History* 24, 53-72

Taylor, J. and Flitcroft, M. 2004: 'The Roman Period', *The Archaeology of Northamptonshire*, Northampton: Northamptonshire Archaeological Society, 63-77

Tebbutt, C.F. 1982: 'A Middle Saxon Iron Smelting Site at Millbrook, Ashdown Forest, Sussex', *Archaeological Collection* 20, 19-35

Terrett, I.B. 1971: 'Northamptonshire', in H.C. Darby and I.B. Terrett (eds.) *The Domesday Geography of Midland England*, Cambridge: Cambridge University Press, 384-420

Thirsk, J. 1964: 'The Common Fields', *Past and Present* 29, 3-25

Thomas, A.C. 1971: *The Early Christian Archaeology of North Britain*, Oxford: Oxford University Press for the University of Glasgow

Thomas, R.M. 2010: 'Monastic Town Planning at Abingdon', *Oxoniensia* 75, 49-60

Tilley, C. 1994: *A Phenomenology of Landscape: Places, Paths, Monuments*, Oxford: Berg

Tipper, J. 2004: *The Grubenhaus in Anglo-Saxon England*, Yedingham: Landscape Research Centre

Tingle, M. 2004: 'Archaeology in Northamptonshire', in M. Tingle (ed.) *The Archaeology of Northamptonshire*, Northampton: Northamptonshire Archaeological Society, 1-14

Tyler, E.M. 2000: *Treasure in the Medieval West*, York: York Medieval Press

Ulmschneider, K. 2011: 'Settlement Hierarchy', in H. Hamerow, D.A. Hinton and S. Crawford (eds.) *The Oxford Handbook of Anglo-Saxon Archaeology*, Oxford: Oxford University Press, 156-171

Ulmschneider, K. and Pestell, T. 2003: 'Introduction: Early Medieval Markets and 'Productive' Sites', in T. Pestell and K. Ulmschneider (eds.), *Markets in Early Medieval Europe: Trading and Productive Sites, 650-850*, Macclesfield: Windgather, 1-10

Van Es, W.A. 1990: 'Dorestad Centred', in J.C. Besteman and H.A. Heidinga (eds.) *Medieval Archaeology in the Netherlands*, Assen: Van Gorcum, 151-182

Victoria County History 1902: *Northamptonshire, Volume I*, London: Institute of Historical Research

Victoria County History 1906: *Northamptonshire, Volume II*, London: Institute of Historical Research

Victoria County History 1930: *Northamptonshire, Volume III*, London: Institute of Historical Research

Victoria County History 1937: *Northamptonshire, Volume IV*, London: Institute of Historical Research

Victoria County History 1938: *Cambridgeshire Volume I*, London: Institute of Historical Research

Victoria County History 1955: *Wiltshire, Volume II*, London: Institute of Historical Research

Victoria County History 1957: *Wiltshire, Volume I*, London: Institute of Historical Research

Victoria County History 2002: *Northamptonshire, Volume V*, London: Institute of Historical Research

Victoria County History 2007: *Northamptonshire, Volume VI*, London: Institute of Historical Research

Vinogradoff, P. 1892: *Villeinage in England: Essays in English Medieval History*, Oxford: Clarendon Press

Vita Sancti Wilfridi, Eadmur of Canterbury (prepared by B.J. Muir and A.J. Turner, 1998), Melbourne: University of Melbourne

Wade, K. 1993: 'The Urbanisation of East Anglia: The Ipswich Perspective', in J. Gardiner (ed.) *Flatlands and Wetlands: Current Themes in East Anglian Archaeology*, East Anglian Archaeology 50, Bury St. Edmunds: Suffolk Planning Department 117–126

Wade-Martins, P. 1974: 'The Linear Earthworks of West Norfolk', *Norfolk Archaeology* 36, 23-38

Wade-Martins, P. 1980a: *Village Sites in Launditch Hundred*, East Anglian Archaeology Report 10, Gressenhall: Norfolk Archaeological Unit

Wade-Martins, P. 1980b: *Excavations in North Elmham Park 1967-1972*, East Anglian Archaeology Report 9, Gressenhall: Norfolk Archaeological Unit and The Scole Archaeological Committee

Wallis, H. 2003: *Excavations at Mill Lane, Thetford, 1995*, East Anglian Archaeology Report 108, Gressenhall : Archaeology and Environment Division, Norfolk Museums and Archaeology Service

Wallis, H. Forthcoming: *Romano-British and Saxon Occupation at Billingford, Central Norfolk*, East Anglian Archaeology

Wareham, A. 2005: *Lords and Communities in Early Medieval East Anglia*, Woodbridge: The Boydell Press

Warner, P. 1996: *The Origins of Suffolk*, Manchester: Manchester University Press

Wass, S. and Dealtry, R. 2011: 'Possible Early Christian Enclosure and Deserted Medieval Settlement at Prescote, near Cropredy' *Oxoniensia* 76, 283-286

Watkins, J. 1896: 'History of Willingham Church', *Proceedings of the Cambridge Antiquarian Society* 9, 12

Weaver, S.D.G. and Hull, G. 2000: 'Saxon, Medieval and Post-medieval Deposits at Waterperry House, Waterperry, near Wheatley, Oxfordshire', *Oxoniensia* 65, 333-343

Webster, L. E. 1986: 'Anglo-Saxon England AD400-1100', in I. Longworth and J. Cherry (eds.), *Archaeology in Britain since 1945-New Directions*, London: British Museum, 119-160

Webster, L. E. and Cherry, J. 1973: 'Medieval Britain in 1972', *Medieval Archaeology* 17, 147

Weddell, P.J., and Reed. S.J. 1997: 'Excavations at Sourton Down Okehampton 1986-1991: Roman Road, Deserted medieval Hamlet and other Landscape Features', *Devon Archaeological Society Proceedings* 55, 39-147

West, S. 1985: *West Stow: The Anglo-Saxon Village*, East Anglian Archaeology 24, Bury St. Edmunds: Suffolk County Planning Department and the Scole Archaeological Committee Ltd

Whitelock, D. 1930: *Anglo-Saxon Wills*, Cambridge: Cambridge University Press

Whitelock, D. 1955: *English Historical Documents, Volume 1, c. 500-1042*, London: Eyre Methuen

Whitelock, D. 1972: 'The Pre-Viking Age Church in East Anglia', *Anglo-Saxon England* 1, 1-22

Whybra, J. 1990: *A Lost English County: Winchcombeshire in the Tenth and Eleventh Centuries*, Woodbridge: Boydell and Brewer

Wickham, C. 2000: 'Overview: Production, Distribution and Demand, II', in I.L. Hansen and C. Wickham (eds.) *The Long Eighth Century*, Liede: Boston, 345-377

Wickham, C. 2005: *Framing the Early Middle Ages: Europe and the Mediterranean, 400-800*, Oxford: Oxford University Press

Williams, A. 1992: 'A Bell-House and a Burh-Geat: Lordly Residences in England before the Norman Conquest' in C. Harper-Bill and R. Harvey (eds.) *Medieval Knighthood IV*, Woodbridge: Boydell Press, 221-40

Williams, G. 2005: 'Military Obligations and Mercian Supremacy in the Eighth Century', in D. Hill and M. Worthington (eds.) Æthelbald and Offa: Two Eighth-Century Kings of Mercia, British Archaeological Reports Series 383, Oxford: Archaeopress, 103-109

Williams, H. 2006: *Death and Memory in Early Medieval Britain*, Cambridge: Cambridge University Press

Williams, J., Shaw, M., and Denham, V. 1985: *Middle Saxon Palaces at Northampton*, Northampton: Northampton Development Corporation

Williams, R.J. 1993: *Pennyland and Hartigans: Two Iron Age and Saxon Sites in Milton Keynes*, Aylesbury: Buckinghamshire Archaeological Society

Williams, P. and Newman, R. 1998: *Excavations at Grove Farm, Market Lavington, Wiltshire, 1986-1990*, Wessex Archaeology Report 15, Salisbury: Wessex Archaeology

Williamson, T. 1987: 'Early Co-axial Field Systems on the East Anglian Boulder Clays', *Proceedings of the Prehistoric Society* 53, 419-431

Williamson, T. 1988: 'Settlement Chronology and Regional Landscapes: The Evidence from the Claylands of East Anglia and Essex', in D. Hooke (ed.) *Anglo-Saxon Settlements*, Oxford: Blackwell, 153-175

Williamson, T. 1993: *The Origins of Norfolk*, Manchester: Manchester University Press

Williamson, T. 1998: 'The "Scole-Dickleburgh Field System" Revisited', *Landscape History* 20, 19-28

Williamson, T. 2003: *Shaping Medieval Landscapes: Settlement, Society, Environment*, Macclesfield: Windgather Press

Williamson, T. 2006: *England's Landscape: East Anglia*, London: RCHME

Williamson, T. 2008: *Sutton Hoo and its Landscape: The Context of Monuments*, Oxford: Oxbow

Williamson, T. and Bellamy, L. 1987: *Property and Landscape: A Social History of Land Ownership and the English Countryside*, London: George Philip

Wilson, D. M. 1976: *The Archaeology of Anglo-Saxon England*, London: Methuen

Wilson, D. M. 1981: *The Anglo-Saxons (3rd edition)*, London: Penguin

Woods, P.J. 1970: 'Excavations at Brixworth, Northamptonshire, 1965-70. The Roman Villa Part 1- The Roman Coarse Pottery and Decorated Samian Ware, *Journal of the Northampton Museum and Art Gallery* 4,

Woolf, A. 2009: 'A Dialogue of the Deaf and the Dumb': archaeology, history and philology', in Z.L. Devlin and C.N.J. Holas-Clark (eds.) *Approaching Interdisciplinarity: Archaeology, History and the Study of Early Medieval Britain c.400-1100*, BAR Series 486, Oxford: Archaeopress, 3-9

Wormald, P. 1983: 'Bede, *Bretwaldas* and the Origins of the *Gens Anglorum*', in P. Wormald, D. Bullough and R. Collins (eds.) *Ideal and Reality in Frankish and Anglo-Saxon Society*, Oxford: Blackwell, 99-129

Wormald, P. 1984: *Bede and the Conversion of England: The Charter Evidence (The Jarrow Lecture 1984)*, Jarrow: The Parish of Jarrow

Wright, D. 2010: 'Tasting Misery Among Snakes: The Situation of Smiths in Anglo-Saxon Settlements', *Papers from the Institute of Archaeology* 20

Wymer, J. 1994a: 'Late Glacial and Mesolithic Hunters', in P. Wade-Martins (ed.) *An Historical Atlas of Norfolk*, Hunstanton: Norfolk Museums Service, 24-25

Wymer, J. 1994b: 'The Neolithic Period', in P. Wade-Martins (ed.) *An Historical Atlas of Norfolk*, Hunstanton: Norfolk Museums Service, 24-25

Yorke, B. 1993: 'Fact or Fiction? The Written Evidence for the Fifth and Sixth Centuries AD', *Anglo-Saxon Studies in Archaeology and History* 6, 45-50

Yorke, B. 1995: *Wessex in the Early Middle Ages*, Leicester: Leicester University Press

Yorke, B. 1997: *Kings and Kingdoms of Early Anglo-Saxon England*, London: Routledge

Yorke, B. 1999: 'The Origins of Anglo-Saxon Kingdoms: the Contribution of Written Sources', in T. Dickinson and D. Griffiths (eds.) *The Making of Kingdoms*, Anglo-Saxon Studies in Archaeology and History 10, Oxford: Oxford University Committee for Archaeology, 25-29

Yorke, B. 2003: 'The Adaptation of the Anglo-Saxon Royal Courts to Christianity', in M.O.H. Carver (ed.) *The Cross Goes North: Process of Conversion in Northern Europe, AD 300-1300*, Woodbridge: York Medieval Press 243-257

Internet References

Ashmolean Webpage 2012: http://www.ashmolean.org/ash/amps/leeds/AS_Oxfordshire/Asthall/asthall_index.html

Atlas of Rural Settlement in England GIS (English Heritage): http://www.english-heritage.org.uk/professional/research/archaeology/atlas-of-rural-settlement-gis/

Cotswold Archaeology Website 2011: http://www.cotswoldarch.org.uk/projects/projects_2010/chelt_academy.htm

Historic Parishes of England and Wales Online: http://www.esds.ac.uk/findingData/snDescription.asp?sn=4348&key=4348

HEFA Website: